"VAQUEROS AND BUCKEROOS"

by Arnold Rojas

This book is a complete, unabridged edition of the original classic by
Arnold R. Rojas (1896-1988). We have kept it exactly as the third
and enlarged edition he published in 1984. Rojas was 88.

The publisher wishes to thank Mr. Rojas' family, especially
Ms. Juanita Montes for help in this project.
We thank you, the reader, for your interest in the work
of this important author.

William C. Reynolds, Publisher
Alamar Media, Inc.
Santa Ynez, California
www.oldcowdogs.com

To Florence, my wife,
in appreciation of her help.
Arnold Rojas

PREFACE

In the following pages, for the second time, the writer has made an attempt to give a factual account of the vaquero and buckeroo from a vaquero's point of view.

Many books have been written on this subject and this book does not pretend to compete with them. Its aim is to present to the reader a simple account of the vaquero's method of working and way of life, and the dangers and hardships he met in following a calling, which in spite of millions of words written in "Western" books, the public knows nothing about.

The writer has endeavored to keep the narratives of the vaquero's experience short, without padding, in a *conte* form, so that they may be read without boredom.

The shortcomings of this book can be laid to the author's lack of schooling, not to the vaquero or buckeroo, whose lives were of great interest; and until some great writer sees the promise for the author in the vaquero's experiences, and writes them, the reader will have to bear with this writer's poor efforts; but if the manner of telling is not all that could be desired, the material can be relied on, for these stories were told from experience and observation, and in no case, second-hand, the object of this writer being to set down facts.

In the following pages, I do not sound the depth of California's Hispanic culture nor trace the currents of the Californian's life, I can only scratch the surface of a rich heritage, because the old people are gone forever. I would leave the task to an abler pen. I write only of those men who rode horses for the ride's sake.

TABLE OF CONTENTS

PART I   Page

Vaqueros and Buckeroos

Part II   Page

The Vaquero

Origins of the Vaquero

Beware The Apaches

In Old Mexico

In The San Joaquin Valley

Old Vaqueros Speak

Vaquero Tales

Part III   Page

More Stories

Part IV   Page

Observations

INTRODUCTION

I wish to thank the many people who have read and liked my book, "These Were The Vaqueros", and who listened so patiently to the long-winded stories of old, broken down buckeroos. In these stories they have ridden the ranges with me, vicariously, of course, in fair weather and in foul; and have seen through the eyes of old vaqueros something of the splendor of those days, though the passage of time dulls the sharpness of visual pictures. I hope they have seen a shadow at least, for there will never be another cattle ranching era in California that produced such men. I hope my readers will hold dear the memories of that great era, for memories are the greatest treasures one can possess.

If I often wrote in lighter vein, it is because most vaqueros and buckeroos never took life too seriously.

If what is written herein is pleasantry, it is because my experiences were pleasant.

If I do not write of "six guns" and shooting, it is because I saw none.

If I do not write of hatreds, it is because I met none.

If the reader will find in these pages nothing of dialect, it is because I heard none. Most vaqueros and buckeroos spoke a decent English, when they spoke it at all. Perhaps a few words of explanation may be helpful to the reader.

IX

To those who read "Westerns" the title of this volume may lead the reader to expect this book to be what it is not, a blood and thunder "Western".

This work does not pretend to fill the picture blood and thunder "Westerns" created, but has remained steadfast to the truth. I have been careful to let the old vaqueros themselves tell the story of what the old West really was. These stories were left in trust to me by old men who held it their duty to pass on the lore of a people who are gone forever, and have left only this heritage of simple tales. In writing them, I am doing a duty to my forebears, and the old men who lived during the era of the great ranches in California. They passed them on to me, to pass on to you.

The vaquero culture was a racial inheritance which had no foreign taint. The truth is more compelling than the fiction of the legend called in late years, the "Western Tradition". The range rider who has become in late years a legendary figure was, perhaps, of greater stature in simple reality than he ever was in the preposterous tales which have arisen of his exploits.

The vaquero did not go in defeat. He was still a first-class horseman when mechanical progress put an end to him forever. He still lives vicariously in the many horse shows and reined cowhorse societies of today. The young men who strive for prizes in the show ring, and travel long distances from horse show to horse show, and work long hours to produce a reined horse, are as dedicated as were the old-timers whose prototypes they are.

Some years ago parts of this book were published under the title, "The Vaquero", and I am republishing it because I was cheated by the man who published it. I never received any money for its sale and I had to hire a lawyer and cancel the publisher's debt to me, to get rid of him.

I am proud to have received this letter from my friend Jim Day, God Bless him.

My Dear Rojas:

I certainly do not brag about any great degree of perception, but I did note during my first association with you that you possessed an innate ability, very uncommon indeed, of a story teller and to some degree, I believed I had a very minor part in fostering that talent. You developed it by persistence and you yourself fostered gradual understanding of syntax and a sophistication of style that became manifest in your writing. These abilities I take credit for giving them their first exposure in print; but that is the only credit I take, for you hoisted yourself by your own western boot straps and are responsible, and to be credited for doing some of the genuinely honest and durable writing of the vaquero. I treasure your books and am honored indeed by knowing you. It is one of the few distinctions I possess. I thank you very sincerely indeed for the gift of the excellent symposium of your work. We have survived to become two old men and in our waning days I wish you *Buena Suerte*.

Jim Day
J. M. Day

XI

SPONSORS

Thirty years ago when the interest in horse shows began to develop in California, I decided to throw in my lot with the men who trained horses for a living, for the handling and working of animals was something I was familiar with. I could shoe horses, break horses, and float horses' teeth, and I thought I could make a living among them. I was not wrong in making that decision, for I have spent a very successful thirty years among horse trainers and have made many friends. Two years ago they presented me with a beautiful silver buckle on my eightieth birthday.

This list includes, of course, horse trainers, horseshoers, saddle makers, and horse enthusiasts in general. When my book "These Were The Vaqueros" came out, I put myself in the hands of my friends. They responded to a man, and undertook to help me sell my book by buying it and recommending it to their friends and clients. These friends each, have sold from one or two to as many as fifty copies. In the following list are the names of those who have made "These Were The Vaqueros" a big success. Without their help and good will, two printings of the book would never have been sold. Besides Chuck Hitchcock who is my distributor of the book, and Lou Hengehold, my old friend of many years, their names are: Lee Dooley, horseshoer; Greg Ward, horse trainer; Frank Rue, cattleman; Jim Albitre, horse trainer; Remick Albitre, cattleman; Mrs. Pansy Brunk and the Brunk Family of Bakersfield; Dick Shrake, horse trainer; Jean Philbrick, horsewoman; Lee Rice, dean of saddle makers; Stan Fonsen, horse trainer; Clarence Chown, horse trainer and teacher; Walter and Leona Cooper, horse enthusiasts; Dave Rhodes, horse trainer; Bill Hughes, horse trainer, teacher; Norman Dunn, horse breeder, teacher; Rusty Paris, horse trainer; Ronnie Richards, horse trainer; Rod Kelly, horse trainer; Frank Craighead, horse trainer; Mrs. Gary Owens, horse breeder; Janet Smith, horse trainer; Bob Robinson, horse trainer; Forest Knott, saddlery; Dick Bailey, college professor; Don Murphy, horse trainer; Bab Verdugo, horse trainer; Bob Tracy, rancher; Flangan, saddlery; El Vaquero Saddlery; Anna Robertson, feature writer; Les and Corolynn Vogt, horse trainers and breeders; Bill Nielson, saddlery; Jim Strong, saddlery; David Silva, saddlery; Cecil Rendon, saddlery; Slim Pickens, actor, saddlery; Lester Garcia, bit and spur maker; Clark Mc Kee, bit and spur maker; Grant Iverson, horse trainer; Duane Pettibones, horse trainer, auctioneer; Gordon Kent, horse trainer; Bill Enk, horse trainer; Jerry Bello, rancher; Beth and B.J. Henning, horsewomen; Kim Anderson, horse trainer; Jimmy Nunes, horse trainer; Jim Vaughn, horse trainer; Bobby Ingersoll, horse trainer; Malcolm Rossol, horse show announcer; Mike Baker, horse trainer; Harold Dakan, Clark's Feed Store; Johnny Bacon, cattleman; Merle Rose, horse shoer; Jimmy Williams, dean of horse trainers; Alan Williams, riding club manager; Mack Lynn, horse trainer; Maria Silva, horse trainer; Mary Gatti, horse trainer; Ray Rich, "Horse and Rider Magazine"; Eddie Griffiths, Bakersfield Californian; California Quarter Horse Review; Bill and Meri Corey, horse trainers; Harriet Landrum, horse show secretary; Harry Forbes, ring stewart; Warren Underwood, ring stewart; Larry Alcorn, Ring master; Peter Looker, ring master; Allen Balch, horse show manager; Bill Martin, horse trainer; Don Wiese, bit and spur maker; Marla Meador, editor; Joe King, horse trainer; George Comfort, artist; David Murray, bit and spur maker; Art Rueter, roper; Peter Cobo, Frank Lane, rancher; Garn Walker, trainer; Ernie Morris, artist, Florence Page, retired educator.

I have tried to list all the names of those who helped. If I have inadvertently missed any, I am sorry.

VAQUEROS AND BUCKEROOS

BLACK BRONCO RIDERS

Sixty years ago, in a drug store in Bakersfield, California, I came upon a postcard with the picture of a black man riding a bucking horse. The horse in the picture was sunfishing and the black man had his mouth wide open laughing, presumably at the horse's efforts to buck him off. The title of the picture was: *Jesse Stahl Riding Glass Eye*.

In after years in browsing through thousands of "Western" books, the thought would recur to me that no one ever thought of mentioning the black man in those stories. This set me to investigating and in time I discovered some very interesting facts. Facts which may be ugly to some people, but let them be facts.

Now, I have always believed that the man who writes, has the duty to tell the truth. For this reason, in *The Vaquero* I brought out the fact that has been hidden for years. This fact was that the real cowboy was a black, that the white cowboy came on the scene when cattle became valuable in the seventies and eighties after the cowboy became romantic in lurid "Westerns" like the "Virginian" and others. The fact was that the Negro being a Cowboy did not set well with some people. As a result, the black man has never appeared in "cowboy" stories. I also stated that the movements of cattle were originally from the West, and not from the South. I also stated that the men painted by the great artist, Charlie Russell, were mainly from the West, Oregon.

My statements brought a tirade from a certain Hutchinson, in a San Francisco newspaper. I am sorry this happened, because I think it a great paper, and have always liked it. This tirade was an excuse for my publisher to say he had not sold any of my books. It seems Mr. Hutchinson took umbrage at my including blacks in the ranks of heroes. Perhaps he could see Negroes as bootblacks, but how dare I say they were heroes, too, like the white cowboys?

Everyone who has studied the matter knows that the black was very much in evidence. Beckwourth, a black, was one of the first to come to California, and in the Gulf Coast States everyone knows about Bill Pickett, who, as "Colonel" Miller said, invented "Bulldogging" — but that he bulldogged a bull of the Spanish fighting breed, I do not believe —.

Mr. Hutchinson not only insults me but also the men who rode in the West, and whom I knew as men who were so serenely sure of their skill that they would cheerfully admire without stint any man, black or white, who could equal them in ability. The vaquero and buckeroo as I knew him, had many faults, even as you and I, but I have yet to know one who would deny a man his just dues because of the color of his skin.

This was proved very conclusively in Bakersfield.

Jesse Stahl, one of the great black bronc riders of all time, came to Bakersfield and entered in the bronc riding contest. He was a sensation, and easily won first money. He might not have been given first money because he was black; but it happened that a first-class buckeroo, and a gentleman, Weef Holloway, — may the grass grow green over his grave — was the judge. He gave Jesse first money despite the howls of those who would keep it lilywhite.

"Westerns" have been laughed at by men of the West and at some of the claims of "Western" writers, but when a man with some pretentions to the knowledge of history begins to take them for truth, it is time to protest.

Since I suffered those insults, I am pleased to say that I have been proven right. Two authentic books have appeared, *The Negro Cowboys,* and *The Adventures of the Negro Cowboys,* by Philip

Durham and Evertt L. Jones, Dodd Mead and Company. The history of Negroes in the cattle industry has been suppressed, though Charlie Siringo and Jo Mora have mentioned them. Nevertheless, they achieved remarkable things under adverse circumstances. The most remarkable being the development of the cattle industry in the Gulf Coast States, and men like Jesse Stahl, Ty Stokes, Sam McVey, Walter Stennet, Harry Gillum, Felix Cooper, and many others have made sure of a place in the history of real cowboys.

Now as to the migrations of cattle and geographic limits of those movements, Charlie Russell completed three thousand five hundred works of incomparable art and never painted a "rimmy" saddle. Surely, those men he depicted must have bought their equipment somewhere besides Pueblo, Colorado.

If one will read the works of Oliver, French, Long, and other Oregon authors, he will find that the cattlemen of that state did not waste any time in crossing Durham bulls with the longhorns brought up from California in 1836. After the Sioux and Cheyenne were put on reservations, men started moving cattle east. These crossbred cattle were called "American" cattle to differentiate them from the longhorn or Spanish cattle. One must not forget, however, that the "Oregon" country included the present states of Oregon, Washington, Idaho, and parts of Wyoming, and Montana. In 1878, 160,000 head of cattle were driven east into the prairie states, and in 1879, 200,000 head were driven east. Long and Ryan were among the many buyers of cattle. Omaha and Kansas City did a thriving business in "American" cattle.

The myth of the cattle drives must be challenged, not only for the sake of decency, but for another crucial reason, namely, historical accuracy, and more important, to combat historical genocide. My purpose is to bring about an awareness to the people who have a Western heritage which could be stolen, ignored, or forgotten. It is an effort to stop people from taking something that does not belong to them.

The Oregon buckeroo, easily the best range rider in the West, has been ignored by historians. He established the cattle industry by hard work and honesty. He did not find established ranches to make his lot easier. He had to build up the ranches with cattle he brought in from far distances and over rugged mountains. With his flat-brimmed hat, his woolly chaps, rawhide riata, and slick fork saddle, he could hold his own in any company. He was always welcome in the vaquero crews of California.

Rube Long, in his book "The Oregon Desert"; Caxton Printers; Caldwell, Idaho, tells two of the best stories of courage I have ever read. He tells of one man who rode five hundred miles to notify relatives of a man who was shot, and of another buckeroo who rode one hundred and fifty miles to get a doctor and saved the lives of many people who had been burned. Both rides were made in subzero weather, neither man slept over four hours during the ordeal.

"La verdad siempre anda sobre la mentira como el aceite sobre la agua."

Cervantes

(Truth always rises over the lie, as oil rises over water.)

HOW I CAME TO WRITE
"THESE WERE THE VAQUEROS"

The San Joaquin was to be my home until forty years later, when the Valley Fever drove me out to seek another climate. The San Emideo was a big ranch, The Tecuya, the Pleito, and the Santiago were included in its area. It had once belonged to the Dominguez family.

From San Emideo I went to work at Buttonwillow, which was the headquarters for the Southern Division of Miller and Lux ranches. Rafael Cuen was the cattle boss. There were two crews, one crew stayed at Deep Wells and worked the cattle in the pastures and unloaded the trainloads of cattle shipped in from other parts of the country. At that time, the Mexican Revolution was in progress and many trainloads of wild, longhorn cattle were shipped into Buttonwillow from below the border. The "chain gang" (the chuck wagon crew) worked the cattle on the outlying ranches. At that time Miller and Lux had seventy thousand head on the Southern Division. The company controlled fourteen million acres in three states: Oregon, California and Nevada.

After I left Miller and Lux, I went to work on the Tejon Ranch. Don Jose Jesus Lopez, the most colorful of the old-time cattle bosses, was the manager. He had been manager for over fifty years. His grandfather, a member of the De Anza Expedition, had superintended the building of the San Gabriel and San Fernando

Missions. Don Jesus, as we called him, had one quality; he would never ask any of his men to do anything he would not do himself, and he would not tolerate any abuse of animals. It was on the Tejon where I worked with Indian vaqueros for the first time, and very good men they were. These Indians were descendents of remnants of tribes which had taken refuge on Tejon Ranch when the whites were slaughtering the Indians for sport. The Indians had their village up Tejon Canyon and made up the work crews on the ranch. I learned much from them. Chiefly, the virtue of patience in handling animals. Some of the vaqueros were Sonorans, sons or grandsons of the men and women who had come over the Devil's Highroad from Mexico in one or another of the colonizing expeditions which followed each other since 1769. Some of the best vaqueros in California rode on the Tejon Ranch at that time (1920's). Some time later I worked for Miller and Lux again, and was there when the company went out of business in 1927.

The cattle ranches were prospering in the 1920's when suddenly in 1929, men went to bed millionaires and awoke next morning penniless. Then came the terrible depression of the 1930's, the hardest years of my life. I learned to do work which I would never have done before. I drove scraper teams, shod horses, worked in the oil fields. If I could get a job that paid a dollar a day I found I could consider myself lucky. In 1934, I went into the stable business. I boarded, broke, and shod horses. It was during that period that I met Mr. Walter Heath, a fine old southern gentleman, who taught me to float horse's teeth. I have been making my living as a horse dentist for the last thirty years.

During the years I was in the stable business, I took an active part in all community parades and celebrations. Once, when I was organizing a parade, I went to Jim Day, the managing editor of the *Bakersfield Californian* and asked him for some publicity for my parade. He said "Go home and write something about your parade, if I can use it, I will thank you".

I had invited a number of very old vaqueros to ride in the parade as guests of honor. I went home and wrote a thumbnail history of each old man. I presented it to Mr. Day. The next day it appeared in his column "Pipefuls". When I went to his office to thank him, he was absent, but Ralph Krieser, the editorial writer, was there, and he said, "That is valuable historical material that you have written. Keep it up". From that day, I contributed the material that is in "These Were The Vaqueros" in serial form to the *Bakersfield Californian*.

One day a priest, Monsignor James Culleton, read some of my writings and undertook to publish them in book form. He published three books, another book was published in Santa Barbara. These four, with one book that had not been published, made up the 528 pages in "These Were The Vaqueros". Some of those books have been out of print for twenty years, and through that time I have had numerous requests for them. This had decided me to publish all my work in one volume.

During my youth, I rode on the Rosedale Ranch with Charlie Hitchcock, a good buckeroo. Through the years, I kept up our friendship, for Charlie was a good storyteller, and some of his stories are in my book. And now, Chuck, Charlie's son, has taken on the difficult job of distributing my book and is doing a very good job of it.

"These Were The Vaqueros" has had such a great success that we have undertaken this book which will be entitled "More Vaqueros and Buckeroos", a sequel to "These Were The Vaqueros".

BITS

We cannot speak of the beginnings of the horse culture, because its roots reach too far back into the mists of time. It came out of North Africa into Spain with the invaders who took root in the Peninsula. Their descendents, each generation in turn, improved it. The Spanish Moors developed it into a fine art, and it was not until after the Christian Spaniards adopted the Moorish system of riding, that they began to win cavalry battles. The Moors and the Gypsies who remained in Spain, fell heir to the horse lore and today still retain the old secrets.

The hand of the Moslem can be seen in the horsemanship throughout Spanish-America, an expression of skills which is still alive in Hispano-Portuguese territory. Striking illustrations of this can be found from Tierra Del Fuego to the Arctic Circle. Yet for all the importance this subject has for horsemen, and for all the vast wordage that has been expended on the "Old Spanish Style", no vital study of it has ever been undertaken.

The bridle bit has developed a false importance with riders who would adopt the "Old Spanish Style", far beyond its merit, because a bit is only a signaling device, nothing more. A bit is not the advent of a performing horse. Bitting has to be learned through careful study of the horse and its movements, its structure and its way of going, before one can become a reinsman. A bit is of no avail if the rider does not stay on the horse's center of gravity and the horse's physical structure is not right.

There are many men who jerk and pull a horse through a performance, and win only because their competitors are even worse.

A teacher can show his pupil how to hold his reins, how to sit in the saddle, how to lay the rein on the horse's neck, to turn the animal around; but he will not be able to teach him how to communicate with the horse. That, he will have to learn by himself; an affinity with the horse cannot be taught.

Of course one man will gain mastery over a horse much more quickly than another, but all men must learn, and all men who ride horses must acquire the knowledge of horses before they can master them.

It is wrong to recommend the use of the spade bit to a beginner, for the simple reason that no two horses are alike. There are differences in the structure of their mouths and in the length and shape of their necks, and their temperaments. Most important, no two pair of hands are alike. There are many men whose hands are not adapted to the use of the spade bit.

This does not come so much from a humanitarian standpoint, but from a practical one. When a horse is hurt, his mind becomes blank to everything but the pain. He forgets everything he had learned in waiting for the next blow. A horse develops so-called bad habits in his own protection. He will set his jaw and go along with his head cocked to one side, waiting for the next jerk. A bit was never intended to hurt, but to signal. As long as a horse is not hurt he will absorb his teaching. Old-timers kept the idea of not hurting their horse uppermost in their minds, and for that reason rode their colts in a hackamore for such long periods of time.

Master workmen through the years have created works of art in bits, but the finest of bits cannot make a reinsman. To be a reinsman, a man must have a knack for communicating his wishes to the horse. True, those old horsemen rode their horses over such a long period of time that the horse would learn each move his rider made, and as a result obey his wishes without the rider's use of the rein.

The best bit makers in the West, at one time or another, worked for G. S. Garcia of Elko, Nevada, who was considered by all riders as the dean of all bit makers. Some time ago, while at the Snaffle Bit Futurity in Reno, Nevada, I met Lester Garcia, son of the late G. S. Garcia, and prevailed upon him to give me a list of the names of the best bit makers his father had employed.

The following list is what he gave me, and I am proud to see that the name of my father's brother heads the list: David Rojas, A. Herrera, Adolf Biacan, Tomas Jayo, Ralph (Filo) Gutierrez, M. V. Hernandez, Juan Estrada, one Valenzuela, Joe Figueroa, Joe Alines, Steve Clark, One Goldberg, Mike Morales, and Manuel Gil.

HORSEMEN

Through the ages, some divine hand or power set the rules which horsemen obey in their conduct in respect to horses. An instinct which was the boon of all men of all countries, of all languages, and all races who handle horses, and that instinct is to make a horse as soft as silk to the rider's hand. This impulse has taken different paths, but all have the same end in view. In Argentina, horsemen have become the greatest polo players in the world. In Chile, the native *huaso* (rider) is the wonder of the southern continent. In Peru, the little horse of unbelievable stamina and endurance has made the Peruvian known the world over.

Charreria (the art of roping, riding, and tailing) is the national sport of Mexico. The Charro is dedicated to preserving the ancient pastoral arts which were brought to New Spain from Salamanca in old Spain. The duty of the charro is to protect the life of the president and to escort the national flag. There is a charro club and *lienzo* in every town of any consequence in Mexico. A *lienzo* corresponds to our arena. Carlos Rincon Gallardo, the Marquis of Guadalupe, was the man who gave *charreria* its impetus. He wrote several books on the subject, and was honored by the King of Spain for his contribution to the history of the mother country.

In California, the first man to realize that the old skills of the horseman were dying and did something to preserve them, was the banker, Marco Hellman. He scoured the country for good horses and bought them. Then he gathered a group of men and dressed them in old Spanish costumes. He went to fairs and celebrations and showed the reined horses. M. R. Valdez, the old reinsman, worked for Mr. Hellman. Now, of course, there are many men who show reined cow horses, and the number is increasing day by day.

The first books to come to the New World on the art of riding were, of course, from Spain and Portugal. But it was not long before books on riding horses began to appear in New Spain. The first one written here was by Don Juan Suarez De Peralta who wrote in 1580: *Tratado De La Caballeria, De La Jineta, Y De La Brida,* (Treatise on the Cavalry, on riding A La Jineta, and on Riding A La Brida). A La Jineta was the style of riding with short stirrups, which was brought by the Moors to Spain. *A La Brida* was the style of riding with long stirrups, which the heavily-armored knights used.

Other works on riding are:

Pedro Fernandez De Andrade: *Tractado De La Jineta De Espana,* 1599

(Treatise on the Jineta Riding of Spain)

Eusebio Manzanas: *Libro De Enfrenar,* 1583

(Book on Bitting)

Francisco De Navarete: *Arte De Enfrenar,* 1626

(Art of Bitting)

Antonio Galvam De Andrade: *Arte De Caballeria Y Arte De Jineta,* Lisbon, 1678

(Art of Cavalry and of La Jineta)

Gregorio Zuniga Y Arista: *Doctrina Del Caballo Y Arte De Enfrenar,* 1705

(Doctrine of the Horse and the Art of Bitting)

Nicolas Rodrigo Noveli: *En Que Se Propone Las Reglas De Torrear Acaballo,* 1726

(In Which Is Presented the Rules for Bullfighting on Horseback)

Jose Vargas Machuca: *Memorial Que Dan Los Caballos A El Entendimiento Del Hombre*

(Briefs the Horse Gives to the Understanding of Man)

Manuel Osorio Alvarez: *Manejo Real, Para Saber Por Si Hacer Un Caballo como Qualquier Picador,* 1769

(Royal Manege, To Know How To Train A Horse Like Any Trainer)

Pedro Manuel De Zurita Haro Y Aunon: *Libro Nuevo Tractado De Enfrenar Caballos,* 1772

(New Book, Treating on the Bitting of Horses)

THE PRODIGAL

Although many of the old vaqueros could not read, and for that reason had never read the Bible, they none the less, had learned its precepts at their mother's knee. I never knew an old vaquero who could not quote Scriptures when the occasion arose, to apply its tenets to his daily life.

One cold November day back in the early twenties, the Miller and Lux chuck wagon vaqueros were camped at the old Chester Ranch on the outskirts of Bakersfield. We were waiting for a trainload of longhorn Chihuahua cattle from below the border. We were just finishing eating the late after-noon meal which is both dinner and supper on the chuck wagon, when a woe-begone boy slouched into camp from the direction of the railroad yards. He had a forlorn, beaten look on his face, as he approached old Santos, the cook. He paused to gaze hungrily at the food in the Dutch ovens which were still half-filled with meat, potatoes, beans and biscuits. Santos pointed to Rafael Cuen, the cattle boss, who was leaning against the rear wheel of the wagon, drinking his fifth cup of coffee. Old Jake, as we called Cuen, had not taken his keen, old, squinting, appraising eyes off the boy from the moment he appeared in camp. As the boy turned from Santos to walk up to him, Cuen pointed to the food in the Dutch ovens and barked, "Eat". The boy's face brightened. He picked up a plate and loaded it with meat, potatoes, biscuits and beans, and began to eat hurriedly. Watching him, we could see that he had been on short rations for many days. His thin, undernourished body, clad in a pair of corduroy knickerbockers, out at the seat and knees, and a grimy flowered, pink shirt, told of hungry days and cold nights spent in barns and box cars without a blanket. His broad face and the kink in his hair said, ''Kanaka'', but his uptilted nose and pale blue eyes said, ''Irish''. It was a Celtic face over an Hawaiian framework. After the second helping of beef, potatoes, beans and biscuits, he switched to beans and ate two helpings of them before he began to slow down. Santo's old Yaqui face beamed, for he loved a good feeder. At last, the boy put his plate down and walked away. Here I must digress to explain about Dutch ovens and fried beans.

A Dutch oven, as all Westerners know, is a large cast iron pot with three, or sometimes four, legs. It has a lid with the edges turned up like the brim of a Mexican hat so that it can hold the coals which are heaped upon it to provide the heat. For a man who has been in the saddle from six to ten hours, no food can have the unforgettable flavor of the beef, potatoes, beans, and biscuits cooked in Dutch ovens over a campfire.

Good chuck wagon cooks were rare, but old Santos was one of the good ones. He could take a couple of Dutch ovens, meat, potatoes, beans, and flour, and put out a meal on which a man could stay in the saddle for many long, weary hours. Santos would roast his beef with that minute measure of garlic and spices which give a hint, but never a taste to good food, then add whole potatoes to bake in the gravy, but beans were his masterpiece. I can remember the taste of them after fifty years.

Frijoles, red beans, often called Arizona strawberries, have been the poor man's standby since the first Spaniards brought them to California. Beans were indispensible to all outdoorsmen, as essential a part of the prospector's outfit as was his burro. The law required the homesteader to live on his claim for three years in order to prove up on it, and often there was little or no money. Few could have lasted if they had not had beans, which were comparatively cheap to eat. Food was the dominant concern in the homesteaders existence. Beans never spoiled, were easily carried, and could be cooked wherever water and wood were found. Much of the early settler's heartbreaking drudgery and toil was done on beans. Santos would boil a batch until they were tender, then set them out to cool. They were better when left to set overnight. To prepare them for riders, Santos would put a cupful of lard in a Dutch oven, let it heat until it began to smoke, then he would ladle the boiled beans into the hot lard. This process sort of French-fried them. They were called *refritos* (refried), and were delicious. When the food was ready, he would set the pots out in a row for the vaqueros to help themselves. Even to the men who had plenty of meat, as the vaqueros did, beans were considered a necessary supplement to their diet - now to get back to the boy, the hungry waif.

I was sitting between old Juan and little Willie and Juan said, "*Dios, como come!*" (Lord, how he eats!). Willie who was only seventeen years old and had been watching the boy in open-eyed wonder, said, "*Ah, es El Hijo Prodigo*" (Ah, he is The Prodigal Son). We had not taken our eyes off the boy. We waited to see what old Jake would do in this pathetic situation. Cuen, we knew could hire him, for that was many years before there were child labor laws. But old Jake could get disagreeably ornery when the notion took him, and do the unexpected.

The boy finished eating at last and walked up and stood before Cuen to ask if he needed any hands. But before he could open his mouth, Cuen frowned fiercely and snapped, "You can go to work in the morning". Then he turned abruptly and walked away, still frowning fiercely. All that day old Jake kept a frown on his face and scolded. Although the longhorns had been unloaded and started towards Buttonwillow in a very workmanlike manner, nothing seemed to please the boss.

Now vaqueros and buckeroos are a thin-skinned class of men and must be handled with kid gloves, so to speak, and do not take scolding, and would ordinarily have walked off the job and left Cuen to drive his herd of cattle by himself. Strangely enough, that day, scold as he might, they only grinned; they knew very well that the old fraud was acting tough because they had caught him showing his soft side in hiring the waif. They all had seen that he wasn't the hard-boiled old cow boss he would have them believe.

Old Jake, whose habit it was to ride a newcomer to see if he had spirit, was surprised to find that the boy had spent some time with the *Paniolas* in the islands. (A paniola is a Hawaiian buckeroo). In the years that followed, the boy developed into a first-class buckeroo and there wasn't a horse on the Miller mounts that could buck him off, or on any other ranch on which he subsequently rode.

There were few, if any better judges of men who would be vaqueros, than old Rafael Cuen. A few days before the advent of the boy, we had been in town with Cuen looking for men. In those days it was not hard to find any number of vaqueros in Bakersfield. Most of the big outfits were still in business, and men were coming and going on the ranches.

We stood in front of the Rex Pool Hall on Nineteenth Street and waited for a stray buckeroo to come by, so that we could accost him and ask if he wanted to work. We had not long to wait. A man came down the street. He was the picture of elegance. He wore an uptilted Stetson, a white silk shirt, and a pair of Pendleton pants. His new boots had underslung heels, and a pair of gloves hung from a back pocket. We said to Cuen, "There's a buckeroo, Jake".

Old Jake grunted and said, "No, too pretty".

"Why too pretty?" we protested.

"Because he won't want to get his hands dirty", the boss answered. "To keep that shirt clean he will want to ride on the point, all the time out of the dust, and besides", he finished, "he will waste a lot of time putting on and taking off his gloves". We looked at each other and grinned in tribute.

We waited and soon another buckeroo came by, but he was the exact opposite of the first one. His hat was greasy and misshapen, and his shirt had never been washed, his pants could have stood up by themselves, and his boots were run over at the heels so badly that he was walking on the counters. "Here's one that ain't pretty, Jake", we said. To our disappointment, Jake grunted again and said, "No, too dirty, a man who is too lazy to wash himself will never wash his saddle blankets, and the result will be that all his horses will have sore backs''.

In the end, we went back to camp with only one new man, and he was an old buckeroo who had worked for Cuen before, but he was a good one.

On payday we would buy a new pair of Levis, and throw the old ones away. The old ones, though only a month old, had been slept in, the legs had been rubbed against the lathered sides of a sweating horse, and were coated with dried sweat. They had been soaked in rains and they were spotted with the blood of the cattle we had dehorned, earmarked, altered, and doctored. They were smeared with grease which had been wiped on them when they had served as a napkin. (Napkins were not found on the chuck wagon). They could have stood upright by themselves, and the prospect of ever getting clean again was remote indeed. The idea of washing them never entered our heads. Washing Levis was a questionable undertaking because they never failed to shrink two or three sizes, and as a result became too tight for comfort. If one wanted pants that could be washed, they would have to buy them two or three sizes too large. But the younger vaqueros and buckeroos didn't want to look like a ''balloon'', as they expressed it. They wanted pants that fit them. So washing Levis was out of the question. Older married men bought their pants so that they could be washed, but they were past the age of frivolity, and didn't care. Of course their wives washed their clothes, but married men were seldom found on the wagon. They got a camp where they had a house for their family, and rode a fixed route to see about water for the cattle and the condition of the fences. Once in a while a married man rode on the wagon. He always went home on payday to take his check to his family. When he returned, he would have clean washed clothes.

Old Jesus was the only man in the crew who wore patched clothes. It was not because he was poor (he owned his own home in the *barrio* in Bakersfield), but because he had a wife who would patch them. On the last payday he had brought back a bundle of clean clothes.

In riches or in poverty, the paisano never fails to follow the example of Saint Martin who shared his blanket with a beggar. He always shares his substance, be it a tortilla or a blanket, for to deny help to one's fellowman is to deny it to God. Old Jesus dug into his warbag and pulled out a pair of pants and a jacket. He gave them to the waif. True, they were shrunken and faded, but they were whole. The boy accepted them with a grateful grin and put them on.

A few days after the boy's arrival on the chuckwagon, Juan and I were riding from Temblor to Pimentel Ranch on the Carriso Plains. Since the road is long and tedious, I turned to Juan and asked, "What do you think brought the kid to the wagon"?

"Now this boy," he answered, "has a stepfather whom he does not like, or who mistreats him, as is often the case with stepfathers. He may have so many brothers and sisters that his parents can no longer feed him, and have sent him out into the world to shift for himself, or then again, he may be an orphan and alone in the world. Here on the wagon, he will have plenty to eat and the old men will teach him how to make his living."

"Vaqueros have a certain delicacy about asking questions; no one will pry into his past. He may have something in his life he may feel ashamed of - *Solo Dios sabe lo que le ha pasado en esta vida* (Only God knows what has happened to him in this life)." "I shall tell you a story of a family who lived in my town and who were ruined by the evil deeds of envious men and involves a witch and a runaway boy".

"The family of Tomas and Sara, his wife, was the most prosperous of the people in our village, and though by no means rich, they, however, owned a few cows more than any of the other families; and although they were respected for their gray hairs and their generosity, there did not lack persons in the village who envied them. One day the devil of envy tempted one of Tomas' neighbors to such a degree that he went to the *bruja* (witch) and asked for a spell to cast on Tomas and his family. The bruja, after she had been paid in advance, of course, demanded a note written in blood, two candles, two black ribbons, and a lock of Tomas' wife's hair. The bruja put all the articles in a basket, and after saying some diabolical words over them, gave them to the envious man and told him to bury them in the graveyard. From the moment they were under the earth the spell began to work, and misfortune fell on Tomas and his family. That very afternoon the watchdog died and the coyotes killed two calves. The next morning Tomas, who had never lifted a hand against any of his children, whipped his eldest son severely. The boy left home vowing to never come back.

"After a few days, the anxious mother could stand the boy's absence no longer. She asked her husband for money with which to travel and seek their son; but Tomas, who had always been the soul of generosity, and had never denied his wife anything, refused to give her money. After the quarrel which ensued, he left home with the family's savings and never returned. The poor mother sold one cow after another until none were left. She spent all the money seeking the boy but never found him. When all her assets were gone, she walked from town to town, begging her way. She finally died in poverty without ever seeing her son again". Juan finished as we came in sight of Pimentel and saw Max Gomez, the Spanish Basque, mounting to ride out and meet us.

"After Miller and Lux went out of business in 1927, Rafael Cuen retired from his position of cattle boss to live in Bakersfield. It was not long, however, before he became bored with doing nothing. Bob Huntington, who had ridden for him on the Miller and Lux chuckwagon, and who was then foreman on Poso Ranch, gave old Rafael a job riding fence.

"Of course Cuen had been offered some important jobs as foreman on several Land Company ranches, but he declined them. He said that he was too old for the strife of being a Cattle Boss, and besides, he did not want to take a job away from anyone. He was content with the humble job of riding fence because it gave him something to do. He rode his fence as diligently as he had worked when he had ninety thousand head of cattle under his care.

"One day he rode his fence and got back to the ranch by ten o'clock. He turned his horse out and put his saddle on the top rail of the corral, as was his habit. He got into his car, and drove to his daughter's home in Bakersfield. He parked the car and went up on the porch and sat down in a rocker to take a nap. His daughter heard him and called to him to say dinner would soon be ready. A half hour later, she went out on the porch to call him to dinner, and found he had died in his sleep. Rafael Cuen had met his death with the same fortitude with which he had for fifty-four years met the task of running a cattle outfit.

"Perhaps this passive courage was a heritage of those old McCuens who had left their homeland rather than suffer the yoke of tyranny, to become the "Wild Geese" who fought in all the armies of the world, but never in their own. In Spain, they dropped the Mc to conform to the Castillian way of speech, and became simply Cuen.

"That superb old horseman, Don Perfecto Cuen, brother of Rafael, had inherited blue eyes, a fair complexion, and a hawk nose from those old McCuens who had come from Ireland. Their motto could well have been that of the "Wild Geese" - "Always and Everywhere Faithful".

DON BALDOMERO IRURIGOITEA

Spain is a land of high, arid plateaus and massive, irregular *cordillera* which crisscross its surface from one end to the other. Because of its topography, many regions are isolated. This circumstance results in peculiar cultures and physical characteristics in the people of each province. For this reason, one can trace the path of each group of conquistadores who came to America from the peculiarities of language and physical appearance of the people. The Basques left a heritage of green eyes, large muscular bodies, light complexions, and long polysyllabic names to their descendents.

He came out of one of the old mining towns of the Sierra Madre. He was green-eyed, broad-shouldered, cat-hammed, bowlegged. His pants of necessity hung down on his hip bones (*pantalones en las verijas*) as vaqueros say, and they were always three inches too long. His name was Baldomero Irurigoitea, a Basque name if ever there was one. He was afraid of nothing. Therefore, he said anything that came into his head whenever the occasion arose for him to speak his mind, in that sardonic turn of phrase which characterizes the vaquero's speech and adds piquancy to his conversation. Whenever anyone asked him where he had come from, his answer would be "*Yo soy de San Miguel donde las mujeres se quedan doncellas para no parir cabrones*". (I am from San Miguel where the women remain virgins so as not to bear billygoats). In this sense the word "billygoat" means something other than the little horned animal of the *genus Capra*. To make him smile I would often say, "*Yo le envidio esas corbas chuecas, Don Baldomero, Usted andubo en muchos caballos buenos para tenerlas asi*". (I envy you those bowed legs, Don Baldomero, You must have ridden many good horses to get them that way). He would chuckle deep in his throat and say, "*Ah como es usted fino*". (Ah, how refined you are).

He had never read Socrates, because he had never learned to read, but somehow down through the ages the aphorism of the great philosopher, "I know that I know nothing", had come down to him. But he applied it in his own way. "You kids", he would say, "in learning to be vaqueros, go through three stages before you begin to learn. The first stage is the period in which you begin to ride on a ranch, and you drive a cow down a lane because she wants to go that way. You think you are a buckeroo and nobody can tell you anything because you think you know it all. The second stage is a short one, and that is when you think you can beat an idea into a horse, but the foreman and old men soon show you the error of your ways. The third stage is the last. It comes sooner or later. It depends on the thickness of your head. It is the stage when you at last find out that you do not know anything. Then you start to learn".

The foreman always put him in charge of us kids, because he had the patience of Job. He taught us many things, and here are some of the pointed precepts we absorbed under his guidance.

"Horsemanship descends from the gentleman, and of necessity the attitude of the gentleman must be maintained in all of one's relations with horses, for only the man with the gentle touch can teach a horse, as one must respect the feelings of the animal. Cruelty and fear go hand in hand, and abuse of dumb animals is the mark of meanness. It is good to be self-confident, but it is also good to be wary, and to study each horse. In a word, be a horse. That is, think like a horse. A man can be killed because of a loose cinch, a broken strap, a stirrup that is not strapped to the stirrup leather to keep it from turning. Too many accidents are proof of ineptitude. A good vaquero has few accidents. He must learn to deal with mean horses, with stupid cattle, with crusty bosses, with saddle-warped, cranky old men who have spent their lives on the range. They suffer from the numerous past hurts and broken bones they have acquired in pursuing their trade. A vaquero must suffer the yearnings and sex hungers of all deprived persons. He must learn to know the gringos, some good, some bad; the silent, aloof, disdainful Indians, and the cynical Mexicans with their bitter, ironical sense of humor.

"He must learn to communicate with his horse, because all the pretty silver-mounted bits in the world will not make a reinsman. To be a reinsman, one must have a bridle hand. A bit is a means of transmitting one's idea to the horse and one bit is no different from another in that respect. There are good bridle hands and bad ones. Good bridle hands do not come from the type of bit one uses, but from a natural aptitude to get one's idea over to the horse. For an example, there was the good vaquero, George Brunk, whose delicate, sensitive, caressing hands on the bridle reins, no horse ever refused to obey.

"There are many old men who would quail at using a spade bit. They would not consider themselves mature enough to use a bit with a high port. On the other hand, there are men who have used one from infancy and will have no other. Of course, a boy's ambition should be to make good horses and to be able to ride bucking horses, that is a *jinete*.

"What makes a good vaquero is not the purity of his blood or the color of his skin; an explanation of his racial background is not pertinent, suffice it that he is a man who pits himself against nature and because he learns its laws, he survives. Courage is a duty that is imposed on him by his occupation. His racial background has nothing to do with his toughness. To be a good vaquero, one must have guts, and the man who lacks them falls by the wayside. He must be tough enough to withstand the hard work, the long hours, the thirst, the hunger, the cold, the heat, the loneliness. He must cover long distances in a day, subsist on jerky and little else for days at a time. He must sleep on the ground and consider the snakes that crawl into his bed as no great danger.

"He must start his education with his first toy which is a

miniature riata and begins to throw his loop at dogs, sheep, goats, pigs, chickens roaming the ranch. He must try to ride a calf and get thrown, until at last he stays with it. Then he must try colts, bulls, anything on four legs, that will make a *jinete* of him.

"And above all, not to forget the vaquero's metaphorical speech in spite of the 'Yankee Schoolmarm'.

"The Thoroughbred horse has a sensitive, nervous system, is unreliable in temperament and disposition, and these traits make him unfit for certain tasks; yet the best running, jumping, and polo-playing horses are Thoroughbreds, and many of the best stock horses in the world are Thoroughbreds.

"It is not easy to train a horse for another person to ride. One man will get along with a horse, while ten other men will not be able to turn him in a city block, as the saying goes.

"One must bear in mind that a horse has a low order of intelligence, is afraid, and does not reason; but a horse can appreciate kindness and good treatment. A horse's chief weakness is fear. Forebearance and patience will do much to mitigate this fault. Punishment will aggravate it. If a man does not understand his horse, it is because he goes about it in the wrong way. He does not gain the animal's confidence, and its intellect is developed in contact with him, if, and that is a big "IF" the horse is treated with kindness. Knowledge cannot be beaten into a horse.

"But let the experts say what they please, nerve is the essential requisite of the rider. All accidents are caused by the fear and indecision of the rider. The horse senses this fear and becomes fearful, too. On the other hand, if the rider is courageous, the horse will sense it and have confidence. Courageous rider, courageous horse. It is as simple as that. If the horse has confidence in his rider, he can be induced to undertake anything.

"Above all, be careful. Risk and danger are factors incurred in handling and riding horses without the rider seeking them.

"The horse's manners, disposition, and actions are governed by the rider's hand, and the rider's seat decides the lightness or heaviness of those hands. A rider who has a bad seat cannot have good hands. By balance the rider can maintain the horse's center of gravity; without balance the rider cannot have light hands. It is light, delicate hands that a horse will obey.

"The balance seat is the seat of Indians, Cossacks and all natural riders. The reins are the means of communicating between horse and rider. They are meant for guiding the horse; they are not intended for punishing and torturing. Cruelty with the bit never cured a runaway or a lugger.

"A tight rein is bad; the constant pull teaches the horse to lay on the bit to numb his jaw. If your horse runs away, stop him by pulling, then releasing the rein. A steady pull will only brace him so that he can run faster.

"Never use a martingale on a horse you are riding after cattle on rough ground; because if a horse stumbles and needs his head to balance himself and cannot lift it because it is tied down, he will fall and perhaps kill or hurt himself and his rider. I have seen three men killed when the horses they were riding stumbled and fell because he could not get his head to balance himself.

"Dolph Short on Tejon Ranch was killed when his horse fell with him. A few weeks later, Joe Alexander's horse stumbled and fell. He was wearing a martingale. Luckily Joe was not seriously hurt. On gaining his feet, he pulled his knife out of his pocket and cut the martingale off the horse. From that day on, he had a horror for that piece of equipment.

"No rider can be a reinsman without effort. A lot of the success in riding is not in the rider's head, but in his hands and in the seat of his pants. It must be done with a light hand and above all, patience; and one day you will discover that you do not need to pull, or jerk, or whip, or spur. You will have developed a bridle hand and an affinity with your horse, and what is more, you will be a reinsman. Reinsmanship, to coin a word, comes with infinite patience and forebearance. Of course, you will need a decent bit, although after a time you will learn that the bit does not have the importance you once thought it had. You will also need a properly rigged saddle; but most important, you will need a horse that has the physical requirements for a spade bit horse."

PIMA PROTEST

In Mexico, the people have the same guilty feeling of having robbed the Indians as the Gringos have in the States. The Indians of Mexico have met the same disregard for human rights as the Indians have met in the United States. The following story was told to me by a man who took much satisfaction in being able to recount how an Indian got justice for himself and his people.

Don Porfirio Diaz, dictator of Mexico, has often been accused of severity toward the aborigines of that country. Several tribes, among whom are the Yaquis, have had good reasons to complain of his ruthlessness. The disaffected, too, suffered at his hands. His rurales (National Police) made his name feared and respected. But Don Porfirio brought law and order out of chaos and internal strife, and welded Mexico into one unit. He gave amnesty to all the bandits who infested the country, on conditions they become the rurales, and with the rurales made Mexico a law-abiding land. This incident occurred when Don Porfirio was at the height of his power, when all opposition had been beaten down, and his rurales had made it safe for a child to walk any road in Mexico without fear.

It is the story of an old Indian who bearded the iron-fisted old dictator and not only lived to tell the tale, but came off with the honors.

Quite often in the history of the Americas, Indians have aided whites against other Indians. These chapters are not uncommon in the history of Mexico, or the United States, for that matter. And perhaps the destiny of that country has taken its course because of that circumstance. The Pimas of northern Mexico many times defended Padre Kino's Missions against the Apaches, and were in a large measure responsible for their survival.

Porfirio Diaz was fighting a losing battle in northern Mexico. He had been wounded, was facing capture and a firing squad, when the Pima Indians entered the battle. They held off the enemy until Diaz's troops could retire. One Pima lifted the future dictator onto his back and carried him off the battlefield to safety. When Diaz came to power, he granted the Pimas lands in a pass in the Sierra Madres. The Indians built their village and lived there in peace for some years. But the demon of avarice never sleeps. A neighboring rancher coveted the Pimas' fertile acres. Each year he would move his fences onto more and more of the Pimas' land, until he had enclosed more than half of it under his fence.

The Pimas protested, but it availed them nothing. At last a number of young men armed themselves and started to the capital to force the government to restore their lands. The men who had fought for Diaz had all died. Only the man who had carried him off the battlefield, survived. This old man watched the preparations of the young men and shook his head in disapproval, but said nothing.

When the young men had been gone three days, the old man armed himself in full war regalia and set out after them. When he came upon them, their ardor had cooled and they were ready to listen to his counsel. The old man offered to take it upon himself to see the president and to get justice for the Indians. The young men turned back to their village, and the old man went on alone.

How long it took him to get to the presidential palace in Mexico City we do not know; but one morning there appeared an old Indian armed in full war panoply who asked to see the president. Of course the guards would not admit him. However, the information that an ancient warrior waited to see him, soon reached the president. He gave orders for the Indian to be brought before him.

The dictator now ruling Mexico was a far cry from the wounded soldier the Pima had carried off the battlefield. Don Porfirio was giving a reception for the representatives of the great powers of Europe when the old warrier stalked into the room. He walked through the groups of ladies and gentlemen and came to a stop before the president. Without a moment's hesitation, he said, "Porfiria, (many Indians in speaking Spanish, use the feminine suffix "a" for all masculine nouns instead of the "o") I have come to ask you now that you are the gobierno (government) why you have discarded the good laws of Don Benito?" (Benito Juarez, Mexico's second liberator and Indian President of Mexico).

The old dictator knew Indians. He had fought with them and he had fought against them. He answered in the same blunt tone, "I have not discarded them. On the contrary, I have made every effort to enforce them."

"Then Porfiria," the old man asked, "why are the lands you granted us being taken away from us? I have come to ask you for justice because though you do not know me, we have been compadres in battle."

Diaz recognized the man who had saved him from capture and probable death before a firing squad. He rose from his seat and embraced the old warrior, then introduced him to the people present, as an old comrade in arms. The president invited all the guests into the palace gardens, and when all were gathered around him, he sat down on a bench and asked the Indian to take a seat and tell him all his troubles.

To the surprise of all, the old warrior ignored the seat offered him and sat down on the bench beside the president! He began his tale and as he talked he would crowd against the president. The dictator of course, would move over to give the Indian room. After the Indian had shoved against him a number of times, the president was pushed off the bench. He stood up and said, "You have pushed me off the bench". The Indian answered, "Porfiria, that is exactly the way the Indians are being pushed off their land".

The old warrior was a guest at the palace for as long as he would stay, and when he left, Don Porfirio sent a lawyer to adjust the Indians' claims. The lawyer forced the landowner to remove his fences and to pay the Indians for the use he had made of their land.

PAPAGO SNAKE SHOW

The little snake charmer in the side show at the fiesta in Magdalena was very pretty with her long-lashed eyes, tiny hands, and tiny, high-arched feet. She was standing in the middle of the pit among the reptiles, four rattlers, an ugly iguana, two big boas, a *chirrionera* (whip snake), a yellowish *sencuate* (this snake is said to wrap itself around a cow's leg, and when the cow is secured, the snake sucks its milk), and a gila monster in a cage.

The snake pit had a platform around it to accommodate the spectators who, for the most part were Papagos. They came from their reservation on the Mexico-Arizona border and were the only Indians at the fiesta who had any money. The Yaquis and Mayos seemed to be miserably poor. The Indians, most of whom were women, crowded up to the platform and stared woodenly. The upland evening had cooled and the snakes had crawled into a mass to keep warm. The little woman had to pull each one she exhibited out of the squirming heap. She handled each in turn, holding it aloft, for the spectators to see. The rattlers, fully five feet long, crawled tamely over her arms without doing more than darting out their forked tongues. The boas made a show of temper, hissing loudly and opening their mouths. The Papagos looked bored.

The little woman placed the cage containing the gila monster in the middle of the pit and opened the door. She darted her hand into the box and caught the squirming monster. She waved it back and forth. The dead-pan Papagos, in a body, gave a violent start. A frightened, horrified look spread over the women's faces, and they hastily placed their hands tightly over their mouths and stared wide-eyed at the reptile in the little woman's hands.

I turned to a Papago youth standing beside me and asked him why the women covered their mouths. "It is a superstition," he answered. "They believe that they will die if they inhale the breath of a gila monster."

The little snake charmer let the horrid, mottled creature crawl up her arm. She stroked it and after an interval, she put it back in its cage, closed the door, turned and smiled at her audience. But the Papagos did not smile back. Staring stark disapproval back over their shoulders, they stalked out of the tent.

Later in the day, I talked with the little snake charmer who told me that the legend of the *escorpion* (as the gila monster is called), comes from the circumstance that it has only one defense, which is its bit. It frightens its enemies by filling its lungs with air and expelling it with such force that it makes a loud hissing sound. Its digestive processes are such that this breath is poisonous, and when it falls on a person's skin, it will raise blisters. That is why the legend of the reptile spitting poison has become current.

"The Gila monster," she went on, "will bite only a warm-blooded creature. Its bite will last for fifteen minutes, and during the time its teeth are sunk into its victim, it is injecting poison into it."

We are told that the teeth of a gila monster are not hollow like those of a rattler, but that the gila is poisonous because of the septic nature of the teeth.

THE GRINGOS

The old settlers of California were an accepting people; they accepted life as it came, "What will be, will be." A fatalism which their Semetic background gave them. A fatalism which was at once its strength and its weakness. The abused Mexican took a little different attitude toward the Mexican-hating gringo than the abused black did.

The gringo who hated him was his enemy, and being an Indian, the Mexican hated him. But he also despised him. It was when he saw the same gringo treat his own people, the Arkie, The Texie and the Okie with disdain, just as a generation or two before, during the Gold Rush, he had mistreated and held himself superior to the poorer, dirtier, smellier, Missourian "Pike", a name he corrupted into "Puke" (vomit). The paisano then began to understand that hate was a disease of the gringo, derived from a background of poverty in the Old World. It was a racial memory brought from Europe. The paisano found that hate was based on economy. The gringo hated himself.

The gringo, when he came to California, found a paradise. Cattle ranches with countless head of cattle, snug ranchhouses teeming with abundance. All he had to do was cheat the rightful owners out of their patrimony, which according to the gringo's own history was no great problem. It was not until after they had taken all the land for themselves, that the gringos met a real problem. There remained a few families, who by some miracle, had retained some of their property. The only way to acquire the land was to marry a daughter of the landowner. But they had already started a campaign of discrimination. They very neatly solved that problem by creating "Old Spanish Families" and thus could marry into them. But those who had no lands left, became Mexicans doomed to work for cheap wages and to suffer discrimination.

Vasquez, whose family came with De Anza, and if anybody could call himself "Spanish" it was he, is never called "Spanish" in all the biased histories or accounts of him that I have ever read. He is always referred to as "The Mexican Bandit".

DEAD MAN'S GOLD

The Camino Del Diablo (Devil's Highroad) crawls its thirsty way from the old Kino Mission town of Caborca, in Northern Sonora, across the uplands and down to Sonoita, where it turns west across the terrible sand desert to the Colorado River. Then across the sand dunes to the *Cerro Prieto* (Black Mountain) and Sentinel, or Mount Signel, on to the Santa Rosas, where it loses its diabolical character, since there is water and timber in abundance in those mountains.

Indians have watched Spaniards, Mexicans and Gringos set out across this desert, and have seen many of them die of thirst since the first dauntless trailblazers, Padres Kino and Garces, marked the overland route into California. These Indians were the Cocopahs who lived in the mesquite thickets along the borders of the Colorado River. They gleaned their meager living from the inhospitable desert.

They had suffered from the atrocities of scalp hunters and other gringo renegades, and had learned to hide from strangers; but they knew all who passed, for they followed each group of travelers across the desert unnoticed. They were witnesses to all the tragedies which occurred along the route. During the Gold Rush period in California, miners returning from the Gold Fields used this route to return East with the gold they had acquired in the mines.

The Indians learned that the men would inevitably quarrel and fight to the death, over possession of the gold. The Indians would wait at the foot of the Santa Rosas and follow each group from one camp to another, until the fight started, but they never interfered. When all were dead, they would gather up the gold and store it in a cave in the mesquite thickets along the Colorado River. One story goes that the Cocapahs once came on five mules laden with miners' possessions. They were all tied together. The men who had owned them had killed one another.

There was a large amount of gold in the *alforjas*. Sometimes there would be a survivor, who never failed to be wounded. He would gather up the gold and start out, but it would be only a matter of hours before he started discarding the booty, and thirst and his wounds would kill him. The Indians never failed to harvest each grain of gold, which they added to the horde in the cave.

Years after the Gold Rush, when towns grew up along the Colorado River, and a railroad crossed the desert, stories were told of an old Indian who would go out into the mesquite, and after a few days return with a large quantity of gold dust and nuggets. Avaricious men undertook to trail the old Cocopah, to find his cache, but the old man always eluded his followers, even when they used dogs. There is a plant which grows in the desert which is very effective in stopping dogs from following a scent. In the end, the men who tried to trail the Indians, gave up in disgust, and like the fox in the fable who said the grapes were sour, because he could not reach them, originated the story that the Dead Man's Gold was a myth.

But stories persist. There was a man who baptized a Cocopah's son and became the Indian's *compadre*. The Cocopah offered to show him where the gold was hidden, but as is usually the case with stories of buried gold, the Indian died a few days before they were to set out on their journey, and the Dead Man's Gold still lies in the cave in the mesquite thickets along the banks of the Colorado River.

HORSES IN BOOKS

Throughout my lifetime, whenever I picked up a book, the first thing I would so was search through it for descriptions of horses. Some were by writers who were not writing about horses, but'whose descriptions were only incidental to the story.

Here are some I have found in a lifetime of searching. Bundeville says - "The Spanish horse, if well chosen, is the noblest horse in the world; the most beautiful that can be, for he is not so gross as the Neopolitan. He is of great courage and docile. Hath the proudest walk, the proudest trot, and the loftiest gallop, the swiftest career, and is the gentlest and lovingest horse, and is the fittest for a king to ride on the day of triumph. He is much more intelligent than even the best Italian horse, and for that reason the easiest dressed, because they observe with their eyes, and their memories are good."

Washington Irving, in his "Legend of Sleepy Hollow", wrote a perfect description of an outlaw bronc. He says, "He was gaunt and shagged with a ewe neck, and a head like a hammer. One eye had lost its pupil, which was glaring and spectral, but the other had a gleam of the genuine devil in it. Still, he must have had fire and metal in his day, if we may judge from his name, which was 'Gunpowder'.

Cunningham Grahame, in his book "Rodeo", describes the Spanish Horse of his day. "They were of the same stamp as the horses Velaquez painted, short-backed, without too much daylight showing

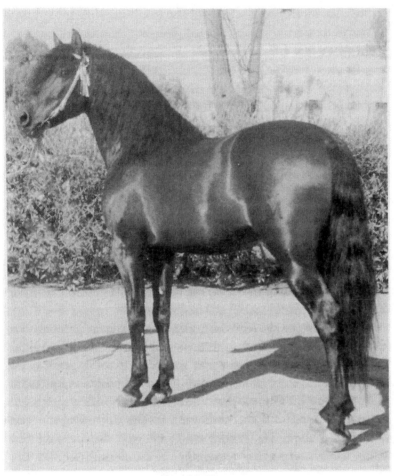

Spanish Horse

beneath their bellies. Their rather lengthy pasterns made them comfortable to ride, and their legs, not too long, and firmly jointed, made them sure upon their feet.

O'Henry, in his "Heart of the West", says of the Spanish Horse, "The Mexicans call him "grullo". He was a mouse-colored, flea-bitten roan dun. Down his back, from his mane to his tail, went a line of black. He would live forever, and surveyors have not laid out as many miles in the world as he could travel in a day."

IN THE HISTORY OF SPAIN
WE FIND THIS ONE

In the year 950 A.D. when Christian Spain was starting the Reconquista, the hero, Fernan Gonzalez rode to the Cortes on so fine an Andalusian charger that the king, Don Sancho, insisted on buying the horse, though his treasury was empty. Gonzalez offered the horse to the king as a gift, but the king would not accept it, and promised to pay as soon as money was available. He also promised to pay double for every day the money was overdue.

The king never paid, and after many years the debt was so enormous, that Gonzalez demanded the independence of Castille from Leon as the price of the horse. Don Sancho granted the demands, much against his will.

Bret Harte, who wrote beautifully of miners and the California Gold Rush says, "She was not a pretty picture. From her Roman nose to her rising haunches, from her arched spine hidden by the stiff *mochillas* of the Mexican saddle to her thick, straight, bony legs, there was not a line of equine grace. In her half-blind, but wholly vicious white eyes, in her protruding under-lip, in her monstrous color, there was nothing but ugliness and vice." *Bret Harte in "How Santa Claus Came to Simpson's Barr"*.

THE TEACHERS

The Sonorans who came to California during the Gold Rush period had a few advantages over the gringos, because they were expert in several trades which the gringos knew nothing about. The Sonorans knew the cattle business, which had been long established in California. Its terminology is still in use in the West. It was the Mexican *arriero* (muleteer) who transported the supplies into the mining camps of the Sierra Nevada. The art of transporting goods on the backs of animals was a heritage from Spain, and brought to America by Sebastian Aparico in 1535 who came to New Spain to teach the natives. The *arriero's* contribution to the success of each individual miner cannot be calculated. The terminology of the present day packer is that of the *arriero*. Alforjas, a word which came from the Arabs, is still used for the bags in which the goods are carried.

In like manner the Mexican *gambusino* (prospector or placer miner), who had experience in placer mining for centuries in his native Mexico, taught the farm boy from the East the art of panning, rocking and sluicing, though he got little thanks for it.

The *talabartero* (leather worker) also played an important part. Most of the early saddleries were established long before the gringos came. Even today, most of the leather workers are from Sonora. The terms for parts of the "Western" saddle are still those used by the early saddlers, such words as "*rosaderos and bastos.*" The reason most of the immigrants were from Sonora and Baja California was that at that time the big land-owners had absolute power over their peons. It was almost impossible to escape from the slavery of the big haciendas. Only those who lived close to the international border could escape into the United States.

I remember a vaquero with whom I worked on the Miller and Lux chuck wagon. We called him "Pelon" (Baldy). Baldness is rare among Indian Mexicans, but Salvador Marques had little or no Indian blood in his veins. In his part of Mexico, no Indian survived the conquest of Nuno Guzman. The people there are mostly of European blood.

One day I asked him, "Pelon, why are you bald, and why is your hair reddish blond and why are your eyes blue? Mexicans are *triguenos* (dark) and are never bald. You must have come from across the water." "No," he answered, "I came from the *Altos De Jalisco* (Uplands of Jalisco) where all the people are fair-complexioned."

Since he was the first man of his type I had ever known, I pressed him to tell me how and why he had come to the United States. "Well," he began, "I was born in *San Miguel El Alto* in the state of Jalisco. My parents were peons on the hacienda of Don Luis Munguia. At that time the terrible *rurales* of Don Porfirio Diaz, the dictator of Mexico, rode the countryside, and woe to any masterless man they found on the road. The captain of the rurales would ask him to show his permit to be away from the hacienda to which he belonged. If he had no permit, the captain would ask him what trade he followed. Then the rurales would escort him to the nearest hacienda and turn him over to the *capataz* (overseer) and tell the captured man to stay there and work at his trade, and to be careful that he was not caught again away from the hacienda without a permit. It was virtual slavery. I determined to escape from peonage, and one night I left the hacienda. I hid in the daytime and walked only at night. It was three months before I crossed the border at Eagle Pass, Texas. From there I came to California."

The last time I saw Pelon was on "L" Street in Bakersfield. He was broke and ill, and since I had just come off a job, I was able to lend him five dollars.

Of late years much has been written and shown on television of the suffering of fugitive slaves in escaping from slavery over the Underground Railroad; but few people realize that men have been running away from the whips of the *capataz* (overseer) on the haciendas in Mexico since 1846, and are still making their difficult way into the United States to find a better life despite the efforts to stop them. The hunger and cold Salvador endured in eluding the Rurales was as difficult and conducive of suffering as were the trials of those who fled from the Simon Legrees in the South.

BUCKING HORSE

The yard in front of the buckeroo barn on San Emideo Ranch where we mounted our horses in the morning was hard and rocky. The thought of being thrown off a horse and landing on its hard surface was an incentive for us to try to stay on our horses whenever one of them took a notion to try to buck us off. Johnny Drayer often said that the hard ground on San Emideo had made a bronc rider of him.

In the old days, before the gringos came, vaqueros never rode mares. Their mounts were invariably geldings, but by the time I arrived on the vaquero scene in 1912 or thereabouts, the vaqueros on California ranches were riding both mares and geldings.

My first job on a big cattle ranch was on San Emideo. I had never ridden a confirmed bucker before I went there. True, I had been on calves and horses that crowhopped a little, and had even ridden hogs. Consequently, since I lacked experience, when Hank Hoskings, the foreman, gave me Golodrina to ride, she bucked me off two times. True, I rode her once, but that was because Antonio Feliz picked her up before she quit bucking. She was definitely getting the better of me. Perhaps I never would have ridden her to a standstill if Salvador Carmelo had not come to ride on San Emideo.

He rode in one night on a sorrel Morgan horse. I liked his broad, good-natured face, with its wide mouth and full lips. It was a self-reliant, competent face. He was an old hand on San Emideo, having

Bud Sherman

Johnny Puget

ridden there when both Antonio Feliz and Juan Valdez had been foremen. I had often heard him spoken of as a good vaquero, and the man who had ridden Barney, a rank bucker, and had made a good horse out of him.

The next morning Hank gave him a string, and he saddled up and mounted in the yard. Hank had told me to saddle Golodrina. I saddled her and led her out. As I have said, she had bucked me off two times, but both times I had twenty-six inch tapadaras attached to my stirrups. The weight of the taps, as we called them, made the stirrups hard to hold. When the horse bucked, the taps would swing and I would lose the stirrup. Then I would get bucked off. I was just a kid and didn't know any better.

The boys had advised me to take the taps off, so the evening before, I had taken them off, and had shortened my stirrup leathers. The fact of the matter was, that I, kid-like, had seen the old-timers ride with stirrups so long that they barely touched them with their toes, and I wanted to imitate them.

Golodrina was one-gutted, that is to say, she had a narrow chest which tapered back to her flanks. She was so small around the barrel that the cinch rings touched the rigging rings on both sides. It was impossible to ride one's cinch, that is, hook the spurs into the bars of the cinch, in the way most riders rode bucking horses in those days. She had to be ridden on balance alone. I was determined to ride the mare to a finish, and without the taps I had a better chance.

She stood quietly while I mounted her, settled myself in the saddle with a rein in each hand, one rein shorter than the other. This was to be able to double her if she should jump or shy. The moment I moved her out she lit into bucking. The shorter rein caused her to buck in a circle. After the first four or five jumps my body began to lean outward and most surely I would have lost my balance altogether, if a stout hand had not caught my shoulder and straightened me up in the saddle. With that little help, I rode her until she quit bucking. It was Salvador who had straightened me up, and it was through him that I acquired confidence, so that I could ride a bucking horse. Afterwards I was to ride worse bucking horses than Golodrina, though I never was a good bronco rider.

Buster Clark

Buster Clark

Johnny Puget

Johnny Puget

Compas

unknown

The vaquero crew which consisted of Hank Hoskings, the foreman, George Hoskings, his brother, Salvador Carmelo, Bill Nichols, who was shortly afterwards killed by a horse falling over backwards with him, Jim Gorman, Jack Emory, Albert Frago, Joe Nicholson, Uel Mathews, whom we called "Booger Red", Bert Galgraith, a Canadian, Johnny Crackenburger, and Johnny Tregea, whom we called "Flaco", were all grinning from ear to ear. Johnny Tregea is the only one of that group whom I know to be alive. Sometime ago he called my distributor, Chuck Hitchcock, and asked him if I remembered him. I assured Chuck that I remembered Johnny very well. He used to ride a lanky sorrel called "Telephone".

I dismounted to fix my cinch, very well pleased with myself; for I had ridden my first bucking horse to a standstill.

Through the years, Salvador and I remained friends even after he was compelled to quit riding, which he loved so well, and go to work in a machine shop, where he could make better wages to support his growing family. He never forgot the morning I rode the bucking horse on San Emideo. Years afterwards when he had retired from the machine shop, and was braiding bridle reins and riatas which were again in demand, I would occasionally send him a client. When the client had told Salvador who had sent him, Salvador would never fail to chuckle and tell him of the time I rode Golodrina that cold morning on San Emideo Ranch many years ago. In his generous way he made me out a much better rider than I really was.

THE WEEPING PHANTOM

Over the length and breadth of the Spanish America from the Columbia, in Oregon in the north, to the Straits of Magellan in the south, whenever the wind, in the stillness of the night in blowing over the land, brings the sound of moans, groans or sobs, to the ears of old wives seated around the hearth, the old women huddle closer to the fire and say, "It is La Llorona weeping for her babies."

La Llorona (the Weeper) has been haunting the Spanish-speaking world since time immemorial. She came to Spain with the first Phoenician traders from the Plains of Canaan. The soldiers of Queen Dido were familiar with the legend of the Weeping Woman when Hadrubal went to Spain to found the City of Alicante. She went to haunt the castle he built above that city, and she haunts it to this day. She accompanied the motley Moslem horde out of Damascus across North Africa, in the first wave of Moslem conquest, and was already an old, old legend to the soldiers of Taric El Tuerto, when he crossed the Straits of Gibraltar to conquer Gothic Spain.

In Catholic Spain, she was an apostate Christian princess who had slain her babies and embraced the Moslem Faith.

In Moslem Spain, she was an apostate Moorish princess who had slain her babies and embraced the Christian Faith. In both legends, she was doomed to haunt the burial place of her infants, and always appeared as a beautiful woman with long hair hanging down to her waist and dressed in a long, flowing, white gown, weeping incessantly.

La Llorona probably had her birth in a nomad society plagued with the problem of infant mortality in a desert environment. A fear of race extinction probably prompted the rise of the legend as a deterrent to infanticide, just as polygamy developed to offset the same nomad conditions.

La Llorona never appeared to men. Only women had heard her sobbing in the night, until Tomas Romero appeared one day to tell his story of an experience. Near the old Mission, there stood some ruined walls of an old dwelling house which had belonged to the once rich Elizalde family, who had long since been despoiled and driven away by the gringos. The house had been left to fall into ruins, and winter rains had washed away the adobe, until only a corner of the wall remained. The walls had surrounded a patio and a garden, and in one corner of what had been a garden, there stood an ancient cottonwood tree which over-shadowed the remaining corner of the wall.

That Friday night Tomas was riding by the ruins when he saw a beautiful young girl standing in the shadow of the tree. She was weeping, and Tomas could hear her sobs over the hoofbeats of his horse. At first he was inclined to stop, then thought she must be crying because the priest had scolded her in confession. He rode on.

It occurred to him that there was no confession on Friday. He passed the place every night and did not see the girl again until the next Friday, when he came upon her in the same spot, weeping.

He stopped his horse and pulled a crucifix from under his shirt, and holding it in front of him at arms length, approached the girl and said, *"Eres tu diablo o santo? Eres de este mundo o del otro? En nombre de Dios Habla."* (Are you devil or saint? Are you of this world or the other? In the name of God, speak.) This exhortation is infallible. No phantom ever failed to speak when abjured in this manner.

"Senor," the girl replied, "I am a poor soul condemned to haunt this spot until the remains of my baby, which lies under that wall, are buried in consecrated ground."

Tomas crossed himself and rode away. The next day he told his story to the people of the village who came in a body with picks and shovels. After digging in the corner of the patio, they found a tiny iron casket. It contained the bones of a newborn infant. They took the tiny body to the churchyard and buried it. The weeping girl must have gone to her rest, because she has never appeared again to anyone in the town of San Antonio.

A SAN JOAQUIN VALLEY GHOST

Ghosts are always associated with buried treasure. The sound of groans, moans, and the appearance of a light, indicate buried gold. Many years ago in "Horcasitas", a ghetto district inhabited by paisanos, in what became the town of Kern, on certain nights there would appear a light which no one could explain, and which the paisanos came to call *La Lumbrita* (little light).

Connie Iverson, who told me this story, says her grandmother owned a house in the settlement, but could not live in it because she was disturbed by the sound of moaning and groaning, heard throughout the night. She rented it to a young couple who were also disturbed by the noises, but instead of moving out, they dug up the entire foundation until they came on a treasure. Instead of sharing it with Connie's grandmother, they bought a house of their own, and left the grandmother's house untenanted.

Connie also knew of a house in Bakersfield where the ghost would crawl into bed with the occupant of the upstairs room during the night, and take all the covers. The sleeper would wake up in the middle of the night from the cold and find a *bulto* (body) in bed with him. Then the whole family would be awakened by a terrified person running screaming down the stairs. At other times the ghost would sit on Connie's sister's lap. She would feel the weight of a body and feel the hot breath of the phantom on her face.

The house had belonged to a gringo family who had rented it to the Morenos. Whether the gringos or a member of the Moreno family had committed a crime which caused the ghost to appear, or whether they had buried a treasure, Connie could not tell me. Suffice it to say that the treasure, if there was one, has not been found.

Connie is sure the house is haunted, because her family had never been in it before, and had never heard of its being haunted until they moved in. Consequently, they were not predisposed to think of ghosts. In fact, before that time, they had never even heard talk of them. Ghost stories were never told in Connie's home.

Another proof is that a cousin of Connie's came for a visit, and before going to bed in an upstairs room, told Connie's dad that if he needed anything to call him.

The next morning the guest came downstairs and said, ''I heard you walking around in the room last night. I went to the head of the stairs and as I stood there, I felt your arm on my shoulders as if you wanted to push me down the stairs. But when I asked you what you wanted, you did not answer.'' He didn't know it had been the ''ghost''.

THE GIFT RIATA

It was an old California custom for a vaquero, when he wanted to make a present of a riata, to hang the riata on the friend's saddle, preferably when the friend was absent. The element of surprise added to the pleasure of receiving the gift. A riata was no mean present. In the Visalia catalog of the 1920's, a riata was priced at 30 cents a foot, and most were over sixty feet long. It took days to prepare the hide, cut the strands, and to braid them. Riatas are hard to braid. The strands must be kept moist, so they can be pulled up tight. Most riata makers choose the winter time to make them, because the foggy weather keeps the strands moist. After the riata is braided, the strands must be hammered down until they lie smoothly. Then the braider must bore four holes in a hardwood post, insert the riata into the holes, and pull it through them until it is smooth, even and polished.

A few years ago I gave a fine riata to Red Jocelynn, the roper. I had picked it up in Sonora. He was pleased with it, because he wanted it for roping horses. Now, every time he sees my car parked, he throws a gift into it. So far, I have received a hemp Porter special, a nylon rope, and another riata, proof of his delight in receiving my gift.

After the terrible depression of the ''thirties'', when the economy began to improve, and the struggle to keep body and soul together was no longer so desperate, when people began to have a dime or two to spend for something besides the bare necessities, it occurred to me to gather up some of the pieces of equipment which had been used by the old vaqueros who were no longer living. As a result, I acquired a Visalia saddle, a Garcia bit, and a pair of Garcia spurs. I found a pair of reins and ramal, but I lacked a riata. That sixty-foot length of braided rawhide, which is so marvelous in the hands of an expert. In order to remedy the discrepancy, I bought a fresh hide from a man who was butchering a steer. I pegged it out in the shade, and when it was ready, I removed the hair with the help of oak ashes, as the old men had done years ago. When I had finished the job the hide was in good shape. I had always been too lazy to learn to braid when the old men had offered to teach me, to my subsequent sorrow.

I rolled the hide up and took it to Salvador Carmelo. He was the only old-timer left who knew how to braid a riata. I left the hide with him and went away to wait until it was made. Some weeks later I got word that the riata was ready. As I arrived at Salvador's house, he was still pulling it through the holes in a post. When it had reached just the right degree of smoothness, he coiled it, but instead of handing it to me, he asked, "Where is your saddle?" I have always carried an old saddle in the car for company or for a conversation piece. I dragged it out and set it on a rack. Salvador walked up, strapped the riata to the fork, turned around, and held out his hand. We shook hands, but I did not offer him any money, because the making of the riata was a labor of love. He was my friend.

Vaqueros — Lakeside Ranch (l.-r.)
Zenon Munos, Frank Feliz, Alfonso Valenzuela, Juan Feliz, Joaquin Feliz,
Foreman

George Knowles, Ed Knowles, John Gomez, Lupe Gomez

OLD PICTURES

I am deeply grateful to the many good people who supplied the old photographs that I used to illustrate my book, *These Were The Vaqueros*. Among them were Salvador Carmelo, Chuck Hitchcock, Lupe Gomez, Catarino Montes, Percy Hoffman, Tex Rosencrans, Ismael Moreno, Evelyn Albitre, Leonardo Chavaria, Adolfo Encinas and Mrs. George Brunk. Some of these kind people have passed away, but their keepsakes live on, a visual part of the Old West. The pictures were lent to me so that my readers might share the mementoes of another day, humble as they were. Taken with a little box camera, the old snapshots lend an element of authenticity to the text.

One day Percy Hoffman came to me and asked, "Do you remember Old Tex Rosencrans?"

"Of course," I answered, "I worked with him on Miller and Lux. He was always referred to as 'Old Tex'. He had been in the country a long time when I came here. He was a garrulous old fellow, but there was no malice in him. I don't think Old Tex ever spoke ill of anyone. He was never cranky and surly like most of the other old men who had been knocked about from pillar to post, from one ranch to another. He was always genial.

"One day," Percy went on, "the old man hobbled over to my shop from the little shack he lived in. He had a cigar box under his arm. He handed it to me and said, "Percy, I can't take care of myself

Klipstein Ranch

Juan Feliz

Vic Huntington

Mr. Jaquine Feliz, Lakeside Ranch

Bole Huntington (left) (other unknown)

Pini

Klipstein Ranch

V7 Ranch, Fellows

Puget, Boggs, Lupe Ortiz, Jesus, Pini

Jaquine and Juan Feliz, Poso Ranch

Nacho Montes, Cat Montes

any more. Today they are coming to take me to the hospital, and I am not coming back any more. I want you to have these pictures. They were taken when I worked for Miller and Lux.'' ''Well'', Percy went on, ''Old Tex never came back. He died a few months later. Take the pictures, maybe you can use them.''

I opened the box reverently, for I was taking a peek into the soul of a man who had loved his calling. These old pictures were all he had to treasure after a lifetime of riding the range. I opened the box and immediately recognized ''Old Blue Dog'', a horse I used to ride on Pimental Ranch. The pictures had been taken on various camps and ranches on the southern division of Miller and Lux, Battenfeld, Swan Wells, Temblor, Salt Slough. True, I had to get Johnny Puget to identify some of the riders in them.

How Do You Do!

FIVE DOLLARS A BRONC

One day, back in the early 'twenties, after a rodeo performance at the old fairgrounds, I was standing on Nineteenth Street in Bakersfield talking to Johnny Drayer, the Irish boy from Butcher Town in San Francisco. He could sing like an angel, and taught me the words to "The Wearing of the Green", "My Wild Irish Rose", and "Where the River Shannon Flows", as we rode the range on San Emideo Ranch. In after years, Johnny won fame as a bronc rider. Al Allen, another bronc rider, approached us and asked, "Do you fellows want a job riding broncs for mount money? I have been offered a job at the Orange County Fair. They need three men. They will pay us five dollars a mount and will let us ride two mounts a day. That will make us ten dollars a day. And ten dollars ain't to be sneezed at", he finished.

Ten dollars a day to ride two bucking broncs from the worst bucking string in the West! They were from the Prescott Frontier Days bucking string. Truly to be a cowboy, as some people said, "One must have a strong back and a weak mind."

That was over fifty years ago, but "Ten dollars a day ain't to be sneezed at" recurs to my mind quite often, and never fails to bring a chuckle of a fond memory.

JOKERS

Anselmo Campas was one of the few vaqueros who ever dared to play jokes on big, burly Frank Urrea. Most men did not care to risk being knocked down with a *surdazo* (a left-handed punch), for Frank was quick-tempered and would start swinging fists at the least provocation. Anselmo, however, was not the least bit afraid of Frank, and never missed an opportunity to tease him. Whenever Anselmo called at Frank's house, he would say to Frank's mother, "*Yo vine a verla a usted tia, y no a este cabron.*" (I came to see you auntie, and not this billygoat), pointing to Frank. This would infuriate Frank. However, the two, Anselmo and Frank, always worked together on ranches.

One summer the two were working on the Olcese Ranch. The weather was hot and the two men slept on a veranda which was built over the river where it broadened out into a wide pool. Anselmo awoke one night and sat up in bed. Frank, whose bed was on the edge of the veranda, was snoring away. Anselmo could not resist the temptation. He tiptoed over to Frank's bed, reached down and grasped it firmly, gave a quick heave, and dumped him into the river. The water was shallow, but deep enough to break Frank's fall. He hit the water with a scream and thrashed about before he was fully awake. He came out of the water roaring and chased Anselmo, calling on him to stop and fight. Finally he wore out, and went back to bed without ever catching his tormentor.

It was a week before Frank would speak to Anselmo. After he had gotten over his grouch, and the two had been on speaking terms for a couple of weeks, Anselmo one day suddenly turned on Frank and said, "Last week you chased me all over the ranch and wanted to fight. Now I've made up my mind. I want to fight. We will settle the matter right now." But Frank did not want to fight, and Anselmo knew perfectly well that he didn't.

But the man who played the best joke on Frank and made the vaquero population of the valley laugh for many days, was a little skinny fellow we called "Tejano" (Texan). Ironically, of course, because he was just the opposite of a blowhard.

One day he was walking through some brush and stepped on a snake. It gave him a start, because it was marked very much like a rattler. When he saw it was harmless, he picked it up and wrapped it in a piece of newspaper, and put it in his pocket. He was not a vaquero, and was just watching the men work cattle. The vaqueros were at the slow work of parting out cows and calves. Frank was sitting on his horse holding the herd while Cuen was parting out. It was a time when the work was tedious, when there was no romance in being a vaquero - if there ever was any - perhaps Frank was just bored or wanted to get the kink out of his legs. He turned his horse toward some trees and bushes and rode to them. Tejano had been watching, he walked toward Frank and met him. He asked, "*Quieres papel?*" (Want paper?) Frank answered, "Si." (Yes). Tejano handed him the snake wrapped in the newspaper.

Frank rode off till he came to a level spot; tied his horse to a sapling, and walked back to the level spot. He dropped his chaps, then he dropped his pants, then he dropped his drawers. They fell around his ankles. He was as effectively hobbled as if he had been shackled with leg irons. He squatted and began to unfold the paper. He could not read, but hoped to look at some pictures. At least he would have a rest. He unfolded the paper. When he came to the last fold he felt a quiver, but he opened it, and there was the snake with its mouth wide open and hissing. Frank yelled, dropped the snake, and jumped. As we have said, he was hobbled. He fell, the snake fell on his bare legs.

He let out a scream and started kicking. The little snake was trying frantically to escape, and crawled over Frank's bare legs. This made him kick and scream more.

Finally the snake crawled off, and Frank saw that it was a gopher snake. He stood up. He pulled up his drawers, then his pants, then his chaps. He shook his fist at Tejano, and in a stuttering scream he said, "Tejano, you - - - - come and fight me, Tejano." When Tejano did not come, he said, "Please Tejano, be a man and come and fight me." Tejano was peeking from behind a tree with a delighted grin on his face. The men who had all ridden up were roaring with laughter. For some weeks Tejano stayed out of Frank's way. He even moved his bed out of the bunkhouse so Frank would not catch him asleep.

PETE RIVERA

One afternoon, I found Pete Rivera sitting on a bench in the warm November sunshine. He welcomed me to a seat beside him. When I had made myself comfortable, he began to tell me of his experiences on the Tejon Ranch in the years he spent riding its range. He mentioned Sutah Coway, the good Indian vaquero, who threw the prettiest loop on the ranch; of Juan Gomez, Navarro Cordero, Luis Zamora, vaqueros, and good vaquero horses, rattlesnakes and other varmints.

"One day," Pete began, "Sutah and I rode into town to get a pair of spurs he had ordered from Garcia. We got the package and after Sutah had unwrapped it, I saw that the spurs had extra long shanks. After he had examined them carefully, Sutah said, "I ordered these spurs to ride this black horse to see if he can buck me off again." Sutah meant to hook the spurs into the bars of the cinch. The long shanks would be a help in hooking the rowells into the bars.

"Before starting back home we went to a liquor store where Sutah bought five bottles of whiskey. He put one bottle in his pocket and packed the others in the saddle bags. We mounted our horses and headed for the ranch. As we rode along, Sutah would take a nip from the bottle he carried in his pocket. We had ridden about three miles when Sutah decided to try out his spurs. At that time most of the roads were not paved. The road we were on was dirt-surfaced. There wasn't much danger of the horse falling. Sutah dismounted, tightened his cinch and mounted. I didn't expect him to be bucked off, because he was a big, strong, young fellow. Of course he was half drunk, but often times I have seen a drunk man ride a horse which he could never have ridden if he were sober, but this time the whiskey was no help. After three jumps, the horse bucked Sutah off, and kicked him as he was falling. He was unconscious when he hit the ground. Luckily, Emiliano Castro was driving by in a wagon. We loaded Sutah in the wagon and Castro drove him to the hospital. I rode on after Sutah's horse and caught him where he had stopped at a gate. The bottles of whiskey were intact. I rode on, leading the horse.

When I came to the last gate, just before reaching the vaquero camp on Tejon Ranch, I thought of the whiskey. It would be sinful to throw away good whiskey, but if I were to take it into camp there would be one uproarious drunken spree, and no work would be done. But to throw it away! Whiskey is sovereign medicine. It is good for snake bites and good on a cold morning. I counted four posts from the gate post, then I buried a bottle at each post and rode into the vaquero camp.

Sutah stayed in the hospital for five weeks. When he came back to the ranch he never mentioned the whiskey. I guess the horse had kicked him so hard that he had completely forgotten everything that had happened to him that day. I never reminded him of the whiskey and it remained hidden.

That following winter was colder and wetter than normal. One evening we rode back to camp soaked to the skin. We had worked in the rain and sleet all day. As we passed the place where I had hidden the whiskey, I asked Sutah if he thought I could conjure a bottle of whiskey. He said it would be a miracle in that kind of weather. I said, "Dig at that post," pointing to one of the four posts. He dug up a bottle and all the crew had a drink. On cold wet days, we would dig up a bottle, and it was almost spring before the whiskey was all gone.

"There were places on Tejon Ranch that swarmed with rattlesnakes," Pete went on, "black diamondbacks in the higher altitudes, red ones in the flat lands, and little, fat sidewinders in the sand over by the Rockpile. One day we came on half a snake; its body had been cut in half and had been carried off, but the half that was left was over four feet long and five inches thick. Some eagle must have carried away the missing part, but how he had cut it we never knew. Whole, the snake must have been over nine feet long. We often saw eagles and hawks carrying off snakes, to feed their young, probably. This one was a black diamondback.

In some years there were more snakes than in others. I don't know why. One day we were riding up a canyon over on the desert side of Tejon when we were stopped by a very strong stench which was coming down a draw. Of course we thought of dead cattle and rode up to investigate. We came on a writhing mass of rattlers. The stench was coming from them. We got off our horses and threw rocks at the snakes until they all drew apart and crawled into a hole in the bank of the draw. I don't want to smell that stench again.

On another occasion we came upon a snake which, as we approached, opened its mouth and made a whistling noise. Immediately, four baby snakes crawled out of the bushes and crawled into the big snake's mouth. It closed its mouth and crawled away. One day we came on a king snake swallowing a rattler. The rattler was twice as long as the king snake. It had already swallowed its entire length of rattler. What it did about the rest of the rattler we never found out. We left it to work out the problem by itself. We never killed king snakes because they prey on rattlers, and are beneficial to humans. Snakes were constantly on our minds, because if one got careless, he could be bitten. *Vibora* was the vaquero's term for the rattler.

AN IMPROMPTU BATH

Motorists driving north on the Ridge Route over Highway 99 will see Castaic Lake across the Freeway from the town of Lebec, just north of Tejon Pass. It is dry most of the time, its surface is covered with a coating of white saline deposits. But in wet winters it will hold water for three or four months.

One cold winter day when the ground was covered with snow and a rim of ice edged the lake, two vaqueros, Chico Martinez, the top hand on Tejon Ranch, and Adolfo Encinas, the best thrower of the rope on Tejon, were riding along the steep sides of the hill above the lake. Suddenly the colt Martinez was riding, shied, jumped, and landed in the lake, bucking. After the first jump, the colt fell into the icy water, soaking Martinez to the skin. The horse floundered around trying to get its footing, until its rider was covered with a coating of mud. The horse and rider were half drowned before they reached the bank again. Even Adolfo did not escape unscathed. He was splashed with mud too.

Jose Maria Valasquez, the caporal who had witnessed the mishap, rode up with a sour look on his face and grumbled, sarcastically, *"Yo no se porque se to antojo banarte en dia de invierno, y cuando estamos trabajando. Uno se bana en el verano cuando no hay nada que hacer."* (I don't know why it has occurred to you to take a bath on a winter day and when we are busy working. One takes a bath in the summer when there is nothing else to do.)

What Martinez answered we do not know. His teeth were probably chattering so much he could not talk.

MORGANS

It was back in the days of my youth, when I worked for Roland and Russell Hill who ran the Tehachapi Cattle Company and bred fine Morgan horses, that I learned the sterling worth of that breed of horse.

Since then I have read many accounts of the origin of the Morgan and all have disagreed. In after years, when I traveled in Europe and studied the Andalusian in Spain, the Lusitan in Portugal, and attended the bullfights-on-horseback, I was struck by the similarity of the Andalusian and the Lusitan to the American Morgan. All three, the Andalusian, the Lusitan, and the Morgan have the same high crest, the same proud carriage, and all three have the courage to face cannon in war as the Lusitan and Andalusian did in the Crimean and Napoleonic Wars, and the Morgan in the Civil War.

The Iberian horse, besides being a war horse, has faced bulls in the arena for centuries. At times while a spectator at the bullfight-on-horseback, I would suddenly be brought back to the old days in the Great Valley in California when the *rejoneador* (bullfighter-on-horseback) rode out into the arena on a horse that to all appearances was a Morgan.

It is my considered opinion - and my reader can take it for what it is worth - that back in that glorious period in United States history - starting with John Paul Jones - which produced that peerless sea dog, the Yankee Skipper, who made America great, and the clipper ship famous, in the annals of sailor men, one of those captains sailing into one of the Spanish ports, found an Andalusian to his liking, and brought him to Vermont to become the father of the Morgan breed.

Clyde Hartman, who had a ranch at Glennville, also bred Morgans. His ranch had been the property of the pioneer Hughes family who came to Kern County in 1869. He bought the ranch from H. Guy Hughes, and it is now owned by another member of the Hughes family, Henry Bowen.

Hartman's stallions were "Will Rogers" and "Captain Jack". For some years I rode colts for Mr. Hartman, and found his Morgans just as good as those of Roland Hill. I had learned about handling horses of that breed from the best vaquero I ever knew, old Teodoro Valenzuela. "You must handle them gently," he would insist, "I know, I broke Morgans on the Cuyama Ranch."

One day, when I was in the stable business in Bakersfield, we were returning from town in a car, when we overtook a young man riding a fine, seal brown colt. We slowed the car to take in the colt's good points, then drove home. We had not been home long, when the young man on the seal brown colt rode into the yard. He was followed by two men in a car. I was pleased to see that one of them was Chris Twisselman, a cattle man from the west side of the Valley. I had known him when I rode for Miller and Lux. His men, Dick Kelly and Charlie Stewart, rode with us on the roundups on the Carriso Plains. I hurried forward to greet him, and he introduced me to his companion, Mr. Anderson, a sandy-complexioned man whose little blue eyes were set in a stern, granite face which reminded me of portraits of Herbert Hoover. But his looks belied his nature, for he was a gentle, kindly man. The first thing he did, was to buy a pair of boots and a bicycle for the little boy who lived with me - But to get back to the Morgans - - -

"This colt," Mr. Twisselman said, "has been ridden only a few times but is very gentle. He is a pure-bred Hartman Morgan. I intended to use him for a stud but he was a little too angular to suit me, so I altered him and gave him to Mr. Anderson. He is in the land department of the Superior Oil Company and lets me graze my cattle on Oil Company land. I have heard that you are a good hand with horses. I want you to ride him and put a good rein on him." I rode the horse for six years. Mr. Anderson, who was a Texan, in all that time rode the horse two times, and one day gave him back to Mr. Twisselman who rode him after cattle for many years.

Because Mr. Anderson had been very kind to the little boy who lived with me, I took special pains with the colt. I rode him in a Jaquima, then in double reins, after Mr. Twisselman had a bit made for him. He took the bit very well. His registered name was "Lynn", but we called him "Percy".

Through the years whenever I needed a horse for any of the tasks for which a saddle horse is needed, I rode Percy. I rode him in parades in Indian costume; I rode him on trail rides in the mountains; I rode him to work whenever the cattlemen needed help; I rode him to wrangle dudes, and I roped on him in rodeos. But the Morgan was at his best as a snubbing horse, when I rode colts.

I rode my colts alone and had to mount them without help. I developed a way of mounting them. I would take a rope, run it through the ring on the snaffle, put it over the colt's head behind his ears, pass it through the ring on the opposite side, then I would join the rope ends and snub the colt up close to Percy and wrap the rope around the horn.

Percy, who in a parade would arch his neck, prick his ears forward, flag his tail, and strut down Nineteenth Street as if he were walking on eggs, oddly enough, when holding a snubbed colt in the corral, became as steady as a rock. He was a stern disciplinarian and would brook no monkey business from the colt. At the colt's least movement, Percy would lay his ears back and bare his teeth in warning, and since horses talk to each other and colts are afraid of older horses, the colt would stand until I was on his back with both feet in the stirrups. Then I would unwind the rope off the horn. Percy would never move from the spot until I had moved off on the colt. After I had ridden that colt I would go through the same procedure with another one. Sometimes I rode five or six colts in a day.

I found out how tough a Morgan could be, one day, when a neighbor came to me and said the wild mare he had in a pasture had gotten out and had taken the other horses with her. This mare had been bought out of a band which had been captured in Nevada. I promised to go after her, and saddled Percy, mounted him, and rode up on the mesa where the runaways had gone.

When I reached the top, the mare spotted me, whirled around and blew through her nose as all wild horses do. She whirled about again and set off for the mountains with the other horses following her. I put Percy into a run and settled down to a long hard ride. They were about a mile ahead of me and we began to gain steadily. I was depending on their tiring sooner than Percy, and not on his speed. Percy settled into a steady run with his nose stretched forward and the nearer he got to them, the faster he ran. We overtook them on the Olcese Ranch near the mouth of the Kern River Canyon. The wild mare was exhausted, she dropped her tail and turned meekly back when I headed her. I had to threaten them with a rope to get them back to the pasture. Percy was not even breathing hard, after a run of fifteen miles. Of course, he had been fed good oats, hay, and grain, while they had been on grass pasture.

THE BURRO AND THE GYPSY

The port of Cadiz in southern Spain has been the crossroads of the Mediterranean world for many centuries, and faces from all the shores of Africa and southern Europe throng its narrow streets. Most of the Spaniards here have lean faces with high-bridged semetic noses, a heritage of the Carthaginians, Arab and Romans, who have sailed in and out of this ancient port of Gades.

But my host at the *Hostal Commercio* was an out and out Celt. He had the upturned nose and ready grin of an Irishman. His physiognomy brought to mind the old legend of Beohan who was said to have taken the first Irishmen to the Emerald Isle from the shores of Spain. He would wait for me in the evening, and tell me of his life on the farm. He had been a farmer in the Province of Hvelva before his growing children had persuaded him to move to the city. I sensed in him a nostalgia for the life on the farm. How he ever learned that I would be interested in his experiences with mules I do not know. Perhaps it was the "Western" hat and boots I left in the room when I went abroad. I never wore them on the street, because to do so was to stop traffic. People stopped and stared at a man wearing "Western" clothes. They have seen too many "Western" movies.

One evening my host told me of the mules and burros he had owned and worked. Spaniards have been expert mule men since that distant time in the past when men learned to cross horses with burros

Spanish Burro

Spanish Burros

to produce the mule, and learn the sterling worth of the long-eared hybrids.

"*Un hijo de caballo,*" (son of a horse) (hinny), he was careful to explain, "is a much hardier animal than *un hijo de burro.*" (son of a burro) (a mule). "The hinny has much more courage and will thrive in the cold winters of our mountains much better than the mule.

I asked him if it was true that all Spaniards hired a Gypsy to buy their animals for them. He chuckled, as all Spaniards do, when a Gypsy is mentioned. Oddly enough, the Spaniard, who toils unremittingly from dawn to dark for his meager portion of bread, good naturedly tolerates the Gypsy, who will not work.

"The Gypsy," he said, "has an oily tongue, and since he will not work, he must scheme. It is true that he will try to make the best bargain for the man who hires him. One of my neighbors had a very fine burro known far and wide for his quality." - Here I must digress to explain to my readers that the burro I found in Spain is not the little scrub burro we find in the United States, the object of ridicule and the symbol of stupidity, though he originally came from Spain. The burro of modern Spain is a big strong animal, often weighing more than seven hundred pounds. He resembles very much the Mammoth or Kentucky Jack, and is very useful to the Spanish farmer.

This neighbor met two Gypsies at a bar during a fair. They invited him to a drink, then to another and another, until my neighbor was mellowed with wine. He sold his burro to the Gypsies for five thousand pesetas. One of the Gypsies left with the burro while his partner stayed with my neighbor and kept buying him drinks. The first Gypsy took the burro behind the building, dismounted and rubbed a dye over the animal's coat enough to alter his color. Then he wound a wire behind the burro's ears to make his ears stay forward. The Gypsy then took off his shoe and drove a nail into the heel, leaving about an inch extending. He mounted the burro and using the nail as a spur, he rode him up and down until the poor animal, who had never been hurt before, was prancing with pain. Then the Gypsy rode him up to the bar, prancing like an Andalusian horse. Of course, his former owner, in his befuddled state of mind, did not know his former burro, and the upshot was that he bought his own burro back for seven thousand pesetas. The Gypsies decamped, my neighbor mounted the little animal which immediately started for home, and did not stop until he came to the door of his stable, which in this case, was the lower floor of his master's home. His wife was standing in the door. The befuddled man said, "Strange, this burro knows where we live." "And why shouldn't he?" the wife demanded, "he is our own burro."

"No," my neighbor answered, "this is an especially fine burro. I paid seven thousand pesetas for him."

But when he removed the jaquima (halter), he found the wire; and when he groomed the burro, he found the holes the nail had made. His lamentations were long and loud. But the Gypsies and the seven thousand pesetas were gone.

VITAMINS

Much of the old Californian's culture came more from the Moslem than from the Christian Spaniard. Customs which had been forgotten in Spain survived here until the Californiano passed into oblivion; although it is not long ago that women covered their faces at the approach of a stranger, in Spain and in Spanish America. But the old Califoriano, despite all vicissitudes, never forgot his *educacion* (manners). Paramount of which was his respect for elders. Children were taught early in life. When a father returned to his home, the children would run out at his approach and kneel down in a row. The father would dismount from his horse and place his hand on each child's head and say, "*Dios te haga santo hijo*" (or "*hija*") ("May God make you a saint son") (or "daughter"). Then each child kissed the parent's hand.

Likewise, when a lovelorn swain asked permission to court the daughter of the house, to show his respect, he would kneel and kiss her father's hand. This was an ordeal for the *novio* (suitor) for those fathers all had a forbidding mien which terrified any brash young man. It was an occasion, however, for much merriment on the part of the younger sisters who were hidden witnesses to the *novio's* trial.

A boy never smoked in the presence of his father, and never left the house without his parent's permission, and by the time he went to work on a ranch the boy had manners. He had learned to address his elders as, "Usted", and not with the familiar, "Tu". He also gave them the "Don" which is the equivalent of "Mr." in English.

The old men were respected because they knew their work thoroughly and had survived the dangers and hardships incident to the life of the vaquero. They had all begun life under severe circumstances, for stout hearts and strong bodies are molded in childhood. They were appreciated for their wisdom and because they took pains to teach the boys who were learning to be vaqueros.

I remember a saddle-warped ancient on one of the Company ranches whom I never ceased to admire, for he was the embodiment of my conceptions of a good vaquero. He was ancient, but he still walked with a swagger, that is, when he essayed to walk. He was at his best on a horse, working cattle, for he never failed to be at the right place at the right time, and that without ever getting his horse into a sweat.

Hilario's wiry, old body had that leanness which generations of starving ancestors had bequeathed him, for it had been tempered in the fires of adversity. It was an open book in which all could read of a hungry childhood, a meager youth, and a manhood of hard, dangerous, illpaid toil, an existence in which the urge to survive was the dominant incentive. By many years the oldest man on the ranch, he could ride longer and farther than any of the hard-riding youngsters who followed his dust on the roundup. Not that they were not good; that ranch was known for its good vaqueros from one end of the state to the other. It was only that Hilario had the vitality of a Mexican mule; heat, cold, sun, rain, wind, hunger or thirst had no terrors for him.

He was grim-faced, squint-eyed, flat-backed and bowlegged. A lifetime spent in camps and bunkhouses had made him chary of speech and chary of mirth. He never laughed and seldom grinned. When the entire vaquero crew was roaring with laughter, a fleeting, sardonic gleam in his eyes, would be the only indication that he was amused. One could ride by his side all day and never hear him say more than a reluctant "Yes" or "No".

It was not until he had told me of the bitter, crushing poverty of his boyhood and of how he had built his undernourished body, and perhaps thus saved his life, by eating the flesh of rattlesnakes, that I began to understand why he was indestructable.

That morning I was shoeing his horse, a chore I always did for him, because old men who have ridden the range all their lives, find it agonizing to bend over and hold up a horse's leg while they nail a shoe on its hoof. He grinned approvingly when I grasped the horse's tail and kept a pull on it while I scraped the mud off his hocks. A pull on a horse's tail when one is working on his hind legs, discourages him from kicking. And this horse would kick.

Later, when I had finished shoeing and I was sitting under a tree, the old man came over, sat down beside me, and told me this story: -

At first I thought he was going to tell me some tall story, for he had the shadow of a grin on his grim old face as he sat down. But as he began, and that bitter, ironic gleam came into his eyes, I knew it would be of some of the struggles of his youth.

"I was watching you," he began. "When you pulled on that horse's tail you reminded me of a job I once had when I was a boy. Every evening I had to tie a heavy stone to the tail of all of the burros which roamed through our village; of course, I had to remove the stone every morning. Sometimes, however, their owners removed them, when they took the burros to work."

"The reason for tying the stone to the burros' tails was to prevent them from braying, and keeping everybody in the village awake. A burro, in order to bray, must first lift his tail. If he cannot lift his tail, he cannot bray. It was as simple as that."

"That was a long time before there were any machines, and all our transport was done with animals. Burros mostly, because the people in our village were very poor."

"I was paid a *centavo* (penny) a week for each burro, but even then, for all the burros I took care of, I did not earn enough to know the taste of meat."

"It was not until I had found work with a rancher, that I ate my first meat. And I wouldn't have eaten any then, on the few cents he paid me, if it had not been for the advice of the *curandero* (healer). The *curandero*, at that time, was called to attend the sick. He cured, or tried to, with herbs, the laying on of hands, or by incantations. The patient lived in spite of the *curandero's* ministrations."

"Most often the *curandero* was a *matasanos* (killer of the healthy). But this man I am speaking of, was sincere and tried to help the people he attended."

"Every morning I had to take a scythe and cut enough hay to feed our animals. The first morning the boss went to the field with me and as I started to work, he said, 'You will run into many snakes in this field. Kill them, but do it before they bite themselves. Snakes that bite themselves cannot be eaten. Save the ones that can be eaten, and I will sell them to the *curandero* to feed his patients.' "

"In an hour I had killed four, and set them aside for the boss to take home. At noon the boss came and skinned and dressed them, carried them to the house, and hung them on a line to dry. By the end of the week we had twenty jerked snakes for the *curandero*."

"He came out to the ranch and bought the snakes. While he was there I got into a conversation with him, and he said, 'I feed this snake meat to my patients, because it has many vitamins, and since their main trouble stems from malnutrition, it helps them. People who do not have enough to eat, would do well to eat the snakes which abound here. They would have better health if they did.' "

"Well, I thought very seriously of what the *curandero* had told me. My younger brothers were thin and sickly. They had never eaten meat. The result was, that the next Sunday, I took the three with me and went hunting where I was sure that I would find snakes. We soon found two fat ones. I was careful to kill them before they bit themselves. I cut six inches off each end of the snakes, because people say that the poison is in the head and tail. We built a fire and roasted them. We ate them, and to our meat-starved palates, they were delicious. From that time on, my brothers and I hunted snakes to eat, and found that the meat was fattening to the bone. We gained weight and grew strong and healthy."

"People called the *curandero* a quack, but in our case, he helped us in the only way he could, by advising us to eat the only meat that was available. I sincerely believe that it was eating the meat of the rattlers that is responsible for my good health, and my ability to ride for a living, at my advanced age."

SONGS

Through the years, one learns snatches of popular songs, which he hums or sings. Then discards them, when a new one appears. Though a song is no longer sung, it is never entirely forgotten. It never fails to leave an imprint on the mind, of some scene in which it was sung. Years afterwards, the tune will bring back old memories, and old scenes to the mind's eye: - Such as the majestic sweep of the snow-covered Sierra, or the vast expanse of the Great Valley, with its hot, burning summer suns, or its cold, clammy, foggy winters, and the great herds of cattle, which are gone forever.

Vaqueros, despite their prosaic existence, were often as sentimental as any other young men in other walks of life. Some, even more so. Perhaps it was the lonely, deprived life they led, with its absence of women and all its resulting sex hunger, that made what we call "Weeping Drunks".

The best "tear jerker" was the song which began with: "I wonder who's kissing her now. I wonder who's teaching her how. I wonder who's buying the wine, for those lips I used to call mine?".

The tears always started, when the singer came to, "I wonder if she ever tells him of me". Tears for a lost love that existed only in the weeper's imagination. Some Dulcinea born of the vaquero's fancy. There were forty men to each woman, and the vaquero's chance of finding one to carry a torch for, was nil. With his meager pay, he had little chance of attracting a girl.

Ramon, when "three sheets in the wind", could be brought to instant tears when someone sang "Cuartro Milpas". This song tells of an abandoned farm, which went to seed when the farmer's wife deserted him.

I'll never forget the summer we sang, "In a Little Spanish Town". We moved cattle out of the valley, across the Alkali Flats, up into the Carriso Plains. It stayed 110 degrees for days in the coolest spot in Bakersfield, which was the old "Union Stable". The pavement melted, and smart alecks fried eggs on the blistering sidewalks.

Whenever I hear snatches of "Alexander's Rag Time Band", a picture unrolls of the creek bottom in Soledad Canyon, with its murmuring stream, and line of cottonwoods, a boy leaving it forever, and starting on the long road across the high desert, to try for a job as a vaquero on the Tejon Ranch. In those days, the Tejon was still a horse and buggy ranch. We traveled in horse-drawn vehicles, or on horseback. The only car was a Model T Ford, in which Don Jesus, the manager, made his trips to Bakersfield.

I never heard a vaquero or buckeroo sing one of the so-called "Western" songs. He sang the current popular song, though he may have learned only a paragraph of it. It was round-up time on the Tejon Ranch when Willie O'Brien brought snatches of a song, the title of which I have forgotten. The words I remember are: "We'll build a little nest somewhere in the West, and let the rest of the world go by".

That was in the era of prohibition, the "Volstead Act" was in force, and someone made a parody of the song. The words were: "We'll build a little still, on the top of some big hill, and let the rest of the world go dry".

It was while I was working for Miller and Lux, that the "straw boss" went to town and met a red-haired woman. It seems she had never told him she was married, until his money was all gone. He came back to the chuck wagon to "nurse a broken heart", as the poets say. We would be riding along, driving a bunch of cattle, when the "straw boss" would burst out with, "Moonlight and roses bring wonderful memories of you. My heart reposes in beautiful thought of you''. He did not have a bad voice, and his singing was rather agreeable.

"Coyote" Joe Nicholson had a high, quavering, nasal voice. His favorite song was, "Frankie and Johnnie". He knew about twenty verses of the song, and would treat us to a concert while we were de-horning R. O. Cattle at the Plecto Ranch. He would go through the twenty verses before he would start over again. He always began with, "Frankie and Johnnie were lovers. Oh my, how they did love. They swore to be true to each other, on earth and in Heaven above. He was her man, but he done her wrong".

Jesse Stahl, Great Black Bronc Rider

JESSE STAHL

It was 1926. We were riding for Miller and Lux on the Carriso Plains, Bill Puget, George Montanio, Salvador Marques, Johnny Light, Miguel Saavedra, and Slim Zimmerman. It was then that Ray Foster told us this story of Jesse Stahl, the great Negro bronc rider.

"Sam Howe and I", Ray began, "were putting Jesse on his bronc in the chute at a rodeo in Priest's Valley. We had lifted him down into the saddle, and stepped down to put his feet into the stirrups, but his feet were too big, though the stirrups were normal-sized".

"Jesse grinned down at us and said, 'turn them sideways' ".

"But what if you get bucked off? That horse will kill you," we protested.

"I won't get bucked off", Jesse answered.

"We turned the stirrups sideways and straightened them around his instep, opened the gate, and let him and his bronc out of the chute".

"Well, he wasn't bucked off. In fact, he never was, unless he was clowning. When the whistle blew, the "pick-up" men had to snub his bronc, uncinch the saddle, and pull Jesse off with it. It took some time to pry his feet out of the stirrups".

CHUCKLES

One day every one of the crew on the Miller chuck wagon got "ringy". The "straw boss" became peeved at Slim Zimmerman and fired him, but a "straw boss" could not write a check, so Slim would not "fire". He stayed on and rode with the crew, saddled his horse every morning, and worked with the men. The crew, of course, rode with the "straw boss". I was the only one who would ride with Slim, so the boss fired me, too. But I wouldn't "fire", either, so Slim and I rode by ourselves. Things were getting bad when Cuen, the cattle boss, arrived, and fired the "straw boss", and left Slim and me to go on working.

CANNY FOREMEN

For many years I have carried a picture of a group of mounted men. Five are sitting on their horses with the reins hanging, but the sixth horseman is mounted on a lean horse of thoroughbred type, which has his neck arched, and seems to be spinning the cricket in the bit. The old snapshot taken about 1917 has been useful to remind me of the astuteness of the old-time ranch foremen, and what good judges they were, of men and horses, for they always rode the best horses.

On the ranch, after the bronco-buster had started the year's crop of colts, he turned them over to the foreman as "broke". The foreman would issue them to the vaqueros. One man would take two, sometimes, but rarely three. Some men would take one, or none at all.

The foreman would watch each colt's progress, but would never try to tell the vaquero how to handle the colt. It was assumed the vaquero knew his business. One day, to the vaquero's surprise, the foreman would ride up beside him, and say, "I will trade you a good bridle horse for that colt".

The foreman could have ordered the man to turn the colt over to him, but he would have risked hurting the vaquero's feelings, for they were very sensitive respecting their skill. When approached with discretion, the vaquero would not feel that his skill was in question, and would cheerfully trade. It is much easier to ride a mature bridle horse, than a colt. One has to be so careful that he does not ride the colt too hard.

The foreman had seen the horse was an athlete and balanced in his movements. While the old-time boss did not know the classical terms used by dressage riders, he knew the colt would make a "spade bit" horse. It is only a horse with a "swan" neck that flexes on the third vertebra that can take such a bit.

The foreman knew, just because he knew. He had watched pack animals traveling over the steep, winding mountain trails, leaning from one side or the other, to avoid bumping into jutting rocks and stumps, to keep their center of gravity. A smart pack animal will bump his pack into a rock or tree once, but only once. From then on, he will twist his body out and around any obstruction and never bump his pack again.

In the old days, men said, to be able to break a horse, one had to have more brains than the horse, and that any fool could break one that was not spoiled, by using patience and common sense. That the real test of a horseman was for him to cure a spoiled horse of bad habits and vices, and that all bad habits came from pulling on their mouths. There are just so many pulls and stops in a horse, just as there are so many eggs in a chicken.

"*No le jales - no le jales*" (Don't pull him - don't pull him"), the old men counseled. "The more you pull, the sooner the horse's mouth will lose its sensitivity, and the horse will start rearing, plunging and stampeding. He will become what the gringo vaqueros call a 'cold jaw' ".

Vaqueros preferred the hackamore to the snaffle bit, because after all is said and done, the snaffle is a piece of iron, and like all bits, will make a horse's mouth hard. The pull on the snaffle is such that it teaches a horse to brace his jaw.

Horses driven in a buggy always become hard-mouthed. So much so, that they often pull the buggy with their jaws, with the tugs hanging loose. This writer remembers Doctor Grinnell back in "the horse and buggy" days in Pasadena, driving up Fair Oaks Avenue on a "hurry" call. His sorrell trotting mare was pulling the buggy with her mouth. The doctor had his feet braced against the dashboard, his bearded chin jutted forward, a rein in each hand, and hanging on for dear life. The very picture of resolution.

True, the snaffle bit was used on many ranches to start a colt, because some require a lot of pulling and doubling. If the rider were to use a hackamore in such a case, the result would be that the colt's lower jaw would become raw and bloody from the constant pulling and doubling. For that reason, those riders used the snaffle bit, until the colt was bridle-wise, then changed to the hackamore.

A horse that has too much pulling, goes "sour". Such a horse was the bay gelding in northern California. He had the bad habit of bracing his jaw, and moving with his head turned sideways, waiting for a jerk. Also, he was ringing his tail, which was caused by the "rimmy" saddle rubbing across his loins.

The trainer was advised to first change the rigging in the saddle, next to throw the snaffle bit away, to put a hackamore on the horse, and a spade bit without reins, in his mouth. Then tie a thin strip of rubber from the bit to the hackamore reins, very loosely, so that there would be but a very slight pull on the bit, just a reminder when the rein was pulled.

Then to select two trees, (many were growing on the ranch) that had low, horizontal branches, and fasten a chain with a swivel to each branch. Get two straps long enough to go around a horse's neck, each with a ring sewed in. Saddle three horses, and fasten two of the horses to a chain. Mount, and work the third horse, but not to spin, or stop him, work him only in a figure eight. Gallop him in a circle, making the circle smaller and smaller. Work him for five minutes only. Then ride him to one of the trees, chain him, and mount the other. In this way, when ridden at five-minute intervals, the horse would never get weary. He would stay tied long enough to get bored, and the result would be, that he would be eager to work again, because a tired horse never learns anything.

In time, the bay horse forgot the pain, and became useful again.

Why the spade bit? The idea behind this suggestion was, that the very slight pressure on the bit, taught the horse that by flexing, he could keep the mouthpiece of the bit flat on his tongue instead of it hitting against the roof of his mouth.

THE FIRST INDIAN RIDER

What must have been his sensation, that first Indian, who mounted the White God's terrible monster, which the invaders had brought in their ships from across the seas?

What courage it must have taken, to even approach the beast! The Indian, we are told by Bernal Diaz, watched with awe and amazement, the skill of those Spanish riders. From this, a longing was born. He began a patient, unrelenting study of the Spaniards and the horses.

Day after day, hour after hour, he watched each move, each gesture, until he knew every motion by heart. At last came the day, when in fear and trembling, he ventured to mount the terrible creature. What iron courage it must have taken, knowing full well it meant death at the hands of the Spaniards, to be caught astride a horse. But mount, he did, and two hemispheres have him to thank, for the propagation of the horse.

AMOR AL GANADO

The mustangs were the worthy descendents of the Iberian horses of Spain, although they varied in type and size. Horses born and grown to maturity in good years, when grass was abundant, were always superior to those that managed to survive the terrible droughts which every now and then visit the range country of California. Those dry years when there was no rain, thousands of horses were driven over cliffs and killed to save the grass for the few cattle that survived.

Naturally, the horses varied much in quality. So much so, that they seemed scarcely to belong to the same breed. But all were good, and could hold their own with any horse in the world of like size and weight, from the fine horses ridden by the old-time dons, whom Walker, the artist, painted in the 1830's, to the little scrub ponies that were a miracle of survival.

Through the centuries of running free, they had learned to take care of themselves, and escaping from predators had sharpened those powers of perception which, later, when caught and tamed, made them the world's greatest cow horse.

Often when a horse showed extraordinary ability and one spoke in terms of praise, the old men would say, "*Al caballo nomas le falta hablar*" (The horse lacks only a voice).

True, in order to attain his maximum development, the horse had to have a rider with the ability to teach him, and not all men on ranches were capable of "putting a rein on a horse". One or two of the men in a crew developed such an affinity with their mounts, that it seemed that the horse could read their minds. Men developed habits in riding and the horse learned each move the rider made. It was a relationship which resulted in a complete acceptance of the rider's guidance. All the horse needed was the slightest of signals, and the vaquero took pains to signal so that no one could see it; such as hitting his spur chains against the metal bottoms of the stirrups for the horse to leap into a run.

The making of the vaquero horse was accomplished over a period of many months. To preclude the possibility of hurting it, the vaquero would ride his colt on the days when there was no hard riding to be done and there was no danger of overriding and hurting the animal. For all vaqueros worthy of the name took great pride in their skill, and the urge to create a good horse was uppermost. Each vaquero put something of himself into his animal. His pride and confidence was evident in the way he sat his horse, and how it performed. It was the instrument of his will and skill.

The vaquero had only to ride into the herd, and indicate to his horse which steer he wanted out. The horse did the rest. The steer was always unwilling to leave the herd and would dodge, twist or turn back, but he could never escape, for with his ears laid back, the very picture of rage, the horse would stay at the steer's tail, often nipping his rump, until he drove him out of the herd. There, one of the vaqueros drove him to the *parada*. The *parada* (the word means literally "stand" like a stand of wheat or barley) in this case, meant the bunch of steers which have been parted out of the main herd.

This quality of working cattle, common to horses that work cattle, was called in Spanish, *Amor Al Ganado* (literally, "Love for cattle") and the horse that lacked this instinct, was worthless in the vaquero's eyes.

Chocolate, a chunky gray horse on Tejon, was one of the very few horses I have ridden that did not have *Amor Al Ganado* ("cow sense", the gringos called it). He had to be turned after a cow. But Chocolate could carry me to the end of the longest, hottest, thirstiest day, and never once falter. Then, after being unsaddled, if allowed to lie down and roll a couple of times, he would get to his feet and be ready to cover the same territory again. Chocolate never "gaunted up" on a hard trip, and was one of the best horses I have had the good fortune to ride.

There is another characteristic of the horse, which is often met with by men who work strange horses, men such as horseshoers and veterinarians. It is the instinct the dog exercises in guarding a house. Although it is not so pronounced in the horse as it is in the dog, it is there.

Once having become accustomed to a place he regards as his home, the horse will defend it; he will show an antipathy to a stranger who undertakes to handle him. The shoer will call him a "barnyard savage" and say he is spoiled by too much petting. But the fact of the matter is, that the horse is only obeying an instinct. If he is taken from a place which is familiar, he will not be hard to handle.

This same instinct works on horses that are in a band. Whenever a strange horse is put among them, those in the band will fight him away. He will be an outcast until another strange horse is put into the band. Then he will join forces with the new horse. When yet another is turned among them, the two outcasts will fight the newcomer away.

Jess Wilkinson (l.), Ab Wilkinson (r.)

In Front of Beale Library — 1901 (l.-r.) Bob Stubblefield, Jess Wilkinson,
Cleve Wilkinson, Ab Wilkinson, Jim Wagey

These five buckeroos drove three thousand head of steers from Cuyama to Belview
Packing Co. in the summer of 1901 and never opened or shut a gate. Jim Wagey owned the
cattle. Jess Wilkinson and Ab Wilkinson, masters at the rawhide work and top buckeroos.
Ernest Morris is the grandson of Jess Wilkinson.

JESS WILKINSON

I met Ernie Morris, the artist, at the Snaffle Bit Futurity, in Reno, Nevada. We had a long visit, and when we parted, I promised to visit him at his home in Templeton.

On my way south, I stopped to see him, and he gave me some pictures of his grandfather, Jess Wilkinson, his uncle, Ab Wilkinson, and another picture of a group of vaqueros taken in 1901.

When I knew him, in 1926, Jess Wilkinson was the vaquero in charge of Chimineas Ranch, which joined the Miller and Lux holdings on the Carriso Plains. Since cattle mix, regardless of fences or property lines, Jess would join the Miller and Lux vaqueros whenever we worked that territory. Jess was an old-time vaquero, who had ridden the range for many years, was a skilled horseman, and did his work well and thoroughly.

While I was visiting Ernie, he told me that his father had been with the crew of vaqueros who rounded up the Tule Elk, in the Elk Hills Reserve. Tule Elk are native to swamp land, and will not live in any other habitat, though efforts have been made to plant them in mountain meadows. They will not stay, and always return to their native swamps.

Pens, with long wings, had been constructed to receive the elk. The vaqueros started from the reserve with Bill Stubblefield in charge. Bill gave strict orders that there was to be no roping. The elk started in a group, and since they run in a straight line, and never swerve, they missed the wings and went on.

Bill forgot about the orders he had given about roping, and instinctively took down his riata. He made a big loop and threw it at a bull elk. The bull's horns were too wide, and he caught only one antler, but he managed to get the bull hog-tied. When he was through, he looked up, and found himself alone on the plains. In the far distance, two men were chasing a cow elk.

The elk that hit the wings dashed themselves against the fencing, and crippled or killed themselves. Those the men roped and tied up, died of fright or rage. Only ten were put into the railroad cars. The bull elk Bill had tied up, attacked a buck deer that was running with the herd. The deer whipped the elk because Bill had sawed off the bull's horns.

MACHOS

The Spanish word *machos*, a synonym for male virility, is slowly being incorporated into English along with *tamales*, *tortillas* and *tacos*. The other day my little fifteen-year-old niece, in speaking of a boy in her class, said, "Oh, he has quite a *macho* reputation in our school."

Her remark brought to mind a story that was told of a group of *caballeros* who owned ranchos and herds of horses and cattle. They fought bulls on horseback and lassoed grizzly bears, and as a result, considered themselves *Muy Macho*.

This group had been bending their elbows in a *cantina* (bar) all evening. It was getting late when the youngest member of the group whom they called "Infant", said, "It's getting late, I think I had better go home."

His cousin turned and asked, "What is the matter, aren't you master in your home?"

"Of course I am," the Infant retorted.

"Poor Infant," the cousin remarked to the crowd, "He is henpecked."

"Judge not rashly," the oldest man in the group, a cynic and the only bachelor, said, "so that you may not be judged."

Then he added, "If the truth were told, no man is master in his own house."

There was a chorus of, "But, I am," "I am," "I am".

"We will prove it," the Oldest Man said with a wicked, knowing grin. "It is one o'clock. We will all go in a group to each man's house. Each one of us will knock on his door and demand of his wife that she serve coffee to all his friends. The behavior of the wife at that hour of the morning will tell us whether the man is master in his own house or not."

As we have said, the group had been bending their elbows and were full of Dutch courage, so they marched off bravely enough.

At the first house, the owner knocked, and immediately the door opened, an arm shot out, and a hand grasped the scruff of the man's neck and jerked him into the house. The door slammed shut, and the nonplused *machos* marched away.

The next house was that of the Infant. His wife was plain, and people had wondered what he had seen in her to marry her, for he had been the catch of the season.

They were soon to know. The Infant knocked. A smiling woman opened the door and said, "Come right in gentlemen. I am made very happy when my husband chooses to bring his friends to our home."

She ushered them into the dining room, seated them and brought them coffee. After coffee, the group marched off to the next house. But here, when the door opened, the wife rushed out and belabored her husband with her purse and drove him into the house, and closed the door.

At the next house the owner knocked, the door opened, and a virago rushed out. "*Boracho*, (drunkard) *vagamundo* (vagabond)," she screamed, "stay with your friends," and slammed the door.

The Oldest Man, with that knowing gleam in his eye, said, "I think that we had better go back to the cantina and have another drink and forget about who is "master".

The few who remained of the group were only too glad to leave their project. They went back to the bar and proceeded to bend their elbows and at last went to sleep on the tables.

A few days later, the Infant's wife was seen driving in a new carriage behind a pair of spanking bays. A present from a grateful husband.

"Truly," said the Oldest Man, after he had sobered up, "there is wisdom in the old adage which says, "*Dios me done con la suerte de las feas, Mas que con las gracias de las bonitas.*" (God grant me the luck of the homely maids, rather than the graces of the pretty ones.)

DANGEROUS DAYS

The only real gun fight I ever heard of, happened in Bakersfield. "The Last Bad Man of the West", Jim McKinney, had holed himself up in the Chinese Joss House on "L" Street.

When Sheriff Kelly of Kern County, who had never seen "High Noon" (television was unknown then), heard where McKinney was, he decided to make him a prisoner. He organized a posse, three members of whom were: Jeff Packard, the City Marshall, Bert Tibbet, a Deputy Sheriff, and Bill Tibbet, a brother of Bert's.

In the battle which ensued, after the Joss House was surrounded by the posse, McKinney was killed at the back door of the Joss House, and Jeff Packard and Bill Tibbet fell mortally wounded in the yard. Thus ended a well-known episode in the history of Bakersfield.

It is, indeed, strange that the man who herded cattle is always depicted in fiction as a killer. The "Western" story is never complete without "six guns", "slap leathers", "fast draws" and "steely eyes". Perhaps they are written on the assumption that a factual story could not be interesting enough to sell without the violence that is in "Western" fiction. As if the daily life of the vaquero did not have enough risk without the added one of flying bullets.

If the truth were told, more men were killed by horses than by Colt revolvers and Winchester rifles, inasmuch as firearms were only an episode in the long history of the herdsman. Even that stylized performance, the rodeo, is an aberration, because the purpose in breeding horses is to use them in herding cattle. Bucking horses were an incident in the life of the vaquero.

Actually, the vaquero and buckeroo were protectors of life. Their purpose on the ranch was to preserve, not to destroy. They often risked their lives to save that of the animals they cared for. Men often sat up all night caring for a sick horse and have ridden all day in a raging blizzard driving a cow to a haystack, so that they could feed her and save her life. They often risked being bucked off a spooky colt, by carrying an orphan calf on the horse to a place where it could be cared for.

There were a thousand ways in which a buckeroo or vaquero could be killed without being shot, and here are a few of them.

To begin with, a rattlesnake could easily crawl into the vaquero's blankets on a cold night, as sometimes happened, and could bite him when the vaquero rolled over and crushed the snake. If he survived the hypothetical snake, after he had drunk coffee, and went out to the corral to catch his horse, the horses could run over him, and his horse could strike him when he went to put the halter over his head. After he had saddled his horse, when he put his foot in the stirrup to mount, the horse could cowkick him as he put his weight in the stirrup. That cowkick which always lands on the groin and cripples the vaquero for many days afterwards - Barney on San Emideo, and Cowboy on Tejon, were two horses that were addicted to that vice. Because *broncos* cowkicked, vaqueros always used blinds when they mounted them.

If the vaquero's horse was a "cinchbinder" he could fall over backwards and break the vaquero's back. The least he could do was to break an arm or a leg. If, by a miracle, the rider escaped injury, the horse would be sure to break the cantle of the saddle, which would necessitate a new tree. Johnny Drayer and Harry Stoy both had their legs broken by a horse falling over backwards with them. Bert Timons had his spleen burst when a blue mare fell over backwards with him at Buttonwillow Ranch, and Dolph Short was killed on Tejon Ranch when a steer hooked his horse and the horse fell over. Bill Nichols died as the result of a horse falling over with him. A horse fell over backwards with Frank Urrea when Frank was fifty years old. His hip was broken, and despite several operations, the bones in his hip would never knit. Frank, a lonely old man, hobbled around Nineteenth and L Streets in Bakersfield on crutches for forty-two years, waiting for death. He died when he was ninety-three.

Pedro Carmelo was riding a horse across a slough during high water. The horse stepped into a deep hole and fell. Pedro was caught under the horse and drowned before the other vaqueros could help him.

If the vaquero made it out of the yard and into the open country, the horse could start bucking. If the rider was alone and the horse bucked for any length of time, the blankets would work out from under the saddle, the saddle would turn, and the vaquero would be thrown, no matter how good a rider he was.

Sometimes a horse would buck the first thing in the morning. Bill, a big bay on San Emideo, bucked so hard one morning that he threw his rider up on the horn of the saddle and tore all the buttons off his jacket, pounded his ribs against the horn so hard that his rider rode bent over for two months afterwards.

The chore of riding over mountain trails and driving all the cattle to the rodeo ground was fraught with many mishaps. The cattle were very wild and did not want to leave their *querencia* (feeding ground). The vaquero had to ride hard and fast to keep the cattle from escaping while he dodged branches, and the horse leaped over brush and cactus, gullies and ravines. If he arrived at the rodeo ground all in one piece, he would have to help the *puestos* (men placed to stop and mill the cattle that were brought down out of the mountains). The ground was pitted with squirrel holes. If his horse stepped into one, he would be sure to break a leg and hurt his rider.

There was danger even in parting out beef. Frank Reese's horse fell over a steer and threw him over his head. Frank died as a result of the fall. When a beef broke out of the herd, it was the duty of one of the men holding the herd to bring it back. If the grass were wet or green, or if there were round pieces of wood or twigs for the horse to step on when he was turning after a cow, he could lose his footing and fall. A man was often stunned when his horse fell with him, and as a result could not get clear when it rose to its feet. The man's foot would get hung in the stirrup, the horse would run off, dragging his rider and kicking at him.

Sometimes the horse kicked over the man and he survived, at other times the rider was badly hurt. Frank Phillips, an Indian vaquero, was dragged for two hours one pitch black night. He did not get free of the horse until the animal was exhausted.

There were always calves that had been missed in the spring round-up. They would have to be parted out, put in a corral and branded. They were big and strong; the vaquero got many kicks and buffetings when he handled them, and ran the risk of the calf's mother hooking him when she heard her calf bawl.

All calves were roped by the hind legs and dragged up to the fire. The man who tailed them and held them by the tail, pulled between their legs and a forefoot, did not have an easy task.

After the work of parting and branding, there remained the job of driving the beef to the pasture where they would stay overnight. If there was no pasture or field, the men would have to night-herd, and there was a chance of being trampled to death in a stampede. Vaqueros liked night-herding the least of all the jobs which made up their day.

Then, when the vaquero's day was done - the day lasted from four in the morning until ten or twelve at night - there was still the chance of the vaquero's dying from acute indigestion after eating the food some of those chuck-wagon cooks prepared.

I have enumerated the risks of only one day in the vaquero's life. There yet remained three hundred-sixty-four days in which to get killed.

BY JACK HITCHCOCK

Author's note: Some time ago I was greatly pleased to receive the following stories from Jack Hitchcock, an old-time Kern County Land Company buckeroo. He worked for Catarino Reese on Bellevue Ranch with Buster Clark, who was also a friend of mine. He depicts Buster just as he was, always ready for a fight or a frolic. Jack's story begins.

"I remember Buster Clark although it is forty-three years since I have seen him. He and I got along very well. He was a good hand and a good man to ride with. He had a horse in his string that was a sure-enough vaquero horse at any part of cow work. He called the horse Red Hogan. He let me use him a couple of times, and I tried to talk him out of the horse, but no way. I think I could have talked him out of his shark-skin boots before I could have talked him out of the horse. He had bought the boots from one of the boys who had shipped out to the Goshen Pens.

Buster had his room at one end of the bunkhouse and I was in the room next to him. That night there was a full moon. Catarino, the buckeroo boss, had two dogs, maybe border-collie and dachshund, anyhow, they were two dogs long and half-a-dog high. One was long-haired and a moon barker. I think every coyote in Kern County was jealous of the way that dog could bay. Well, along about ten o'clock, that dog started yapping. He woke me up and I could hear

Buster cussing at the dog. He reached out and grasped the first thing that met his hand and threw it. It was his clock. The dog was quiet for about ten minutes, then started again. Buster reached out again and threw what his hand had grasped. It was one of his prized shark-skin boots. The dog ran off, then returned and ran off with the boot. Buster, wide awake now, looked out and saw it was his boot. He ran out in his bare feet. The dog escaped into a cockle-burr patch where Buster could not follow. We found the boot later.

We were a happy bunch on Bellevue Ranch and got on well together. I remember a rider, I think his name was Jim MacNeal. He had a Model A Ford car. When the wrestling matches were on, he would take Buster, Johnny Dallas, Broadway and me to the wrestling matches.

There was a big wrestler who was the villain and always won. He made the crowd so mad that they wanted to lynch the referee for giving him the decision. Buster used to get so mad that he wanted to get into the ring with the villain. I had boxed for a season or two, so I became Buster's trainer and manager. 'Buster,' I said, 'your name is too tame, we'll have to change it to something tougher!'

Catarino said, 'What are you going to call him, Jack?'

''Muscles Clark, the Bellevue Terror.''

Mrs. Reese said, 'You are good at naming, what are we going to call you?'

'Oh,' I said, 'you can call me Handsome Jack.'

Now to get back to Buster and his boots. I had a pair of Blucher boots from Olathe, Kansas, I paid twenty dollars for. I wanted to keep them kinda new for a while, so I sent to Lee Bergen, a friend, who owned the Visalia Stock Saddle Company in San Francisco, for a pair of black boot-shoes I saw in his catalog, size eight.

When I received tham I liked their looks, for they were neat with a nice undersling heel. But they must have been made of boa-constrictor hide the way they pinched my feet. I filled them with gyp corn and poured water on the corn so that it would swell and stretch them. I struggled along for five days, then gave them up. They had gotten my feet so sore, that I went to town and bought a pair of plough-boy shoes size nine-one-half, so that my feet would get over hurting.

The next day we were working over at Goshen and I was wearing the big shoes. Buster and I were riding side by side ahead of the crew when Buster stopped his horse and called back, 'Hey fellers, get up here and get a look at this!' When they rode up he said, 'Look at the pretty *tapaderoes* Jack bought.' He meant my oversize shoes.

A few days later he asked me if I wanted to sell the black underslung boot-shoes. 'No,' I said, 'but you can have them if you want them.'

Buster was a big man, but he wore a number seven-one-half boot. He figured he could wear those pretty underslung boots.

That day we were riding in from Canfield Ranch when I met Catarino. He turned his horse around and rode on beside me. As we rode along, he saw Buster approaching. He burst out laughing and said, 'Look at Buster's feet.'

Buster had tied the pretty shoes to the saddle and was riding in his stocking feet. He couldn't handle those pretty shoes either. For years afterwards, I wondered if anyone ever wore those shoes.

Slim Roberts was another good guy. He was also a very good buckeroo. He could play the mandolin and yodel. He could not sing because a horse had kicked him in the mouth and knocked his front teeth out. Slim had a string of horses that weren't too much, all except one, that was an outstanding cowhorse like Buster's Red Hogan. This horse was called Prince. Catarino said that when Slim got his string he got one real cowhorse, 'No calf will ever get away from that horse even if he has to follow one down into a squirrel hole.'

About a month later I got to see what Catarino had meant. I didn't see the horse go down a squirrel hole, but I saw him do something I have never seen a horse do before or since.

We were coming from Canfield Ranch with a good-sized bunch of cattle. When we came to the weir on the canal, we saw that there was a big hole about twenty feet deep and full of water. About twenty cows and calves crossed the canal and Slim went with them. Catarino, Buster and I, were on the drag when Catarino said, 'Watch out, Slim!'

Just then a big bull-calf that could really run, broke out along the canal.

Now Slim liked to chase bunch-quitters. He hollered to his horse, 'Bend her, Prince, bend her'. The only way that horse could turn that calf was to pass it on the outside, as there was no room between the calf and the water. Just as he was passing the calf, it turned and jumped into the water, and before Slim could stop his horse, Prince jumped right into the middle of the water after the calf. After all these years, I can still see Slim on Prince, sailing through the air. Slim, with both hands on the horn, landing in the middle of the water with a splash, and letting out a yell, then sinking out of sight. Before he went under, he yelled, 'Gosh Amighty damn!'

When he came up he was still on Prince, so they were able to get out. Slim got off his horse and sat on the canal bank and poured the water out of his boots. He looked like a drowned squirrel.

Johnny Dallas and I went up to Tehachapi to work for Bob Cooper. Bob backed his Packard out of the shed and told me to drive it to Tehachapi and get Johnny and a bad dog that the Marshall said had menaced several people.

I got Johnny at the hotel and when he got into the car, the dog jumped in his lap and bared his teeth and growled every time Johnny moved. He said that was the scariest ride he had ever had.

I used to get letters from Johnny, but after World War Two I never heard from him again.

To get back to Buster Clark, he never did meet that wrestler who was such a villain. Maybe it was a good thing for that villain. Buster could get rough when he got riled.

The more I write, the more I remember, but I must quit now."

Your Friend, Jack Hitchcock

Part II

THE VAQUERO

by Arnold Rojas

Preface

With the publication of this book, *Vaquero*, A. R. Rojas completes the demolition of a mountain of apocrypha hitherto burying the truth about western horsemen and horses. Mr. Rojas' three earlier books, a trilogy of notable literary achievement, were successful precursors of this final definitive volume. I believe him to be the foremost authority on the tradition and history of the western horseman. *Vaquero* gives more information about the genesis of the western horse and the western horseman than any other book within my experience.

There is so much fiction, so great a mass of erroneous matter in connection with the vaquero and that misnomer, the "cowboy," that it is a fine thing a genuine vaquero of fifty years in the saddle—for such is Rojas—has been at pains to set down the facts. It is a partucularly happy circumstance, one of those fortuitous things we encounter in life, that Mr. Rojas, a man of practically no formal education as a writer, has the talent of being able to write well. He has a delightful style reminiscent of the late Cunningham-Graham, and he is that very rare man indeed, a natural story teller.

Mr. Rojas is a master of the "conte" form of writing, a brief story of cleverly selected details and single, strong impact. In this book are a number of such charming stories embellishing the history of the horse in the West and the Spanish tradition of its rider.

It will be a very useful publication indeed, for it will set the record straight for those perceptive enough to read it with respect to the "boloney" perpetuated by "western" movies produced in a rigid pattern of literary cliche at almost complete odds with the western horseman as he really existed since the origin of western horsemen with the Spanish Conquest and the end of it in the 1920's when cattle handling was changed on the great ranches.

J.F.M. (Jim) Day
Managing Editor
Bakersfield *Californian*

Introduction

The vaquero, as I knew him, was the embodiment of all the heroes that I had read of in books.

In the years since Miller and Lux and other great cattle outfits passed out of existence, millions of words have been written about the West, but little about the real vaquero or buckaroo.

Much valuable history has been lost because of the inability of the vaquero, under the handicaps of language, lack of schooling, or indifference on the part of those who could have written them, to get his experiences into print.

I have managed to salvage some of the lore, although I met the vaquero, as my friend Arthur Woodward says, "at the tag end of a great era in California history." I managed to make contact with some of the men who had lived during the Gold Rush period, and who remembered the tales their great-grandfathers and grandfathers had told them. They were natural story-tellers whose talents went back many generations to the Arabs, the fathers transmitting it to sons from one generation to another. The *viejos,* the old men, I knew had a gift for capturing the mood of the vaquero, his joy and his grief, his humor and his sorrow, his nostalgia and his pride. I have no individual heroes or heroines. I but tell of things as they were and of men as they were—of simple men who toiled, hungered, froze, or scorched in doing a job which required skill and courage.

It has been said that we learn more of history from fiction than from our schoolbooks, that fiction has a wider influence than generally accepted historical accounts. This may hold true in one respect, that is in the influence of fiction on the reader, but it is not true that it teaches facts. He who writes of incidents as they happened has no need of fiction.

If this narrative had been a work of fiction, I could have followed the rule of the "Western" writer and shaped it in a different fashion, but in dealing with facts we cannot let our imagination run roughshod over truth.

In undertaking this work I hope to right a common misunderstanding. I saw that the vaquero was almost universally confused with the cowboy, and that the actual Westerner, the vaquero or buckeroo, was not given his rightful place in history. Having shared his tobacco, I must out of loyalty defend him. No one can expect to portray the whole pattern of the vaquero's life. In a factual book such as this there can be little continuity; the events did not happen so. At best the sketches must be short. The events described here are true as they were told to me, and accurate as I can make them. Whoever reads this will know that this is the way it was in the old days.

Some of the men who told me stories have risen to wealth or high station, but having once been vaqueros or buckaroos, they must, in memory at least, remain vaqueros all their lives.

The stories of bandits and the legends, many of which had their origin in Spain, were so much a part of the vaquero's life that his story would not be complete without them. They may be history, legend, or tradition; they are tales which changed in name and locale with each telling.

This book in not an attempt at history. It is just one man's picture of a time which has passed and will never come again. It is a picture of the men with whom I worked, talked, and lived. It is an effort to bring to the printed page old California in an era full of epic heroism, of which the heroes were totally unaware.

Little of what I write here was learned from books. I write of what I have learned on the range, at the campfire, in the dust of the corral, and the reader can trust what he reads in this book, because this is the only way these indicents could have happened.

Vaquero is, in part, the story of the men who herded cattle in the Far West, of the men who rode far and hard and suffered many hardships in making their living. But hardships, however painful to endure, are pleasant to look back upon, and old buckaroos have told these stories with a fond retrospective chuckle. Time rubs off the sharp edges, and even the roughest experiences on the cattle ranges are remembered with the strongest interest and nostalgia—and sometimes exaggeration.

The horse lore comes from men who have studied the history of the horse in Spain and Spanish America, from students of hippology who have pored over many old records from throughout the Spanish speaking world to find a thread of truth in a mesh of fable. The lore has been traced through words written in English, Spanish, and Portuguese.

Much has come from Spain, Argentina, Mexico, Brazil, Portugal, and from men who have studied the actual history of the West. Besides the good people in Europe and Latin America who have supplied me with information, I am indebted to Mrs. Bernice Harrell Chipman, Walter Kane, Jim Day and and Ralph Kreiser of the *Bakersfield Californian,* without whose help, constant friendship, and encouragement this book would never have come into being.

Arnold R. Rojas

Calexico, California
January 28, 1964

THE VAQUERO

LOYALTY

Although the terms "cowboy," "vaquero," and "buckaroo" have in the past been used interchangeably and indiscriminately, to do so is not, as a matter of fact, wholly accurate. They are not actually synonymous, because there is a vast difference between the cowboy and the vaquero or buckaroo.

This may sound contradictory to those who are not familiar with the terms used in the actual West. To explain the difference in terminology we must go back into early history. In the United States there are two systems or styles of working cattle, or, rather, two kinds of herdsmen. One, the vaquero, is Hispanic in origin; the other, the cowboy, is African in origin. The herdsman of the North is a composite of the two styles.

By vaquero or buckaroo is meant the original rider - Spaniard, Mexican, Indian, or Anglo - who herded cattle in the far western states and the territory of Hawaii, that is to say, in California, Nevada, Oregon, Arizona, Utah, and Washington, and in parts of Idaho, Montana, Wyoming, and British Columbia.

By cowboy is meant the Negroes and whites who herded cattle in the southern states, from the Atlantic seaboard to the eastern base of the Rocky Mountains, and from the Gulf of Mexico to Canada.

The vaquero or buckaroo is a Westerner in fact. The cowboy is a Southerner, however people may call his territory the "West." The rider of the northern states, like the buckaroo of the Pacific slope, is of Yankee stock. Although there was a great Irish migration into the Northwest, the culture of the real or actual Westerner is entirely Yankee.

The cowboy's territory is east of the Rockies; the vaquero's is west of this great barrier. The vaquero or buckaroo is unlike the cowboy in many ways: their racial background, lingo, character, methods of working cattle, and conception of what a horseman should be are different, even when the vaquero, buckaroo, or cowboy happen to be Anglo, Negro, Spaniard, Mexican, or Indian.

Vaqueros, buckaroos, and cowboys drove the same Spanish cattle, rode the same Spanish mustang, met the same dangers and difficulties in their work. They ate the same kind of food, suffered the same hardships, yet were as far apart as East and West.

The vaquero's pride was in having a bridle hand; the cowboy had to have a horse that knew more about working cattle than its rider. That is to say, the horse worked cattle of its own accord, without the guidance of its rider. This instinct, however, is common in all horses that work cattle, from Tierra del Fuego to Canada.

The difference was that the vaquero's and buckaroo's horse, besides having *amor al ganado*, love for cattle, as this instinct is called in California, also had a trigger rein and could be turned against his instinct to close with a grizzly bear. Lassoing bears was a common enough vaquero sport.

The vaquero has had some influence on the cowboy - especially the northern one - but the cowboy has never had any influence on the vaquero or buckaroo, regardless of what "western" writers may say on the subject. These writers have confused the terms "cowboy," "vaquero," and "buckaroo" either from ignorance of their subject, chauvinism, disregard for truth, or plain malice. Most motion pictures, television shows, and popular books on the West have served only to obliterate the truth.

The vaquero or buckaroo, the real Westerner, was a cultural force that writers have ignored. He never had a true history written about him while, on the other hand, the Gulf Coast rider or cowboy has had his chroniclers by the score.

The buckaroo who drove the Oregon cattle into Montana, with his long riata, and single-rig, center-fire saddle, has been immortalized on canvas by the great artist, Charles M. Russell. But there has been little worthwhile prose published on the subject of vaqueros or buckaroos.

Will James, in his *Cowboys North and South* is highly readable – but all wrong. There are only western and eastern herdsmen. James split it the wrong way.

Jo Mora in his *Trail Dust and Saddle Leather* made a great and sincere effort, and his illustrations were authentic. But in his effort to translate vaquero terms into English he used the lingo of the Gulf Coast which was not typical of the West Coast. In other respects he had great merit as a historian. Neither Will James nor Jo Mora was a vaquero and neither of them knew the craft at first hand.

It is not my intention to prove that one system or style is better, or which herdsman is superior. But in justice to the men who developed the cattle industry in the far West before the "cowboy" was ever heard of, I must correct some errors that have marred the true story for years. I speak as a vaquero – and I know whereof I speak.

As nature segregates and forms distinct groups from creatures of a common stock, so the Californiano developed into a type of his own differing from those of his background in Spain. To understand who and what the vaquero or buckaroo actually was, and why he was found with a distinct culture differing from that of any other herdsman, even from those who spoke the same language and were neighbors – English in the United States and Spanish in Mexico – we must go back to Cristóbal Colón, to the fifteenth century Spain of Fernando and Isabela.

Since the Castilian Isabela either financed or permitted Colón to make his expedition of discovery (we do not know since accounts and legends differ) only the subjects of the Castilian crown were permitted to go to those regions where gold was to be found. Thus it was that the Castilian, Andalusian, Extremaduran, Basque, and Portuguese had a free hand in pillaging the fabulous El Dorado of the New World. The subjects of Don Fernando – the Aragonese, Catalans, Valencians,

Murcians, and southern Italians - had to stay at home, being refused the opportunity to share in carving up the golden pie.

By the time northern New Spain (what is now western United States) was colonized, however, some of the stay-at-homes could come to America, and the men who guarded the first colonists on the journey across the desert into Alta California were Catalonians.

These Catalonians brought the art of *La Jineta* from Spain and transplanted it in California. There the system of riding was much modified from La Jineta of the fifteenth century Andalusian which prevailed in central Mexico. We thus find the California rider distinct not only in costume, custom, speech and character, but also in nature, from the other riders or herdsmen of the New World, including those of central Mexico, even before the gringo came to the West Coast or went to the Gulf Coast states.

The central Mexico rider is a leverage-bit man. His steel curb-chain is still the iron-ring curb of the Moors. On the other hand, the Californiano is a palate-bit man. He uses a leather curb-strap. He does not depend on leverage so much as on the signal of the port touching the palate. The only thing the central Mexico vaquero and the California vaquero or buckaroo have in common is that they both wrap the rope around the horn of the saddle to hold a beef when they lasso it.

The California vaquero was born when Don Juan Bautista de Anza led his colonists across the desert into California in 1776. These Catalans had centuries of hand-to-hand combat on horseback in their background; and when they hung up their *chaquetas de cuero*, their leather jackets, to settle on the ranchos and raise cattle they kept alive their pride in an ages-long tradition of horsemanship. The Indians they trained as vaqueros became converts and disciples of the same proud tradition and often exceeded their masters. Some of the very best reinsmen were Indians.

From the beginning the vaquero followed a pattern furnished him by his ancestry in the Old World. He never subordinated his conception of a gentleman on horseback to that of a herder of cattle - a precept which all vaqueros, no matter of what race, have followed religiously in California. And to this day the art of riding is affected by the ancient military tradition, although it has passed through successive modifications.

The vaquero's horse was trained first as a cavalryman's horse, and as a cattle horse afterwards, even though the vaquero's worst enemy was usually nothing more than a maddened bull or an enraged grizzly. That the vaquero's horse was trained for war was proved at San Pasqual in 1846, when the Californians (the majority of those who fought that battle were Sonorans, however) made a brave defense, with riatas and lances, against a seasoned regiment of United States troops.

When the Yankees came around the Horn in sailing ships to California, the *paisano*, the native, called them *marineros*, or mariners. They were of the best Anglo stock and became pupils of the hard riding Californians. To their credit let it be said that they loyally adopted the Spanish tradition. They called themselves vaqueros, pronounced it *bukeras*, and later corrupted it to buckaroos.

When the paisano put the New England sea-dog on horseback and taught him the vaquero's trade and the Spanish style of horsemanship, this gringo became the first buckaroo, and while adapting the sober, prosaic Yankee to the Spanish tradition, the paisano took him out of character enough to imbue him with a touch of Don Quixote. The transplanted sea-dog absorbed his teaching so well that he often carried the passion for decorating himself and his horse with silver trappings to further extremes than the proverbially ostentatious paisano. Observe any parade in any western town.

The gringo immigration began in the 1830's and in time these Yankees and their sons and grandsons spread the longhorned Spanish cattle of California from the Mexican border to British Columbia, and from the Pacific to the continental divide.

Their cult of Spanish horsemanship was, as late as 1910, as clean as it was when the first cavalrymen rode into Alta California, and its influence has been so all-prevailing that as long as men ride horses with curb-bits and drive cattle in North America they are paying tribute to the Spaniards.

Andalusian Horse

Elk-necked Spanish Horse

Draw a line on the map of North America, starting in Old Mexico at the southern tip of the peninsula of Baja California. Draw the line a little south of Culiacan in Sinaloa to the Sierra Madre Occidental, then north through this sierra to the border of the United States where Arizona and New Mexico meet, then along this border to that of Utah and north to the corner of Wyoming. From here follow the western base of the Rocky Mountains into Canada. This is the American West, the territory of the vaquero and buckaroo. Of course the vaquero drove cattle over more territory; but to be specific we will say three states and one territory in Mexico – Sinaloa, Sonora and Baja California (the state and the territory), and California, Nevada, Oregon, Washington, Arizona, Utah, and parts of Idaho, Wyoming, and Montana in the United States. Or, roughly, the part of North America lying west of the Rocky Mountains, and the part of Mexico lying west of the Sierra Madre, from the Tropic of Cancer to Canada.

The vaquero and his counterpart, the buckaroo, plied their trade from the Hawaiian Islands to the prairies of central North America, where he was taken to rope buffalo. *A palate-bit man first, last, and forever, while pursuing his calling, he never forgot, wherever he found himself, that merit lay not only in what he did, but also in how he did it.*

Those who wrote of early California are unanimous in saying that the vaquero's skill was marvelous, and although this subject does not come within the scope of this work— nor does the author feel qualified to expatiate on the general history of California - it must be said in passing that, unfortunately, these same writers copy each other in saying that the Californian lost his lands and cattle to the gringos as a consequence of his love for ease and gambling. This is an unjust slander. There is no truth in it.

When the gringo took over the land, the paisano –if he did not migrate to Mexico, Chile, or Spain – gathered what few cattle were left to him and disappeared into the most distant and isolated places he could find in the West, as far away from the marauding bands of gringos as he could get. Where is he now? Ask the lonely canyons and deserts of the far places. They could tell if they could talk.

So much for the vaquero; let us return to the cowboy.

The cowboy still exists. He can be found at any of the numerous "rodeos" staged in many cities and towns of the United States. This rodeo is not a "gathering of cattle." That was the original meaning of the word. The rodeo is now a stylized performance to which admission is charged. Bucking horses and Brahman bulls are ridden and calves and steers are roped against time in this rodeo by men who are called "cowboys."

These cowboys are not herders of cattle, they are rodeo followers. They have more the character of performers than of herdsmen. Some of these cowboys may have come originally from a ranch, but more often than not they have never worked on one.

Although the rodeo had its birth in the southern states, modern rodeo performers come from every state in the Union. One top performer learned to ride bucking horses on a dude ranch in the Adirondacks of New York.

These men are an aberration. Their calling serves no useful purpose and is more brutal than that of the bullfighter. However, in justice to the rodeo cowboy, it must be said that he can ride anything that wears hair, the worst bucking horses and the meanest Brahma bulls, and he is afraid of nothing but an ambulance. Although conversationally the present day rider does not compare with the "old time" rider, the records and the size of today's horses prove the reverse.

This cowboy is indebted to the Negro for his culture. The African was a herdsman in his native habitat. The African status symbol was cattle. It still is in many parts of Africa. The Negro handled great herds of cattle and made a virtue of necessity to develop methods of handling cattle without a horse. Some of the practices of today's rodeo come directly from Africa and are in use there to this day.

The original cowboy came from the Atlantic seaboard and was frequently a Negro or poor white who was not always supplied with a horse by his cavalier master. As a result, the system of bulldogging, flanking, working cattle in closepens and chutes - and the sports of the rodeo arena — were developed. The fastidious vaquero or buckaroo called this "wallowing in manure."

When the United States took possession of the vast territory east of New Mexico and north of the Rio Grande, the Anglo from the South (as always in our reference, this is a loose term, since there was a heavy Scotch and German migration into that part of the Union) found himself in possession of vast herds of cattle which he could have for the taking.

When he came to work these cattle, some writers would have us believe, he would not adopt the Mexican's way of working because of his hatred of Mexicans. Actually he adopted all he could, the two-cinch saddle of central Mexico, the lazo, and the curb-bit.

The bondsman dumped from the English convict ships was a snaffle-bit man; he tied his rope, not because of a disregard for consequences, but because he had to have two hands to guide his horse. He could never learn to take turns around the horn to hold a beef. The truth of the matter is that the cowboy adopted the methods he used, not from choice, but from the pressure of circumstances.

The first cowboy was poorly mounted. The horse he rode, contrary to tall tales of wild white stallions, was never more than a pony. The assertion of Will James that the horses of the Pacific Northwest were the best mustangs in North America is true. And it is also true that the mustangs of Texas, New Mexico, and the Mexican states that border the United States were the poorest.

When the first herds of cattle were driven from the Gulf Coast into the Pacific Northwest, it was found that the horses often gained as much as two or three hundred pounds of growth after a year or two there. This was so even when they had, presumably, reached their full growth in Mexico or Texas. Grass and water can do wonders.

While it is treason to depart from the incredible pattern of the "western" yarn immortalized in so much printed matter, it is nevertheless true that the cowboy waving a sixshooter did not win the West. The cowboy never got to the actual geographic West. If anyone is to have the credit for the winning of the West, it should be the United States Army private.

The cowboy got as far west as central Arizona. There he met the buckaroo. There the two systems—one Spanish, the other African—clashed.

It was in the nature of things that when the West Coast rider met the Gulf Coast rider there would be friction. The buckaroo looked down on the man who would dismount and wrestle cattle afoot while his horse stood around with its reins dragging in the dirt.

Ironically, it was the Anglo rider representing each system who upheld the superiority of his way of working cattle and handling a horse; this to the great astonishment of the tolerant paisano.

The West Coast rider abhorred the plain equipment of the Gulf Coast rider; in it he found no silver, no beauty, no pride in possession or profession. The Afro-Anglo idiom jarred with the Hispanic-Anglo terms. Besides, the low port bits favored by the cowboy spoiled horses' mouths.

The buckaroo and the cowboy quarreled and quite often fought. The excuse was that one used a single-cinch saddle and the other used a double-cinch saddle, or that one used a high-port bit and the other used a low-port bit.

It makes a man stop and think about the actual history of our West when he pictures two men fighting, one Anglo fighting another Anglo, one for a culture he got from the Spaniard, and the other for a culture he got from the Negro. These clashes did not occur on the Gulf Coast or on the Pacific Coast, but in Arizona, Nevada, and Montana. And it is a fact that the many fights and quarrels which resulted from these differences of opinion were not fought by the Hispanic Californian on the one hand and the Negro on the other; the contending Anglo riders were descended from Yankee stock on the one hand and from Southerners of the other. However, this was the general case. There were all sorts of exceptions to the rule. The men who were on one side of the fence or the other were not all descendants of Yankees or Southerners. And one fine old gentleman, to whom I am indebted for much of this material – a staunch old buckaroo whose lip still curls at the sight of a ''rimmy,'' a two-cinch saddle – is a grandson of Tenneseeans.

Just remember that the environment of the old time cattle ranch was a close one. It bred strong loyalties.

VAQUERO

I do not come from an "Old Spanish Family." Old Spanish families are an invention of the gringos. They are a myth which the paisanos have come to believe themselves, as Sancho did his enchantment of Dulcinea in *Don Quixote*. My father was of Sonoran stock and of clerical people, that is to say, there had been priests and nuns in his family. He had enough education to act as interpreter in court, as he was sometimes asked to do. He was a skilled craftsman who made silver mounted bits and spurs for the trade in his own shop. Besides that source of income the financier Lucky Baldwin paid him one hundred dollars a month to make the plates for and to shoe his favorite race horses at Santa Anita Rancho.

My mother's mother, Rita Ruiz, was born in Los Angeles and had come to Rancho San Pasqual (which is now the city of Pasadena) after the gringos had disposessed her. That was before my mother was born and when Tia Concepcion, Aunt Concepcion, the second child in my mother's family, was yet a babe in arms. Tia Concia, as we called her, in later years told a story of having been driven away from home by gringos, and of her and my grandmother being without food or shelter when Vasquez, the bandit, found them and fed the mother and child. My grandmother's parents had come from the old colonial town of Alamos, Sonora, while Don Pablo Sola, the last Spanish governor of California, was still in office.

There were two Spaniards from Extremadura, and two Yaqui women on my father's side of the family, two Catalans and two Mayo women on my mother's side. So if I now and then take a dig at the Spaniards or at the Indians, I am exercising an inalienable right. I am speaking about my own family.

Mother, having been born after the gringos took California, could speak English, though she could not read or write. Although we spoke Spanish at home, the Yankee schoomarm was already an influence, because we brothers and sisters spoke English among ourselves and had a leaning toward the gringos. My first actual contact with them was at the Garfield School on California Street in Pasadena. The teachers were kind and from that childhood impression I have had a high regard for the gringo teacher.

Mother died when I was a child, and as a result we were all five small children sent to orphanages. I spent four years in one, then ran away and was never caught. I was in the third grade then and have never gone to school since. Although I was subsequently sent to other orphanages, the authorities were never able to keep me in one for more than a few weeks at a time.

I lived with my aunt Concia in Pasadena, but never liked it. Perhaps I would have vegetated there and never known about vaqueros if it had not been for my uncle Jim McFall. He came to Pasadena to visit my grandmother, and when he went back to his ranch in Soledad Canyon I went with him. Uncle Jim was my mother's oldest brother. When ten years old he had gone on a trail drive which crossed half the continent. Grandmother told us that he had run away from home in 1860 and did not return to southern California until he was middle-aged.

He had joined a company of gringos—though Aunt Concia said that it was Vasquez with whom he had left—who were driving horses east into a middle-western state. Grandma could not tell us the name of the state. Perhaps she could not pronounce it. All she knew was that it was a land of *chubascos*, blizzards, *muy lejos, donde habia puros gringos*—far away where there are only gringos. It was most probably Nebraska. It was during the late 1850's and early 1860's when the vast herds were driven out of California into the eastern states, after the members of the best families in California had emigrated to other lands and left their herds and ranchos to be despoiled by the gringos.

My uncle Jim was a neighbor of Don Leonardo Ruiz who was a relative of my grandmother, Rita Ruiz. Don Leonardo had lost his property on the coast and had come to Soledad to grub out a living. He was a kindly old man, and because he never scolded me as my uncle Jim did, I went to live with him.

It was on his *ranchito* that I stumbled, so to speak, on the trade I was to follow throughout my lifetime. It was to be my work, my hobby, my study. Don Leonardo had a fine background, both practical and historical, in Spanish horsemanship, even if he was too old to practice it. He opened a new world for me. From him I learned that we had a Spanish tradition of horsemanship, the antique Arabic-Moorish Hispanic art of La Jineta. *Cosas de muy lejos atras*, things of the distant past, as he expressed it.

I shall always cherish the memories of the long winter nights on the little ranch, when the wind howled out of the Mojave and we sat by the fire of black *chamiso* roots which burn like coal, and listened as Don Leonardo told of *garanones Guzmanes y Valenzuelas*, stallions of Guzman and Valenzuela breeding, from which descended the Carthusian chargers which the breeders of Jerez and Sevilla cherished. From these war stallions came the Isabellas (palominos and buckskins) of Andalusia from which the mustangs that ran wild in the New World were descended. These *destriers* were bred and trained by priests and monks in Carthusian monasteries, and took the name of that order. They were sometimes called the ''monk's horse'' or ''monastery horse.'' The equestrian monks and priests who came to the New World and taught the ancient Hispano-Arabic hippology of which they were masters were probably Carthusians.

I have often pondered on the perversity of fate which sent Don Leonardo, such a fine old gentleman, to that lonely, sterile desert canyon, so aptly called La Soledad – the Solitude. He was so out of place there. Perhaps I have given Don Leonardo attributes he did not possess, but this he did for me: He taught me the value of things which link us to a bygone day, and placed before me a cavalcade of horsemen which has been passing now for fifty years.

It was there on the ranchito that I began to worship the men who rode horses and to envy them their bowed legs. There I decided never to go back to the town of my birth. I would seek out a ranch where there were vaqueros and I would learn to ride. True, it was poorly paid work, and there were many risks and dangers incident to the life of a vaquero, many hardships to be endured. But at least I would be on horseback and would not be looked down upon.

The great ranches were in the San Joaquin Valley, so I decided to go there and see Don Jesus Lopez, manager of the Tejon Ranch. Don Leonardo gave me the old hump-backed, hip-shot pinto mare and the saddle with the broken tree. It was all he had to give.

I shall always remember my first interview with Don Jesus Lopez at the vaquero camp on Tejon Ranch. After I had told him I had come to the ranch to look for work, he looked for a long time at the hump-backed mare, then at the saddle, than at the bit. Then he turned to me and asked the question which has made many good men hesitate to answer, "*Y tu, hijo, eres vaquero?*" And you, son, are a vaquero?

Young as I was I had sense enough to answer, "No, *pero puedo aprender.*" No, but I can learn.

The next question was another which many good vaqueros have been loath to answer: "*Y si un caballo repara, hijo, te tumba? Aqui hay caballos muy malcriados.*" And if a horse should buck, son, would he throw you? There are horses here that are very rude.

"*Pues,*" I answered, "*depende en los reparos.*" Well, it depends on the bucking.

Don Jesus turned and looked again for a long minute at the hump-backed mare, at the old saddle, then at the skinny kid before him. He assumed a very serious expression, and said, "*Bueno, como buen paisano te voy a dar trabajo. Pero yo no quiero muchachos que maltratan y estrujan caballos. Todo que te pido es que cuides tus caballos, pobrecitos.*" Well, as a good fellow townsman (he was from Los Angeles) I am going to give you work. But I will not have boys who mistreat and abuse horses. All I ask of you is that you take care of your horses, poor things.

The horses Don Jesus gave me were Chocolate, a gray; Kelly, a sorrel; White Stockings, a stocking-legged sorrel; Smokey, a brown; and Horcado, a gray. They were the best horses I have had the good fortune to ride.

THE SPANISH
CALIFORNIA DIALECT

In these stories I use the Spanish of the vaquero, who is now gone forever, even if the dialect does not conform to the best Castilian. The reader will, no doubt, search through Spanish dictionaries for some of the words. He will either fail to find them or they will have definitions which do not agree with those in the text; because of that circumstance, some explanations are in order.

The Spanish spoken in California was a dialect of old Castilian which was brought by the Catalonian soldiers who accompanied the missionaries into this part of New Spain. Even today the paisano counts his money in *reales*. Often the vaquero adopted terms to suit the occasion or circumstance. The word *nuqueador* — one who slaughtered cattle by stabbing them at the base of the neck, the *nuca—* is an example.

Many of the words used here had gone out of use in Spain long before the gringos came in 1846. From that time the paisano's language began to die out in California. Few of the old people could read or write, but spoke a clean, simple Spanish; and it was not until the gringos erected schools and the paisano sent his children to them that the young ones began to interlard their speech with English words. Those who retain fragments of Spanish today speak it with a Yankee accent.

The children did not have a chance. In the hands of that peerless civilizer, the Yankee schoolmarm, they were taught the three R's - and to think in English. It is safe to say that the school, more than the barbed-wire fence or the plowing up of the range, was responsible for the decline of the vaquero.

It is not true that many Indian words were used, as some writers assert. About the only Indian word (said to be derived from the Yaqui and that is debatable) is *pochi* or *pocho*, lopped off or bob-tailed. A bob-tailed horse was called "El Mocho" by Californians, and "El Pocho" by Sonorans. Californians became "pochos" or "pochis" when Alta California was severed from Mexico.

Another word of doubtful etymology is *coche* or *cochi*. In Spain it means coach, in Mexico an automobile, but in California it meant hog.

The word *bravo* is often translated as brave in English. In California it was used in the sense of fierce. A *toro bravo* was a fierce bull, not necessarily a brave one. The word also meant sharp or keen. A knife with a fine edge was said to be *brava*, barbs on fence wire were *alambre bravo*, rock which cut up a horse's feet was *piedra brava*, and an awl with a fine point was *brava*. Anything that drew blood or would attack, as a wildcat, was *brava*. Even chili, when extra peppery, was *chili bravo*.

The best interpretation of the term *bravo* I have ever heard was given by Russell Hill, who spoke Spanish fluently.

A rodeo was in progress at the old fairgrounds in Bakersfield. One of Russell's vaqueros was standing under the grandstand. He was holding a lady's hand and looking into her eyes, probably telling her she was beautiful and that he couldn't live without her. Russell, mounted on one of his fine Morgan horses, rode by, and seeing the soulful little tableau, said, warningly, "*Muncho cuidado, es muy bravo el marido.*" Look out! The husband is very fierce.

Whether the lady had a husband, we do not know. It is very probable that Russell was joking.

The vaquero never used the proper *mucho*, much. He said *muncho*.

The cowboy expression "broke in two" may very well have

been derived from the vaquero's *se mocho*, meaning a horse bucked, and similarly, the phrase "part out," to separate cattle, came from *apartar*.

Whenever a vaquero plunged after a runaway beef, or raced after an animal to lasso it, it was said he *arrebato una res*, assailed a beef. The same term arrebato was used when one person attacked another.

Quite often the vaquero, when at a loss for a word, called a thing he had no name for by an unchaste name, as people call a thing that has no name a "doohickey" or a "hootenanny."

The *Californiano* – writers on California to the contrary – called himself a *Sonoreño*. I have heard third or fourth generation descendants of members of the De Anza expedition (Don Jose Jesus Lopez for one) say, "*Nosotros somos Sonorenos. Sonora es nuestra tierra.*" We are Sonorans. Sonora is our motherland.

This prideful distinction stemmed from having descended from the actual colonists, not from the convicts who were introduced in subsequent expeditions.

The gringo vaqueros – by gringo vaqueros I mean the Anglos, sons of Yankee parents, who could handle a sixty-foot riata and a full spade bit, and there were many who could – interlarded their speech with Spanish words, and more often than not used them correctly.

Whenever they became loosened in the saddle and they were forced to grab the saddle horn, as sometimes happened, the gringo vaqueros would say that they had "grabbed the apple." The paisano's equivalent for this term was, "*agarrar la comadre*," clutch the comadre. Perhaps they called the horn "comadre" because the word means literally co-mother. The comadre is the woman who sponsors one's child when it is baptized. Since a comadre or *compadre* would never fail one in time of emergency, it was quite logical that the saddle horn should be called "la comadre."

There were many stout youngsters on the ranches who could rake a bucking horse from shoulder to flank with their spurs, and hit him with their hat at every jump, but it was no disgrace to clutch the horn when the rider felt himself getting loosened in the saddle, because he "had bought the horn when he bought the saddle." Sometimes, however, a rider did not have time to grab the horn. He often found himself on the ground twenty feet away, with a handful of dirt.

Every now and then in some musty old Spanish book one meets with the word *jinete*. In Spain and Latin America jinete means simply a man on horseback, but in the language of the vaquero it has much more significance. To us a jinete is an expert rider of bucking horses. No ordinary rider who just managed to stay on a bucking horse was called a jinete in California; such a person was merely a *travieso*, a mischievous one, a rapscallion. Used in the sense of a verb, *jinetiar* meant to ride a bucking horse.

At the vaquero camp on Tejon Ranch one day many years ago, the following conversation took place between Don Jesus Lopez, the mayordomo, and Don Porfirio Valencia, the *caporal*, or foreman. The object of their discussion was a new vaquero who was as yet untried.

Don Jesus: *Y ese vaquero, podra andar en El Canelo?''* And that vaquero, will he be able to ride the Roan?

Don Porfirio (By the way, Don Porfirio lisped.): ''*Pues, el dice que es jinete y amansa caballos.''* Well, he says that he is a bucking horse rider and tames horses.

Don Jesus: ''*Bueno, bueno. Vamos a ver.''* Good, good. We shall see.

Don Porfirio: ''*Adolfo dice que esta enfada de andar en ese caballo.''* Adolfo says he is fed up with riding that horse.

Don Jesus: ''*Si, si. Pobre muchacho.''* Yes, yes. Poor boy.

The outcome of this conversation was that the new vaquero was given the Roan, and in the course of events was thrown ''as high as a kite.''

THE INDIAN VAQUERO

When a vaquero was especially skilled, and he was asked how he had reached such a degree of proficiency, his answer would invariably be: *"Me crie entre los Indios."* I was raised among the Indians. Or when some vaquero had performed his work with great skill, the other men would look at each other, smile approvingly, and say, *"Se crio entre los Indios pues."* Well, he was brought up among the Indians.

Contrary to a lot of false statements, a man took pride in calling himself "Indio." The Indian vaquero was highly respected for his skill and good qualities – that is, by those who knew him. And the proof is that very few of the men who have ridden on the Tejon stayed there any length of time without becoming *"Indios del Tejon,"* Tejon Indians, whatever their true race may have been.

At night around the fire a note of awe would creep into the old man's voice, as he told of hard riding Indian vaqueros who had roped grizzly bears and led wild cattle out of the Sierra, men who had become legends on the Tejon Ranch.

Cattle ranching was the Californiano's preferred – his sole– occupation for the first hundred years after the state was founded. Indeed, from 1769 until the turn of the present century, cattle raising was the most important industry in California.

In the beginning the ranches were Spanish and Mexican land

grants. After California became a part of the United States, big cattle companies formed the greatest cattle ranches in North America. The Tejon, Kern County Land Company, and Miller and Lux are examples of these huge ranches.

It was boasted, in his many bunkhouses in California, Nevada, and Oregon, that Henry Miller could ride from the Mexican border to British Columbia and sleep on his own land every night, change horses every day from his own *caponeras* (a *caponera* is a band of horses, usually geldings, kept for the use of the vaqueros) and eat beef from his own herds on the entire journey. Of course this was an exaggeration, but nevertheless the Miller and Lux holdings were enormous.

One might say that cattle ranching in California did not lose its paramount importance until after 1927, when Miller and Lux started selling out their land. The Kern County Land Company with its three and three-quarter million acres is still the largest producer of range beef in North America.

The vaquero or buckaroo who herded the cattle on the ranches of California was sometimes a Cahuilla, a Piute, a Mission Indian, or a member of one of the other numerous tribes which populated California. Sometimes he was a Sonoreno, that is to say, a native of the state of Sonora in Old Mexico, or a descendant of Sonorenos born in California. Sometimes he was a Californian of pioneer colonial stock, like Don Jesus Lopez. At other times he was from Baja California like Frederico Lamas, and sometimes he was a gringo. Once in a while a Chilean was met among the vaquero crews.

The vaquero of California was the North American counterpart of the Argentine *gaucho*, the Brazilian *vaquiero*, and Chilean *buaso*. But our histories have ignored him. This rider was called a "vaquero," a word derived from *vaca*, cow. He was never called a "cowboy." In fact, the Anglo rider of the West (if an Irishman can be called an "Anglo") particularly of California, Nevada, and Oregon, so disliked the word "cowboy" that he coined the term "buckaroo" from vaquero, and by this he was known.

Perhaps this Hispanicization came from the padres who were the vaquero's teachers. They were almost invariably good horsemen and could balance a lance or throw a *lazo*, a lasso, with the best leather jacket soldier. Indeed, they sometimes solved the problem of bringing their neophytes into the fold by lassoing them. Often some recalcitrant Indian, who later became a good vaquero of the mission herds, got his first object lesson in throwing the lazo when a zealous padre rode after him and roped him, thus literally leading him into the bosom of Mother Church.

It is doubtful whether the first padres brought vaqueros with them from Velicata. The first cattle were probably driven into Alta California by *harrieros*, muleteers, and cavalrymen. The padres trained native Indians as vaqueros as the herds increased, despite the Laws of the Indies which forbade Indians, on penalty of death, to ride horses. The Spaniards feared the Indians would become warriors like the Apaches. Subsequent events proved that the Spaniards were not wrong. The padres were good teachers. A few years after the arrival of the first cattle there were a number of good Indian vaqueros at Monterey.

The *rancheros*, the ranchers, of the old Spanish and Mexican grants used Indian vaqueros almost exclusively until the Gold Rush period. Then Sonorenos who had migrated to California to seek gold began to take over the herding of cattle. Some ranches, however, use Indian vaqueros to this day, as do the Tejon Ranch and the Paubo Ranch. The Santa Margarita used them until it became Camp Pendleton. The vaqueros who drove the first great herds out of California in 1836, when Ewing Young began supplying the Oregon ranchers with cattle, were probably Californians and Indians, but when Pete French and John Devine stocked the eastern Oregon and western Nevada ranges with California cattle their vaqueros were Sonoreños.

The gringo came into the vaquero picture in numbers after the 1850's and from his advent the crews became mixed. These riders were, for the most part, sons of immigrants or small ranch owners. These gringos had been reared with Spanish speaking children and, more often than not, spoke Spanish. All riders, no matter of what racial background, used the same type of equipment – spade or half-breed bit, rawhide riata, ''shotgun'' or ''wooly'' chaps, and flat, hard-brimmed hat.

It would be unjust to say that men of one racial group were better at the work than those of another racial group. There were good Indian vaqueros, good Mexican vaqueros, good Californian vaqueros, and good gringo vaqueros, and the only Negro vaquero this writer ever knew was a good one too. He would ride any of the other vaquero's broncos for ten cents. If that price was too high, he would ride the bronco for a sack of Bull Durham tobacco which cost only a nickel, and few if any horses could buck him off.

It is only when they have ridden together stirrup to stirrup, and depended on each other in the thousand emergencies which arise when working wild cattle or riding bronco horses that men really know each other. Differences in race are forgotten as they learn each other's worth.

Contrary to the ''western'' writers who have written so much of hatred between the Anglo and the Latin peoples of California, the relations between the gringo and the paisano, as far as the vaquero and buckaroo were concerned, were good. The skilled men of any race were respected and usually had a large following. Such men were Juan Olivera, Lupe Ortiz, Juan Gomez, and many others. By the same token the Bowers, the Hathaways, the Brunks, the Roses, and the Pascoes were respected as first-class buckaroos. As a matter of fact, a man took more pride in calling himself *Indio* than in calling himself anything else. Regardless of what malicious writers may say, the Indians were liked, by those who knew them, for their good qualities. The Indian vaqueros Carlos Valenzuela, Bill Nichols, Vic Cordero, Nacho Montes, and many others earned the respect of all men.

The Indian vaquero was sparing in speech, and serene under all circumstances. He was pithy in all his expressions and often spoke in metaphor or ironically. One would have to be well acquainted with him to know his meanings. He had a knack for giving names which never failed to correspond to something risible in their owners. His nicknames told the characteristics of the victim. There was a man in

Bakersfield who every year managed the Frontier Days parade. He had a long, thin, straight nose and little blue eyes. He would have filled the description of Ichabod Crane in *The Legend of Sleepy Hollow*. Agustin Hinio named him *El Pajaro Carpintero*, the Woodpecker. A vaquero stationed at Fort Tejon liked to ride up and down Highway 99 so that the people could admire his figure on horseback. The other vaqueros named him "Highway Bill."

To a man whose color approached that of roasted coffee, the Indians would apply the term *El Guerro*, the Blond, or *El Gringo*, the Gringo. Or if the luckless one happened to be of Yaqui extraction, which was quite often the case, he would be named, *El Yori*, the White Man. To a man on Tejon who rode humped up over his horse the other men applied the name *El Tacuachi*, the Possum. They would say of a man who showed much Indian blood in his makeup, *Ese no le debe ni los Buenos Dias a los Espanoles* —that one doesn't owe even a "good day" to the Spaniards. Or if person's hair was stiff, they would say, *Ese lo tienen que peinar a martillasos* —that one has to be combed with a hammer.

THE VAQUERO'S SADDLE

The Iberian invaders from Andalusia and Extremadura brought the high-peaked Moorish saddle of which the big-horned saddle of central and southern Mexico is a modification. The Spaniards from every part of Spain who settled in Mexico over a period of three centuries had very little in common with the first *conquistadores* in respect to styles of riding and horse equipment. As a result, "Mexican" saddles, bits, and spurs vary in type, style, and period.

The California vaquero's saddle is not adapted from the Moorish saddle. It is a modification of the Persian saddle which was brought to the New World in later years. However, Moorish, Persian, and "Mexican" saddles are basically the same. They have the same side-bars, high fork, and steep, high cantle, and the stirrups hang at the same angle.

The Persian saddle was adapted for use in hot country. It was a skeleton tree with a detachable housing called a *mochilla* in Alta California and a *cojinillo* in Baja California, Sonora, and parts of Sinaloa. It was the saddle that the Spaniards, who went to the Hawaiian Islands in 1808, took and introduced there. This saddle is still used on Hawaii's Parker Ranch.

In Alta California it went through succeeding modifications. The detachable mochilla and cojinillo were discarded and a permanent cover was put on the tree. This original tree was the model for the

Old Vaquero Equipment

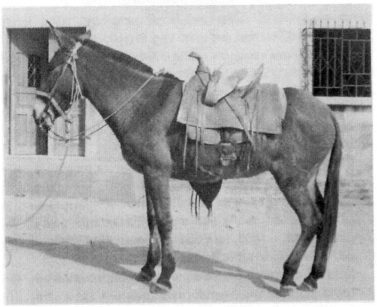

Ring Bit and Center-fire Saddle

Visalia, Taylor, and Ledesma trees which spread over the West in the last century. It was the best saddle in the world for practical use.

Here we must digress to explain why the vaquero abhorred the two-cinch or double-rig (rimfire) saddle and despised the man who rode one. The double-rig originated in Mexico in the days of the colony. It was in use there until by brutal trial and error it was found that it inflicted unnecessary pain on the horse and was inefficient besides; the vaquero discarded it.

The early vaquero was an observant man. In the course of his work he found that the forering on the double-rig saddle was so placed that it acted as a pivot between the cinch and the fork. When a rope was attached to the horn and a pull was exerted, the fork of the saddle would tilt forward, and the sharp ends of the side bars would be driven into the horse's shoulders. The mechanical principle was the same as that of a plow. Indeed it had the same effect as a plowshare. The back cinch, being loose, served only to hurt the horse's belly muscles.

On the other hand, the center-fire, single-cinch saddle had the ring placed in the center of the tree. When a pull was exerted on the horn, the pull would be equal from front and back of the saddle and, as a result, the saddle would not tilt. However, the center-fire had one bad feature. It had a tendency to slide forward and needed constant attention. This constant "fixing" had its benefits. The fixing kept the saddle from bearing too long on one spot, and thus prevented many a sore back.

Back at the turn of the century the "rimmys" started coming out of the south and often there were mixed crews on the roundups in Montana and Arizona. Men who rode double-rigs were on roundups with men who rode single-rigs. The foreman, when he had assembled the crew before sending them out to gather cattle, would say, "All you buckaroos riding center-fires get off and fix your saddles. All you lazy sons of bitches riding rimfires can stay on your horses."

This riding in mixed crews made the vaquero and buckaroo cleave all the more to the center-fire. Those riders who had wandered away from the home range to ride in other climes came back to California and told around the campfire of the customs and methods of the rimfire men.

Antique Spur

1860 Spur, Rowell —7¼ inches

"Those cowboys," they would say, "never got off to fix their saddles. When they pulled them off in the evening, they took off half the horse's hide with the saddle. The reason they had to have so many of those little horses in their strings was that the horses had to have time between saddlings for their backs to heal."

In like manner the old-timer clove to the slick-fork. The swell fork, sometimes eighteen inches across the swell, "beat a man to death" when a horse bucked, and the swells were in the way when a rider leaned down to avoid obstacles such as tree branches.

So the vaquero used the California saddle with single rigging, that is to say, one cinch. The ring extends from the center of the saddle. The single-rig is better from a humane and from a practical standpoint, because a horse, in order to move in comfort, must have freedom at the shoulders, and anything that binds that part of the animal's body, as the double-rig does, will interfere with the animal's movements. The single-rig saddle also came to the United States from Mexico, where both styles were used until the double-rig was discarded.

Another advantage of the single-rig over the double-rig is that the stirrups hang slightly forward, and thus the weight of the rider and the pressure of the stirrups equalize the load on the horse's back. The length, width, and shape of the bars distribute the load over the horse's back; a tree that is too long is better than a tree that is too short.

Because no two backs were alike, each horse in the vaquero's string presented a different problem. There were high and low withers, broad and wide backs, long and thin backs, "hump" or "hog" backs. The hog back and high-withered back were anathema to the vaquero. Kidney sores result from hog backs, caused by the side-bars digging into the back when the vaquero rode too much on the cantle. Low, sloping cantles, much in use today, were scorned by the old-time vaquero. He knew their evil. The straight, high, broad cantle had a purpose; it kept the rider where he belonged in the saddle. The muscles which propel the horse press against the ends of the bars, and a thin horse will bruise more easily than a fat one.

But of all sizes and shapes of horses' backs, the low-withered back was the bane to the life of the man who had to keep a saddle on it. The low-withered horse required a cinch to be kept excessively tight. Of late years saddle makers have come out with a contraption they call a "quarter-horse-tree"; this, however, does not solve the problem of low withers.

Another troublesome type of horse was the "one-gutted" animal. A one-gutted horse had flanks so narrow that they let the cinch slip or drop back. Such a horse could hardly be ridden without a breast-collar and was such a "poor keeper" that his rider "would have to tie a knot in his tail to keep him from going through the cinch" before the day's ride was over, as the gringo buckaroos expressed it.

Careless cinching was cause of galled horses. Riders differ in their methods of cinching. Some cinch loosely, then tighten up after the horse has traveled a while and warmed up. Others cinch up tightly when they first saddle up. Some horses fall over backwards when cinched up the first time in the morning. The belief was common among riders that a "cinchbinder," as the gringos call a horse that falls over backwards, would never have acquired the vice if he had been cinched up tightly from the beginning of his training or breaking. Horses that have been broken with a loose cinch invariably buck or fall over backwards when they are cinched up tightly.

Good vaqueros never failed, when the opportunity presented itself, to dismount, loosen the cinch, raise the saddle and blankets and let the air pass over the horse's sweaty back for a few moments. But they never removed the saddle from the horse's back until the animal was cool, believing that a horse would chill if its wet back were exposed to the wind. They never turned a saddle blanket over once it was shaped to a horse's back; nor would they ever wring out a wet blanket. Wringing broke the threads.

Ranchers who kept the same breed of stallions and mares over a period of time were not troubled with back problems so much as were the ranchers who bought their saddle stock wherever they could get it. Ranchers who bred their own saddle horses could breed for certain type and breed out faults in conformation. Each ranch bred for a certain type; in the days of great ranches in California, a person could determine where a vaquero rode by the appearance of his horse. At a gathering of vaqueros or at a rodeo, a Kern County Land Company horse could be easily distinguished from a Miller and Lux horse. And a Tejon horse could be distinguished from as far as the eye could see it; and, for that matter, so could a Roland Hill Morgan.

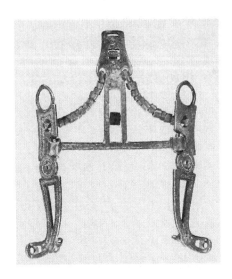

Sonora Spade

Bridle which saved Jose Juan's Life

THE VAQUERO'S BRIDLE BIT

The bridle-bit was the most important piece of equipment in the vaquero's outfit. Without a good bit he could not work a horse properly, and unless a vaquero had a good bit a mayor-domo worthy of the name would not hire him. It was as simple as that. And it was just as important that the vaquero know bits and their function.

The California vaquero never used a low-port (grazer) bit, nor one with abnormally long shanks or jaws. He learned very early that such bits would spoil a horse's mouth. The curve in the mouthpiece of the low-port grazer clamped a horse's tongue, and the animal learned to ball its tongue and brace its jaw in self-defense. The grazer was deficient in leverage and as a consequence the horse learned to bear on it and thus became hard mouthed.

The long shanked bit with "enough leverage to lift a boxcar," as the gringos expressed it, either pulled a horse's head up too high or pulled it down into his chest. In any case, a long shanked bit was sure to cut a horse's tongue.

For these reasons the vaquero used the high port bit, either the spade or half-breed. However, the bit did not make the horse. The horse was made before a bit was ever put in its mouth. No bit in the world can make a mouth. The horse was made with the *jaquima*, or hackamore, a band put around its nose in order to school the animal. The jaquima saved the mouth because it accustomed the horse to obey the rein without hurting it as would be the case if it were to be pulled with a bit in its mouth. The jaquima was not removed until the horse could stop, turn, and back perfectly. The bit was then used to maintain the condition into which the jaquima had put the horse.

In the old days vaqueros never started to break a horse until it was five years old. The reason was that a vaquero never liked to put a bit in a horse's mouth until it had its "bridle teeth," the canines. Vaqueros believe that a horse cannot be bitted successfully until it has all its permanent teeth. A colt changing teeth will not pay attention to the pull on the rein because of the pain. Another reason vaqueros would not put a bit in a horse's mouth until the animal had adjusted to carrying a load on its back was that a colt will stumble and have to be pulled, or will shy and have to be doubled. If the colt were wearing a bit, doubling and pulling would hurt its mouth.

Most old-timers who had colts in their strings rarely rode them more than two or three times a month. Actually it was only a short period that a colt was ridden with a jaquima. During much of this period it was ridden with double reins, with both bit and jaquima. The reins of the bit were not pulled, however.

From this practice, no doubt, has come the myth current among dudes and aficionados of the spade bit and "California style" of today that the old Californianos rode a colt two and three years with a jaquima. These people never take into account that a horse is a creature of habit, that the longer one wears a jaquima the more habituated to it the animal will become. As a consequence it will be just so much harder to accustom to a bit.

The mouthpiece, of whatever form, has nothing to do with the severity of a bit. The length of the shanks or jaws of a bit decides the amount of its leverage or severity. Actually, however, the weight of the rider's hand decides whether any kind of bit is mild or severe. The leverage or curb bit is actually a lever. The mouthpiece is the fulcrum or prop, the shanks or jaws are the lever lifting against the chin or curb strap. It operates on a principle of mechanics. Originally the spade bit (in Spanish *paleta*, diminutive of *pala*, spade) had only two or two and a half inches of leverage. When bit makers lengthened its shanks and made a leverage bit of it, they spoiled it for the purpose for which it was designed.

To be effective in the function for which it was designed, the port of the spade bit must be at an angle where it will signal the horse just as the curb tightens. Careful adjustment of the curb strap is very important. The Californiano never used a curb chain on a spade bit. He believed that a chain calloused the chin-groove and as a result the horse lost the sense of feel in that part of its anatomy. The vaquero used a leather curb strap. The secret of the spade bit is that a horse never learns to lean or brace on it and as a result never has a hard mouth. Contrary to present day opinion, spade bits were not intended for nor used on hard mouthed horses. The old-timers often said that a spade bit was the only bit that fit a horse's mouth, and that the braces were responsible for this result. Contrary to those who exhibit ideas about bits nowadays, not all vaqueros were enthusiastically dedicated to the use of the spade bit. Many of them preferred a half-breed bit, yet the fact remains that they too rode good horses.

Good spade bit men were rare, even in that era of good reinsmen. Those who were outstanding were men who devoted themselves to putting a trigger rein on a horse. This bit was for those men who prided themselves on having a "bridle hand." Someone once asked Juan Olivera why he used a spade bit when the horse Juan rode would have obeyed with a silk string in his mouth to control him. Juan retorted that it was not a matter of strength, but a matter of pride in having a bridle hand. However, many old vaqueros had no bridle hand, and perhaps that is the reason the Creator imbued the mustang with *amor al ganado* or what buckaroos call "cow sense." The horse taught himself to herd cattle. There is an old saying, born of Spanish equitation, that "*El caballo de rienda: no se hace; el nace.*" The reined horse is not made; he is born.

Of late years there have been many tirades against the spade bit, and by the same token, many encomiums bestowed on it. But those who censure or praise it don't know what they are talking about. The men who could handle a spade bit died out long ago.

The teeth have much to do with the way a horse obeys the rein.

Horses that slobber, throw their heads, pull to one side, or go frantic when ridden with a tight rein, do so for no reason other than their teeth are sharp on the outside edges. The horse's upper jaw is wider than the lower, and after the animal is five years old, the upper grinders wear to a razor edge on the outside. In using a curb bit with a curb strap the pull on the reins presses the bit against the side of the horse's mouth. This in turn squeezes the flesh against the sharp points on the teeth, cutting gashes into the flesh. Riders often blame the bit for the horse's erratic behavior when it is the teeth that are causing the trouble. Horses with mouths that have been neglected never fail to have old scars in the mouth where they have been cut. The contraption called the "hackamore bit" which exerts a squeeze on the horse's nose and jaw seems to have been designed to slice the side of the horse's mouth.

LOVE OF CRAFT

More often than not the vaquero and his gringo counterpart, the buckaroo, stood the long hours, bad food, extreme heat and cold incident to his calling because of his love for horses. Surely in the southern San Joaquin Valley of fifty years ago there were jobs that paid more money and were much less strenuous. The oil fields were booming; even the farmer paid better wages than the cattleman. But the vaquero was a romantic. He liked to make his living riding a horse even if it entailed hardship and suffering.

Moreover, he was a perfectionist. His way of life was passing, but he still tried to perfect himself in his work. Though the ranch management frowned on the practice, he would put his rope on anything that walked and often with dramatic results. Many of the most comical situations the vaquero found himself in came from his penchant for experimentation. He would rope a grizzly bear, wild horse, wild cow, buffalo, wild hog, elk—even ostriches on the Tejon and Tracy ranches—and work out the problem of extricating himself as best he was able. He roped wherever he could, whenever he could, whatever he could with a serene disregard for consequences. The results were seldom if ever tragic. There is a providence that protects children, drunkards, vaqueros, and buckaroos.

Coyotes were the hardest of the wild animals to rope and the man who caught one was respected far and wide as a *lazador*, a roper. But when a vaquero snared one, while he took justifiable pride in the feat, he would say with becoming modesty, "*Ese fue un sapo*"—that was a lucky throw.

Whenever the vaqueros caught a coyote they would mark it in some way. Once a coyote was caught on the plains west of Los Banos by Miller and Lux vaqueros. This time the vaqueros branded it with the S Wrench, bobbed its tail, and put the Miller mark in its ears. This coyote was caught in a trap two years later on the Tejon Ranch by Jerky Johnson, who was trapping for Tejon that year. The distance from where the coyote was caught and branded to the place where it was trapped is well over a hundred miles.

Once it came to the attention of Henry Miller that his men were chasing coyotes. He waited until they were all together. Then he stormed into their camp and at the top of his voice, screamed that he was not raising horses for buckaroos to stove up chasing coyotes. But the men would never stop trying to improve their skills. There has never been, in the history of the world, a man who took more seriously the skills of his craft than the vaquero; and though the range rider has been depicted as a man of violence, that is far from the reality of the true vaquero.

The vaquero spent hours in preparing his riata, stretching and smoothing it with loving care. He knew that the condition of the rope would decide whether the throw would be accomplished successfully. There are several ways to throw a riata. The whirling of the rope overhead, horizontally or vertically decides where the loop will meet its target. *Mangana*, from *manos*, hands, is the skill of lassoing an animal by the forefeet, and *pial*, from *pies*, feet, is the skill of catching one by the hind feet. These, of course, were in addition to the skill of catching an animal by the horns.

But all this must be done gracefully. A vaquero was proud of being able to lasso his animal without undue haste. To the vaquero it was undignified to throw a rope hurriedly. The loop could be thrown crossways, from the left, from the right, underhand, overhand, or backwards, but it must be done without hurting the animal roped or the vaquero's horse. This to the vaquero was of the utmost importance.

Although he often did not know it, the vaquero's beliefs, myths, and superstitions about horses came from the Arabs and their influence was predominant in all the vaquero's relations with his mount.

The Arab's belief, shared by the vaquero, was that a horse had more than forty whorls or verticils— circlets of hair radiating from an axis, that is, spots on the horse's coat where the hair is in spiral form or pattern—and that of those forty, twenty-eight were lucky and the rest were unlucky, depending on where on the horse's body they appeared.

If he came upon a horse that had more lucky spirals than unlucky ones he would try to get that horse in his string. Unlucky spirals are found just above the cheek, on the hip, beside the tail, and on the inside of the leg. Fortunately, there are more lucky spirals than unlucky ones. Those that are on the ears, neck, belly, and flanks are all lucky.

Another Arab tradition the vaquero believed in was the worth of certain colors in horses. Dark shades were preferred to light ones. Light colored horses were distrusted. The old Arab prejudice against the spotted or yellow horse with white man and tail prevailed among the vaqueros, although pseudo-Hispanophiles, in writing of the early history of California, disseminated the myth that Californianos preferred the palomino. The California vaquero preferred the chestnut, *alasan tostado*, above all other colors in horses. The black came next, then the gray. However, the tradition that no Arab chief would ride a yellow horse or allow one to remain in his stable overnight, was unknown in California.

This third-hand belief—from Arab to Spaniard to Californiano— that it was a despicable act to ride a yellow horse with white mane and tail was not widely accepted in California, perhaps because the Spaniards that came to California were not Moorish Spaniards, but Catalans. The stamina of the yellow horse with black mane and tail, the buckskin or *bayo*, was proverbial among vaqueros.

A horse of solid color without a trace of white was a prize, indeed. Though Arab traditions and myths are not pertinent yet it still holds that there is no bad color on a good horse and that a perfect horse is hard to find.

White feet meant white hoofs, which are inferior to black hoofs. The Arabs believed that a horse with one white forefoot and one white hind foot was a lucky horse, since they could mount on a white (good) omen and dismount on one. A horse with white hind feet was preferred to one with white forefeet.

The vaquero, like the Arab, believed that a horse had three ages: the first seven years of the animal's life was the period in which it could be left with the trainer. A horse is never fully developed before the age of seven. The second seven are the best or prime years of the animal's life, and then the owner should use it. According to the Arabs, the horse should be lent to an enemy the third seven years, if he can be prevailed upon to accept it.

But if the horse had a good mouth, it could be of any color and have only three legs for all the vaquero cared. A good mouth was the vaquero's greatest pride. A horse that would not turn, stop, or back at the slightest twist of the rider's wrist was worthless in the vaquero's eyes.

However, in judging the vaquero's horse we must take into consideration the fact that the vaquero and his horse had been together over a long period of time and in many a tight squeeze. Through association the horse had learned every mood and quirk of its rider and could, to a large extent, read its rider's mind and from the rider's movements anticipate his slightest wish. This affinity between horse and rider was what made good horsemen. It also was the reason a vaquero stayed on a ranch year after year. He did not want to leave a string of good horses.

This applied only when each rider used certain horses exclusively. The old adage that two of the best riders will spoil the best horse is true in the sense that the horse will be confused by different signals, since no two men signal a horse in the same way.

To slide to a stop, back at a trot, and spin to the right or left without opening its mouth or throwing its head was the test of a good horse. And all this with only a slight pull on the reins—an open mouth indicates a hard tug on the reins.

Here we must digress to speak of open mouths on horses that are ridden with a bit that has a high port. A high port does not necessarily make a horse open its mouth. A hard pull on any bit will do the same thing. This writer has many pictures taken over all the world showing horses being pulled, and it seems that horses that are ridden or driven with straight or snaffle bits seem to brace their jaws and open their mouths even more with bits that have no ports at all.

We shall not undertake in this work to give instructions on how to stop and pull a horse. That has been covered by experts in many other books and it would be superflous to include it here. The good Lord did not make two sand grains on the seashore alike so it follows that there are no two horses alike. This circumstance renders all these instructions useless and the books worthless, since the writer of such books cannot set down the dispositions and characters of the horses the trainer will meet.

Of course, being human, a vaquero would be more skilled in one thing than in another. One was better at riding bucking horses, another was better at throwing the lazo, or at teaching horses to rein; but this does not mean that they were specialists. They could handle all the skills of the trade with more or less expertness. It has often been said that a *jinete*, a bucking horse rider, was good for nothing else; but that is not altogether true. There were good reinsmen on the ranches that a good bucking horse would have trouble in throwing.

One of the skills of the vaquero, that of throwing a beef by a pull on its tail, though common in early California, had gone out of practice at the turn of the century. Although old vaqueros speak of it as often done on the ranches, the last time this writer saw it attempted was on the Tejon Ranch in 1920. The attempt was a failure. When the vaquero, Mike Tapia, bent down to grasp the beef's tail, his horse, El Machucado, lit into bucking. The rider straightened up and grabbed the saddle horn to stay aboard. Nepomuseno Cordero, who did not like Mike, for a long time afterwards would give us instructions on how to tail a beef. He would wait until Mike could not avoid seeing him and then go through the exact motions Mike had gone through. This made Mike angry but there was nothing he could do but *pelar los ojos* – show the whites of his eyes – at Nepomuseno.

George Hoskings, who worked for the Kern County Land Company at Bellevue and at San Emideo, was very skilled at doing this trick, and often gave proof of his ability by turning some refractory beef heels over head. The skill had its risks. If the tailer did not have a hazer he had to crowd the beef. If he permitted his horse to lag, the beef could cross in front and cause a pile-up. Perhaps the introduction of modern beef, tamer but much heavier than the Spanish cattle, made it risky to continue the practice. Hereford and Durham cattle did not need the rough treatment the Spanish cattle got. Besides, they were too valuable.

Of late years the San Joaquin Valley has become a cotton producing country. The farmers of the Buttonwillow area have brought in large flocks of geese to eat the weeds which grow in the cotton. So my friend Buford Fox acquired a large flock of geese. True to the western tradition, he looked around for someone to herd them. He went into Bakersfield and there ran into the old vaquero Adolfo Encinas, and offered him the job of herding geese. Adolfo's daughter, Carmen, somewhat dubious about her father's being able to cope with the new job, warned Buford, saying, "My father doesn't know about geese. All he knows is herding cattle and breaking horses."

But Buford put Adolfo's bed in the pickup and took him out to Buttonwillow. Buford raised Arabian horses then (he has quarter horses now), so he mounted Adolfo on one of his Arabs and turned the geese over to him.

I learned about Adolfo's new job one day and was surprised to run into him the next day, back in town. So I asked, "How come?" Adolfo is a good raconteur but this time he would not talk. All he would say was, "*Esos gansos estaban locos.* Those geese were crazy. They would run here and there like sheep. I couldn't drive them."

And that was the end of his goose buckarooing.

ORIGINS OF THE VAQUERO

ORIGINS OF THE VAQUERO

The legend that the native-born vaquero developed the bit, spur, saddle, and method of riding used in the Americas after the arrival of the Spaniards is an old one. But, alas, it is only a legend.

The riding equipment and the method of guiding a horse by pressure on the neck were centuries old before Colon ever sailed from the port of Palos in Spain. The Crusaders had met with this style of riding in the tenth century when they fought the Saracens.

The hero gods in Hindu mythology roped the wild Cebu cattle; the ancient Persians used the lazo as a military weapon; the Spaniards were adept at using the running noose, which was one of the classic uses of La Jineta, long before the rape of the Aztec empire. The word jinete is said to come from the blue-eyed Berber tribe that supported Abderaman in his struggle for the Caliphate of Cordova.

The saddle used here was adapted from the one in use in the Egyptian Sudan which originally came from Persia; and for that matter, so was the spade bit. Spade bits are found over all Sonora, parts of Chihuahua, Sinaloa, and Baja California. Many have been dug up in the ruins of town and buildings which the Yaquis destroyed long before Gaspar de Portola ever brought the first riders and horses into California.

Two styles of riding existed in Spain at the time of the Conquest, La Jineta and La Brida. Bernal Diaz says, ''The Conquest was made *a*

La Jineta." The two styles were diametrically opposed. Differences were in the bits, spurs, and saddles, but the chief one was in the length of the stirrups. Since the vaquero's style of riding was adapted from La Jineta, and since La Brida had no influence whatever on the Latin-American rider, we will speak no more of it.

True, in later years the New World rider lengthened his stirrups, but that was because he had let his charger run wild and multiply. He could not mount a bronco with the short stirrups of La Jineta. So by the time the Spaniards came to California they rode with long stirrups. Those old horsemen were toe riders and prided themselves on the extreme length of their stirrups.

The guiding of the animal by holding the reins in the left hand, that is to say, by pressure of the rein on the neck, was the swordsman's way of riding, and the use of the rider's feet as an aid in the control was conducive to the maximum speed and dexterity in turning, which was vital in individual combat. Indeed, this starting and stopping the horse and the speed in the dashes and starts decided the outcome of battle.

When the first Spaniards came to America their horses' speed, dexterity, and aptitude for racing was noted faithfully in Diaz's *Historia Verdadera*. Diaz called such a horse "*revuelto*" – well-turned or well-reined. In the kingdoms of Castile, Valencia, and Aragon since ancient times – probably before Hannibal brought his Numidian cavalry across the straits-short races called *cosos*, from the Latin word *cursus*, were popular. One may well say that the original Spanish horse was a "short-distance" racer, or that the original "quarter-mile" horse was s Spanish horse.

The term La Jineta was applied to the equipment used in this style of riding. There were Jineta spurs, saddles, bits, and other articles. From them came the vaquero's equipment, and, for that matter, that of the *huaso* of Chile, the *gaucho* of Argentina, the *vaquiero* of Brazil, the *charro* of Mexico, and to some extent, of the cowboy of the Gulf Coast, and the *panieola* of Hawaii.

The Jineta saddle was square, strongly made, with both high pommel and high cantle. The rider was literally boxed in without much risk of being ejected during the violent movements of racing, bull-fighting, or skirmishes with the Moors, from whom the Spaniards had adopted this type of fighting. The height of the pommel and cantle permitted the rider to stand in his stirrups and wield sword and lance without danger of falling out. The broad flat stirrups supported the feet firmly, which was a help in wielding the sword.

The influence of La Jineta spread into the far Northwest. Charles M. Russell, that peerless observer (who, incidently, never painted a cowboy, only buckaroos) speaks of those old center-fire, slickfork, spade bit, rawhide riata men as watching their shadows as they rode along, admiring their figure in the saddle.

The horseman's seat was like the light cavalryman's. It was called the "hunting seat" in Europe, which is simply what is being introduced today as the "forward seat" or "balanced seat." It was the jockey seat before Tod Sloan invented the "monkey on a stick" seat used by the present-day race rider. It is the seat which the Arabs, Moors, Tartars, and Cossacks, all natural horsemen, use; it permits the ball of the foot to absorb the shock. It was used for centuries among horsebreeding peoples, and developed through generations of living in the saddle. It was what a buckaroo would call "riding one's stirrups."

In La Jineta the *alludas*, the aids, such as the use of the feet and legs, or shifting of the body, were used to change pace or action, as the present-day *rejoneadores* do in the bull ring.

The La Jineta and La Brida schools of riding were so distinct that the old Jesuits, in listing church property, were careful to place each item in its respective category. There are still extant in musty church records long lists of articles such as a Jineta spur, a La Brida stirrup, a Jineta saddle. The *fiador*—theodore to the gringos—was another Arab, Moor, and Persian piece of equipment which the vaquero inherited.

Oddly enough, the *Tira de Bocado* — indispensable to the Argentine gaucho and called *barbuquejo* in California - was a piece of La Jineta equipment never adopted here, though the Plains Indians used it exclusively in place of a bridle. It is a strip of cloth, a strap, a string of rawhide, or a cord tied around the horse's lower jaw. The reins are attached to this and it is used in place of the bit until the colt is broken.

The Plains Indians acquired horses soon after the Conquest and learned to use the lazo after the classic style of La Jineta. This was long before the vaquero had cast aside the *baston*, or cane used to place the loop over an animal's head, and learned to whirl and throw his lazo as the present-day riders do. The northwestern tribes who met the vaquero driving cattle north out of California in the 1830's learned from them the art of throwing the lazo.

Another heritage of La Jineta was the prejudice extant among *caballeros Ibericos*, the Iberian gentlemen, of the sixteenth century that made them consider it *altamente deshonroso montar en yegua* - highly dishonorable to ride a mare. This prejudice has endured in California to the present day. Perhaps this is why the vaquero referred to the bands of horses from which he drew his string as *La Caponera*, from capon or gelding.

An ancient book on the classic uses of La Jineta says, "The reins must be carried in the left hand. Over the shoulder of the same side as the lance the jinete should wear the cape, the hood snug. The knees tight against the saddle; the feet parallel to the horse's body; the heels down. The spurs should be buckled firmly to hang below the stirrups. This article, in the conception of the author, should be heavy."

The La Jineta bit called *freno de candado* had a high port, fixed bottom bar, very short shanks curved in the form of an S. The shanks of the bit are the two parallel bars of metal which terminate in rings in which the headstall and reins are attached. Forged to the mouthpiece, the shanks make up the sides of the bit, and act as levers when the reins are pulled.

A small wheel, the roller or cricket, placed in the port, turned on a pin at the movement of the horse's tongue (from habit showing either pleasure or displeasure). The noise made is proportionate to the size of the silver conchos which amplify the sound. This in some Latin-American countries is called *freno de buen eco* – bit of a good echo. These bits were so extensively used in all Latin America that manufacturers in France, Belgium, and England produced them for the American trade. The type was called in California *freno Chileno* ("Mexican ring" by the gringos), and *freno de argolla*, or ring bit. Its original name, however, was *freno de la Jineta*. In Mexico today one can still find stacks of old worn-out ring bits, which proves how extensively this bit was used.

Bits as depicted in the paintings of Velasquez and other Spanish painters are so like many of the present-day ones that they seem to have been forged by the same hand, though they are centuries apart. They are *frenos forjados por muy capaces maestros* — bits forged by very capable masters — and those painted by Walker and Russell could well have been forged by the same hand as those depicted by the old Spanish masters.

The Jineta spur had no rowels. It was a gaff in the shape of a sparrow beak, a *pico de gorrion*, sometimes called *asicates*. The use of the rowel became universal in New Spain soon after the arrival of the Spaniards. The *asicate del Moro*, or Moorish gaff, was a long spur without rowels. Later the pico de gorrion had a small rowel. The spurs the conquistadores used had no rowels.

One page in an ancient Spanish book has this to say about spurs: "Spurs are a necessary aid to the *lazador* (roper), and to all who work on horseback. He who uses them wisely will not have to trade off his horse. He who rides without them commits a fault; for him they are as shackles to a prisoner."

The same old author remarks further, "The vaquero though rustic had the innate courtesy acquired from Spanish ancestors to remove his spurs before entering a house." Then he added as an afterthought, "Besides, the large rowels scoured the earth or dirt floors."

Bits and saddles, as time passed, were adapted to the climate, terrain, or to the type of horse the vaquero rode.

The spade bit came with the first Spaniards to northern New Spain. Like the original freno de la Jineta it had but one or two inches of shank or leverage. However, this bit had a four- or five-inch port.

The spade bits dug up in old adobe ruins in Mexico never had more than two inches of shank. These were made before Alta California was colonized. The bits that came to California later had the same measurements from side to side, from the bottom of the port to the top, and from the bottom of the mouthpiece to the bottom of the shank. Later the bit makers in California, perhaps because of the change in the type of horses the vaquero rode, made the spade into a leverage bit and spoiled it for the purpose for which it was originally intended.

During the nineteenth century the mines of Sonora prospered, and the saddlers and bit makers produced much fine work. Finely carved saddles and elaborate bits found a ready sale. For that reason many of the old bits found there show skilled workmanship.

Most of the saddlers and bit makers in Alta California were from Sonora, a few from Baja California. They came to work in the mines or to take up their trade here. Marteral and Herrera came to seek gold. They found riches in the saddles they manufactured for the men outfitting for the gold fields and cattle drives out of California to the East and Northwest. When the great cattle ranches were set up in the San Joaquin Valley they moved there. But by that time the miner and would-be miner had scattered the California tree over half a continent. Ladesma, Moreno, Wilson, Walker, Brydon, Garcia, Alberto Cuen, (brother of Rafael Cuen, the Miller cattle boss) were some of the old-time saddlers.

Famous bit makers included Tapia, David and Abran Rojas, Gutierrez, Figueroa, Amistosa, Espinosa, Madueno, Bob Pini, Harry Malone, and A. B. Hunt, who was a pupil of Madueno. Hunt was still making bits a year or two ago. Tapia, in this writer's opinion, was the best workman of them all and Madueno was the poorest. When this writer came on the vaquero scene about 1910, and began to take an interest in bits and pore over saddlery catalogs, Garcia and Sterns produced the best work. Later Manuel and Pasquel Gil, brothers from the old colonial town of Alamos, Sonora, were the best in the country. Bit makers worked for different saddleries at different times, so as a result, the quality of the work varied. But G. S. Garcia in Elko, Nevada, always had good workmen.

Though of late years his bits have become collectors' items, Madueno always made his bits too short above the mouthpiece. They required a very tight chin-strap to keep them from rocking. He hammered out a piece of iron and bent it upward in a half circle to form the shank. He probably was unique in using this method; but the assertion that he invented the spade bit is preposterous. The shanks of his bits were always beveled. The most useful bit he ever made was owned by Emiliano Cordova and is now in the possession of a man in Vista, California.

David Rojas made bits in San Luis Rey from 1888 until 1900 when he went to Elko, Nevada, to open Garcia's shop. He died in 1902. He and his brother Abran made light, thin, narrow shanks. But Tapia did the most beautiful work of them all. The bits could be identified by the class of silver and the engraving.

While to riders of other climes a bit was just a bit, the California rider laid much stress on his bit; he demanded, and would be satisfied with nothing but the best.

In speaking of the origins of the vaquero we must not forget to mention in passing the first horses to come from Spain. They came with the first Armada, and were such faithful, heroic horses and played so important, though innocent, a part in the conquest, that a list of them should be included in all books of the American horse. There were sixteen mares and stallions, mostly grays and sorrels, in the original conquest of the New World.

Bernal Diaz gives their colors and the names of the most outstanding. Two were of the famed Valenzuela breed of Spain. There were *El Harriero*, the Driver; *Motilla*, Little Tuft; *El Romo*, the Roman Nosed One; *La Rabona*, the Rat-tailed One (she was the "good gray mare" of Valasquez de Leon). *La Rabona* was probably an appaloosa because the rat, or stub tail, is a characteristic of that type of horse, and prevails on the appaloosa from Tierra del Fuego through South America, Mexico and western United States to Canada. Diaz called her a gray, but there are many shades of gray and some of the appaloosas are a mottled color which closely approaches, or is, gray. The "blunt old soldier" says of *La Rabona*, "when the battle was going against the Spaniards and the men were weakening, Valasquez de Leon would appear on his good gray mare, and the men would take courage."

The Indians' belief that man and horse were one (the centaur myth) was true in the sense that there existed a perfect affinity between horse and rider. This affinity has never been better exemplified than in the Conquest, where man and horse made one terrible creature.

The fabulous amount of gold which the Spaniards took from the New World had at least one benefit to posterity. It brought to America the finest horseflesh to be found in Europe. These horses were shipped to New Spain and in time sired the great-hearted mustang, the vaquero's horse. True, before the vaquero went out of existence he rode horses of many breeds and mixtures, but the mustang was the perfect horse for working cattle – sure-footed, utterly loyal, tireless, patient and brave. He was the welder of two continents, a worthy descendant of the Andalusian barb.

The vaquero while working cattle rode hard and was hard on horses, but he never abused them to make a spectacle. The way the vaquero went about taming a horse was not always gentle, but he was not deliberately cruel. He had applied his military riding to the herding of cattle and the roping of grizzly bears, Tule elk, and wild hogs. He never overestimated the intelligence of his mustang, and had studied the degree to which a horse could be taught. He had learned that patience and repetition were the only means to success in teaching the horse. He never asked the animal to do more than could be expected of it.

The blood of caballeros, bullfighters, Jews, Moors, Basques, and Indian heros ran in the vaquero's veins. He was a strange mixture of races. He admired his Iberian father, but sided and sympathized with his raped Indian mother. If food was short he fed his horse before he fed his wife. Though often a strange contradiction, he was, without doubt, the most interesting man in the New World.

He was a descendant of the old conquerors, and retained the language of Spain. In living the free life of the nomad he imitated the Spaniard in the trappings of his horse, and the Indian in his abode. He spent his wealth on silver-mounted bits and spurs and often left his home destitute of necessities. He slept on the ground, but rode a silver-mounted saddle. He may not have combed his hair, but his horse's mane was trimmed, with one tuft for a colt and two for a bridle horse. He was named after the saint's day on which he was born; it was often Jesus who was the most proficient in stealing cattle.

The vaquero would lie on the ground with his saddle for a pillow even though the rain was falling, and sleep without a word of complaint, yet he would grumble when his saddle-blankets got wet. Wet saddle-blankets make a horse's back sore.

The vaquero's way of life gave him virtues which do not exist in this modern day, and at this distant time no man can judge a man of that era. His life was hard. He would stand shivering in the early morning cold, holding a cup of coffee in his shaking hand, then sit a horse all day in the driving sleet, chilled to the bone. He would ride from dawn to dusk in a cloud of alkali dust, his tongue parched and swollen, with rippling water in a mirage shimmering in the distance, with visions of all the water he had ever drunk or seen wasted haunting his memory, for memory plays queer, cruel tricks. The want of water was the vaquero's greatest hardship in the burning heat of a San Joaquin Valley summer. He often rode in a daze with visions of springs of cool water bubbling out of the pine-scented Sierra, of canals of water from which he had never bothered to drink. And when he came to drink it would more than likely be out of a reeking waterhole that contained the putrid remains of some animal.

But there was another side. A matchless sky overhead. An expanse of wild flowers that spread over the great valley like a purple carpet, so vast that a day's ride would take one only to the middle of it. The bold, brooking Sierra standing in grim outline that stretched away to the northern horizon. A wild chase down a mountainside in the fall when the air is like wine and life is good. The feel of a good horse between one's knees as he sweeps and wheels around a herd of restless cattle. The evening campfire when men broil *costillas*, ribs, on chamiso root coals, and gather around to tell tales of long ago, of Murrieta, Vasquez, and Garcia.

COLORS OF HORSES

Some quaint and curious beliefs regarding the colors of horses have come down to us from medieval Spain, and the vaquero still puts faith in them.

One of the old beliefs is that the color and markings indicate the horse's temperament, that the horse of solid color, without a touch of white is bad tempered and treacherous. Such a horse never fails to have a bad mouth. However, now and then, one found a chestnut of solid color that was well reined and useful. Chestnut horses are more spirited than those of other colors. The redder the color the more pronounced this characteristic becomes.

The bay is spirited in proportion to the amount of black in his color scheme. The blacker the markings, the better his temperament. On the other hand, the black with no white markings is seldom other than quiet and gloomy.

Another belief, not quite so widespread, is that all creatures are composed of the four elements earth, air, fire, and water, and that a horse's characteristics are decided by the proportions of these elements contained in its body.

Spanish horses were of all the colors of the rainbow, yet many old vaqueros held to the belief that there were thirty-five colors of horses, each of which had four or five different shades. I have yet to find a vaquero who could name all thirty-five colors.

Buckskin Horse with the Honorable Marks of Service

The Palomino Horse (second from left) is a Pure Blooded Barileno Mustang
(from a 1901 photo)

Whenever I have asked one of them to name all the colors, he would tell me that there was only one man in the two Californias who knew them all, and there came a day when even he failed to name a certain color. This vaquero was much sought after when horses changed hands. He named the color that was put down on the bill of sale. One day he was hired to attend a sale where a large band was being sold. For hours, one after another, the mayordomo, the manager, parted out broncos, and the man called out each one's particular hue.

The band had dwindled down to a few head when a horse of a very original shade was parted out. The man who knew all the colors was at a loss to name this particular one. Never in either of the two Californias had such a shade been seen. The horse was of none of the known colors; yet he was of all of them.

Immediately the work stopped. The mayordomo waited. The vaqueros gathered around the odd-colored bronco. This man said he was of one color, that man said he was of another. None agreed. The mayordomo called a consultation of the oldest vaqueros. They could not agree.

So the bronco was turned back into the manada, and the expert on colors, *con mucha verguenza* — covered with shame — rode home.

I had been thinking of that story. So I went to Francisco (Chico) Urrea and asked him to tell me what were the colors of the horses that he had ridden back in the last century, when the greatest cattle outfits in the world were operating in the San Joaquin Valley. Chico is one of the old-school vaqueros, one of the last three left alive in the Great Valley, and perhaps in all of California. He said that the Miller and Lux horses which were ridden by the vaqueros on the southern division were all S-Wrench mustangs, and they came from the White Horse Ranch in Nevada and from the Malheur and Harney ranches of Miller and Lux in Oregon.

These mustangs are not to be confused with the southern range ponies which the gringos called "broomtails." The Oregon and Nevada horses were of the best Spanish stock, the best range horses in the West.

Nevado, Best of Carthusians

Carthusian Horse

Among them, Francisco says, were *bayo*, buckskin; *rusbayo*, light buckskin; *bayo Zebruno*, zebra stripped buckskin; and *grullo*, crane colored, or slate gray (these never failed to have a black line down the back). Palominos were scarce, though *jilotes*, flaxen-maned sorrels, were frequently found among those mustangs. There were many variations of roan: *canelos, rosillos, sabinos* cinnamon, rose red, strawberry. Grays predominated: *moros*, iron grays; *tordills*, light grays; *moros obscuros*, dark grays; *moros claros*, blue grays; *tordillos dorados*, dappled grays; and *tordillos manchados*, fleabitten grays.

When a horse turned white with age, he did not become a *blanco*, a white; he remained a tordillo. Vaqueros from Lower California called a fleabitten gray an *escarchado*. Why? I do not know. *Escarcha* means frost. Perhaps they meant hoary with age. *Quien sabe*? Who knows?

The term blanco was applied to a horse with a white skin, whether its eyes were white (albino) or dark. An albino horse was called *guerro*, blond. *Zaino* means bay in California, Lower California, and Sonora, whether the horse has white markings or not, though this term is used for a horse of any solid color in some parts of Mexico and Latin America.

Retinto, brown, also had several shades. When a black horse faded out in the summer he became a *retinto quemado*, a burnt brown, or *prieto quemado*, burnt black. *Prieto*, jet black that did not fade out, was very rare. *Alasan*, sorrel or chestnut, had many variations in shade: *alasan tostado*, toasted or liver chestnut, was by far the most popular among vaqueros, and there were few of them who did not know the centuries-old verse

> Caballo alasan tostado
> Muere antes que ser cansado.

Which was to the effect that a horse of chestnut color expires before he tires. A sentiment no doubt inherited from the Moors.

There were also *alasanes obsuros* and *alasanes claros*, dark and

Dominguez Mare

Andalusian Horse

light sorrels. *Castano* is another term for chestnut, but it was used only by Spaniards in Spain, never in California. The Californiano clung to the Moorish alasan for sorrel.

A spotted horse was called a *pinto* whether he was skewbald or piebald or whether the spots were large or small or any color of the rainbow. The odd colored appaloosa, though often met with, had no special name; he was a pinto here, though there are other terms for that color in Mexico and Spanish America.

A *lucero* had a star in the forehead; a *cara blanca* had a bald face and a *pico blanco* a white muzzle. An *un-albo* had one white stocking or sock; a *dos-albo*, two; a *tres-albo*, three; and a *cuatro-albo* had four.

The *caballo alasan cuatro-albo* or four stocking-foot sorrel was very popular among the younger, flashier *vaqueritos.* "Vaquerito" is a term applied to a young fellow who has not quite acquired all the skills of a full-fledged vaquero. To call a boy a good vaquerito was a compliment; but to call him a vaquero was to give him the accolade. He had won his spurs.

Chico Urrea says that when Miller and Lux took possession of the Spanish Ranch in the Cuyama Valley about the turn of the century, the company bought all the horses and cattle the ranch carried. Among the horses acquired were two little black *chinos, muy buenos caballitos* - very good little horses. There were also a very good gray and a very good sorrel in this manada. *Chino*, in the dialect spoken in California, means curly; a curly-headed person is a chino, and so is a curly horse. The chino horse was often met with among the mustangs, but now seems to be extinct. The last chino horse this writer remembers was a leggy brown on Tejon Ranch along about 1919 or 1920. The horse, at that time, was ridden by a man we called *El Molacho*, the Toothless One. The chino's hair had a pronounced curl and would never lie flat, not even in the summer when the hair was short. The mane and tail had a curl or wave, sometimes so perfectly marceled that a woman could well have envied it. The chino was a distinct type like the appaloosa and was never found among the horses descended from those brought by the gringos. This type occurred in horses of Spanish strain only. Like the alasanes, bayos, and grullos, the chino had a reputation among vaqueros for being *muy guapo*, very tough, either in the sense of being tireless on long hard rides, or in bucking long and hard.

"One day," Chico says, "I was riding the gray at Salt Slough. I lassoed a very fierce Chihuahua bull. I had to throw that bull about ten times before he would stay down long enough for me to take my riata off his horns. He seemed to be made of rubber. He was the toughest bull I ever put a lazo over. I would hold my horse and let the bull charge toward me, when he had two or three feet over the riata I would take a run and throw him. But he would bounce up again.

"But the little horse never failed me. He never got tired. *Ah! que buen caballito era* —Ah! what a good little horse he was."

A *caballo romo* was a roman-nosed horse or ram-headed horse. This horse was also considered to be muy guapo. Like the mean horse, the roman-nosed horse was obstinately tough.

BLOODED HORSES

Writers on the West for many years have been in the habit of calling the range rider's horse a "pony." This term may hold true in southern or prairie states; but in the far West the rider, vaquero or buckaroo, never rode a pony.

True, in the southern or Gulf Coast states the horses were little better than ponies, and were so small that each man had to have ten or twelve in his string and changed mounts two or three times a day. These were little horses that disappeared under the bulk of saddles which often weighed over forty pounds. The riders believed that the bulk of the saddle was a benefit to the horse, that on long journeys the ease of the saddle compensated for the added weight, and that large saddles distributed the weight of the rider over a larger portion of the horse's back. As a consequence of this practice and belief, when working cattle the ponies had to be changed two or three times a day, depending on the class of work.

In California, Oregon, Nevada, and Washington the range riders were mounted on horses, never on ponies.

California has always had the best of Spanish horses. For over a hundred years men who wrote of this state have praised the California mustang. As early as 1840 blooded horses were coming to the West over the Oregon trail. In the southern San Joaquin Valley J. B. Haggin and Bill Carr established the Kern County Land Company. They brought thoroughbreds from Kentucky, and at one time had as many as six hundred brood mares. The vaqueros rode horses culled from this stock.

Men from Argentina and Chile have come to the Carr and Haggin breeding farm to buy horses. Lucky Baldwin acquired horses at this farm, horses which made the name of Santa Anita famous over the world.

Roland Hill of the Tehachapi Cattle Company for many years bred more Morgan horses than any other breeder. His vaqueros rode the best of the Morgan breed.

Miller and Lux, with its control over millions of acres in three states, needed thousands of horses to mount the hundreds of riders in its employ. Henry Miller imported the finest coach stallions to be found in Europe, and these bred to Oregon and Nevada mares produced good saddle stock.

On some of the ranches, Buttonwillow for one, there were as many as five hundred saddle horses, and the roar of their pounding hoofs as they were driven into the corral in the morning was an unforgettable sound that never failed to bring the vaqueros out of their blankets. It would have awakened the dead.

The Tejon Ranch, after the passing of the Barileno mustang, bought seventeen mares and three stallions of Carr and Haggin breeding from Charlie Kerr. These stallions and mares produced the saddle stock on the Tejon until the ranch management imported an Arabian stallion, one of the first in the southern San Joaquin.

In the southern part of the state, ranchers were using fine stallions to breed saddle horses as early as 1849.

One of the factors responsible for the skill of the vaquero was the breeding of the horses he rode. The quality of the horse made the vaquero famous as a reinsman over the land.

AHIJAR

Abu Khalil, the blue eyed Arab, spoke perfect Spanish. He had lived in Spain, Morocco, and Egypt. He was an old man and in poor circumstances when I met him, but friendly and genial. Every now and then I would invite him to eat with me.

It was not altogether hospitality which prompted me, however. I wanted to ask him questions in respect to the etymology of Arabic words which the Spaniards had inherited from the Moors, words which are still used in California although they were brought from Spain centuries ago, and which have been adopted into the gringo buckaroo's vocabulary.

Such words are *moro*, gray; *cincho*, cinch; *alasan*, sorrel or chestnut; *jaquima*, anglicized into "hackamore" by the gringos; and *barbiquejo* or *barbuquejo*, the string which goes around the chin to hold a hat in place and the thong which is tied around the horse's lower jaw to serve as a bridle. This was the Plains Indians's method of bridling, which like the practice of using a cane or pole to place the loop over the head of the animal to be roped, as the present-day Mongols do, was one of the classic usages of La Jineta. It was adopted from the earliest Spaniards, probably from Coronado or his contemporaries, long before the method of swinging and throwing the loop was developed in the New World.

Abu Khalil said that the old proverb we have already quoted,

Caballo alasan tostado muere antes que ser cansado, the horse of dark chestnut color dies before he tires, had its equivalent in Arabic. This accounts, in some measure, for the veneration the paisano had for certain colors of horses. It was a survival of an ancient hippology which had its roots far back in Central Asia.

The gray color must have predominated in the horses the Moors rode into Spain, and the Spaniards associated the color with the rider and *Moro*, Moor, became a synonym for gray.

Cincho still remains "cinch" in the gringo's vocabulary for all the influence of the Anglo-Saxon and his girths.

Abu Khalil said that *ahijar*, the practice of engrafting a dog onto a goat, so that the dog would grow up and stay with the flock and protect it from coyotes, wolves, and other predators, was as old as Father Abraham and his son Ishmael. This system of inducing a dog to adopt a goat as its mother was the same in old California as in Arabia. The Spaniards brought it to the New World.

"In order to accomplish this task one must wait until the bitch has a litter of pups. Then one must search for a goat which has had a kid on the same day as the bitch. Then one must take a pup before its eyes are open and put it to suckling the doe. But first one must take care that the milk of the goat has the same richness and fat content as that of the dog; otherwise the pup will not thrive."

But how the ancient herdsmen decided this question without instruments, Abu Khalil did not tell me.

SPANISH BITS

It was a time of great riches in Spain. The *escudero harto pobre y humilde* had come back to Spain, loaded down with the gold of the Aztecs. Adventurers without a centavo in their ragged pockets but with larceny in their hearts were eager to sail for the New World where Cortez had found a cacique from whom he had squeezed a room full of gold.

In hopes of finding another Montezuma or Atahualpa, hordes of avaricious men set out with expeditions in which they had sunk every centavo they possessed or could borrow. Many of these expeditions met with failure, and thus much of the blood-stained gold brought to Spain went into ships and armaments which were lost or destroyed in the New World. The legend of El Dorado died with the last conquistadores and dreams of gold soon vanished before the greedy and sinful eyes of rude soldiers. Men fought like tigers not for freedom, nor for any noble end, but to free themselves of penury in Spain.

Though some of these robber groups reached their objective, there never was another golden Mexico or Peru. The later arrivals came to guard the mines already established. In many localities Europeans were needed because the local Indians the Spaniards recruited as soldiers were no match for warlike Yaquis, Apaches, or others.

The Spaniard who led the expedition that brought the spade bit to the New World must have come directly to Northern New Spain, because the spade bit is not found south of Sinaloa. He must have recruited his soldiers in some isolated part of Spain close to the Basque country. From the evidence we must assume that he was probably one of the soldiers of Urdaide or Ybarra.

This man's name is unknown to history. Perhaps he was some out-at-elbows relative or younger son of a noble house, made bold by poverty, but sharp enough to grasp and hold his share of golden loot after the disaster which befell Pizzaro. Or perhaps he was one of the few who were too smart to be cheated by the sly Cortez as were many of his followers such as Bernal Diaz del Castillo. He was, no doubt, a black-bearded rascal with olive skin and Moorish eyes, but a horseman to the very *tutano*, the very marrow.

THE FIRST CATTLE DRIVE

Ewing Young may well be called the father of the great cattle migrations over the American West. The first cattle drive in the history of the West started from San Jose, California, in 1836. These cattle were driven to the Willamette Valley in Oregon. Young had contracted to supply the ranchers there with breeding stock. This was thirty years before the Texas trail herds are claimed to have started moving north.

This herd from San Jose was the first of the large scale movements in which thousands of head of cattle were handled. Subsequent trail drivers over all the West learned to handle big herds from those pioneer cattle drivers.

These men rode for months in an endless monotony of landscapes, of swaying backs, tramp of hoofs, clash of horns; of bawls, smells, dust; of footsore horses, footsore cattle, or exhausted animals left to be devoured by wolves; an endless monotony of solitude, of herds of elk, antelope, deer, and great gray bears.

There were no towns or villages on that trail from San Jose to the Willamette Valley, only tribes of stolid Indians who stared at these gaudy riders whose ornate trappings filled the red men with wonder.

But these men had no quarrel with the Indians, rendering it necessary to take their lives. On the contrary whenever the riders met the Indians, the vaqueros curried their friendship and with presents of meat averted hostility. The vaqueros respected the Indian's right to human dignity, and as a result records show that there were few if any differences with them.

These vaqueros were always on the alert, never sleeping their fill, only dozing with one eye open for crawling things whose bite was fatal, dozing with the ever present dread of the wild stampede sweeping over them. They were afraid to die in this savage land lest they be buried in unhallowed ground like a heathen, far from the prayer of mother or sister.

At night the vaqueros crawled into damp blankets to dream of fiestas and fandangoes in a sunnier clime, before suffering had made those old scenes so remote as to be almost forgotten. These vaqueros, born in the serene South, were to know the howl of blizzards, the pelt of hail, the chill of snow, and in the North the endless, cold, clammy mist that was almost, but never quite, a rain, that hung on day after day and wet the riders through and through.

Riding day after day, in the chill of dawn or blaze of noon, riding through pitch black nights or glaring days, riding in wet weather or in dry these men helped make possible the settlement of the West.

BEWARE THE APACHES

The Old Pueblo of Alamos, Sonora

ALAMOS,
MOTHER OF CALIFORNIA

After hearing Mass on September 29, 1775, there left from San Miguel de Horcasitas the expedition commanded by Don Juan Bautista de Anza, who had drawn *un buen contingente*, a good company, of colonists from El Fuerte, Ures, San Miguel de Horcasitas, and Alamos. Alamos contributed twelve families, making forty-nine persons in all. On leaving Horcasitas the men waved their sombreros and the women their mantillas, saying "Adios" to the residents who had followed them to the edge of town, calling the usual warning of the time:

"*Cuidado con los Apaches.*" Beware the Apaches.

Brave Alamos, who from behind her grilled windows and blank walls bore the onslaught of fierce warriors and yet sent her sons through the gantlet of Seri, Yaqui, and Apache to carry the banner of Castille and Leon over half a continent.

Colonial Alamos, priceless legacy of the Moor and Goth, where the whispering spirits of long departed conquistadores haunt the narrow, lonesome streets and stir restlessly at the hollow ring of footsteps. Here is the same oriental atmosphere that clings to the somber old missions of California.

The soul of Alamos abides in her ruins, and one comes very close to the spirit of old mother Spain in her empty patios. The forlorn *portales*, roofed porches, fall in ruin. They bespeak the fate of the

Old Salamancan Spain

Moorish Tower in Spain

Saint James, the Moor Killer (Santiago Malamoros)

Moor; but the old stone church stands firm against the ravages of time, as a grim Gothic warrior faced the hosts of Islam. The proud, haughty spirit of northern Spain still lives in the buttressed old pile. Unyielding as the mountaineers that built her, she stares at the empty houses and the people who shuffle to and fro across the plaza, where the world of today is the world of yesterday.

In contrast, the portales were fashioned by no hand other than one fresh from the building of such as the Alhambra. The fine old buildings of Alamos are empty and dilapidated. The inhabitants have drifted into a currentless backwater of life and are probably unaware that from here rode forth, "all fire and thread-bare velvet, the finest horsemen in the world" to make the tradition of the West. Men still ride mules and horses with high-horned, center-fire saddles along the narrow, cobbled, old-world streets between blank, windowless Arab houses.

Senor Palomares showed me an old spade bit that had belonged to his father's grandfather. Don Romulo Feliz had another antique bit.

"*Son cosas de los viejos*," things of the old people, he said of the silver mounted, well made article.

"*Desgraciadamente*, unfortunately, this fine inlaid work is not made here any more. Nobody has the money to pay for it."

The crumbling tombstones in the ancient Campo Santo are inscribed with old names such as were brought to California by the *fundadores*, the founders. They are commemorated in the towns and streets which bear the names of those colonists: Palomares, Feliz, Cantua, Valencia, Ibarra, Vasquez, Ruiz, Chavez, perhaps the very brothers of those who lie at rest there. They tell the story of a people who carried the embers of European culture from one frontier presidio to another across the New World to Alamos which was the outpost of civilization, and from Alamos, Padres Kino, Salvatierra, Garces, and other pioneer priests pushed their missions and "little cattle ranches" into the frontier.

Though poverty and distress remain where pride and pomp once reigned, Alamos in her decline is still an enchantress. She still casts her spell across the far reaching deserts to the great cities in California of which she is the mother.

THE DEVIL'S HIGHROAD

In the northwest corner of Old Mexico, in the state of Sonora bordering the Gulf of California, lies a vast, forbidding desert. It is a land of contrasting landscapes, of odd and varied aspects. Its topography in part is made up of great level plains covered with loose sand where a horse sinks to its fetlocks. Here the winds blow the sand into dense yellow clouds, drift it about, and finally lay it in dunes and long, twisted ridges like snowdrifts.

Some plains are covered with *cholla*, a growth of stunted, twisted cactus, and brush. There are other plains where the land is bare and covered with glaring white alkali. Here the mirages can lure an unwary traveler to his death. Immense areas are covered with black lava which at some remote period was spewed from the bowels of the earth. There are chains of bare, burnt mountains with ridges that suggest the scaly legs of some giant sleeping lizard. These *cordilleras* extend across the desert for interminable miles, with their peaks standing clearcut against a flawless sky. Down from these mountains come great *canones* and *barrancas*, canyons and ravines, deep and awful to behold, cut out by torrents in some prehistoric age.

There are solitary hills, buttes, pinnacles, and flat-topped mesas which stand apart in lonely grandeur and rise abruptly out of the flat plain.

There is a dusty, tortured, lonely road that crawls across this land

The Cordillera along the Devil's Highroad

from Sonoita to the Colorado River and beyond into far California.
Men risked their lives to cross this desert, and the demon of thirst has
strewn the white bones of hapless travelers along the stretch from the
little village of Sonoita to the Sierra of California. In two hundred
miles there was but one water hole.

The road has been called *El Camino del Diablo*, the Devil's
Highroad, since friendly Indians led Padre Garces over its route. It
was this far-ranging explorer who mapped it for Sonora's greatest
son, that intrepid *hombre de buena cepa*, man of good family, Juan
Bautista de Anza, who led the way across it in the first overland
journey into California.

This inhospitable land had its denizens. They were the Papago
and Cucapa tribes, and on its far western edge, where the waters of the
Gulf lap its shores, lived a remnant of the once warlike Seris. These
Indians traverse this land in small groups, subsisting on scanty roots,
seeds, rodents, reptiles. Food gleaned from the desert is scarce at
best.

There was another Indian, distinct from those mentioned, who also ventured into this land. This was the Apache warrior. As the wayfarer plodded over the Camino, the warning, *Cuidado con los Apaches*, which he had heard at every stop on his way across Sonora, rang ceaselessly in his ears.

Many men have come over the Devil's Highroad – priests, soldiers, colonists, and gold seekers – but the most outstanding was the martyred Padre Francisco Garces. Though he laid down his life more than a century ago, he is still honored. Along the great highway that runs north through the central valley of California a statue of the pathfinder has been erected where travelers may see him gazing down into the heart of Bakersfield.

Padre Garces, Martyr

THE LITTLE BAND

They had opened the route overland to California across the burning sands. And now, the "Little Band" stood on the banks of the Colorado, to find that after the perils of the waterless desert, they had fallen *de las llamas al brasero*, from the flames into the brazier.

Between them and the life-giving water stood a host of Indians, eager to spill the blood of these strange white men, to learn if the blood of the man in the torn, threadbare robe was of the same color as that of the captain in the plumed hat, he who ride the fine horse and carried the ornate sword.

Don Juan Bautista de Anza and Padre Francisco Garces, the leaders of the Little Band, were pre-eminent among the daring men in an age of great adventure. They bade their soldiers stand firm and wait. Men of that era had great faith, and these were confident of yet finding a way out of this new peril.

A veteran of many a pitched battle, the captain carefully scanned the enemy, noting his arms and numbers. De Anza and Padre Garces noticed that for all their enmity the Indians seemed hesitant to attack. In looking for an explanation for this attitude, the Spaniards saw that among the Indians a number of men carried *cruzitas se carriso*, little crosses made of reeds. So the Little Band knew that this adventure would end well for them. The Cross planted years before by the far ranging Padre Kino had borne fruit in this barren desert.

Appy Mule

Mexican Hinny

It is many years since "el hombre de buena cepa" opened the route into California. But every now and then the shifting sands to this day uncover the whitened bones of some long-dead animal, with those of his luckless rider lying close by. They are mute evidence that men stayed alive on the Devil's Highroad only as long as their mounts lived.

"When the mule one rides over the Camino becomes mad with thirst and fights to turn back to the last place it had water, let it go," the men who traveled its burning length said, "One will find only death on the road back. The animal will come to the end of its strength, and lie down and die long before it reaches its last watering place."

From necessity and from experience, the king's soldiers and their descendants turned to the long-eared hybrid as best suited to the conditions of the desert. Here the mule survived long after the Andalusian horse was dead. Many weary miles of cactus and sand would never have been covered in early days if it had not been for the stamina of that unsung hero, the perverse, intractable mule.

Though a prolific mother, Sonora, due to its geographic location, is often cursed with drought. The poverty of moisture brings hunger to her children. As a result, they have drifted periodically, a stream of woebegone humanity and animals, down the barren tableland to seek sustenance in the great valleys or coastal regions to the northwest. They ran a great risk of death from thirst and from the arrows of the world's greatest warrior, the Apache, to reach California far across the sand dunes.

While they accompanied the Cross, they brought cattle and brood mares through the desert, ever on the alert for the menace of the Apache that dogged their footsteps. They would end one thirsty *jornada*, or stage, to begin another at the same monotonous two-mile-an-hour gait, day after day, months on end, over half a continent, in oven-like heat or bitter cold and always in suffocating dust. It was an epic of dauntless men and brave animals of immense vitality who brought the cattle industry to California and the western United States. They were humble, resolute men who took danger as it came and savage, sudden death as it found them.

THE LAST RIDE

As we have seen, beginning in 1774 and continuing for more than a hundred years, Sonorenos traveled on horses, mules, and burros over the Camino del Diablo into California. The knowledge that many thousands of travelers lost their lives on that *Jornada del Muerto*, that Route of Death, never deterred others from venturing over it. However, since the beginning of this migration there have been but few who have not yet yearned to return to Sonora when they had come near the end of their days.

This urge was so strong that when an old man felt that his time was near, he would leave everything he owned - his house, his herds, his children - to return to his homeland to die.

Alfredo Bohorques and I were talking of the old days and of old-timers, those iron-willed men who crossed wastes of burning, shifting sands and lived when mules and burros died. And Alfredo said:

"There was an old man of my acquaintance who had spent his youth searching for gold in the placers of the Sierra Nevada. He had managed to accumulate enough of the elusive metal to establish a little ranch and to stock it with animals. He specialized in the breeding of saddle mules. The mules he bred had a reputation for being mean and hard to handle, but they were not entirely without virtue. Their reputation for meanness was compensated by their excellence under the saddle and their endurance on long, hard roads.

"The old man had five strapping sons, every one capable of handling the mules his father raised.

"One morning the old man awoke with the feeling that his life was coming to an end, and that it was time for him to prepare for his journey into the next world. He decided to go back to his birthplace to die. He informed his sons of his intention. They remonstrated, but to no avail. He was determined to make the journey.

"He ordered them to comb the manadas of mules and find an animal strong enough to carry him across the desert which stretched for many miles between the ranch in California and his destination in Sonora.

"The only animal stout enough to survive on that terrible road was an eight-year-old bronco mule which had escaped from the ranch and had been running with wild mustangs on the desert. The old man's sons had but recently captured it.

"The sons lassoed and threw the mule, and after much struggling strapped a saddle on its back, put a jaquima around its nose, and blinds over its eyes.

Mula

Muletos

"The old man strapped his belongings to the saddle. These consisted of a blanket, an *anfora* or *bota* - a leathern water bottle - a sack of *pinole*, which is made of either wheat, corn, acorns, or even mesquite beans, toasted and ground into a meal, and mounted while the mule was still on the ground.

"The mule got to its feet bawling and bucking, pawing at the jaquima around its nose, and biting at its rider's legs. But the old man weathered the storm. When the mule at last assumed a horizontal position, the old man got it into a run and headed it south. The last the sons saw of their parent and his recalcitrant mount was their forms disappearing in a cloud of dust.

"Some weeks later the sons received a letter which told them that their father had arrived in the town of his birth, and that he had died a few days after his arrival; that the mule was thoroughly broken-in and had become so attached to its old master that it had refused to eat and had brayed forlornly for days after the old man's death.

"The sons were convinced that the old man had willed Death away for as long as he had to stay on the back of that wild mule, crossing the Camino del Diablo."

JOAQUIN MURRIETA

The old stone church in Alamos, Sonora, faces the plaza and frowns down on the boys and girls who, serenely indifferent to its disapproval, walk round and round the brave little cluster of vegetation that serves as a park.

The girls chatter as they walk arm in arm. Each girl carries a flower. The girls walk counterclockwise, the boys walk clockwise to face the girls. Each boy also carries a flower.

When a boy meets a girl who pleases him, he offers her his flower, which the girl never refuses to accept. If the boy is to her liking, she will keep the flower and give him hers. On the other hand, if he does not please her, on the next turn around the plaza she will return his flower, and in this delicate way close the matter between them.

It was in the momentous year of 1849 in this oldest pueblo in northwestern New Spain that Joaquin Murrieta humbly offered his flower to Rosita, and was accepted. The records of the old church attest to their marriage before its altar.

Shortly after this important event in their lives Joaquin and Rosita set out to seek their fortune in the gold fields of California. They crossed the Devil's Highroad, and after weeks of travel arrived in the gold fields. They found riches, nuggets of gold, but they also found disgrace and death.

The Grave in Cucurpe where Joaquin Murrieta is buried.

Joaquin had gone to work on his placer claim, leaving his young bride alone. Thirteen gringos came to the cabin. The thirteen men found Rosita without a defender. They must have beaten her into submission before each one of the thirteen ravished the poor little-girl bride. Joaquin came on the scene in time to find them robbing his house and his wife breathing her last. He fought, but to no avail. The thirteen men beat him until he no longer moved. Then they left him there for dead.

But Murrieta did not die. While the desperadoes were beating him, he had kept his senses long enough to impress on his memory the features of every one of his wife's murderers. He would recognize each one again whenever he should meet him.

He lived from then on for revenge. When, after many days, he could ride again, he set out to do the task for which he thenceforth lived. For many weary, desperate years he hunted down his wife's ravishers. He searched from one mining camp to another until, one by one, he found them all, and the last of the thirteen died begging for mercy.

Murrieta, his work done, went back to Sonora to live out his broken life, not with gold, a wife, children, happiness, but with bitter memories.

How long he lived in Cucurpe after his return from California, we do not know. When he died the compassionate people of the town laid him to rest in the old cemetery with a prayer that this much abused man might now sleep in peace after a ruined life.

But it was not to be. The gringos who had never been sure whether they had actually killed the nemesis of California's gold rush days, or an innocent man, learned of his death and burial. Still in keeping with their earlier acts of barbarism, they denied him, to the very last, the right to human dignity. They committed the last indignity by an act of desecration of the dead. They dug up his bones to measure his cranium!

Murrieta, after a hundred years, still remains a legendary figure, and as long as the Spanish tongue remains in California, his tragedy will be remembered.

Among the men who followed Murrieta out of the Sierras, over the desert, and across the Colorado were Avilez, Pinto, Arbiso, Sesenia, and Duarte. There was a substantial amount of gold among the articles carried in the *alforjas*, the pack saddles, with which the mules were loaded. Murrieta divided it among the men who had followed him. There on the east bank of the Colorado the men disbanded, each to go his separate way and lose himself in the many villages and hamlets of Sonora, never to be heard of again, except for the tales which rose over the length and breadth of Sonora as the smoke rises from its many hearthfires.

Only Manuel Garcia, also called Three Fingered Jack, was ever heard from again. That desperado came to the violent end of his bloody trail, perverse and unrepentant to the last. He looked into the muzzle of the revolver which was to take his life and scoffed:

"You may shoot me, but I still have the best of the bargain. My one poor life is but poor pay for the many I have taken."

CALIFORNIA HERB MEDICINES

A good vaquero "never had time to get sick." Few if any germs had effect on his weatherbeaten body, and except for the knocks, bruises and cuts which were so much a part of his day's work he seldom was ill. However, he had his nostrums.

Gavino Garcia wore buckskin *armitas*, a sort of apron which takes the place of chaps, he said, because buckskin would cure his rheumatism.

Jose Dominguez, whose mother had been a sister of the bandit Tiburcio Vasquez, would turn his shoes upside down and cover them when he went to bed. This procedure was supposed to prevent them from "catching cold."

In the infrequent times he needed medicine the vaquero used herbs, which grew everywhere and could be had for the taking. Some had been used for centuries in the Old World. The first Spaniards found herbs which they had used in Spain growing abundantly in America.

We read in Cervantes of the shepherd using *Romero*, or Rose mary, common in California, to heal the torn ear of Don Quixote, after that mad gentleman's fight with the Biscayan.

The vaquero's *Esteafeate* (Artemisia Mexicana) was the *Ixtahuatl* of the Aztecs, and was used by them to treat bowel disorders.

Saffron, the Arab's *zafaran* and the Spaniard's *Azafran*, was used to flavor food. It was also used in bath water to cure rheumatism.

Rosa de Castilla (Castilian Rose) was used as a purgative for infants.

Yerba Buena, literally Good Herb (Mentha Piperita) common mint, was a universal tea. It was the first herb planted whenever the paisano established a new home. It would grow wherever the ground was kept moist and when crushed had a very pleasing odor. It was used to flavor food, and gave *menudo*, a tripe stew, a distinctive flavor.

Ruda (Ruta Graveolens) was picked, crushed, and applied locally to relieve pain.

Cilantro (coriander) was another plant which was used for food and for medicine.

Hojasen (Florrencia Cernica) was used as a physic.

Sauco (elder blossoms) were gathered in the spring. When they were steeped into a tea, they were used in cases of fever and to treat children who had measles.

In speaking of the many herb remedies used and relied upon by the paisano, Dan Castro says that *Yerba del Pasmo* (Waltheria Americana), *Canutilla* (squaw tea or Ephedra Californica), *te de Aliso* (tea made from the bark of the sycamore tree), and *Yerba Mansa* (literally Tame Herb, Anemopis Californica) were the favorites. Yerba del Pasmo was a universal poultice.

Canutilla, Dan says, would make a man as skinny as a rail if taken over a period of time. The herb was brewed into a tea.

Te de Alsio was purple in color. It was used as a specific in the treatment of blood ailments. Paisanos drank it to enrich their blood.

Yerba Mansa was found in all creek bottoms. It was chewed to relieve colds. Some vaqueros said it would cure tuberculosis. It was brewed into a tea and used to bathe wounds. Vaqueros tied a piece of the root to the mouthpiece of their horse's bridle-bit to prevent the animal from becoming wind-broken or to cure that condition-whether this practice had the desired effect, I do not know. Yerba Mansa had a very astringent effect and would pucker the mouth.

IN OLD MEXICO

Baja California Vaquero

BAJA CALIFORNIA VAQUERO

There is a legend to the effect that when Don Gaspar de Portola saw Baja California for the first time he wept because Spaniards had to live in so desolate a land.

Father Francisco Palou complained that the mules which had been taken by Father Junipero Serra on the expedition to Monterey were badly needed at Loreto and that the raising of cattle in Baja was hardly worth the effort, since beef did not bring in enough money to pay the vaquero's wages. Brush and cactus grow so thickly there that there is hardly room for grass.

Baja California is, however, a fertile ground for the student of the history of the far West, for it is part of the territory where the spade bit and Spanish spur were used. It cannot be ignored by the historian who seeks to establish the exact limits of territory over which that type of bit and spur were used in Mexico and the United States. Much of the Baja vaquero's equipment in use today is like that which was brought to Alta California in 1769.

The Baja vaquero is an anachronism. His saddle has not changed in two centuries. He wears a *cuera*, a tunic of buckskin, that is no different in design from those worn by the *soldado de cuera*, the leather-jacket soldier, who guarded Padre Serra. The Baja vaquero wears the same *bota* they wore. This bota is a sort of legging which he wraps around the calves of his legs to protect them from thorns. He wears a hat made of buckskin. He puts a heavy leather housing over his saddle tree, and folds it back over his legs. He calls this housing *armas*, or armor.

But the Baja California vaquero is worthy of respect for he is the granddaddy of the Western American vaquero and buckaroo; moreover, he is a skilled workman. The Baja vaquero is of necessity a "brush popper"; for there is no rougher terrain or denser vegetation on this continent than on the peninsula of Baja California. It is actually a mountain range sticking up out of the water. Everything that grows there has thorns: cholla, ocotilla (palo adan), brasil, mesquite, cacachila, unia de gato (cat claw), palo zorilla, palo blanco, palo verde, long boy, to name a few. This "long boy" was named by the English pirates or buccaneers who waited along the coast for the Spanish galleons in order to rob them.

The Baja vaquero's horse must of necessity be small, a pony in fact, for he must be able to follow the cattle into any hole through the brush the pursued beef makes. The Baja vaquero does not carry his rope fastened to his saddle. It would be torn off before he got well started. In fact he has no use for a long rope. He does not have the time nor room to rope a beef as the vaquero farther north does. He carried an eighteen-foot rope fastened around his waist and so adjusted that he can release it in an instant. If he can rope a beef before it gets into the brush, well and good; otherwise he follows the beef into the brush and when he is close enough, he reaches over the horse's ears, grasps the beef's tail, raises his leg to clear the horn, and slides down the horse's neck to the ground. With a quick jerk he throws the beef to the ground and ties it. The vaquero's little horse or mule is trained to follow his master when he dismounts so that in the event the vaquero fails to throw the beef and it escapes, he can mount the horse and take up the chase again.

EL BARROSO

I met him in the *bosque*, the backwoods, of Baja California, almost at the end of the peninsula. He popped out of the brush and cactus, leading a wild cow.

Cattle are shipped out of Baja by boat. They are led into the surf and herders in a rowboat tow them, swimming, to the ship. There they are hoisted out by a crane and lowered into the hold.

This was the last beef to go on the ship, so when it had disappeared into the hold, he invited me to his camp. His camp consisted of a *ramada*, a sort of arbor made of brush, under which was a table and a bench. A circle of stones served for a stove and the cooking utensils consisted of a coffee pot and another pot which contained beans.

He made a fire and put the coffee pot on to heat. Then he cut some slices of meat, sprinkled them with salt and pepper, and wrapped them in a cloth. When the coffee was boiling he took it off the fire. There was a fine bed of coals left on which he put the meat to broil. When it was done he dug up some tortillas which he had stored away safe from animals. The tortillas were fresh, which meant that some woman had made them for him in the last day or two. They were not the large-as-a-hat, thin-as-paper tortillas of Sonora, but the small, thick *gordas*, or fat ones, of Baja California. He placed the food before me and said, "*Coma.*" Eat.

The meat was fat, juicy, delicious. I ate one of the best meals I have had in years.

In my travels I always carry two or three cartons of American cigarettes for just such occasions as this, when it would be an insult to hospitality to offer money and when words are inadequate to express one's appreciation for courteous treatment. I opened one of the packages and offered him one. After he had lit it I gave him the carton and said:

"*Estos son para usted.*" These are for you.

He filled his mouth with smoke, expelled it through his nostrils, and said, "*Ah, tobaco Americano, que sab roso.*" Ah, American tobacco, how flavorful.

He put the carton of cigarettes away, then sat down again to talk. This is the story he told me as we sat under the ramada and waited for the tide so the ship could sail.

"The Spaniards, like the slave holders of the American South, bred their own slaves. My father was a Spaniard, my mother was the daughter of a vaquero on the rancho, so I became a *pistolero*, a gunman.

Modern Mexican Longhorn (Chihuahua)

"The Spaniards had many illegitimate sons, and while the fathers never recognized them legally, the sons knew who their fathers were. When such offspring grew up, the Spaniards took advantage of this relationship and used the sons as their personal bodyguards.

"I was twelve years old when I went into the service of Don Fermin, the owner of half the valley. Don Fermin was the last of the old-school dons. He was a hard master but he was just. When we did anything well we were paid, either in money or in praise, which is at times worth more. Don Fermin could ride as well or better than any of his vaqueros, and would never hesitate to show us how to throw the lazo on the wildest bull, or how to mount and ride the wildest mustang. In a word, he would never ask a man to do a thing that he would not do himself. He rode just as hard and just as far as his toughest vaquero.

"In time I acquired a measure of fame as a bull rider and the name of 'Barroso' which means clay-colored (*barro* means clay) in this way. One day a young Spaniard from a neighboring estate came to visit our patron. He was riding with us on the morning that a wild, clay-colored bull followed a heifer into a big stone corral. Don Fermin ordered us to ride into the corral and to close the gate so the bull would not escape. When we were all inside, Don Fermin said, 'Two of you throw a lazo on that bull and stretch him out so that Jose may ride him.'

"The bull was soon roped and stretched out on the ground where I mounted him. He was very active. He bucked across the corral and when he came to the stone wall, he jumped it and carried me across a field and under a tree where I caught hold of a branch and pulled myself off his back. I stayed in the tree until the vaqueros drove a couple of *cabestros*, lead oxen, up and led the barroso bull away. When I got back to the corral, Don Fermin and the young Spaniard both gave me a present of money.

"The young Spaniard stayed some weeks and rode with us every day. He seemed to have taken a liking to me because he always chose me for a partner whenever the vaqueros roped in pairs. One day in speaking of me to Don Fermin he referred to me as 'El Barroso.'

" 'El Barroso, cual el Barroso?' Don Fermin asked. El Barroso, which El Barroso?

" 'El muchacho del toro barroso,' the Spaniard replied. The boy of the clay-colored bull.

" 'Ah!' Don Fermin exclaimed, 'Jose. Si, si. Jose.' Ah, Jose. Yes, yes. Jose.

"From that time on I was known as El Barroso.

"Many years after I had left that ranch, I returned for a visit. Don Fermin had long since gone back to Spain. The place had changed owners. The vaqueros were working cattle in the corrals, so I took my place near the gate. I had been standing there a few minutes when someone called, 'Barroso!'

"I turned to answer the call when to my surprise a young fellow also answered. There was another Barroso on the ranch. I had a tocayo, a namesake.

"Just then an old man came up to me and said, 'I know you. You are the old Barroso, the pistolero.' He had spoken so loudly that the vaqueros crowded around us to see who I was. The old man - he was the caporal - turned to the vaqueros and said:

" 'This is the original Barroso. He was a great jinete de toros, rider of bulls, and a man who could be trusted to guard a man's back in a fight.'

"The boy who was called Barroso came up to greet me. He had wild, yellow eyes and a lanky, cat-hammed cuerpo de jinete, horseman's body.

" 'Este muchacho es tu tocayo,' the caporal said. 'Lo nombramos Barroso porque es muy horqueta.' This lad is your namesake. We named him Barroso because he is a good rider.

"Just then the patron came up to see who I was and the caporal introduced me to him. The patron told me that I was welcome back to the ranch, that I could work there if I wished, and that I could stay as long as I liked.

"But I did not stay there long; for as you know when a man has a reputation there are always young men who will test him to see if what is said of him is true. And if a man stays too long in one place he is sure to get into a fight and kill somebody.

THE YAQUI WARRIOR

I was attracted to him the moment he came aboard the train in Guadalajara; and as he stood in the aisle, a short, broad figure, I noted every detail of his appearance. I saw at once that he was a Yaqui, and from his erect carriage and square shoulders that he was an old soldier.

His eyes were those of a man who had never flinched; they were the eyes of a man who has no imagination, that is to say, no fear; for fear is but imagination.

One might say that his face was grim, but by no means stolid. He had those features which proclaim unsullied Toltec blood: the straight nose, thin lips, and square chin of the pure-blooded Yaqui.

He found a place in the rear of the car and sat down. Every little while I would turn around and stare at him, until at last I decided that I must talk to this old warrior. I sensed that there was a story behind his resolute, inflexible, impassive air. I got up, walked back to his seat and sat down beside him.

He had been expecting me. He greeted me with a wide grin which reminded me of another Yaqui, Mariano Sanchez, the friend of my boyhood; he had grinned like this old man.

Perhaps it was some atavistic urge which attracted me to this man, for we had nothing in common. He had been born in the wild reaches of the Sierra del Bacatete, had led a primitive life, and had

Yaqui Indian Dancer

Yaqui Indians

known bitter, unrelenting struggle to survive racial extermination, while I had been born in a city in comparative comfort. All I had had to worry about during my boyhood had been getting enough to eat, which in the United States, at any rate the part I was born in, was no great problem.

All the Indians I had known heretofore had been of a peaceful race. All I knew of Indian strife was what I had read in books, and I only half believed what I had read.

As the train crawled across the barrancas and through the mountains of Jalisco and Nayarit, en route to the States, I listened to the saga of the reluctant warrior who had wanted to live in peace and had spent a lifetime fighting. For this was Exciquio Chavez, the Yaqui who rose from peon to brigadier general against his will. I listened attentively and respectfully; this man was of a race which had defied the Aztec, set limits for Spanish territorial expansion, and fought Spaniards, gringos, and Mexicans for generations.

In good but curt and simple Spanish which ran in typical Indian monotones, he began the following recital:

"When the Yaquis *se alzaron*, rose against the government - or, to use an American term, 'went on the warpath' - I was sixteen years old. I did not want to fight. That I might live in peace I left the town of my birth and went to Ures, Sonora. There I found work as a peon on a hacienda.

"I had been there only a few days, when as I was busy shelling corn, a squad of soldiers came and suddenly siezed me. I asked them why I was being arrested and the *cabo*, the corporal, answered, 'We are making prisoners of all the Yaquis alzados.' (An *alzado* is an Indian on the warpath.) 'They are to be hanged or sent to Yucatan.' A Yaqui sent to Yucatan was sent to his death. Few Yaquis born on the uplands or in the mountains of Sonora could survive, for very long, the tropical climate of that peninsula.

"I protested that I was a working man, that I earned my living honestly, and that I had never taken up arms against anyone, much less the government. But it was to no avail. I was marched to the *comandancia*, the office of the district, and before an officer who said, 'You are an alzado, if you will tell me where you have hidden your arms, you shall not be hanged. You shall be sent to Yucatan instead.'

"I protested again that I had hidden no arms, and that I had never been an alzado.

"The comandante said. 'Bueno! If you will not tell, you shall be hanged as soon as we can find a tree high enough to raise you off the ground.' "

Here the old Yaqui grinned broadly and went on with his tale.

"I was sixteen years old and *muy tonto*, very stupid. So I answered him with, '*Ah ---- me van a matar!*' Ah ---- you are going to kill me!

"My remark made the comandante laugh uproariously, but I was marched away nevertheless. I was put into a group of other captives.

"Of course the only crime these men were guilty of was that they were Yaquis. Many of them had not been alzados at all. We were herded out of town and traveled half the morning before we came to trees which could serve as gallows.

"When we finally arrived at this forest the soldiers wasted no time. They pulled a man out of the group of captives, adjusted a loop around his neck, threw the end of the riata over a limb and pulled him kicking and struggling into the air, as we watched. They left him hanging for what seemed a long time, then they suddenly released the rope and dropped him to the ground.

"When he had quit gasping and had recovered his breath and could talk, the cabo asked where he had hidden his arms. But like all Yaquis he was *cate monte*, he would not speak.

"The soldiers strung the man up again and left him hanging, then pulled another man out of the group. They used the same routine with all the captives, but none told where they had hidden their arms - that is, if they had ever had any.

"Because I was a boy, I was left for the last. When all the other captives were hanging from the trees, the cabo came to me and said, 'Now, alzado, it is your turn.'

"I had two pesos secreted in my clothes. I pulled them out and said to the cabo. 'Here are two pesos, I will give them to you if you will give me something to eat. I do not want to die hungry.'

"The man accepted the money and laughed. Then he said, 'We will not take time to hang you now; you may go back with us. You shall be sent to Yucatan instead.' "

The old man paused in his narrative to chuckle, then continued.

"Whether it was consideration for my youth, or the two pesos, or whether it was for the lack of a riata with which to hang me, I do not know, but I went away from that grove of trees alive.

"Back in Ures I was held in a *corralon*, an inner courtyard, and after more Indians had been brought in, I was taken with them to Hermosillo, the capital of the state.

"In Hermosillo I was taken before the comandante of that district. After he had asked me some questions, he said, 'I do not believe that you, muchacho, have been an alzado, therefore I am not going to send you to Yucatan. You may stay here and work on the prison we are building.'

"The men brought in with me were put to work on the prison. I worked there for two years, and when the building was completed, I was released.

"I found work in a flour mill in Hermosillo. My mother came to keep house for me. But I was not to live in peace, much as I desired it. One day a cabo came to me and said, 'You are ordered to report for duty at the *cuartel*, the barracks, as a soldier of the revolution.'

"I was content with the work I was doing and did not want to leave it. I ignored the cabo's orders and went on working at the mill.

"Two days later I was returning home from an errand for my mother when three men accosted me. They were Yaquis and each carried a rifle. They told me to go with them. I was taken to a house near by and one of my captors said, "We are going to kill you for not obeying orders. Why did you not go the barracks?' Luckily, I had the order from the comandante for my release from work at the prison in one of my pockets. I pulled it out and showed it to my captors. I said, 'Here is the reason why I did not report.'

"The Yaquis could not read, but they were impressed. One of them said, 'Bueno, compadre.'

" 'Compadre,' in the vernacular, is the equivalent of comrade, so I was safe for the time being, anyhow. After some more questions the man said, 'You may go.' My mother asked me what had kept me so long. I told her I had been visiting a compadre.

"A week later the same three men came to my house, and the one who had acted as spokesman before said, 'Compadre Chavez, you have been chosen to gather the tribesmen to fight the enemies of the revolution. You shall take ten men and provisions and bring in the warriors.

"Two days later I left for the Yaqui country. There I was so successful that I returned to Hermosillo some weeks later with five hundred men. I delivered them to a cabo and went home. The next morning I went back to my work at the mill, hoping that I was done with military life. The comandante awoke the next morning to find his army of the revolution swelled by five hundred fighting men. When he was told who had brought them in, he sent for me. He thanked me for my help, and I told him that I hoped he would find a man to put in charge of them because I was needed at the mill. With that I went back to work.

"But the men I had brought in would have no other leader than me. They said that I had brought them and that I was the one who should lead them. The consequence was that, very much against my will, I was made a captain.

"My men were such good fighters that in the very first battle we engaged in, we defeated the enemy and took a huge store of arms and horses.

"Pancho Villa with four thousand men attacked us. I had four companies of Yaquis. We dug in on a hill, and when the battle was over the 'Centaur of the North,' as he has been called, was defeated and in retreat.

"General Obregon in gratitude for the services they had rendered his cause ordered that all Yaquis who had been banished to Yucatan during the Diaz dictatorship should be brought back to their original home. I was ordered to go to Yucatan and invite all the tribesmen there to return to Sonora. In Merida we found that the governor there had recruited two companies of Yaquis. He had equipped, trained, and armed them, and was using them as palace guards. They were well disciplined, first-class soldiers.

"Two officers and three men had come with me. We presented General Obregon's orders to the governor. He promised to turn over the command of the Yaquis the next morning. He assigned us to quarters in an old hotel near the palace.

"We were preparing for bed that night when two Yaqui women married to two of the governor's guards came to us and told us that the governor did not want us to take his guards away, and that he was going to have us shot when we went to take over the command of the Yaqui soldiers. After the women left we talked over our predicament. We resolved to fight for as long as we could. We supposed that the Yaquis would take the part of the governor.

"Early the next morning we loaded our guns, set up a barricade in the vestibule of the hotel and walked out and stood facing the street. Soon we heard the sound of marching men and the guard came into view in formation. Three officers were in the lead. The soldiers wheeled and came to a halt in front of us. Just as one of the officers raised his sword, we fired. Our volley killed the three officers.

"We retreated into the *saguan* and knelt behind and waited. As the first Yaqui entered we held our fire. He advanced until he saw us behind the barricade, halted and called out, '*Que cham alea compa?*' How are you comrade? Then we knew that the Yaquis were not going to attack us. More came in and they too were soon greeting us.

"The people of that town barricaded their doors and stayed in their houses until I had gathered all the other Yaquis living there, commandeered a train and took my tribesmen back to Mexico City, and finally to Sonora."

LITTLE BAY HORSE

He was a chunky little bay mustang. The strain of the original Spanish horse could be discerned in the set of his "sheep" head, little pin ears, and coyote hips. He was blindfolded; and when the Judas on his back reined him into the path of the charging bull, he obeyed the rein. As the horns struck, he braced his legs and never gave an inch. Here was an "honest" horse, a dream horse which a range rider always seeks, but seldom finds.

When he turned into the path of the bull, he was obeying an instinct inherited from generations of ancestors that had been reined into Aztec spears by Spaniards, and into herds of countless buffalo by Indians through the centuries since the first horse came to America. He was faithfully going to his death in this dilapidated bull ring.

When the picador turned him around, we saw that his hip was covered with brands. How many times he had changed hands for better or for worse only he could have told, and now he faced an ignominious end to a useful life.

He was draped with the mattress-like padding which protects the horses from the bull's horns. His stubby, hairy legs gave him the appearance of a robust man in shorts, wearing a kitchen apron.

When the bull charged the second time, he pricked his ears forward at the sound of the pounding hoofs and braced himself. We hoped fervently that he would come out of that slaughter pen without being gored - bulls sometimes lower their heads and get under the padding to gore a horse. And luck was with him. When the crowd filed out after the fight, he was still on his feet.

It took us two days to find his owner and one more to find a man who could buy him for us for what he was worth. His price was one hundred pesos.

The little bay horse is safe now from the sharp horns of fighting bulls. Now he has a home on a ranch where a baby boy rides him around and around the yard. When the little boy slides to one side of his fat back, the little horse stops and waits until the lad is astraddle again. Then he starts walking around the yard once more, pricking his ears forward and setting his feet down carefully lest he jar the child he is carrying.

IN THE SAN JOAQUIN VALLEY

Burt Snedden's riders at Santa Barbara Canyon

OLD SAN JOAQUIN BRANDS

Gringo brands in the southern San Joaquin, with but few exceptions, date from 1849. Of the many hundreds of brands in California the Tejon's Cross and Crescent is the oldest. It has been in use over a hundred years. It is made up of the oldest religious symbols to come out of Asia, the cross of the Christian Spaniards and the crescent of the Moslem Moors.

In the early days Tejon Ranch vaqueros held their rodeos over four counties and ran cattle over a range of two hundred miles. They would start their rodeo where the present town of Palmdale stands in Los Angeles County, and end up on the San Joaquin River in Merced County. The Tejon vaqueros gathered cattle on the Mojave Desert, in the Sierra Nevada, and on the plains of the central San Joaquin.

J. B. Haggin and Bill Carr, who organized the Kern County Land Company, used Haggin's initials JBH for a brand in California only. They had several different irons: the Diamond A in New Mexico, the ZX in Oregon, the Wagon Rod in Old Mexico before the Madero revolution.

Harrell's brand, the Shoe Sole, was a "forty-niner" brand, and so, for that matter, was the JF of John Fancher. He brought the first red Durham cattle into the southern San Joaquin.

Francisco Temple was ranching as early as 1840. He ran his Diamond P iron on Spanish cattle on the San Emideo.

Bob Pini, Santa Margarita

Bob Pini, Santa Margarita

Bob Pini, Santa Margarita

Ed Knowles, (l.), Juan Gomez (r.)

Branding, Dale Vuelta

Dale Vuelta

Joe Smith (l.), Willia Lanas (r.)

Porter, Tip, Cat, Tip (l.-r.)

Jack Sutherland ran his Scissors brand in both Kern and Tulare counties.

The Cross C of George Crossmore and the Wine Glass of John Montgomery were worn on the hips of cattle from the Kern River to the San Joaquin River.

R. L. Stockton's CT was a pioneer brand; so was Roland Hill's Circle H. Roland, however, was better known for his breeding of Morgan horses than for his cattle ranching operations. Although he pioneered the baby beef feed-lot operation in California, he was twenty years too early. People were not quite ready for baby beef in the early twenties.

Jesus Garcia ran his JG on the Carrizo Plains. His ranch was called the Saucito.

Goode and Peacock, another pioneer outfit, ran their V 7 near Cholame in San Luis Obispo County, though they were a Kern County firm.

But Miller and Lux was the greatest of them all. Their brands H H connected and S Wrench were worn by more cattle and horses than any other brand in North America, even if we include the enormous herds of Don Luis Terrazas in northern Mexico.

Willie Araejo   Jose Messa, Poso Ranch

Roundup 1921 − 2400 Head − Miller and Lux

Tex 1921, Miller and Lux Rodeo

CATTLE KING

We were talking of the old days, when Henry Miller controlled fourteen million acres in these states.

Catarino Reese, as a young man, was for a number of years in the employ of Miller and Lux, and, as a result, had many opportunities to study the Cattle King's singular character. He has many vivid recollections of the old man's eccentricities.

Miller was a far cry from the novelist's characterization of a cattle baron.

"He was cranky," Catarino said, "and gave a man hell for no reason that I could see. I guess he did it to let the man know who was boss and to keep him under control. I don't know what else he did it for. Both Miller and his foreman, Rafael Cuen, had one thing in common. Neither one had any use for a man who did not talk back.

"One time a vaquero told Miller to go to hell. Miller raised his wages. At another time he said to a man, 'You are a teef.'

"If I were as big a thief as you are,' the man retorted, 'I would have a lot of cattle.' Miller walked off chuckling.

"Rafael and Miller quarreled all the time, but Rafael was loyal and Miller trusted him implicitly. When a superintendent (over Rafael) was incompetent, Rafael would get Miller to fire him. This is the way Rafael would go about it: The superintendent would give certain orders about the cattle. Rafael would obey them to the letter.

Tex on Portugue 1922

When the cattle would arrive at Los Banos, Miller would see them.
He would immediately go to Buttonwillow and jump Rafael, but that
worthy would be ready. He would say that he had followed orders, so
there would be nothing left for Miller to do but to fire the
superintendent.

"This roundabout way of doing things could have been solved
by simply making Rafael superintendent. But that was out of the
question. Rafael could neither read or write."

"One day," Catarino went on, "the vaqueros were branding
cattle on one of the numerous camps or ranches which made up the
vast Buttonwillow Ranch when Miller drove up in his buckboard.

"He was evidently in very bad humor because he got out of the
buckboard and went up to the fire, which was made on the bank of a
ditch filled with water, and stood looking down at the branding-irons
which were heating.

"Suddenly he started kicking, and kicked the burning logs and
irons into the water. The men who had been tailing the calves as they
were dragged up to the fire, stopped working and grouped around the
remains of it. The vaqueros who had been doing the roping coiled

their lassos and waited. Miller suddenly realized that the men were idle and that he was losing money. There was a Japanese kid working as wrangler. Miller ordered him to retrieve the irons. The boy waded into the ditch and fished them out. Miller then turned around, walked to his buckboard and drove away muttering.''

The old Dutchman must have let off a lot of steam by kicking things around. Being a Cattle King must not have been all fun, and even what appeared to others as simple little matters just might cause an explosion when viewed through the eyes of one such as Henry Miller.

For more than two hundred miles north and one hundred miles west, and over millions of acres, cattle with the Double-H-connected brand of Miller and Lux ranged and multiplied.

The three chuck wagons that covered the Southern Division of Miller and Lux ranches had made camp at Salt Slough, where they were lined up in a row.

One morning the three wagon bosses, Tom McRaff, Bill Stubblefield, and Rafael Cuen, had stayed in camp; they had sent their respective crews out under Catarino Reese to make a rodeo.

Catarino was far out on the west side of the valley and had already sent out all the men but one. They were spread out in an immense circle and were driving the cattle within it into the rodeo ground, when Catarino saw Henry Miller in his buckboard driving toward him.

All of Catarino's meetings with the Cattle King had been disagreeable - Miller had scolded each time the vaquero had been unlucky enough to meet him. Once started on his tirade Miller would not let up until Catarino would become angry and tell him to see the bosses about the matter, and not him - he was only a hired hand. Whereupon the Cattle King would walk away mumbling to himself.

Seeking to avoid him this time, Catarino rode into a draw, but Miller cut across and intercepted him.

"Vot you do me mit the cattle?" he asked, as he drove up. Catarino explained that he had orders to gather cattle and hold the rodeo at Salt Slough where the wagon bosses were waiting.

Miller ordered him to send the men back to camp. The one vaquero who remained with Catarino was sent out to inform the men of the changed orders. Miller, with Catarino riding beside the buckboard, went back to Salt Slough.

Since there were three crews, there were three cooking fires, one behind each wagon. Miller went from one fire to another, lifting the lid off each pot and examining the contents. When he had peered into each of the pots, he went to the wagons one after the other, and looked through the supplies of food carried in them.

After he had looked into every corner of the wagons, he turned to one of the cooks and asked, "Where is the meat?"

The cook pointed to the side of a wagon, where a greasy gunny sack hung from a nail. Miller jerked the sack off the nail and peered into it. There were four scrawny, dried up strips of jerky in it. Miller threw the sack on the ground, then gave it a kick. The sack sailed through the air and landed in the dust. The Cattle King followed after it, and he kept kicking it until the jerky fell out and he was clear of camp.

All through this proceeding he kept muttering, "No meat in camp. No meat in camp." Still muttering, he walked to where the three bosses were lying on their beds and said, "Go bring a cow for meat." Rafael Cuen mounted his horse and beckoned to Catarino who was still on his horse. The two were riding away, when Miller called to them and said, "Take six men, take six men."

When the cow (of course it was an old one, a heifer would never have been slaughtered while the Cattle King was in camp) had been brought in and butchered, Henry Miller got into his buckboard and drove away.

THE TEJON RANCH

The Tejon Ranch lies in a corner of the San Joaquin Valley, and spreads across the Sierra Nevada and into the Mojave Desert. It is made up of four ranchos granted by the governors of Califoria during the period of Mexican rule - Rancho Castaic, Rancho Tejon, Rancho la Liebre, and Rancho Alamos y Agua Caliente.

The vastness of its area covers various types of climate. On the south side lies the high arid plain, where a forest of giant cacti, relic of some prehistoric age, raises its grotesque limbs like arms in pain or supplication. Antelope once abounded here and horses of purest Andalusian strain roamed its vast expanse.

On the northwest side of the ranch is the great valley of the Tulares (San Joaquin), and between the desert and valley the Tehachapi Mountains stand as a barrier. There is a pass over these mountains. It is the southern gate into the San Joaquin Valley, and many adventurous men, priests, scalp hunters, trappers, colonists, and soldiers, have passed over it.

Much of the ranch is occupied by the massive Sierra Nevada, with its frowning peaks and its sides covered with pine and oak trees. The great *Oso Pardo*, the California grizzly, once roamed in vast numbers through its meadows, and Indian tribes fought each other to the death for possession of the fruit of the mighty oaks.

Along the western base of the Sierra are the foothills where once the redmen drove the Tule Elk into canyons and slaughtered them with reed arrows shot from elderwood bows.

To the northwest lie the great plains where the streams flowing out of the mountains sink into marshes in the floor of the valley.

In the year 1772 Don Carlos II ruled in far-away Spain and George III sat on the throne of England. On the eastern coast of North America men were dreaming of a free land released from the yoke of the motherland. In Virginia a man named George Washington was gathering fame as a leader.

From the Asiatic mainland the Russian Bear had reached across the Bering Strait and laid his huge paw on the opposite shore; already new Russian blockhouses were being built farther south along the Pacific coast. Far to the south, across the drifting sand dunes, De Anza was fighting Apaches and waiting to fulfill his destiny by crossing the Devil's Highroad and founding the great city by the Golden Gate.

In this same year a travel-worn Spanish captain paused on the crest of the Tehachapis and gazed down on the oak groves and *cienegas*, meadows, in the little valley below him. He was the first man of European blood to set foot on Tejon Ranch.

He had come a long way in the service of Spain, from Barcelona in his native Catalonia to Mexico and now to California. He had traveled thousands of miles over bleak highlands, through lush tropic

Indian Graveyard on Tejon Ranch

jungles, warm seas, and forbidding deserts.

The long arm of Spanish authority in the person of the Catalan, Don Pedro Fages, had reached out across the Colorado desert, over the San Bernardinos, through Cajon Pass and across the edge of the Mojave. He was searching for deserters, and now here he was, at last, in the mountains where the fugitives had taken refuge among the Indians. Whether the Spaniard found the men he was seeking in that time so far away, we do not know; but he was the first white man on record to gaze on the San Joaquin Valley.

Four years later one of the greatest trail blazers in the history of the New World, Padre Francisco Garces, came. He was the second white man to cross over the Tejon Ranch. He was at his everlasting task of searching out and mapping the route for the colonists sent out by Spain to hold the frontier against "The Bear Who Walks Like a Man."

We do not know how long the rancho has had a name, but as early as 1820 Padre Mariano Payereas recommended "the place we call Tejon" as suitable for a mission.

The Tejon Pass was already well known before Edward Fitzgerald Beale, "the lord of all he surveyed," as Lincoln was said to have called him, came to the Ranch of the Badger.

There are many Spanish names listed in the records of the ranchos which make the present Tejon. Jose Maria Covarrubias was granted Rancho Castaic. A member of his family, Don Nicolas won fame as the finest horseman in the Pueblo de los Angeles. Ignacio del Valle, listed as one of the fundadores of California, had come over the Camino del Diablo with Juan Bautista de Anza. With Jose Angel Aguirre he was granted Rancho el Tejon. Pio Pico, last Mexican governor of California, granted Rancho la Liebre to Jose Maria Flores.

Rancho Alamos y Agua Caliente was the property in part of Francisco Lopez. Don Chico brought the first Spanish horses to Antelope Valley. They were called *Barilenos* - mustangs. Elizabeth Lake was then known as Laguna de Chico Lopez. Don Chico had the distinction of having discovered the first gold in California, in Placeritas Canyon while he was pulling *cacomites*, wild onions, out of the ground.

CUMMINGS

California's pioneers came from every part of the globe. One youngster, still in his teens, left his native Austria and embarked on a sailing ship bound for California by way of Cape Horn. When he found he could not enter the country without a guardian, the captain of the ship adopted him, and bestowed his own name, George Cummings, on the Austrian lad.

Young Cummings spent some time in the gold fields, and in the late 1850's he drifted into southern California. There he found the dons with enormous herds of cattle, but no market for them.

Some five hundred miles north lay the city of San Francisco. Its thousands of miners needed beef, so Cummings became a dealer in cattle. He married the daughter of the mayordomo of San Fernando Mission, Don Francisco (Chico) Lopez.

Cummings bought his steers in southern California and drove them north through the San Fernando Valley, over Fremont Pass, up San Francisquito Canyon to Elizabeth Lake, and across the desert to Willow Springs. From there he drove over Oak Creek Pass, through the valley that bears his name and down into the San Joaquin Valley, skirting tule marshes for hundreds of miles before he came to the end of his drive in San Francisco or at one of the mining camps in the Sierra north and east of Sacramento.

How and when the forty-niner chose the site of the present

Cummings Ranch we do not know, but we can easily see why. The ranch sits at the foot of majestic Cummings Mountain, with the valley, which is also named after the pioneer, spread below and Bear Mountain towering in the background, a panorama which can hardly be excelled in all of California.

The Cummings Ranch never grew to the size of some of the ranches of that period which were larger, in some instances, than European principalities. It remained a small ranch, yet it was well known, perhaps more so than many of the larger ones. And that was because every homeless person who came into the Tehachapi country could find hospitality at the Cummings Ranch.

Throughout the years Cummings and his son Ed made welcome everyone who came to their door, though their kindness has often been abused and they have been paid in *mala moneda*, bad coin, as the old people say.

Ed Cummings, the pioneer's son, is well past eighty. He was born on the ranch in Cummings Valley. A white-haired old man with the air of a benign patriarch about him, his sense of humor is still keen, his memory still bright. He remembers many laugh-provoking inconsistencies of the early day Angelenos.

Vasquez the bandit, he says, was a crack shot. The men who made up the posses which periodically chased him out of Los Angeles were very careful to stay back out of range of the bandit's rifle. They would stop whenever Vasquez stopped to fix his saddle or to breathe his horse. They were also careful to wait until he was well on his way before they took up the chase again. This lack of enterprise in the face of danger, when revealed by some irresponsible babbler, never failed to provoke laughter in the City of the Angels.

The posses always turned back when the bandit reached Laguna de Chico Lopez (Elizabeth Lake), allowing him to ride unmolested into the Sierras. They would show the same lack of determination whenever the Indians, who rode into southern California to take horses away from the ranchers, reached the lake with the horses. The posses never followed them past that point. It was Indian country from there on.

Tehachapi was so tough a town that Ed's mother, in constant fear because of the shootings and brawls, was driven to leave the ranch and return to Los Angeles to live.

"Don Jesus Lopez, manager of the Tejon Ranch, was my second cousin, but I called him '*tio*,' uncle. You see," Ed said, chuckling, "he had money."

In the wintertime Ed's cattle would drift down out of the mountains into the Tejon Ranch's range, so Ed attended the rodeos on that ranch when the vaqueros worked the county adjoining the Cummings Ranch.

Ed could never get used to going without eating from four in the morning until eight at night and sometimes later. So one morning he asked Santos Montano the *cocinero*, the cook, for a lunch. The lunch consisted of three strips of *tasajo*, jerky, and a couple of *semitas*, unleavened biscuits, which he tied behind him on his saddle.

The Tejon vaqueros eyed the package tied to Ed's saddle, looked at each other, grinned, but said nothing. They knew what it contained. At twelve o'clock they gathered around Ed and asked, "*Onde esta el lonche, pues?*" Well, where is the lunch?

Ed untied the package, opened it and hospitably passed it around to the self-invited guests. By the time the three strips of jerky and the two biscuits had made the round of the assembled company, there was hardly a morsel left for the reluctant host.

After this experience, whenever he carried a lunch while riding with the vaqueros on Tejon Ranch, he ate it before he got to where the vaqueros were gathered.

Ed's son, who is known as Buddy (he was a football star at Santa Clara) tells of the time when he, too, attended the rodeos on Tejon Ranch, and of the hard work tailing calves that were to be branded. Tailing calves fell to the lot of the boys on the crew, while the easier job of lassoing was left to the old men.

This was rather an injustice to the youngsters, because the old men, after a lifetime of using the riata, were good ropers, while on the other hand, the boys needed the practice.

On Tejon Ranch calves were roped by the hind legs and dragged up to the fire. One of the boys, who was tailing would take hold of the calf's tail, give a pull and throw the calf. The man on the horse, who had roped the calf, would ride his horse away from the calf to help the man tailing throw it. Then the man tailing would bring the calf's tail between its legs, hold it close to the flank, kneel on the animal's side and grasp a foreleg to hold it while it was being branded, earmarked, and if a male, altered.

The man on the horse, meanwhile, had brought his horse up close to the calf, and taking his turns around the horn, would hold the calf with the rope around the hind legs.

The man who roped could help the man who tailed by pulling with his horse away from the calf. Or he could let the rope slacken, making it hard or impractical to throw the calf. It was exhausting work under the best conditions.

Buddy remembers very vividly Sutah Coway's stoical behavior under pain and injury. Sutah was a native Indian and one of the best ropers on the Tejon. One day he was roping and Buddy was tailing calves. Buddy had caught a calf by the tail and pulled to throw him, when the rope went slack. He looked up to remonstrate with the roper, and saw blood streaming from Sutah's hand. His thumb had been cut off.

The Indian dismounted leisurely, tied his horse to the corral bars, then slowly, as if he had all the time in the world, gathered some foxtail grass and made a little pile of it. He then asked Buddy for a match and lit the grass. When it had burned down to ashes he gathered them and applied them to the stub of his thumb. He did this to stop the flow of blood. Sutah then wrapped his hand in a red bandanna kerchief, got on his horse, and went on roping.

"My Gosh!" Buddy exclaims. "No antiseptic, no doctor, no medicine, no nothing!"

HAUNTED HOUSE

Over on the west side of the Great Valley, against the foothills which buttress the vast expanse of the Carrizo Plains, close to a spring of brackish water, stand the walls of an old adobe. The house stood beside the Old Road to Los Angeles -*El Camino Viejo a Los Angeles* as the paisanos, who often gave fanciful but otherwise pertinent names to places, called it.

One night forty years ago when we were holding rodeos on the Carrizo Plains, I mentioned the ancient adobe as we sat around the campfire. And this is the tale an old vaquero told about it.

"The rains have all but washed away the walls of that old house; it was deserted during my grandfather's time. It was during his boyhood that the old man who lived there alone and who never spoke to anyone, was found dead in his bed. It has been haunted ever since, and because of the sad circumstances connected with it no one would ever live in it again. It has deteriorated as empty houses that have lost their souls do.

"Ethnographers never have pieced together the scanty scraps of information in the records which the old padres left. They know that many groups made up the colonists who came to California: crossbreeds of Moor, Berber, Catalan, Basque, Celt, Arab, and Jew; Yaqui, Mayo, Opata, Piute, and Mission Indians. Suffice it to say that this particular ranchero's name was Martinez, an old Castilian name if ever there was one. He was one of those hardy herdsmen who prefer the perils incident to the life of a cattleman, one of those souls who hover on the fringes of civilization, never at ease in towns.

"His cattle ranged into the tulares of the Great Valley that geographical history tells us was, in the time of my grandfather, an immense swamp; that an unbelievable luxuriance of grass and flowers grew during the wet seasons; and that it was a desert spotted with leprous alkali patches during the seasons of drouth, where heaps of bones marked the deaths of thousands of animals, victims of thirst and hunger. It was a place into which cattlemen did not venture too far, for fever lurked in its tule swamps.

"The ranchero lived with his two sons, having lost his wife when the boys were mere children. The wants of this little family were met by the sale of his cattle which he drove to market in the mission town of San Luis Obispo. But as time passed an enterprising Prussian came into the Great Valley and drained the tule swamps. The town of Bakersfield came into being. The town thrived from the very beginning, not only in point of population but in the number of homicides. Not even the fabled Bisbee, Tombstone, Abilene, or Dodge City of the western writer's imagination could compare with Bakersfield as it actually was. It was said that men never rode under a tree near Bakersfield lest their heads strike the feet of the bodies hanging from its branches. Bakersfield was a roaring cowtown and groups of gunman - and just plain cattle and horse thieves - employed by the big cattle companies swaggered through its red-light district which covered six solid blocks. But, fortunately, California historians, unlike those of other states, have seen no glory in the departures from decency of the state's early citizens, and have tried to play down the more lurid history of our state.

"In time Bakersfield became a market for cattle and Martinez sold his beef to a buyer from there. The buyer brought his vaqueros and Martinez went along with the drive to collect his pay for the cattle. There were no incidents other than those met in driving and moving cattle. He arrived in the town and was paid in gold coins. Martinez then bought a few presents for his sons, consisting of clothing which could be carried tied to the saddle strings. He started back home.

"He had kept his business secret and so when night came he camped along the road and slept soundly. The next day he had traveled about three hours and was looking forward to seeing his own roof when suddenly his horse shied violently, almost unseating him. Two men wearing masks jumped out of a ravine and leveled guns at him, demanding his money. Martinez thought quickly and moved slowly. He untied the bags which were fastened to the saddle horn. Then he took a bag in each hand and tossed them on the ground in front of the robbers. The shiny gold pieces were spilled and the robbers, showing their inexperience, took their eyes off their victim and stooped to gather up the money. Martinez, who had his revolver stuck in his waist, drew it, and with two quick shots killed both assailants.

"He dismounted and went up to the first robber and uncovered his face. He must have given a deep cry of pain, for looking up at him was the dead face of his younger son. With a great dread in his heart he walked to the other body and uncovered the face. It was his elder son.

"Two vaqueros riding toward the coast found the old man bent over the bodies of his offspring and babbling over and over again, '*Aqui esta el dinero si lo quieres. Aqui esta. Aqui esta.*' Here is the money if you want it. Here it is. Here it is."

COOKEE

Fifty years ago the cooks found on the camps and ranches of the southern San Joaquin Valley, were, for the most part, Chinese. The chuck-wagon cooks, however, were always of some other racial stock because a "Chinaman" could never be found who could drive four mules, the chief requirement in a chuck-wagon cook.

The Chinaman was a reliable employee. He seldom went off on a drunk, and he would stay on the job year in and year out without missing a day's work. His meals were always on time. But that was as far as his virtue went. The Chinese camp or ranch cook was a copyist, a creature of habit and routine. He had no originality; his food was dreary and monotonous. He cooked each thing in just one way and every time he cooked it he would cook it exactly as he had the first time. He never varied in the smallest pinch of salt or drop of flavoring. His purpose was to duplicate.

After one had eaten a Chinaman's cooking for a week, one would know what he would get for breakfast, for dinner, and for supper each day of the week, of the month, and of the year. Day in, day out the food would taste the same, smell the same, and look the same.

A good Chinaman was a blessing to the ranch housewife during the busy season. He was a cheerful worker and more often than not possessed a sense of humor. His remarks were always sing-song laconisms, full of wit.

I remember a Chinaman who came to work for Dick Brite one summer. This cook asked Mrs. Brite to bring out some food article from town. She either forgot it, or it was too high priced for her purse.

I was standing in the doorway when the cook asked her is she had brought the article. When she answered that she had not, the Chinaman, in a high-pitched sing-song entirely devoid of passion, but without hesitation said, ''You son-a-bitch, you too stinch (stingy).''

Of course Dick had to fire him. But I think he did it regretfully.

BEDROLL

The buckaroo called his roll of blankets a bed, but it was his wardrobe, suitcase, and safe-deposit box rolled into one. It consisted of blankets and quilts wrapped in a heavy canvas. A mattress was rarely used by the buckaroo; it made the roll too cumbersome for use in camp life. Some bosses like Rafael Cuen, however, by virtue of their position, sometimes included a mattress in their roll. A big bedroll took up too much space in the wagon and caused the cook and horse-wrangler to grumble when they had to lift it into the wagon when camp was moved.

Besides the blankets and quilts, the roll contained the buckaroo's extra clothing and a sack "warbag," as the gringos called it, in which was packed a razor, soap, towel, and his supply of tobacco, which was more often than not a carton of Bull Durham. Odd pieces of equipment such as bits, spurs, and ropes were also wrapped up in the bed. Sometimes a book or a magazine was carried. The book, though, was usually a saddlery catalog.

The bedroll was the safest place to store anything of value or that was fragile. Rolled up in the blankets the article could never drop out even over the roughest roads, and the thickness of the bedding protected it from breakage.

A sheet of eight-ounce canvas sixteen feet long and six wide was used as an outer covering for the roll. This canvas shed water and kept the rider's "forty years gathering," as he called his possessions, dry. It also kept out much of the cold.

When the bed was spread out on the ground, one half of the sheet was on the bottom to keep out the dampness of the ground and the other half was folded over the top. The sides, which were equipped with snaps and rings, were folded over and the snaps fastened into the rings. The buckaroo thus would be snug for the night.

The canvas was the rider's most important piece of equipment, and was one of the first considerations when buying an outfit. A man could not work efficiently without a dry bed. When there was snow, sleet, or rain the buckaroo would prop up the top sheet with a stick so it would shed water. On such nights he could build a big fire and stand as close to it as he could, for as long as he could stand the intense heat. When his clothing was steaming or scorching, as the case might be, he could run to his bed and crawl in. In this way he would not have to lie and shiver until his body heat overcame the cold, if it ever did on a freezing night.

The buckaroo's preparation for sleeping consisted in taking off his boots and putting them under the warbag which he used for a pillow. This was to keep them dry and to prevent packrats or other night prowlers from carrying them off, and to eliminate the possibility of rattlesnakes, scorpions, or centipedes crawling into them.

Every morning the buckaroo rolled up his bed so that it could be loaded on the wagon which took it to the next camp.

Ready to gather in the High Sierra

COW HORNS

In the old days before the coming of the Hereford to California, vaqueros in gathering their herds would, in certain localities, come upon cattle which had horns of abnormal length while others of the same Spanish breed on neighboring ranges would have normal horns. This curious circumstance caused some controversy among the riders. Some vaqueros contended that these conditions were not the result of breeding but of certain substances contained in the grass the animals ate or in the water they drank which promoted the extraordinary length of horn. Others believed that the continual friction against the branches and limbs of underbrush as the cattle forced their way through heavy growth was responsible for this development. However, the latter contention does not hold true in tropical country where cattle in heavy jungle do not grow horns of unusual length.

The occurrence of long horns in herds of cattle ranging in areas widely separated was not limited to the western United States but was common to all Latin America. The elements which were responsible for these abnormalities seemed to be most abundant in the grasses or water in the State of Chihuahua in old Mexico. The cattle which made the longhorn famous in song and story were brought from that part of Mexico.

Guy Hughes at Granite Station Ranch June 10th, 1959

Frank Smoot (l.), Clarence Allen (r.)

GLENNVILLE: A PILGRIMAGE

I have gathered the names of vaqueros and buckaroos who rode the ranges of the southern San Joaquin and its surrounding sierra, and though the list exceeds five hundred names, it is not now, nor will it ever be, complete. The list goes as far back as the memory of the oldest old-timer, Francisco Urrea, and includes the names of men active in the trade to about 1930. The old-time vaquero and buckaroo has just about passed out of the picture since then. My "census" included only professional vaqueros and buckaroos who had worked for the big cattle companies with headquarters in the valley.

Up in the Sierras there were men who owned small herds of cattle, to whom cattle ranching was not a full time occupation, and who held their rodeos in the spring and fall on a community basis. But for that, they were no whit less salty than the professional riders. As a matter of fact, it took an extra good valley man to stay in their dust in rough mountain country. Quite a few of these mountain boys had reputations as vaqueros and buckaroos which many valley men might well have envied.

A listing of vaqueros and buckaroos without the names of the mountain men would be entirely too narrow. The place to go to gather their names was Glennville, because, through the years, it has remained a cowtown. There the old-timers congregate once a year for the town's annual rodeo, to spend a day renewing old friendships, and

Ready for the Roundup, Glennville

Laurie Richards

go away in the evening smiling and looking forward to next year's celebration. Glennville is still an old western town where the spirit of neighborliness has not died, where the word neighbor is still used in its older, truer, honest sense. This spirit is a survival of pioneer days when neighbors shared joys and sorrows, famine and plenty, when a man, called in the hour of need, never failed to go to the aid of his neighbor.

The road to Glennville winds from Bakersfield up out of the floor of the valley, over rocky hills into the Sierra, and on into the little town nestling in a draw between pine covered mountains.

On the road I met Remick Albitre. Here was a man who was qualified to give me the names of mountain riders. His father, Bautiste Albitre, had come into the mountains in the early days, and had been R. L. Stockton's foreman. But the Albitres go back much further than the last century. When Padre Junipero Serra left his little token mission of San Diego de Alcala to go to Monterey in 1769, he left four rickety, scurvy-stricken soldiers to guard it. One of these soldiers was Bautiste Albitre, ancestor of Remick, and the first Albitre in California.

Remick has attended every rodeo in the Greenhorn Mountains since he was a boy. (By this "rodeo" I mean a gathering of cattle, not a wild west show which is also called "rodeo.") He promised to meet me later in the day, and I drove on into the town. At the little church I met Superior Court Judge Warren Stockton, who had once been my boss when he was running cattle near Buttonwillow. Reminiscing of the days when he was a rancher, Judge Stockton mentioned old Bruno Contreras, who lived to be well over a hundred years old and was an active rider up until the time of his death. In his youth Bruno had been a vaquero for Pio Pico, last Mexican governor of California. Old Bruno, the Judge said, would never speak English to a man. If a gringo spoke to him, it would have to be in Spanish, but whenever the old man had to speak to a woman or child who did not know Spanish, he would relax his rigid idiosyncrasy and courteously use English.

The Judge said further that all the vaqueros and buckaroos who had worked for him or his father, R. L. Stockton, had one characteristic in common: They were never anything but loyal to the man who paid their wages. He added, too, but somewhat mournfully, that he could never get any practice lassoing calves because he was the boss and had to stay afoot and mark, alter, and brand the calves while someone else did the lassoing. (The old-time gringo in California always said ''lasso,'' he never said ''rope.'')

I found Remick at the rodeo grounds. Jesse Stockton, the Judge's brother, had come along to help him in remembering names for my list. I wondered what the Kern County Superintendent of Schools had to do with the names of vaqueros and buckaroos. I was in for a very big surprise. For a time the names came thick and fast, as Jesse wrote them down. I soon learned how good the vaquero or buckaroo was, or had been, by Remick's grin. The better the vaquero or buckaroo, the wider the grin.

It seemed to me that as a name came up, Remick's memory would flash back to some incident in the past when the rider mentioned had ridden some hard-bucking horse or lassoed some wild outlaw steer on a rough mountainside. Jesse would suggest a name tentatively. If the man mentioned was only fair, Remick would give a hesitant, ''Yes.'' If the man was not up to his standards of what constituted a vaquero or buckaroo, he would put his chin in his hand, frown deeply, study a while, then very reluctantly say, ''Well.''

What was surprising was that Jesse, who has spent so many years as an educator, could remember as many names as Remick, who has spent his lifetime among the riders of the Sierras.

My friend, H. Guy Hughes, should be included in the list, as he was a native of the Glennville area and a fine Vaquero. He lived in the mountains and was considered an excellent horseman.

OLD VAQUEROS SPEAK

JUAN BRAVO

"Every man" said Lupe, "who ever worked on the Tejon Ranch and rode colts during the course of his stay there, got thrown from a horse, no matter how good a rider. Juan Bravo, the jinete, came up from Chihuahua about 1900. He was a relative of Terrazas and came with a shipment of longhorn cattle from one of their ranches. *Hay! come eran malditos.* My! how mean those cattle were. I was caporal when the cattle arrived and when they were unloaded Juan asked me for a job. I took him to Don Jesus who said, 'If you can ride bronco horses I will give you a job.' Juan assured him that he could do this. In fact, he was a very good jinete, but like every other man who ever rode on the Tejon Ranch, he too was bucked off.

"One day we were holding rodeos in a territory which had many wild cattle that had escaped the rodeo for several years. Don Porfirio ordered Juan and me to stay with the *puestos*, the men posted to stop and hold the cattle that are driven down out of the mountains by other members of the crew. 'If any wild cattle come down,' he said, 'don't let them get away.' Juan and I promised that none should escape.

"While we were waiting two wild cows came down together in one of the bunches. When they got to the *parada*, the herd, they went through it and struck out for the mountains. Juan and I were ready. I took after one and he the other. I lassoed mine and tied her. Juan roped his but she proved to be very active. He would throw her but she

— 257 —

would bounce up on her feet before he could get her tied. He was riding a colt which he was breaking for Dick Dougherty. The horse got tired of being jerked around and lit into bucking and Juan was thrown. The cow got away with his riata. I chased her and lassoed her just before she got into the deep brush. By that time she was pretty tired so I had but little trouble tying her. When I got back to where I had left Juan he had caught his horse and was mounted. 'Where is the cow?' he asked. 'Didn't you catch her?' Just for fun I said, 'No, and you will be fined five dollars to buy whiskey for the men for letting the cow take your riata away from you.' Juan said disgustedly, '*Que vaqueritos de cincuenta pesos estos.*' What little fifty-dollar vaqueros these are.

"By that time the rest of the crew had all come in with their cattle and I said to Don Porfirio, 'There is a wild cow in the brush tied up with Juan's riata.' Juan, who was near, said eagerly, '*Onde? Onde?*' Where? Where? We rode over and led the cow back to the herd.

"Some time later, when we got back to Lebec, Juan bought a gallon of whiskey and treated the crew because he had lost his riata."

Jack Leiva told another story of Juan Bravo.

"He was a famous bronco buster in his day. He had a deep bass voice and was always threatening someone with death, but he never hurt anyone. His bark was worse than his bite. When Juan came to work he was assigned a room in the bunkhouse. The rooms were shared by two men, but Juan had this one all to himself, for reasons which will be explained later on in the course of this story. He rode through the spring and fall rodeos and stayed that winter. In the spring he left the Tejon to go to Walla Walla, Washington, to break army horses.

"In all the time he had slept in the room he had never swept it out. When the next man to occupy it opened the door and saw its condition he was appalled. Vaqueros do not have access to laundries, nor do they have wardrobes, so Juan had worn his clothes until he could wear them no longer. When he took them off and put on new ones, the possibility of soap and water having any effect on them was so remote that the vaquero threw them in a corner. The old clothes could stand upright. They had been so molded to the vaquero's body from having been slept in and worn in the rain, that a sculptor could have modeled an exact likeness of their owner from a study of his cast-off clothes.

"During the winter Juan had tracked mud mixed with manure into the room and a layer of it covered the floor. Bunches of hair he had scraped off rawhide strings, and strips of unused rawhide, buckskin, and leather left from the reins and riatas Juan had made and repaired during the winter were strewn over the floor.

"In a corner was a pile of 'long-handled' underwear, socks, and pants he had discarded as he had acquired new ones. The degrees and color of the dirt on the clothing could have told how long the vaquero had been out on rodeos and on which part of the ranch, as the age of a tree can be told by it rings.

"Into another corner had been thrown old saddle blankets, burlap sacks, an old hat, and worn-out boots with their tops cut off - the tops were cut off and made into a bag in which was carried a hammer and staples. This bag was tied to the saddle and carried when the vaquero was sent out to ride fence. But, strangely enough, Juan seldom if ever used up the staples. He could never find a broken place in the fence which could be fixed on horseback. If the boots had no stitching, as those made by Buckingham and Hecht, the tops were cut into strings and made into bridle reins.

"To get back to Juan and the room, the new man called the other members of the crew. They came to the door and looked in, then looked at each other. One of the riders stood looking into the room for a while, then he turned and went out. He had been struck with an idea. He returned in a few minutes with a box, a rake, a scoop shovel, and a broom. Then he got some newspapers and lined the box. He then proceeded to sweep and rake up the room. One of the vaqueros asked him if he was going to preserve the trash, and he answered, 'Juan will be lonesome for this stuff so I am going to send it to him.'

"The rest of the men immediately went to work to help him. They picked up every bit of litter and put it in the box. They swept up every bit of dirt and put that in the box. When the room had been cleaned and all the litter carefully packed, they nailed a cover on the box and shipped it C.O.D. to Juan in Walla Walla, Washington. The charges came to sixteen dollars and some cents.

''When Juan came back to the Tejon the following year, he tried to find out who had played the joke on him, so, as he said, he could kill him. But everybody just looked innocent and went about their work.

'' 'Sure was a *dirty* trick,' they sympathized.''

CATARINO

In more than fifty years in which Catarino Reese has been foreman for the Kern County Land Company, he has taught many kids their trade. There also have been several superintendents who are indebted to him for whatever knowledge of beef they may have, however little they acknowledge the debt.

The kids who learned to be buckaroos under him called him "Pop," because he always had their interests at heart. Though the older members of the crew often disapproved of his actions, he would put a kid to doing some job wich was usually reserved for an experienced older man. Catarino would order some green kid into the herd to part out beef, telling the kid to not be afraid to bring out whatever beef he thought was fat. "I will tell you whether the steer is good or not," he would say.

One day Catarino, riding a green colt, along with another vaquero on a green colt and a boy riding a gentle, well-broke horse, came upon a wild Chihuahua cow that had got out of a pasture. The wild cow would not drive back through the gate into the pasture, so it became necessary to lead her back.

Catarino turned to the kid and said, "You have a good, gentle horse, so you will have to lasso her. First get off your horse and tighten your cinch."

When this had been done, Catarino said, "Now you are going to rope that cow, and if you follow directions, you will not have any trouble. I will yell directions so you won't have to look up. Now when you throw your rope, throw it good and hard. When the loop is around the horns, jerk it up tight, then take three turns around the horn and let it run just a little. Don't let it slack because if the cow steps over it she will be tripped and will fall. Do not look at the cow, but keep your eyes on the gate that you are going to lead the cow through.''

The boy threw his lasso around the cow's horns and took his turns as directed.

Then Catarino yelled, ''Turn your horse toward the gate.''The boy did so.

Catarino yelled again, ''I am going to get off my horse and start the cow. When she starts, head for the gate, and don't stop.''

Catarino rode off a little way and dismounted. He pulled the blinds down over his horse's eyes and walked toward the cow. He put himself between the cow and the kid who had her roped. The cow charged him.

''Get going,'' he yelled to the boy.

Before the cow could reach him the boy put spurs to his horse and pulled her through the gate. She passed within two feet of Catarino.

Catarino mounted his colt again and rode through the gate to where the cow and boy had stopped.

He said to the kid, ''Throw your rope behind her and go on past her.'' The boy did as directed and threw the cow.

Catarinio dismounted and blindfolded his colt again.

''Now,'' he said, ''I will get hold of her tail and hold her down while I take the rope off her horns and put it aroung her hind legs.''

After he had caught her tail and placed the rope aroung her hind legs, he said, ''Bring your horse up close to the cow, so that when she moves the horse will back up to keep from being kicked and will hold her.''

Catarino mounted his horse again and said, ''Now slack your rope suddenly, so that the cow will rise free from it.''

The boy obeyed and the cow got up. By that time the vaqueros had ridden away and left her to join the other cattle in the field.

THE IMPENITENT PENITENT

This tale came from Sonora, and was told to me by my friend, Alfredo Bojorques. The name Bojorques is included in the list of fundadores of California. A member of Alfredo's family came with De Anza in 1776.

There was once a timid man who suffered so much from the depredations of one of his neighbors that in desperation he went to a compadre for advice on how to deal with his problem.

The compadre was a man of little patience. When told of the circumstances he said, "The next time you find one of your calves branded with his iron, following one of your cows, kill him - the neighbor, of course, not the calf."

The timid man hesitated before he asked, "Oh! I could never bring myself to do so violent a deed."

"Well," the compadre answered, "if you are afraid to do it yourself you can very easily find a man who will do it for you for a hundred reales."

The timid man hesitated before he asked, "But where could I find such a man? That would be hard indeed."

The compadre snorted. "Bah," he said, "this is very simple. Go to the church in the morning and look for the man who is praying the loudest. He will be the man who has committed the greatest crimes and the one most willing to execute your commission."

Accordingly the timid man went to the church the next morning. After listening to the various moans and lamentations he located a man who was scourging himself with a bundle of nettles, wearing a necklace of cactus, and crawling down the aisle on his knees.

"Surely," the timid man thought, "this man has sinned greatly. He is the man for my purpose."

He waited until the man was outside the church and then approached him on the matter of eliminating his rapacious neighbor.

The compadre had been right on the matter of finding a man for the job in a church, but wrong on the price he would demand for his services.

After much haggling the price was set at five hundred reales, half the amount to be paid in advance. The timid man paid the amount demanded and went on his way.

"Now," he thought, "my troubles will be over." His property would henceforth be safe from his rascally neighbor. He ate a big supper and went to bed.

But "conscience is a hungry dog that gnaws and gnaws." He could not sleep. He asked himself many questions. What would become of the neighbor's family? If he were killed his children would be orphans and his wife a widow. They would starve without a father to protect them.

True, the timid man would not do the actual killing, but since he was having it done, he would be guilty of it. He would be just as guilty of the crime as his hireling.

The next morning, anxious and sleepless, he arose and went to the church to find his man, his hireling, repenting louder even than on the day before.

The timid man rushed to him and said, "I have changed my mind. I don't want my neighbor killed. His wife and children will suffer if they lose him. You may keep the money I have paid, but please don't kill him."

But to the timid man's consternation, the hireling said, "I am indeed very sorry, but I cannot do as you ask. Even if you don't want him killed now I must go through with it. You see, I have just finished doing penance for killing him."

MARTINEZ

"Francisco (Chico) Martinez," said Lupe Gomez, "was the son of old *'Cachcuero'* (Teodoro Martinez). He was one of the best vaqueros on the Tejon ranch, and for many years was the *amansador*, the trainer, there. Some of the colts he broke were ridden five times, others were ridden ten times, and yet others had to be ridden by the amansador for months before they could be turned over to some vaquero as properly broke.

"When broke these horses were supposed to have no vices; however, they often displayed whims and vagaries. Every morning we paid them the compliment of assuming that they could buck us off. We rode out in the gray dawn with a firm hold on our reins and with all the slack out of them.

"One of the first lessons Martinez gave a colt was to rope a beef on it. However, the fact that Martinez could rope on a horse did not mean that just any other vaquero could do so. Once in a while one of the horses would buck his rider off. If Don Jesus Lopez, the mayordomo, happened to be present and witnessed the incident, he would hurry to the fallen man, help him to his feet, brush off his clothes, and ask in a surprised voice, *'Pero que tiene ese caballo, hijo? Martinez lazaba en el!'* But what is the matter with that horse, son? Martinez lassoed on him.

"All the horses on the ranch bucked now and then, even the old

Guadalupe "Lupe" Gomez

ones. But we would have ridden no others, for we knew their virtues. That little tendency to 'break in two' did not prevent them from being faultless vaquero horses. They were the best horses that I have ever had the good fortune to ride. Sure-footed, tireless, loyal, they would race down slopes of the Sierra where one would not dare go afoot.

"The Tejon was known from one end of the state to the other for its good horses, and the reason they were good was that the vaqueros and buckaroos were always good men. Taken as a whole - gringos, native Californians, Sonorans, and native Indians - they were as good as any in the West.

"I don't know what it is that transmits the instinct for working cattle from one mustang to another, but this amor al ganado is common in all horses that work cattle. It is much stronger in some, however, than in others.

"On cold mornings our horses would all leave camp with a hump in their backs, looking for an excuse to buck. Some young fellow would be riding an old reprobate that had had a bad reputation in his colt days. He would be going along with his ears laid back, *pelando los ojos* - showing the whites of his eyes - as if daring his rider to slacken the rein.

"One of the other riders would say, '*Afloja le la rienda, vale.*' Slacken the rein, pal. But the man on the old reprobate would do no such thing. Instead he would hold his hand palm upward, bring the tips of his fingers together, back and forth, in a repeated motion and say, '*La familia no me deje,*' which could be translated as 'The thought of my family will not let me.' But it meant that he had no faith in his ability to stay on that old reprobate, because the horses *eran muy enchilosos*, were very peppery.

"The best horses on Tejon, during the years I spent there, were *El Mostela*, the Weasel; *El Espanol*, the Spaniard, who would start bucking the instant his rider put his weight in the stirrup to mount him; *El Jabalin*, the Pecary, who was untrustworthy; *El Clavo*, the Nail, who bucked with Chamale Montes and threw him; *El Naranjo*, the Orange - no doubt because of his color; *El Gallineta*, the Guinea Hen - Why? *Quien sabe*?; *El Patas Coloradas*, Red Legs; and *El Mira Lejos*, He sees Far, because he carried his head stretched forward, as if he were looking at something in the far distance.

"There were also *El Membrillo*, the Quince; *El Soldado*, the Soldier; and *El Censontli*, the Mocking Bird. Don Toribio, the caporal, was one day racing after a beef on Censontli. The horse stepped into a squirrel hole and fell. Don Toribio's hip was broken in the accident.

"Our horses had to be good in those days. The Tejon had fifty thousand head of cattle; besides those which strayed onto the ranch from Walker's Basin, from the Miller and Lux and the Kern County Land Company ranches, and from ranches in the Tehachapi Mountains, the Coast Range, and the Sierra Nevada. Riders from three counties met at the Tejon rodeos. As a result we had a lot of fun - fun meaning seeing a horse break in two with its rider.

"When one horse lit into bucking there would be a chain reaction. Three or four others would follow the first one's lead and go into action. Then there would be horses without their riders going in all directions. Of course we would have to lasso them, and that was fun too."

AFICIONADO

"Sometimes a man will carry his *aficion*, his special enthusiasm, even past the grave,"said Jose Juan. "There was a man who liked horse racing so well that he took his passion for that sport into the next world.

"When he arrived at the gates of Heaven and knocked for admission, Saint Peter opened the gate a crack, looked out and said, 'There is no room for you; the place is filled with horse race enthusiasts like yourself.'

"The *difunto*, the deceased, peered in through the crack and studied the great crowd. He recognized some of his old cronies, so after a few moments he turned to the Saint and said, 'If I get rid of most of them will you let me in?'

" 'I most certainly will,' Saint Peter replied.

"The difunto announced in a loud voice for all to hear, 'There is to be a great race down in the Other Place, and all of you who miss it will have cause for regret.'

"As he had foreseen,there was an immediate rush out of the Pearly Gates down into the Other Place.

"When the last of the aficionados had passed out, Saint Peter said, 'Now there is plenty of room and you may come in.'

"But to the Saint's surprise the difunto did not enter. He stood staring at the disappearing crowd of aficionados rushing down to the Pit. Then he turned to the Saint and said, 'That race may be as good as I said it would be.' And without even saying 'Adios' he hurried after the crowd."

EL CHIQUITO

The colt was clumsy, big-footed, and awkward. We sat, backs against the shed, and watched the kid who was breaking him. He would gallop the colt from one corner of the corral to the other, where he would stop him against the bars and try to lift him in a spin backwards.

Mariano, who had been watching the longest, shook his head at the kid's efforts and said disgustedly, "It is useless to try with such a dunce. It is hard to teach even a good horse; and one must search long and hard for a colt that will take a good rein, for they are precious few.

"This reminds me of a *cuento*, a story, which is apropos of the matter in hand. It is about the fatherless Chico, his burro El Chiquito, and the bars of silver.

"Chico lived with his mother and sister. He managed to support them by hauling wood and charcoal with the burro and selling it from door to door. He never overloaded or beat the little animal and so, because of the good treatment, the *burrito* stayed fat and sleek and free of saddle galls.

"As he was very timid, El Chiquito soon learned to run to his master for protection from the fiercer members of his breed. Since all animals ran at large about the town, he was often chased home by one of the other burros.

"In those days, the gringos had not yet brought screens to

California; so in hot weather the doors were left open, and ninos, chickens, goats, and calves went in and out at will.

"One day El Chiquito ran home, chased by a big black burro. As El Chiquito approached the house, his master failed to come to his rescue and drive off his assailant, so he ran into the house. His pursuer, who was nipping at his fat rump, followed through the door and hemmed him against the *hornilla*, the oven. There he spun around and was showering a rain of kicks against El Chiquito's ribs when the women, who had been away gossiping, returned and drove off the pursuer.

"When Chico returned home he was met by the scolding women who told him that there would be no supper until the hornilla, which the burros had demolished, was repaired. Being very hungry, the boy set about fixing the stove.

'He picked up a brick which, oddly enough, had not been broken, and on examination found that it was black and of solid metal. He carried it outside and showed it to his mother. She took one look at it, and grasping his arm, led him back into the house.

"Safe from prying eyes and ears, she said, '*Santo Nino bendito*! It is silver. It is an *entierro*, a buried treasure. An old entierro.'

"They uncovered a small fortune in silver bars. The old house had once been occupied, so it was said, by the lady friend of an old-time bandit.

"The little family knew that it would not have the silver long if the officials of the town learned of the find, so the mother went to Don Fermin who had a shop and lent money at usurious rates. She told him about the bars of silver. Don Fermin rubbed his hands, and with a greedy gleam in his eyes he said, 'Bring me the silver and I will exchange it secretly; no one will know. Bring me the boy and I will send him to school and make him a partner in my shop.'

"So Chico went to school and his mother and sister were doled out enough money to barely keep body and soul together. The boy was kept at his books and became an expert at accounting. El Chiquito, the burro, gained the most from all this because he was never loaded again and lived, fat and sleek, to a ripe old age.

"When Don Fermin died his heirs denied any knowledge of the silver, and because Chico persisted in his claims, they turned him out without a cent. From this reverse of fortune Chico became mad and the butt of those who had envied him in the past. However, he never lost his knack with figures, and whenever he passed a band of sheep or herd of cattle he looked each animal over carefully.

"He would then estimate the weight of each animal and compute the gain each one would make when fed so much for so many days, for such and such a price. When his figures were completed, he would write below them, 'In order to make this gain they must be sold for cash.'

"So, by the same token," finished Mariano, "to make a reined horse, you must first find a colt that has the capacity to learn."

OVERHEATED CATTLE

"One day," said Catarino Reese, the old Land Company foreman, "the vaqueros from Bellevue Ranch were ordered to ride toward Goose Lake and meet the vaqueros from Poso Ranch who were driving a herd of steers from the lake. The Bellevue riders were to take over the cattle when they met the other crew. The cattle were to go to Buena Vista Ranch.

"It was a very hot day even for the southern San Joaquin, so you who have spent forty summers here can imagine how hot it was.

"About half-way between Goose Lake and Buena Vista we met the men driving the steers from Poso. It was still early in the day. In fact, it was far too early for them to have covered as much distance as they had. But when I reached the herd I saw why they had made such good time. The cattle had been driven too fast.

"Francisco Urrea was in charge of those riders and cattle, and I don't know why a man of his experience could have let them get into that condition.

"I took one look at them and I said to Urrea, 'These cattle are overheated. You drove them too hard; and I will not be responsible for the ones that are lost.'

"The vaqueros from Poso turned their horses and went back to Poso, leaving us with our problem.

"First we tried to let the steers stop and spread out, so they could cool off; but they would only crowd together and bawl. Then we tried to move them at a slow walk. But they would not start out at a walk. When they moved at all it was at a run.

"A steer would be standing still; then, all of a sudden, he would throw up his head and run. He would run about a hundred yards or so, then drop dead. The cattle were terribly frightened and in a panic. We lost ten head before they cooled off, and it was late evening before we would move with them at all.''

OLD BRONCO RIDERS

I asked Lupe Gomez if it was true that *Cachecuero*, ''Rawhide Sheath,'' as old Teodoro Martinez was called, rode bad horses after he was ninety years old.

''*Pues*,'' Lupe answered, ''*en 1900 estaba muy viejo y todavia amansaba caballos.*'' Well, in 1900 he was very old and he still broke horses.

''One day Don Jesus, an impish look on his lean old hawk face, approached Cachecuero and said, '*Te voy a dar otro caballo para que no estes apie.*' I am going to give you another horse so that you will not be afoot.

''Now being *apie*, afoot, did not mean that a man was walking. It was an ironical term that meant that a vaquero's horse was old, lame, poor, or sore-footed, or had a sore back. A man could be mounted and still be 'afoot.' When some man was riding a 'poor keeper' the other men would remark that he would be 'afoot by noon.' It meant that the horse would gaunt up so much that the rider would be laughed at on account of his horse's condition.

''To get back to Cachecuero. Don Jesus gave him a mean horse. A big bay which we had named *El Toro*, the Bull. Cachecuero wrapped his *ramal*, his rein end, around the horn of his saddle and using this for a hand-hold, he rode the horse. El Toro just couldn't shake him loose.

"All those old men could ride a bucking horse. The fact that the horse was mean did not bother them in the least.

"Don Luis Lopez had a horse in his string that we called *El Catrin*, the Elegant One. El Catrin bucked every time the old man mounted him. This, of course, never deterred Don Luis. El Catrin got ridden whenever the old man decided to throw a saddle on him."

There were lots of old men among the vaqueros who could put the youngsters to shame. Old Don Antonio Leiva rode with his stirrups so long he could barely touch them with his toes. It was the style of riding peculiar to the old Californians, and Don Antonio, being of that race, would never shorten them no matter where, what, or how he had to ride.

The young men on the ranch, who had not known him in his youth, often wondered what the old gentleman would do if a horse were to buck with him. Don Antonio one day put their minds at ease in respect to this.

Even the old horses on Tejon Ranch would buck on occasion, and Don Antonio had one in his string that would hump his back every morning. The old vaquero would ride out holding his rein tight until the horse's back was warm. The younger vaqueros would watch the performance and look at each other and grin.

One morning Don Antonio woke up with his *santo ladiado*. In the vernacular this means he got up on the wrong side of the bed. He saddled and mounted.

One of the vaqueros said, "*Cuidado, Don Antonio, se va mochar ese caballo*." Look out, Don Antonio, that horse will break in two.

Don Antonio snorted an unprintable reply and slacked the rein.

The horse lit into bucking. The old man stood up in his stirrups and rode the animal to a standstill. During the bucking, the bridle slipped off the horse's head, and with the headstall around his chest and his head between his legs he was free of any restraint. But Don Antonio, in spite of that, weathered the storm.

When he dismounted later, he came to the surprised and awed youngsters. "Muchachos," he smiled, "he is merely a horse - and am I not a vaquero?"

VAQUEROS BUENOS

Lupe Gomez can well be proud of the title of vaquero. He has ridden wild range horses and tamed them, and has lassoed wild cattle on the steep, rocky slopes of the Sierra, led them out and yoked them to oxen.

He was telling of the times back in the last century when he was young and thousands of cattle ran wild in the mountains.

"There were five head of *cabestros*, lead oxen, on Tejon when I went there as a boy. They were kept in a little pasture near the vaquero camp.

"In the morning, when we were all mounted and in a group waiting for orders, Don Jesus Lopez would say, '*Muchachos, vamos a bajar ganado bronco de la sierra ahora. Lleben los cabestros.*' Boys, we are going to bring wild cattle down out of the mountains today. Take the oxen.

"We obeyed orders with alacrity, because we were sure to have a lot of fun that day running in the Sierra. We would drive the oxen to a spot as near to the wild cattle as we could, and leave them there. They never strayed away, and when some vaquero led a steer out they would be there waiting to be yoked to the wild one.

"*Pero los vaqueros buenos eran contados.* But the good vaqueros were few. The men on the vaquero crew who could, and would, venture to lasso and tie a wild steer in the rough terrain of the

Sierra Nevada could be counted on the fingers of one hand, even on the Tejon which was known far and wide for its good vaqueros. *Porque les hacia cinco.''* This is an untranslatable term which means that some of the men were afraid. Here Lupe turned his hand palm upward and brought his five fingers together in the vaquero's age-old manual sign for fear.

"Did you tie your riata to the saddle-horn when you dismounted to tie a steer?" I asked.

"Of course not," Lupe snorted, "I never tied a riata to the horn in my life. That was a despicable thing to do, because if the steer should get up with the riata tied, the horse would be at the mercy of the steer. The rider could get to safety while the poor horse was being gored, tangled up in the rope, or at least jerked around.

"Whenever a vaquero lassoed a steer, and it was *patas arriba*, legs in the air, he would drop his riata on the horse's neck, dismount and tie the beef. He usually had plenty of time. In the event that the steer got to its feet before the vaquero could reach it and get its tail between its legs to hold it, he could mount his horse, pursue and tail it, or pick up his rope and throw it again. But a vaquero *never* tied his riata," he ended emphatically.

"Tying the hind feet was enough; the beef could not get away with its hind feet tied. Sometimes an active beef would have to be thrown two or three times before it would lie still long enough for the vaquero to dismount and tie it.

"*Juan Viejo*, Old Juan Leivas, taught me to lasso and tie wild cattle in the Sierra. '*No tengas miedo apiarte*,' don't be afraid to get off your horse, he would say.

"Don Luis Lopez would also help me. He would say, '*Pon cuidado como hasen los viejos.*' Heed the old men's methods. '*Mirando los viejos se apriende.*' One learns by watching the old men.

"In those days any vaquero could tail a steer and it was often done to stop a runaway or to take the starch out of a mean one. But the hardest part of the chore of capturing wild cattle in the mountains was not the roping and tying, but that of leading them out to where the oxen were waiting. If the oxen were too far away, one could tie them to a tree and let them fight the rope until they got sore around the base of the horns. If one undertook to lead one that hadn't been treated in this manner, it would sit back on the rope and refuse to lead.

"One day we were at Los Lobos when Ed Conley, the cattle buyer, borrowed El Naranjo from Don Luis Lopez. Ed and I rode out of camp together. In the course of our ride we came upon a bull *sestiando*, or drowsing, under a tree.

"Ed, who spoke perfect Spanish, said, '*Vale, vamos coliando ese toro.*' Pal, lets tail that steer.

"I answered, '*Bueno, pero primero compon tu silla.*' Good, but first fix your saddle. - El Naranjo was a 'one gutted' horse.

"In his excitement, Ed disregarded my advice. He at once got his horse into a run after the bull, which had awakened on our approach and was making off. The cattle buyer's horse was in a fast run when he overtook the bull. Ed leaned over and grasped the tail; as he went to straighten up, the saddle turned. Of course, Ed was thrown. He landed on his head and El Naranjo ran off kicking at the saddle hanging under his belly."

VAQUERO TALES

EL MOLACHO

El Molacho, the Toothless One, told many entertaining tales of incredible doings which had happened only in his fertile imagination, or he attributed to himself the more interesting incidents which had befallen other people. No one can say with certainty whether he believed them himself, but that did not matter. His tales never hurt anyone; he had no malice. He told them to prove the fertility of his imagination and theatrical instincts, because he had nothing else to do to relieve monotony, or just for the hell of it. His repertoire of yarns was quite ample, to say the least, and covered every subject under the sun.

He told the following tale as we sat throughout the day at Commanche waiting for the sun to go down so we could move on to the next camp with the beef we were driving to the railroad.

"Everyone knows," he began, "that rattlesnake meat, ground and sprinkled over a leper's food, will cure him of the disease. The same is true of buzzard meat. I once cured a man with a broth made of buzzard, though the treatment was very severe.

"The lepers in the old days, when their disease began to be obvious, would take up their abode in the town's cemetery. If they did not go there voluntarily they would be stoned out of town.

"When a boy of my acquaintance contracted the disease, a friend and I undertook to cure him. First we set about catching a buzzard. We got a fishhook and baited it with a piece of meat, then set it out in the sun to ripen. In a few days the buzzards were attracted to it, so we threw it out to them as bait. A big fellow grabbed it. When he had swallowed it hook and all we pulled him in and tied him securely.

"We went in search of a pot with a tight cover. When we had found the pot we filled it with water. Then we made a fire and set the pot to heat over it.

"We put the buzzard into the pot, feathers and all, and sealed the cover on the pot with dough so that the steam would not escape.

"We let the pot boil until we thought that the buzzard was dissolved. Then we took the pot off the fire, uncovered it, and looked into it. The buzzard had boiled down into a broth of about a cupful and had turned a dark green. We strained it through a screen and put it in a cup. Then we squeezed enough lemons to make a cupful of juice. This, with a cupful of sugar, we set near us ready to hand.

"We found the boy in the cemetery sitting on a tombstone.

" 'Come with us,' I said. 'We have a medicine that will cure you.'

" 'No,' he answered, 'leave me to die in peace.'

"My companion took hold of him and held him firmly while I pried his mouth open with a stick. I poured the broth down his throat, and so that he wouldn't spit it out, I worked his tongue as one does when one drenches a horse.

"When he had at last forced all the green stuff down his throat, we poured the lemon juice into his mouth. When this was down we poured in the sugar for dessert. He rolled his eyes around, shuddered, and passed out. We left him there and rode away.

"Four days later we rode by. We found him sitting on a tombstone and strumming a guitar. In two weeks he was back in town, to all appearances a healthy man."

"Speaking of rattlesnakes," El Molacho went on, "one day I was following another boy through some bushes when he suddenly jumped into the air and screamed, '*Me pico una vibora*,' a rattlesnake bit me. I ran after the snake, and as I passed it I made a wide sweep around it and met it coming toward me. I faced it because a snake can strike backwards much faster than it can forward. I killed it and went to see if I could help the boy, who had sat down in the trail.

"Just as I reached him, a man appeared around a bend in the trail. He was carrying a mattock. I told him what had happened and he said, 'Quick, we must bury the bitten leg in the ground. Help me dig a hole!'

'We found a soft spot of ground and quickly dug a hole about three feet deep. We put the boy's bitten leg into the hole, filled the hole with dirt, and with a stick tamped the dirt around the leg.

" 'There,' the man said, 'let him stay there for four hours.'

"He went on his way, and I stayed with the boy. In a little while he quit moaning, but it was late in the evening before I dug his leg out of the hole. The pain and swelling were gone, and he was able to walk home."

However, I liked El Molacho's stories about *diableros*, men possessed of the devil, and about witchcraft much more than I did the ones about his nostrums. They were not as gruesome.

"*El Guerro Rosalio*, Blonde Rosalio, had strange powers, for he had sold his soul to the devil. He could throw a bull by simply lifting it by the tail. He would stand in the middle of the round corral and ask us to drive the broncos around the corral in a fast run. One moment we would see him standing there and the next we would see him astride one of them. We could never understand how he did it. He would ride this wild horse out of the corral without saddle or bridle and work cattle with it. In a day or two he would turn this horse over to us thoroughly broke. He never ate meat. He never cooked food. He would go to one of the many women on the ranch and ask her for tortillas and beans from the pot. That is, beans that have not been fried. Or he would ask for salt and sprinkle it on the tortilla, roll it up, and eat it. He never slept in a house. He built a nest in a tree and slept there, away from the other people on the ranch.

"El Guerro Rosalio would catch fish without a hook and line. One day a woman asked him to catch one for her. He went to a puddle by the horse trough and pulled an enormous trout out of it. The woman was afraid to take it. She said it was a devil. But one of the vaqueros, who was afraid of nothing, took the fish to another woman, who fried it for him. He ate it with great gusto.

"El Guerro Rosalio would disappear for days at a time. He would turn himself into a coyote and run with the packs. No one dared shoot at the coyotes seen on the ranch for fear that one of them might be Rosalio.

"When he died we laid him out on a bed made of rawhide strings laced lengthwise. When our work was finished we all went a short distance away and made coffee. We were sitting around the embers of our fire when we saw one corner of the house in which the body of Rosalio lay catch fire. Then the flames jumped to the next corner and burned there. Then they jumped to the next, then the next. The house burned to the ground in two hours.

"When the fire had died down enough for us to approach it we went to where the body lay. To our surprise, the bed on which the body lay was not even scorched. The blanket which covered it did not have ashes on it.

"We went back to our fire to wait for morning. When it came we approached the bed to carry the body to the cemetery. But El Guerro Rosali's body was gone. It had been spirited away from under our very noses. We never found a trace of it again."

The best tale Molacho told was the one about the bucking bull," he began, "that bucked so long and so far that I would have starved to death if the vaqueros in the crew hadn't taken pity on me.

"A wild *barroso*, a clay colored bull, had followed a heifer into the corrals at the home ranch. We knew he came from a wild band because he bore no brand and had never been seen by any of the vaqueros on the ranch.

"The boss ordered the men to lasso him, and when he was down we branded and earmarked him. I jumped on his back as the men let him up. But I was to wish that I had stayed off. He bawled and bucked across the corral and when he came to the bars he did not stop. He jumped them and struck out across the valley.

"He would buck for a while, then he would run for a while until, bucking and running, he had crossed the valley and got into the mountains. I clung to his back and thought he would never stop. At last when he had reached the desert and had run under a number of Joshua trees in an effort to brush me off his back, he turned back toward the home ranch again.

"I had now been on his back five days and was beginning to get a little hungry. As the bull raced along I suddenly espied a package hanging from the limb of a tree. I snatched it as the bull tore by, and when I opened it I found it contained *burros* of meat and *frijoles*. (A *burro* is beans, meat, or other food wrapped or rolled in a *tortilla*.) I had finished devouring them when I saw an *amfora*, a water bottle, hanging from another tree. I managed to get hold of it, too, and drink the water it contained. The vaqueros from the ranch had followed the bull's tracks into the mountains, and there lost them. They had then hung the packages of food on the trees on the chance that I would see them.

"Some weeks later when I rode that bull back to the home ranch he was thoroughly tame. He became the pet of the children who fed him *panocha*, brown sugar."

THE LOST BULL PUP

Whenever I pass through the town of Tehachapi I stop for a chat with Jack Leiva, who is in business there. He never fails to tell me a story of his old vaquero days on Tejon Ranch, when Don Jesus was manager of the ranch.

Jack is a good story teller and like the other old vaqueros remembers the humorous incidents of earlier days on the Tejon. With something of nostalgia, he says:

"Oh, if only those days when Don Jesus Lopez was the boss could have lasted forever! Those were the happy days." There is always a chuckle in his stories, though it stems frequently not from the sense of the comic but rather of the ironic.

"One day," he once told me, "we were riding on the plains near Rose Station when one of the boys saw a small animal, about the size of a rabbit, under a bush. The vaquero saw at once that it was not a wild animal, so we rode over to investigate. We found, of all things, an English bull pup. To all appearances it was a purebred dog and we were at a loss to determine how it happened to be on the plains of Tejon Ranch, far from any human habitation or people who would own such a dog.

"We sat there on our horses looking at the forlorn little creature, then suddenly Chico Martinez said, '*Mira, hay esta el Dyner.*' Look, there is Dyner. Curiously enough, the name stuck. From then on the pup was known as Dyner.

"My father - Don Antonio Leiva, the caporal - dismounted, picked up the pup, put it inside his shirt, and mounted again. He carried it in his shirt all the way back to the vaquero camp. Every little while on the way back he would pull the puppy out of his shirt, talk to it, pet it, and then put it back in his shirt again.

"On our way we were conjecturing on how the pup had got to the place where we had found him, when we came upon some wagon tracks. We saw in the distance a number of Gypsy wagons moving in the direction of Bakersfield. The pup had evidently fallen from one of the wagons.

"The pup grew up at the vaquero camp and was a favorite with everyone. He was always as fat as a seal because everyone at the camp would take meat from the table and feed him.

"At that time a number of greyhounds were kept at the ranch. We used them to run the numerous coyotes. The bull pup would run with the hounds, but of course he could never keep up with them. He would arrive at the kill panting for breath and long after the coyote was dead. He would immediately attack it, growling fiercely, much to the amusement of the vaqueros.

"Of the men in the crew, Willie Husband was the dog's favorite. Willie would take the dog to his camp where he let him sleep in the house. On some nights Willie would quarrel with the dog and put him out, but the pup would create such a racket that Willie would let him in again. Men riding by the camp late at night would hear Willie arguing with the pup, and think that Willie had another man in the house with him.

"The bull pup was full grown, and had been running with the hounds all the time he had been on the ranch, when one day they all turned on him and killed him. We could never figure out why.

"We had a lot of fun with those hounds. The water from Tejon Creek would spread out into ponds when it reached the floor of the valley. A dense growth of cockleburs would grow in those wet spots. The coyotes would hide in them as they afforded the only cover on the bare plains. We never failed to scare up one of the predators there.

"One day I was alone with the hounds, following at some distance behind them. They were chasing a coyote, when it suddenly disappeared. The hounds stopped and stood about in a circle, barking. When I rode up to them I saw that the coyote had fallen into an abandoned well which had been filled with trash and dirt to within six feet of the surface of the ground.

"I dismounted and went to the edge and looked down. The coyote was huddled against one side of the hole trying to avoid the five rattlesnakes that were striking at him. So far none had reached him.

"I took my riata, dropped a loop around his neck, and hauled him out to the surface where the hounds immediately attacked him. They worried him until he lay still, then they left him and went to the trough and lay down in the water from the trough's overflow, leaving the coyote stretched on the ground with my riata around its neck. While the hounds were cooling off I looked around and found an old shovel. I was busy chopping up rattlesnakes with it when I happened to look up and saw the coyote making off with my riata still around his neck. He had been playing possum.

"I called to the dogs, and at long last one of them saw him and gave chase. When the dogs caught the coyote the second time, I made sure that he was dead and that my riata was off his neck before I went to exterminating rattlesnakes again."

In speaking of the stoical, dauntless old vaqueros he knew, Jack said, "I do not believe my father ever feared anything in his life, judging from the stories I have heard of him and from my own observations. The only time he ever showed emotion was on the day I left to join the Army in the First World War. He was afraid I would not come back."

CHUCKLES ON THE RANCH

One day, on San Emideo Ranch, the buckaroos were butchering a steer. Ernest Brunk was sitting on his horse, a brown called *Boracho*, Drunkard, watching the men work when he should have been helping. He had a rope in his hand and every time one of the boys bent over at his work, Ernest would hit him across the posterior.

Alfred Frago got tired of Ernest's playing. He cut a piece of the beef's liver, and turning around slapped it on Boracho's nose. Boracho had not earned his name for nothing - he bucked in a weaving, staggering way. He snorted, reared and pawed at the liver sticking to his nose, then spun around and bucked off across the field, bellowing and pawing. Of course Ernest got bucked off.

*　*　*

Joe Nicholson was tall and skinny. He brought to mind the story of Ichabod Crane, especially so when he was on horseback. His feet were so big that he had to shop for extra large stirrups.

Joe was riding down the trail into Pleito camp on San Emideo Ranch when Alfred Frago, whom we called Frager, saw him. Joe was some distance off and Frager had time to hide in a thicket of pomegranates which lined the trail. Joe was riding a mule named Tony. Tony was as gentle as a lamb, but like all mules he would sometimes shy and "swap ends," as the buckaroos say.

Fiesta, San Emideo Rancho

Antonio Feliz

Chief Juan Losada and his wife
Tejon Ranch

Just as Joe on the mule passed him, Frager let out a war whoop and jumped out of the bushes. Tony "swapped ends" and Joe's feet went through the stirrups. He grabbed the saddle horn with both hands and as Tony stampeded toward the corral where the other men were working, Joe yelled, "Help me, help me, help me!" When Tony reached the corral the men caught him and extricated Joe from the stirrups.

Frager made himself scarce until Joe had got over his fright and anger a little, and when Joe did finally find him, Joe said in a hurt, complaining voice, "You son of a bitch, you could have got me killed."

* * *

"Whenever," Catarino said, "I told some rider to be careful, or that the horse he was riding would buck him off before the day was over, my prediction never failed to come true.

"One day Ramon, who thought he was a great horseman, was riding a brown colt. When he had mounted that morning, the colt had given a few crow hops, and Ramon was grinning around at the men as if he had made a great ride.

"I did not want my horses spoiled so I said to him, "Don't think that horse can't buck. If he does really turn it on he will throw you so high the birds will build nests in your ears before you come down!'

"Sure enough, about the middle of the morning, the horse broke in two with Ramon and bucked him off so hard that we lost an hour waiting for him to get up off the ground.

"That night he quit because, he said, I had put a curse on him and caused the horse to buck him off. But the truth of the matter was simply that Ramon was not as good as he thought he was."

* * *

Salvador Carmelo

Frisco, Sal Carmelo, John Gomez, Jake Smith, Jim Loveal (left to right)

The mishaps his vaqueros suffered often made Don Jesus Lopez laugh despite the seriousness of the situation.

One day Campas, a vaquero, was hung in the stirrup when his horse fell with him. The horse ran off across the plains dragging poor Campas over brush and cactus.

Don Jesus was sitting his horse, talking to Don Porfirio Valencia, the caporal. As he watched the horse running and kicking at the dragging Campas, he turned to the caporal and said, "*Mira, Porfirio, est Campas ha de querer mucho a ese caballo, porque no lo quiere soltar.*" Look, Porfirio, this Campas must love that horse very much because he does not want to leave him.

* * *

Henry (Hank) Hoskings asked Salvador Carmelo for a chew of tobacco. Salvador handed him the plug. Henry put it between his teeth and was pressing down on it when a rope, on a cow they were doctoring, got under his horse's tail. Bill, the horse, clapped his tail down on the rope and went bucking off across the field with Salvador riding behind, yelling, "Bite it off, Hank, bite it off." But Hank, in one of Bill's hard jumps, had swallowed the plug, and was sick afterwards.

* * *

Juan Bravo was a crack shot. One day he was sitting in the shade of a grape arbor. A rooster came by. Juan drew his gun and shot the rooster's head off. The noise the rooster's body made jumping around brought a woman to the door. She asked how the rooster got that way. Juan drew his gun, shot the head off another and said, "This way."

On another occasion Juan was out on the range with two other men. They had been riding since dawn without food and one of the men complained. Now the vaquero never likes to hear one say he is hungry when there is no food to eat. It goes against his grain to hear useless complaints.

Sal Carmelo (l.), Jimmy Campas (r.)

Lupe Galvan

Augustine Hino

So when in the course of the ride the men came upon a snake, Juan shot it. He got off his horse, made a fire, skinned the snake and roasted it.

When it was done to a turn he told the man who had complained to eat. The man refused. Whereupon Juan pulled out his gun and told the man to eat it or he would die on the spot. The man ate the snake. He never complained in Juan's presence again.

* * *

The smell of garlic never fails to remind me of the day, back in the early twenties, when Henry Hoskings, Bert Hobbs, Uel Matthews, and I rode to Salt Creek Camp near Tecuya.

We had dinner with Joe Nicholson, who was stationed there. The dinner consisted of enormous steaks which Joe had smeared with garlic. While we were eating, Henry, who was the foreman on San Emideo then, never ceased complimenting Joe on his skill as a cook. That individual, very pleased, grinned from ear to ear and boasted, "I never took a back seat for any man when it comes to cooking."

After dinner we started back to San Emideo. We had traveled about five miles when the garlic began its work and we became sick and remained so all the way back to the ranch.

As we made our woeful way along belching garlic, Uel Matthews, whom we called Booger Red, would say every little while, "And Hank said Joe is a darn good cook," imitating Hank's voice and trying to spit the taste of stale garlic out of his mouth.

* * *

ELK AND COYOTES

Old vaqueros never liked to run their horses. They never got them out of a walk unless it was absolutely necessary. They saved them as much as they could. Those who did like to *correr como los muchachos*, to run about like boys, were looked upon as being not quite grown up.

No doubt this practice of saving the horse for some untoward emergency was a survival from the days of the Apache, when it was certain death to be surprised by an enemy when one's horse was tired or jaded.

For many generations, since the coming of Father Kino, Sonorans have fought Indians. Even today the word Apache is imbedded in the vaquero's vocabulary. It is often used as a synonym for implacability. A fighting, striking, kicking, squealing bronco would, quite often, be named El Apache.

Whenever a beef had to be roped in an open field, an older man would hold his horse in and wait until some young blood took after it. When the youngster had thrown his loop and, of course, missed, the older man would cut across into the beef's path and lasso it. This was not conducive to good humor in the vaquero who had missed, but it saved horses.

Catarino Reese always starts his stories with, "It tickled ta hell out of me." He was telling of his days as foreman for the Kern County

Land Company, in whose employ he spent fifty-four years. During this time he never wore a ten-gallon hat, or wore or fired a revolver in the line of duty.

However, he had many and varied experiences; all his tales have a touch of humor. It is to be remarked that all old-time vaqueros and buckaroos had a good measure of this quality in their makeup.

"One day," he began, "we were riding along on our way to work some cattle, when we came on a herd of about five hundred elk. There were about eight men in my crew, and all of them became excited and started chasing the elk.

"I was riding ahead of the crew when I heard the commotion behind me - the elk running, the buckaroos yelling and swinging their ropes.

"There was a boy riding along with me. He was very willing and always obeyed orders promptly, so I turned to him and said, 'I will stop those darn fools from raising hell. You get on one side and I will get on the other, so the elk will run between us.'

"The boy did as I directed, and as the elk passed I threw my loop on a big bull and pulled him out of the herd's path. I then waited for those darn fools to come up.

"The elk fighting at the end of my rope stopped the crew. They left off chasing the herd and turned to help me take my rope off the big bull. It took some time to do that little chore, but it got their minds off chasing elk and running their horses down, and back to the job on hand.

"Although a buckaroo, whenever he saw an elk, would chase it, an elk was very seldom lassoed by overtaking it. It was too fast. When pursued by a mounted man the elk seemed to be going at a slow lope, but the pursuer would have his horse in a dead run, spurring and whipping in an effort to close in for a throw. If the horse was fast enough to close in, which was seldom the case, the elk would lengthen his stride just a little and easily draw away from the horse just as if the horse were standing still.

"This does not mean that we rode slow horses. We rode some of the finest horses in the country. Sometimes when I was riding one of

Willie Tevis's polo ponies, and all conditions were in my favor, I would overtake an elk. But that was seldom."

Catarino chuckled again. "One day a buckaroo was chasing an elk. He was nowhere near it and the chances of his catching it were hopeless. He was losing ground at every stride.

"I got in the elk's path - they always run in a straight line - and as it passed I lassoed it. The buckaroo was very angry with me. He felt that I had cheated him out of the glory of lassoing an elk.

" 'Did you really expect to catch that elk on that horse?' I asked him.

" 'Yes,' he answered. Some fellas never learn." Catarino chuckled at the memory.

Coyotes are as hard to catch as elk. One day Catarino was riding on the range west of the Company fence when he saw a kid on a pot-bellied mare chasing a coyote. He was a long way off, but approaching rapidly. Catarino took down his riata and waited for him to approach.

"I expected the coyote to run away from the mare. But to my surprise, as the chase wore on, the mare closed in on the coyote. She was crowding it when I threw my loop and caught it.

"The coyote was played out but the mare was not even panting. She was breathing as if she had not run a yard! I asked the boy how he expected to catch the coyote without a rope. He said that he didn't need a rope; that he often killed coyotes by running them down on the pot-bellied mare; that when she had overtaken one she would paw it to death."

This time Catarino's laugh exploded loud enough to break up our quiet conversation about the good old vaquero days.

JAKE

Around 1918 there were thirty or more dogs of every mixture and breed on San Emideo Ranch. There were two Russian wolfhounds, several greyhounds, an airedale or two, and some bird dogs. The only one worth anything was Shorty, half English bulldog and half great Dane or St. Bernard or some other big breed, because Shorty was a big dog. His usefulness consisted in catching a steer by the nose and hanging on until it was exhausted. Sometimes he would throw the steer. He could never be persuaded to let go.

There were many more cats on the ranch than there were dogs. At noon when the men gathered at the cookhouse to wait for the bell which announced that the meal was ready, the dogs and cats would gather there, too. The reason the animals did this was that some of the men would adopt one of them and take food from the table to feed it.

The instant the bell rang the thirty or more dogs would start barking. Then each dog chose a cat and chased it up a tree or into the grape arbor. This cat and dog routine was performed every noon.

One day the ranch management decided to cut down on the number of cats. Two men were delegated to do away with them. When they were through they piled, Ed Norton told me, seventy-five cats in the wagon used by Jake the stable buck. Jake's last name was Smith or Schmidt. He was a Dutchman and couldn't read or write. He had been stable buck on San Emideo for twenty years and the wagon was the vehicle used to haul away the manure and trash from the stable and corral. Before he came to San Emideo Jake had been a prospector in Arizona and had left a partner there to whom he sent a grubstake every payday. Once a month, just before payday, this partner sent a sample of ore which Jake would forward to an assayer in Los Angeles. Of course the sample would have no trace of precious metal.

The men on the ranch said that the old Dutchman was being swindled, but Jake never lost faith and through all the years he spent on the ranch he never failed to send his partner money after every payday. If I remember rightly, it was twenty dollars which he sent. At that time such an amount was almost enough to keep a family in food for a month, so the partner had a very good thing of it.

To any man willing to act as secretary Jake would dictate a letter to the assayer. The wording never changed. The letter always read like this: "I am sending a sample of ore for you to assay. I am sending five dollars. If it is not enough let me know. If it is too much have a drink on me. Jake Smith."

On payday Jake took a bath. There were two bath tubs for the men to use. After filling a tub with water, he took all the clothes he had worn for the month - socks, long handled underwear (worn winter and summer), overalls (bib variety) - into the tub with him. As he sat in the tub he washed the clothes and himself, using a sock for a wash cloth. Jake affected loud colored socks and with the red underwear the resulting laundry was streaked with several colors and never failed to have more than a trace of tattle-tale gray.

RIDING COLTS

Contrary to general belief, there were many good vaqueros and buckaroos who couldn't ride a bucking horse, that is to say, one that bucked hard. As a result, they would try their best to keep one from bucking. This caution was common not only among poor bronco-riders. There were many vaqueros whom ''it took a good horse to buck off'' that did not like to have a horse buck because it spoiled the animal. They, too, tried everything in the book to keep a horse from bucking.

On the other hand, there were men who welcomed strife and liked to have a horse buck; but those riders spoiled horses. It was seldom that a *jinete*, a bucking horse rider, turned out a good vaquero horse. Most of them spoiled everything they rode. All they taught a horse was bad habits. On the other hand, the men who were not combative, those who never let their colts buck, turned out the best working horses, and that is the mark of the good vaquero.

''When we rode colts out in the early morning,'' Lupe Gomez said, ''we would sit up stiff and straight in our saddles, with one rein shorter than the other, so that we could double our colts if they were to 'break in two.' Our eyes were glued to the colt's ears, because the position of the ears indicate the horse's mood.

''The colts would travel with their ears laid back flat against their head, *pelando los ojos*, showing the whites of their eyes, the very picture of malice and bad humor, as if daring their riders to give them an excuse to buck.

"It is the first jump the bronco makes that is the hardest. If the buckaroo stays after the first one, he will most probably weather the storm.

"After we had traveled two or three miles, the colts' backs would begin to get warm and the humps would settle down to normal. Their ears would start moving back and forth, an indication that they were in good humor at last. The vaqueros would relax, slacken their reins, and start rolling cigarettes and telling lies."

They had got through the critical period of the morning without having to ride through an equine earthquake.

PENANCE

The fat cattle we gathered during the summer and fall were held in a pasture near the vaquero camp until the buyer came and parted out his choice of the beef. When a number were ready for shipment, we drove them to the corrals at Caliente and loaded them on the cars.

When we were through with the work of shipping, Don Jesus would invite us all to the one saloon in town for a drink. One round of drinks was all he would buy, no matter how much we hinted for him to buy another round. Immediately after we had finished our one drink he would order us to mount our horses and go back to the camp at Los Lobos.

On one occasion Jose Maria Velasquez and Nacho Montes disobeyed orders. They stayed in Caliente and went on drinking. When they finally started back to Los Lobos their horses somehow got away from them and they arrived at camp on foot. Jose Maria's horse made his way back to the ranch in good order, but Nacho's was bleeding from a deep gash across the chest. He had been caught in barbwire.

Some days later, when we had got back to headquarters, and the men were all gathered at the corral to catch their horses, Don Jesus arrived and ordered the caporal to catch a certain *tordillo* (gray). When the *tordillo* had been led up Don Jesus turned to Nacho, who was still *muy crudo*. To be *muy crudo*, very raw, is to have a bad hangover. *"Ahora, por boracho, me amansas este caballo,"* said Don Jesus. Now, for being a drunkard, you will break this horse for me.

The gray was *muy maldito*, very mean, and Nacho, though he was one of the best Indian vaqueros on Tejon, had a lot of trouble with him. The horse was very tall and Nacho very short, so he had difficulty in mounting. Perhaps Don Jesus had taken that circumstance into consideration when he gave Nacho the penance.

BURRO MEAT

Rawley Duntley and I were discussing the merits of beef, venison, pork, and even - ugh! - mutton. After all had been passed upon, he said, "Do you know that burro sometimes makes good eating?"

"One year we were preparing for our annual barbecue," he went on, "and when everything else was ready for our celebration, we found that beef was not available at any price. Rather than disappoint a lot of people, I sent some boys out on the desert to shoot a number of burros.

"They shot four nice fat ones, dressed them out, and brought them home. The lads meant well, but in dressing the carcasses they cut them up crosswise, as one would chop up a snake.

"However, they barbecued well, and when served on the day of the celebration, a woman came up to me and said: " 'Oh, Mr. Duntley, this meat is so delicious!'

" 'Yes,' I answered, "burro makes good eating.'

" 'Burro!' she said, 'Do you mean to say that this is burro meat?'

" 'Of course,' I said, pointing to a chunk of meat on the table, 'can't you see the prints of hobnails on that piece where the prospector kicked it?' "

QUERENCIA

The homing instinct that draws all dumb creatures back to the place of their birth is so pronounced in some cases that it is a cause for men to marvel. An animal left to itself more often than not will return to its home pasture no matter how many miles away it may be. Paisanos call this instinct *querencia* from the verb *querer*, to love, and have so much faith in its power that, when lost or unsure of their route, they will leave the finding of the way home to their mount.

That the swallows return to the mission of San Juan Capistrano on St. Joseph's Day every year has long been known to all the world, and is one of the most interesting features of that mission. However, the *golondrinas* are not the only creatures that have developed an intense love for that particular part of California. There was a sorrel horse that escaped his groom three times and each time made his way from San Francisco back to his home pasture at San Juan - a distance of nearly five hundred miles.

For many years over the seven western states, the sorrel horses bred by Don Chico Forster of San Juan Capistrano were known for their superior qualities. The sorrel color predominated because at one time the Forsters had acquired a fine stallion and he had stamped most of his descendants with his color. The cavalrymen who pursued the Apache chieftains, Victorio and Mangas Coloradas, over the desolate plains and hills of Arizona were, for the most part, mounted on horses bred by Don Chico Forster.

The Army remount buyers were not the only ones who appreciated the good qualities of these horses. Among those who sought the best in horseflesh were the purchasing agents of the city of San Francisco. They bought horses from the Forsters for the renowned mounted police of that city.

One day an order for a select number of colts was received from the bay city and the vaqueros combed the bands for the best. They were justifiably proud of the record their horses had made with the mounted police. Among the colts parted out was an outstanding sorrel. He stepped higher, moved faster, and carried his head more proudly than any of the others. He also fought the rope harder and bucked higher and longer. One of the sweating, swearing vaqueros struggling with him remarked, *"Este alazan esta bueno para el capitan."* This sorrel will do for the chief. And as chance sayings often take root, the horse became known as *El Caballo del Capitan,* the Chief's Horse.

The horses were sent to San Francisco and the sorrel entered into the intensive and intricate training required of a police horse. Nor did he escape the chief's discerning eye as later on he lived up to his name and in reality became the Chief's Horse.

Winter passed, spring came and went, the golondrinas had long since returned to Capistrano when one morning a four-year-old niece of Don Chico awoke and got out of bed She walked to a front window and looked out. There, standing at the front gate, was the Chief's Horse. His *querencia* had brought him back. How he had escaped his grooms in the bay area and avoided capture on the five hundred miles of road home, no one will ever know. But here he was.

In that era when horses could often be had for the asking, an animal's only value was the time spent in its training. A police horse, because of a long and complicated schooling, was a valuable animal. The same applied to his contemporary, the fire horse.

The sorrel was sent back to San Francisco and affairs at San Juan resumed their usual routine until the horse appeared at the Forster Ranch again. How he had escaped his grooms a second time is a matter of conjecture. He had completed his training for police work so there was nothing to do but send him back despite whatever feeling Don Chico and his vaqueros might have had in the matter.

Time passed. One season came and went, then another. It was late fall and the rodeos were over in Southern California. Don Chico's vaqueros had pointed the beef herd north to market and had them strung out in a long line, traveling freely, when the vaquero on the point saw a riderless horse coming toward him. When it had come near enough to be recognized the man saw that it was the Chief's Horse. He had escaped for the third time and was making his way back home again. We do not know, but perhaps Don Chico prevailed upon the police chief to let the horse stay at San Juan. This is a reasonable assumption as men who know and ride horses never fail to have that streak of sentiment which makes them all kin.

One summer during the Old Spanish Days in Santa Barbara, Jimmy Rogers and I were sitting in the grandstand and talking of the range rider's sense of humor and of campfire tales in general when Mr. Beale, who was present, told us the story of the Chief's Horse as he had heard it in San Juan. So one day while passing through the town I stopped at the Tom Forster Ranch. Mr. Forster informed me that the little girl who had seen the horse from the window had been his aunt, the late Mrs. McFadden. Mr. Forster and I talked of vaqueros and horses, of stories and story tellers. He told me this tale about Juan Manrequez, one of his father's vaqueros. Juan was entrusted with the messages sent from the ranch and made many trips to Los Angeles. He was very popular with the children on the ranch and on his return from a trip they would crowd around him; for he always had an interesting story to tell of his adventures while away from home. These adventures came out of a fertile imagination and the children were fascinated with the tales.

"*Ustedes no van a creer lo que les voy a platicar de lo que me paso; pero es la pura verdad.*" You won't believe the things I am going to relate; but it is the purest truth, was always the prelude to one of Juan's stories. Here is one of them:

"As you know, the patron sent me to the *pueblo*, to Los Angeles, the other day on a very important mission. I started at a gallop and my horse, El Liston, ate up the leagues. I had covered almost all the distance and it was not yet daylight when I came to the Rosa de Castilla hills near Los Angeles. There my horse went lame. After I had examined him I saw that he could never reach the pueblo, so I started looking for a horse that I might rope to carry me the rest of the way. There are many range horses in that part of the country so after urging my limping mount only a little farther along, I came upon a flat where I saw a little horse moving across the trail. He was short and round, had a sharp pointed muzzle and little pin ears. I thought he was an odd looking horse. He traveled in an awkward shuffling gait and I said to myself, 'I am lucky to have chanced upon *el caballo para ir a traer el cura*, the horse on which to bring the priest.' ''

Here we must digress to explain to the gringos who are not of the initiated the meaning of this term. A *caballo para ir a traer el cura* is a pacer. Pacers originally came from Spain and according to the old people were the palfreys one reads about in old books. Vaqueros never liked to ride them because their feet were always in the wrong position when one went to turn them. Anglo vaqueros called them "side wheelers." Pacers were called *generoso* by the paisanos and before the gringos brought buggies to California they were ridden by women because of their easy gait. On those occasions when some paisano was on his deathbed the caballo generoso was used to mount the padre who was brought to the rancho to help the dying man prepare for the next world. Not that all padres were poor riders. But they lacked practice and it was not fitting that they should ride a hardgaited horse. Now, to get back to Juan and his tale...

"I threw the lazo around his forelegs and threw him. While he lay there I fitted the Jaquima around his nose and put the *tapa-ojos*, the blinds, over his eyes, then let him get to his feet. While I was saddling him I noticed that he had short, stiff hair and that someone had hogged his mane, no doubt to make a hair rope. His owner had not intended to ride him. No one would ever think of cutting off a horse's mane if he intended to ride him because, as you know, a horse's mane, like a woman's hair, is its crowning glory.

"Before mounting I tied a stout limb of a tree across the saddle next to the fork as we all do when we ride a bronco. This was to keep my leg from being broken or pinned under the saddle in case the bronco threw himself and tried to roll. I mounted, but instead of bucking, the animal turned and bit my leg and growled. This surprised me very much since I had never heard a bronco growl before. I kicked his head around and got him into his peculiar shuffle and rode on. It was broad daylight when I reached the *plazita* and as I passed the Church of Nuestra Senora the people who were going to mass stared at me. This surprised me as men riding wild broncos in the City of the Angels were a common sight. But the more people I passed the more surprised they appeared so at last I looked down at my mount and saw that I was riding a grizzly bear!''

Mr. Forster says that Juan would get up and walk away immediately after he had finished his yarn and before the children had recovered enough from the sensational details to start questioning the truth of it.

EPILOGUE

It is a matchless summer day in beautiful Santa Barbara, California.

The bright warm sun beams down on the groups of people who are massed for the Old Spanish Days. They are all in costume, and though there may be some incongruities in their dress, they make up in enthusiasm for whatever they may lack in conformity to period, for it is fiesta time, that week in August when the *Barbareno* gracefully lets the present slip back into the past to pay tribute to the fundadores of California.

The marchers are taking up their positions when an old vaquero, on an ancient sorrel horse, rides up and takes his place in the line of march. He is a man out of the past, a figure of legend. He stares straight ahead, seemingly indifferent to the many eyes that are upon him. This old vaquero represents the horsemen of an era that is past. And today Santa Barbara, and in spirit all California, pays tribute to a tradition of horsemanship which his ancestors brought from Spain - a superb art which every man, be he Spaniard, Mexican, Indian, Anglo, who has taken it for his own, has cherished and been faithful to.

The old vaquero's saddle, bit, spurs, reins, and hair rope are old, but well made. The silver on the bit, spurs, conchas is fine, white. The saddle has acquired that mellow tint which only loving care and pure castile soap can impart to California oak-tanned leather.

But the old vaquero's hat, shirt, denim pants, and boots are new, unfortunately. The clothing which would have been in keeping with the old equipment went out of style fifty years ago and has not been manufactured since.

The band begins to play; the five flags which have flown over California move up the street. Spanish Santa Barbara is passing in review. The old vaquero, his reins nipped delicately in the fingers of his left hand, moves them ever so slightly, and the sorrel, good vaquero horse that he is, takes the signal. He senses the old man's pride, and perfectly in keeping with his rider's mood, arches his neck and, stepping as if he were walking on eggs, struts up the street, spinning the cricket in the bit for all the world to know that he is content under the hand of his old master.

The old vaquero rides on up the flag-lined street and out of sight. He is lost in the groups of riders that follow him. All too soon the pageant is over. Santa Barbara has come back into the present and the old vaquero has ridden back into history. Perhaps, *con el favor de Dios*, if it pleases God, we shall see him again an another such beautiful August day during Old Spanish Days next year, when the spirit of old mother Spain returns to hover for a few brief hours like a benediction over Santa Barbara.

We shall scan the groups of riders in search of the old vaquero, for he is a symbol of a time which will never come again. And though there may be "cowboys" in this speed-mad world, the vaquero is gone forever from the soil of California.

Part III

MORE STORIES

7440 AlexanderCourt,
Fair Oaks, California.   95628
February 11, 1981.

Dear Mr. Rojas:

This morning I received my copies of your two latest books These Were the Vaqueros and Vaqueros and Buckeroos and I wish to thank you for inscribing them for me. I hadn't expected this so it was an added pleasure. I already have your books Bits, Bitting and Spanish Horses; California Vaquero; Last Of the Vaqueros; Lore Of the California Vaquero and The Vaquero in addition to two magazine articles in Horse and Rider and the American West.

In skimming through the pages of the two books I received this morning, I recalled my meeting with Don Jose Jesus Lopez in 1934 when he lived in Bakersfield and what a pleasure it was to talk with him. As I also recall, it was not too long after that that he passed away. I came to 6alifornia in 1934, as the aide to the Superintndent of the Sacramento Indian Agenɾy, having been transferred from the Northern Pueblos Agency in New Mexico. During the depression years, I became quite well acquainted with the Allens, especially Mrs. Allen who was very interested in the Indians in Tejon Canyon and it was through her that I was able to get enough money to build seferal small cabins in the Canyon for the aged Indians who lived there.

Henry Miller Bowles, one of the heirs of the Miller and Lux estate is also a friend of mine as are Betty and David Potter (Visalia Saddlery) and Dave Silva who lives not too far from where I am. I must also admit that my very good friend is the Hutchinson about whom you speak disparagingly in your Vaqueros and Buckeroos, on the subject of negro cowboys. I think if you ever met Hutch personally you would like him, perhaps not as much as I do, but some.

One time when I was on the Tejon I had to see a man who I understood was the ramrod - the Indians called him an Apache. Do you know of or recall such a man when you were on the Tejon?

Well, that's enough"paper talk."   Keep well and let me know if and when you publish more broks.

Sincerely,

MICHAEL HARRISON

"Miguel"

Mr. Arnold R. Rojas,
c/o Mr. Chuck Hitchcock,
620 Munzer Street,
Shafter, California. 93263

Lupio & Rea Orteja are also long time friends of mine.

—314—

Arnold R. Rohas   March 24, 1965
                                                     Box 357
                                                     Hatch, New Mexico

Dear Sir:
Please excuse the delay in this letter. I was not acquainted with the American
West publication until this year and having gotten the back issues just now read
your excerpt from the Vaquero that was in the volume 1 no 2 issue: American West
Spring, 1964.

I dont normally write letters to editors or publishers but took exception to some
statements you made in the article. You imply that all the millions of cattle
that were marketed on the eastern slopes of the rockies from Texas, New Mexico,
Colorado, Kansas, and Wyoming were taken there by "rodeo cowboys". This seems
a bit hard to take as many of these were as fine a herdsman as could be found
any where. They certainly knew more that the "rodeo" fellow and certainly many
of these came from ranches. I grant there are difference in dress and saddle
preference coming out of needs of the different areas. The good old working
buckaroo had little use for the fancy silver trappings, worn by the mexican,
while he was doing his job.

Mr Remington, who knew the horse very well and painted them very well, gives
the mustang of this area much more credit than do you. They may have been
smaller and not as fat but for stamina they were hard to beat. I would suggest
you read some of Remingtons bits about horses.

Lastly, you leave some of the wildest and best country out of what you call the
true american west. Being born in California you would tend to draw the line
further west than we do, but omitting the likes of New Mexico, Colorado and Wyoming is a real sin. We here in New Mexico include ourselves in the real west as
those of southern California would include themselves in the southwest. As to
the southwest, we draw the line from Yuma to Flagstaff, to Durango to Tucumcari,
and on to Alpine, texas. This leaves out all of California which we call the
west coast.

Our "cowboys" may not be vaqueros but we feel they are as good as your "cowboys"
since the only real vaqueros seen these days are in parades.

                                     Very Truly Yours

                                     C.R. Hall

Coyote Chasers - Land Co. Ranch

Buckeroo shack at Carneros Rocks - Miller & Lux

WATER, GRASS AND CATTLE

Spaniards, Portuguese, Frenchmen, Englishmen and Russians have come to the Americas and have found them good. But it was the Andalusian horse and long-horned Spanish cow, that met the best welcome; for it was on the plains that stretched from horizon to horizon, that nature spread the finest banquets of grass. Natural pastures she had been preparing for untold centuries where horses and cattle could roam at will and multiply into countless thousands.

After he had acquired his lands in California, Henry Miller set out to find more range land for his cattle. He came upon hidden valleys, high in the mountains, between the deserts of Oregon and Nevada. In one way or another, he managed to buy the land that controlled the water.

Once in control of the springs, creeks and rivers, he would have the use of millions of acres that would be useless to other stockmen, who owned no water rights. Much of the land Miller used for his cattle was either leased or free range.

He had developed a cross between the Red Durham and Hereford, which would thrive on the roughest terrain. These he used to stock his Oregon and Nevada ranges. Among his proudest vaqueros were those who pushed cattle from the valleys of California across the Sierras into Pisen Switch on the Walker River in Nevada and up into the White Horse, Harney and Malheur, in Oregon. Open range

Carneros Cow Camp, 1884

Miller & Lux Barn

Carneros Rocks - Miller & Lux

ranches where the chuck wagons started rolling in the spring and stayed on until snow began in the fall. The nearest shipping point was Winnemucca, Nevada, sometimes 500 miles away and after weeks on the drive the beef steers were loaded onto the cars.

There was a story told around the campfire to the effect that when Henry Miller bought the Panama Ranch from Don Ventura Cuen, it was stipulated in the deed that the sons of Don Ventura would have a job with Henry Miller for as long as they lived. One might think that such a stipulation would at some time in the course of events become embarrassing to Henry Miller, but such was not the case. Among the thousands of Miller's employees, none was more faithful than Rafael Cuen. No man in his employ was more worthy of the old Deutchman's trust in the fifty-four years Rafael Cuen rode for him.

Twisselman's Chuck Wagon

SAN EMIDIO RANCH

The ranch of Johnny and Cathy Tregea sets in a fold of the mountains of the Coast Range, two-thousand feet above sea level. The surrounding slopes are dotted with massive oaks and pale green buckeyes.

It took an hour of driving along a winding mountain road before I came to the gate that leads to the house. I counted eight does and fawns that had ventured timidly out of the covert into the flat in front of the house.

Johnny is eighty years old and his wife is seventy-nine, yet he and his wife are running their cattle ranch very efficiently. In fact, Johnny was recently named "Cattleman of the Year."

When I drove up to the house, Mrs. Tregea was preparing a lunch to take to the men who were working with her husband up on the summit of the range. She packed the basket of lunch into the jeep, told me to get in and drove off on some tracks that had been made by wagons years before she came there. We went up steep mountain sides and across gulches and ravines.

I marveled at her expertness in handling the jeep. Her reflexes were still those of a young person.

When we reached the spot where Johnny and his men were working, he recognized me immediately and greeted me cordially. The last time I had seen him was on Chester Ave. in Bakersfield twenty years before. He and I are the only survivors of the vaquero crew that was on San Emidio Ranch sixty years ago.

My visit to the Tregea's came about because of some old pictures. One day I was talking to a young friend, Philip Mello, and I said, "Philip, if you had red hair, a turned-up nose and freckles over your face, you would look like a boy I used to work with."

"Was his name Alfred Fraga?" he asked.

"Yes," I answered, "but we called him Frager."

"He was my grandfather; my brother, Ron, has all the pictures Grandpa got when he rode on San Emideo, my Grandmother gave them all to Ron."

San Emideo Ranch - Kern Co. Land Co.

I had been looking for old pictures of vaqueros and buckeroos to complete a work I was doing. Up to the time I talked to Philip, I had not found any. Although from my own experince, I knew that many of the boys, like myself, carried a camera among their belongings. Usually it was a Brownie box camera, which cost about a dollar at that time (1920). I remember that Bert Galbraith, a Canadian, took many pictures while he was on San Emideo.

(l. to r.)
George Hosking
and Alfred Fraga
at San Emideo

We drove to Ron's house in McFarland, where he showed me the pictures. All had been taken on San Emideo. Unfortunately, I could recognize only George and Henry Hoskings, Pete Rivera, Juan Reyes. The rest I had forgotten. As I have said, John Tregea was a survivor. He might be able to recognize the vaqueros in the pictures, but after I had driven to his ranch and had shown them to him, he couldn't recognize any more than I could.

He let me make copies of his pictures and in one of them, I recognized myself in one of the groups. I bade Johnny and his wife goodbye the next morning and thanked him heartily for his help in bringing back memories of the big ranches in the Great Valley and its Sierras. I also owe a debt of gratitude to Helen Albiso for her kindness in lending me copies of pictures taken on Tejon Ranch, when her late husband, Frank Albiso, was a vaquero there.

Henry Hoskings was foreman on San Emideo when Fred Rush was superintendent. Henry and his brother George had come up to Kern County from Julian in San Diego County. Their father, old George Hoskings, was the cattle buyer for the Hardy interests in San Diego.

George, Henry's brother, was the superintendent at the abattoir on Bellevue Ranch. Later, he returned to San Diego and managed the abattoir in National City. Both George and Henry ("Hank", as we called him), died young. They were good vaqueros.

Johnny Krackenburger - San Emideo

"Coyote" Joe Nicholson - San Emideo
The chaps are batwing angoras

Diamond A Cattle - San Emideo

Doctoring - San Emideo

Alfred Fraga at the squeeze chutes on Pleito Ranch - San Emideo

Pete Rivera - San Emideo

Stretched Out - San Emideo

Parting Out - San Emideo

Mules - San Emideo

San Emideo

San Emideo Canyon

Disaster! Packing fence posts into the Mil Potreros

RO cattle shipped in from Spain

Vaqueros - San Emideo

Holding Herd - San Emideo

Hank Hosking up on Kangeroo near old Spanish adobe - San Emideo

George and Hank Hosking (center) others unknown - San Emideo

Pete Rivera, horse's name is Bill - San Emideo

Alfred Fraga (Frager)

The day we counted 9,000 head of cattle through a gate into San Emideo.

Hank on Kangeroo

Breaking - San Emideo

Remick Albitre

Shadows on San Emideo

CATTLE RANCH (The Tejon)

My dreams of what an old-style cattle ranch should be were fulfilled when I rode into the vaquero camp on the Tejon Ranch. It was late September and the bunkhouse, cookhouse and corrals drowsed in the afternoon sun.

I rode up to the hitching rack, unsaddled my horse, turned him into the corral and found a seat under the cottonwood which shaded the cook shack and waited. I had not waited long, when a group of men came riding in. I was instantly alert.

These were the men I had been seeking — vaqueros. They rode in, the horses eagerly lengthening their stride to end their day's labor sooner. Each horse spinning the cricket in his bit, the spur chains striking against the stirrups and the tapaderos tapping in rhythm with the horse's walk. Every man sitting erect in the saddle to hide his fatigue, his reins nipped delicately in the fingers of the left hand.

The Tejon was an old ranch, situated in the corner of the Great Valley. It had once been an Indian Rancheria. The people had driven the Tule elk up the canyons to be slaughtered by bow men, hidden behind the ridges. The Indians, besides being hunters, were weavers of water-tight baskets and makers of tough pottery. After the Spanish came, the Indians became the best of vaqueros.

In the years when the elk became scarce, they ate acorns, locusts, but bear meat they never ate, for the formidable grizzly was

Juan Gomez (r.) -
Tejon Ranch
Man on left unidentified

Halter breaking -
Tejon Ranch

beyond their skill. It was not until the Spaniard came, with his horse and lazo, and after the Indian had become a vaquero, that he was able to tackle a grizzly with success.

Then came "the Lord of all he surveyed" and bought the four Spanish grants which compose the present day ranch. It was a Spanish Ranch founded by a gringo. But the Tejon's founding by Fitzgerald Beale did not make it a gringo ranch. It was the most Hispanic of any ranch in California and it was Don Jose Jesus Lopez, whose personality gave the ranch its atmosphere. Even as late as 1937, it was run in the old Spanish way.

Don Jose Jesus Lopez
Manager, Tejon Ranch
Retired 1937

Catarino Montes, Phillip Crosswaite, Frank Albiso - Tejon Ranch

Willow Springs Resort circa 1890 - Tejon Ranch

Modern Buckeroos.
Middle man is author's grandson, Leonard Montes

Chris Montes
Great grandson of Nacho Montes

Leonard and Levi Montes

Stretched out - Tejon Ranch

Cowboy in trouble

Castaic Lake - Tejon Ranch

TEHACHAPI CATTLE CO.

Russell and Roland Hill, brothers, were born and raised among Hispanic and Indian Vaqueros. The Hill Ranch near Tehachapi bred the finest Morgan horses. Once broken and trained these horses were sold for enormous prices. Mr. Hill was, in fact, the largest breeder of Morgan horses in the United States.

The names of his stallions are in the pedigree of all prize winning Morgans in present day horseshows. They had the best horses because the Hill Company hired only the best vaqueros. They expanded later to become the Tehachapi Cattle Company.

Juan Reyes, the dog's name is "Shorty" - San Emideo

Juan Reyes

JUAN REYES

I knew Juan Reyes years ago when I worked on San Emideo about 1918 or 1919. Through the years, I would see him in Bakersfield every now and then. He worked for Bert Snedden who ran cattle in the Mootaw and Lockwood Valleys behind San Emideo.

The last time I saw Juan he was sitting on his horse atop a hill and laughing uproariously at a Miller and Lux horse, which, with ears laid back and teeth bared, was parting a cow out of the herd.

Juan belonged to the old Reyes family who had lived in Santa Barbara Canyon for a long time. A good vaquero, Juan Reyes. The steer in the picture was a Diamond A, dehorned longhorn. The dog's name was "Shorty."

EARLY VAQUEROS

As the Indians were slaughtered by the Whites or died from disease or starvation, Hispanics began to appear in the vaquero crews on the ranches. The reason was that the Hispanics dutifully followed the Biblical admonition, "Be fruitful," and obediently were astonishingly prolific.

Big families were the rule and as a result, numerous youths had to find a source of income and since there was no other work, they became vaqueros.

Jose Ortega was one of twenty-one children and he himself, fathered twenty-one. One Maldonaldo had thirty-one and one Castro was the father of twenty-six, while Juan Cota left five-hundred descendants. And why not? The pastures teemed with cattle and sheep and for a mere scratching with a wooden plow, the land gave an abundance of fruits and vegetables.

The *ninos* flourished on a diet of beef. Feeding the numerous children was no problem. While it was beneath the dignity of the *hijo del Pais* to toil in the field, he did not consider it degrading to herd cattle, since he could practice some of the skills he had inherited from the cavalryman.

The result was, one often came upon a younger son of an old colonial family riding the range. Don Pedro Yorba, Don Luis Lopez, Don Victor Ortega, Juan Olivera to name a few. All were first-class horsemen.

Frank, Ramon, Joe, Vicente
Vaqueros - Tejon Ranch

Frank Albiso and Don Toribio Cordova
Don Toribio was head vaquero on
the Tejon for many years

Ben Ali Haggin, said to be of Turkish or Kurdish extraction, came from Kentucky and joined forces with larger landowners, the homesteaders and squatters, until they owned millions of acres. They acquired lands in New Mexico, Arizona, Oregon and even in Old Mexico, where they controlled many acres of land which they had to abandon after the Madero Revolution. One of their ranches in the San Joaquin Valley had eighty sections in alfalfa.

The average person in the United States would think that the largest cattle ranch in America would be the King Ranch in Texas. It is not even the third largest. Miller and Lux was several times larger, until it went out of existence. The Kern County Land Company was almost twice as large, after it had sold an immense acreage in the last thirty years. It still has 1,869,776 acres under its control.

The offspring of the Indian vaqueros learned from their parents and readily adopted the vaquero tradition for their own. "An indolent, feckless people," Bernard De Voto called them. But Bernard De Voto never had to break and train a bronco horse, nor did he ever rope and spread-eagle a thousand-pound grizzly bear and kill it with a knife.

Writers who have never been west of the Mississippi River, expound about the people in California, but these selfsame writers never rode in a roundup for days and nights. They try to dismiss the native peoples, but the fact remains that long after the land grabbers had stolen the land, the few surviving Indians and Sonorans were still herding the cattle in the West.

Hard-riding, tough, and efficient men of Indian blood were the best in the world. These riders had acquired a skill which they had begun to develop when mere babies. As toddlers, their first toy was a miniature riata, with which they began to practice, and they were expert by the time they were ten years old. Their skills developed from constant practice and dedication to the vaquero tradition which were always subject to the corrections of older men.

The vaquero's work was the most complex and hazardous of any of the risky occupations men followed in a frontier environment and certainly the most intricate. The lassoing of grizzly bears was a daily chore, in which the risk to their lives was commonplace. While the

Indian vaqueros resting against the bunkhouse - Tejon Ranch

vaquero acquired skills, he also acquired a sagacity which was the result of a broad experience in avoiding mistakes handling animals.

It is not too much to say that the vaquero's work required a skill as intricate as that of medieval man at arms. Certainly it was as complex as any of the occupations in America. They were men who could use their handmade tools with the deftness and artistry of a master. It is to the padres that we owe the development of the vaquero, finished horsemen many of them, who taught the Indian to be a vaquero, in defiance of the "Law of the Indies."

The Spanish established the cattle ranges of the West and their cattle and horses were the nucleus of all the cattle and horses which enriched this nation. Here lived the vaquero and his counterpart, the buckeroo. These tales of their adventures are true, quite true. Many of the first colonists brought no women. The result was marriage with Indian women.

The cavalrymen had to be Spaniards (Christianized Meztizos), to be able to ride a horse, for the law of the Indies forbade Indians the use of horses.

The Spaniards, after ruining the Jews, who enriched them, after expelling the Moors, who civilized them, came to America to enslave the Indians. However, they did not slaughter them as Gringos did.

The great Scot man of letters, Robert Louis Stevenson, on a trip to California, said, "The Padres who have passed away, have been succeeded by greedy land grabbers and sacrilegious pistol shots. It is a matter of perpetual surprise to find a people full of deportment among so many mannerless Americans. The Mexicans have a name for being swindlers, but certainly the accusation cuts both ways. In a contest such as this sort, the entire booty would scarcely have passed into the hands of the more scrupulous race (The Gringos)."

Chief Juan Losada and his family

Chief Juan Losada

CHIEF JUAN LOSADA

He was the most respected of all the Indians on the Tejon Ranch, for his skill as a vaquero, and his character as a man. For many years he was the Chief of the Indians on Tejon Rancheria.

Juan Losada was very old and had long been retired as a vaquero, when I was there for the first time, but his exploits during the years he rode the range, were still spoken of around the campfire.

One of the legendary good vaqueros, he had won fame as a roper and tamer of wild cattle, for he was a master of animal psychology.

The Tejon had a number of tame oxen (cabestros), which when yoked to a cimarron (wild steer or cow), would lead it out of the mountains and into the home pasture, not however, without a long struggle.

Juan never used the oxen, but developed a method of his own. When he left camp in the morning, he carried a razor-edged hatchet and a number of rawhide thongs which he had soaked overnight in water. The thongs were carried in his chaps' pocket.

When he had roped and thrown a cimarron, he would take an eight or ten foot branch of a tree, and lash it to the horns, across the forehead of the wild cow or steer. The rawhide being wet, would shrink and hold the pole tight, indefinitely. The pole would extend the horns four or five feet on each side of the animal's head. Then Juan would release the steer and it would run for the timber and dive at a hole in the brush, but the pole would hit the brush on each side of the hole and the steer would bounce back. It would try to break through until it was exhausted and then lie down. Juan would then remove the pole and drive a much subdued steer to join the herd.

Sometimes he would rope a steer that was such a fighter, he would ride off and leave it with the pole lashed to its horns for a day or two. He knew the steer could not leave the locality, as the pole would prevent its progress, through the underbrush. Juan was sure to find a much tamer cimarron after a couple of days.

I remember back in the early thirties, when Juan, a dignified old gentleman, past ninety, would come into Bakersfield to ride in the Frontier Day's Parade. His eagle-feather war bonnet and buckskin costume and the way he sat on his horse, never failed to bring a round of applause as he rode down Nineteenth Street.

Once, during the Lion's Club Rodeo and Fiesta in Bakersfield, the old gentleman had a chance to show us not only what a great hunter he had been, but also saved us from total ignominy.

During the rodeo performance, the Indians rode past a target set up in front of the grandstand and shot at it with their bows and arrows. All missed. Juan, who was sitting in the grandstand, shook his head and muttered.

That evening, we all attended the banquet at Hotel El Tejon. During a lull in the entertainment, I asked the old chief to show us how he killed Tule elk in the swamps where Bakersfield now stands.

The old man did not hesitate. In full war bonnet and buckskin costume, he rose and tottered from his seat, taking the bow and arrows I handed him. We had set up a target in the dining room. It had a three-inch bullseye in the center. The old chief put six arrows, each one evenly spaced, around the edge of the circle, and the seventh in the exact center!

For many years now, Juan has been sleeping in the Indian graveyard on the Tejon Ranch. The Indians have moved away, the only ones left are those who sleep with him in eternal rest.

GRINGO VAQUEROS

In many of the following pages I have been compelled to bear witness to the skill on horseback of the Gringo vaqueros or as they styled themselves, "buckeroos," to whom the Hispanic California culture had become second nature. I have never lamented that they became as expert in a calling as the people who taught it to them.

Therefore, it pleases me to chronicle the doughty deeds of good Gringo buckeroos, good Mexican vaqueros and good Indian vaqueros.

I feel that it is fitting and proper to make my readers acquainted with the West as it really was and if in some small measure I have been able to do so, my work has not been in vain.

Along the coast, in Mission towns, there were Gringos who were raised among the natives and who were taught by the older vaqueros. These Gringos, many of whom spoke Spanish, became intimate friends of the natives and the result was, no discrimination. But there were some who did not follow this pattern and were insulting. Those who treated the natives well, were repaid a hundred-fold, for they were the men who learned the skills of the vaquero, who possessed a valor hardly comprehended.

Catarino Reese was one of the men who taught many of the vaqueros the skills of good horsemanship and they in turn, taught others. Thus the Californians were indebted to men like Catarino Reese, a fine vaquero.

HAZEN COWAN
on
BOXING JIMMIE
BAKERSFIELD RODEO
1919
MARCELL

LLOYD SAUNDERS
"BULL-DOGGING"
BAKERSFIELD "RODEO"
1919
MARCELL

NORMAN COWAN
on
DOUBLE
GOFF
BAKERSFIELD RODEO
1919
MARCELL
PHOTO # 5
1919

Slim Pickens - buckeroo, rodeo bronc rider, rodeo clown and movie actor.

Slim Pickens comes from a long line of pioneer cattlemen and was raised in the cattle country east of Fresno in the Sierras. After years spent as a buckeroo, he followed the rodeos as a bronc rider. Later he became a rodeo clown, a job requiring no end of guts. The very dangerous Brahma bulls had to be lured away from fallen riders by the clowns to prevent injuries or death. Rodeo men say that Slim Pickens was a good clown.

Broncs for the Wild Horse Race, Pendleton

PINI

Pini was a "Roman-Swiss" and a good fellow. He never failed a friend in need. When a buckaroo had gone broke and asked for a loan of a couple of dollars, Pini would say, "What! You in need and you never told me. I know you would share your last fifty-cents with me and you know it. So would I with you, so should I with so good a friend as you are."

"If you were eating an orange, you would share it with me and give me half."

Then Pini would share the two dollars. He was wise enough never to carry more than two dollars but he always gave half of what he had in his pocket.

Like all the Italian-Swiss who came among Hispanic vaqueros, he became fluent in Spanish after a short time. He worked on most of the big ranches, Tejon, Miller & Lux and others. He left Bakersfield to work on the Santa Margarita in San Diego County. Somewhere on the many ranches, he learned how to make bridle bits which he always stamped with his name, "Pini." He also learned to braid bridle reins, hackamores and riatas. He contracted asthma here in the valley and left to live on the coast.

One black night, I drove into Paso Robles fairgrounds and while groping through the barns for an empty stable, I ran into a man in the dark. It was Bob Pini. He helped me find a stall and after the horse I had hauled in had been stabled, he took me to his cabin to sleep. Bob has been dead for years now, but every now and then, I run into a bit with Pini stamped on the mouth piece and it never fails to bring back a fond memory of a good fellow.

When he was a young man, he was "as strong as an ox," and one day on the Tejon Ranch, he was able to prove it. It was the custom on the ranch to name a colt after the man the colt had bucked off.

There was a sorrel horse on Tejon that had bucked off a vaquero named Noriega. He was given to Pini, who saddled him one cold morning. He mounted and had hardly gotten away from the corral when Noriega started bucking. Bob was never a bronc rider, so after a jump or two, the horse threw him out of the saddle back over the cantle. Bob managed to grab on to the horn, and weather the storm. Noriega did not buck him off. It was his great strength which had enabled him to stay on the horse.

PROSPECTORS

I was a fourteen-year-old boy riding along an old dirt road in San Bernardino County enroute to a sheep shearing camp, when darkness fell. In order to get to the camp I needed daylight to find my way, so I began to look for a place to spend the night. I had traveled a mile or two in the dark, when I came upon the prospector.

He had started out his burros, had cooked his supper and was setting out a couple of pots on the grass, as I rode up. He looked up and said, "Get down, get down and haf some supper." I dismounted, unsaddled and hobbled my horse. He was an old vaquero horse which had grown too old for ranch work and had been given to me by a rancher. Although a little stiff, he was sound and could carry me easily. He immediately began grazing after I carried a bucket of water to him. By the time I got through with the horse, the old man had set out two tin plates and some cold biscuits and said, "Come and eat." One pot contained jackrabbit stew with dumplings, the other pot, brown beans.

The old man ladled a big helping of rabbit and dumpling and one of beans onto my plate.

As I have said, I was fourteen years old, with a castiron stomach and a faultless digestion. I ate my fill and when I was replete, I said, "You are a good cook."

"Yah," the old man answered, "I lif on fife dollars a month, and I don't lif on sawdust, either."

All prospectors are talkative, even garrulous from being alone, so I listened to the old man, who was a Deutchman. He had four burros and when I asked him how long he had owned them, he said, "I haf had the two blacks and the blue one for fifteen years, but the grey, he is just a young fellow. I haf had him only fife years."

We separated the next morning after a breakfast of flapjacks and coffee. The old man had to go on to San Bernardino to get supplies. I rode on to the sheep camp.

Through the years, I have met prospectors, but none have stayed in memory like the old Deutchman. Probably because he fed me when I was hungry.

Later, when I was grown, I met another prospector, who has stayed in my memory. He was known as old man Jackson and the area of his wanderings was the Sierra Nevadas and the upper deserts.

Back in the "twenties," people of the valley did not have refrigeration or cooling systems and in the hot weather were forced to sit out in the yard in the evening until the house cooled enough for them to go to bed. Those who could afford to do so, would go to the mountains or the coast. Many had summer cabins on Mount Breckenridge.

One summer I went to Delonagha Hot Springs during the hot weather. To go there was much harder than it is today. The modern road built by the convicts was yet to be constructed and one had to take the route that skirted Breckenridge Mountain to reach Kern River at Democrat Springs or go by Poso Flat and up and over Greenhorn Mountain. Then down the old stage road which had not been used for years and on to Delonagha. There were a number of buildings there which had once been a hotel. The owner had abandoned it with its furniture and one could use the buildings.

That summer a friend took me to Delonagha in a Model T Ford. I planned to walk down the canyon to Bakersfield when my food supplies were exhausted.

Through the summer a number of families camped there, but I had been alone for two weeks, when one evening the old prospector came down the train leading two burros. I invited him to share my supper, which he did.

Mr. Jackson had been out in the desert and not spoken to anyone for a month. He was hungry for speech, so we sat and talked on a number of subjects, for the old man had read many books. About two o'clock in the morning he made a pot of tea. After we drank it, he said, "Now a lot of people don't believe in God, but I do and the way of proving that there is a God, is to do this."

He took me by the arm and led me out on to a little knoll and pointed to the northern sky. It was a beautiful, clear, summer night and the stars shone brightly.

He said, pointing to the North Star, "Do you see the Big Dipper? If you had a watch that could run for a thousand years and you could live that long and if you knew enough of astronomy, you could set that watch by those stars and in a thousand years, those stars would be in their exact position to the second and such a system did not just happen. Some divine Hand runs it according to established laws."

ART RUETER

He was born one hundred years too late. Although most of the cattle ranches had long since been subdivided or planted to cotton or potatoes, Art Reuter (Arturo to his friends), persisted in being the most enthusiastic afficionado the vaquero way of living and working.

What drew me to him was the delight he showed in anything pertaining to horses or cattle. He owned a horse and went to every "roping" in his neighborhood. (A place where a man could practice for 25¢ a throw.) Oddly enough, through diligent practice, he attained a degree of skill in throwing the lazo. The men who attend these "ropings" are sometimes better ropers than those riders who work on a ranch. They are called "Sunday Ropers." During the week they are carpenters, plumbers, undertakers or professional men. One dentist became so skilled that he qualified in the largest rodeos in the West.

Arturo was an avid reader and a student of all authentic publications which dealt with horses and horsemanship. In a sense he was an anachronism, but if he realized it, it did not dampen his ardor. No rodeo, horse show or bullfight on horseback, was too far away. I once went with him to Tijuana, a distance of one-hundred and fifty miles, to see Carlos Arruza fight bulls on horseback.

PIONEERS

The experiences of pioneers are replete with incidents of trials and disappointments. This story of a pioneer woman is typical of all the struggles encountered by the men and women who came to the West in the last century to establish cattle ranches as a way of making a living.

Where some were more successful than others in terms of wealth, it was only a matter of degree. They all met hardships in the struggle to gain a foothold in a new and hostile land. Some won, some lost, but all fought a worthy battle. In their humble way, they are a part of the history of the West.

The lady who told the story of her mother's courageous struggle in founding a home, lies blind and helpless in a hospital, but she inherited her mother's dauntless spirit. She married a cattleman and when the chips were down and he needed help, she never hesitated to don chaps and spurs and ride with her husband to share the toils and dangers incident to the handling of cattle in a mountainous terrain.

Her mother was handicapped by two small children, weak lungs and a persistent cough when she came to the West. She had some education and training as a teacher, but not enough to teach in California. She journeyed to San Francisco and enrolled in a normal school. Her finances were so short that she would take her two small daughters to a little French restaurant and order a twenty-five cent meal and divide it among the two children and herself. Luckily, the waiter would dish up "big helpings" as one of the daughters would say in later years.

She went to San Luis Obispo after her period of schooling and finding nothing there, hired a wagon and driver, piled her few belongings, herself and her children into the wagon and came to Kern County. Mr. R. L. Stockton, the County Superintendent of Schools, gave her a first chance at teaching in a school in the hills where the sun shone brightly every day and her lungs could get strong again. One daughter said, " After that, we were never hungry again."

She was lent a deserted homestead cabin in which to live. The shack had not been lived in for years and was in bad condition.

We set about scrubbing the floors and washing the windows until they were crystal clear," her daughter remembers. "We took burlap sacks, opened them, washed and ironed them, used them for wallpaper and carpets. Then we cut pictures out of magazines and papers, and pasted them on the burlap." Water for the household had to be pumped by hand and carried in buckets from the well.

"We made mattresses out of denim and stuffed them with grass." After laboring so long and endlessly, they came to love the place. In time, the mother bought it. At last she and her daughters had a place to call "home."

Being a woman of culture, her first purchase or extravagance was a piano. It brought much enjoyment in the long, lonely, winter nights.

Pupils of the school brought the little family black mission figs, purple grapes and quinces. She fried the quinces and believed the eating of them was instrumental in curing her weak lungs.

In some years, rattlesnakes swarmed over the area and her main concern was to teach her pupils how to cope with them. "Don't let a child run who is bitten. Keep him as quiet as possible. Lance each hole in the flesh made by the fangs so it can drain and apply a tourniquet above the wound to keep the poison from spreading."

She was among ranchers who raised cattle and she saw that the cattle business was the best way for an unskilled woman to make a living and put together a competence. She started to acquire pieces of land, a plot here and a plot there. After years of drudgery and saving every penny, she managed to acquire enough land to run her cattle.

She bought a small bunch of cattle. A neighbor gave her an old vaquero horse which taught the two daughters to herd cattle. The cattle she bought were sold at a profit and she bought more.

In the winter she cleared land, foot by foot. She would wrap her and her daughter's feet with burlap and carry sackfuls of hay to the cattle standing in the snow and she saved all of them. She also bought a horse and buggy.

A homesteader that had relinquished his claim, sold her a milk cow, a team of gentle work horses and a flock of chickens. But the ground squirrels killed her chicks by catching them and sucking their blood.

She got a start raising hogs, with one pig, but the coyotes ate the pig. She started the task of fencing her ranch, a task that took years to finish.

She set out an orchard, but the cattle ate the young trees, so she fenced it. Then one daughter began teaching school and at last life became easier. Worn out by overwork, plagued with rheumatism, she went to Delonagha Hot Springs, where, after taking the hot sulphur baths, she was relieved of her aches and pains.

Now that she had enough land on which to run cattle, the heartbreaking labor was by no means over. Running cattle along the Kern River, contrary to TV and "Western" movies, was no picnic. They would get down the river, but there was no way of driving them up or down, for the course of the river was blocked with bluffs and boulders. Cattle had to be driven across and up a mountain and along a ridge, to get them out.

Two groups would station themselves on each side of the river. Vaqueros would all rush them across. The two groups stationed on the other side would keep the cattle from going up or down the river. The entire group of riders would rush them up the mountain until they were far enough to be held there. Then the riders would go back for another bunch.

When the road was built from the mouth of the canyon up Kern River by convicts, the ranchers were saved from all this labor, for they could use the road.

In dry years, the ranchers would be compelled to drive their cattle out of the mountains into the valley, where they could rent stubblefields to run them through the winter. It was always a problem of survival for the ranchers. Year in and year out, the rancher moved his cattle from the mountains to the valley and from the valley to the mountains, in rain, sleet, snow or summer heat.

When there were no men available to help, the wives would mount a horse and help. Often they were more efficient than men. When there were no fences, it meant riding herd day and night to keep the cattle from straying.

In bad years, when cattle were starving, the government men shot them, then paid the owners. The cattlemen would not have survived if there had not been meadows in the high Sierras, where they could run their stock, with a permit and where they could be fattened on the lush grass.

Loading cattle
aboard ship

FALLING HORSES

There have been many incidents of a horse falling and leaving his rider to die on the plains. Sometimes a horse would fall, gain his feet and run off before the stunned vaquero could recover enough to grab the reins and prevent the horse from leaving him afoot. Also, a man's foot might hang in the stirrups and he would be dragged to death, as was Tommy Newcomb and others who met the same fate.

No sailor left adrift in an open boat in mid-ocean, would be in worse condition than a vaquero left afoot. Wild cattle would attack him and the only way to save himself was to lie motionless on the ground. The cattle would approach and smell him. If he lay perfectly still, as if he were dead, the cattle would go away in time and leave him to make his way as best he could to some ranch house or water course. (He could follow a stream to get help). Sometimes the vaquero managed to reach a ranch, but more often than not, his bones were found bleaching in the sun, months or years afterwards.

One day Juan Gomez, who had only one leg, was riding on the plains near the sinks of Tejon, when his horse fell. It recovered its feet and ran away before Juan could prevent it. When Juan did not show up at the vaquero camp that night, the men saddled up and rode out to find him. The Tejon covered eighty miles of territory and at that time it took in the land where the towns of Arvin and Weedpatch now stand.

The men were not successful until mid-morning, when they saw smoke rising out on the plains. Juan had gathered grass and weeds and with his knife had cleared a space and set fire to the grass. The weeds being green, had made a thick smoke which was seen by the riders who immediately converged on it and found Juan, sitting there, waiting. He had cleared enough space with his knife so there was no danger of starting a grass fire, the dread of all vaqueros.

To fight a fire, the vaquero must dismount, take a wet burlap sack and beat out the flames. It entails much walking in tight, high-heeled boots before the average grass fire is extinguished.

BANDITS

The name of the guerrilla fighter Murrieta (called a bandit in California), is an old Basque surname and has been called "Murrieta" for centuries. The first Murrieta in Northern New Spain was one of the sixty Basque soldiers of Martinez De Ituralde, who came to Sonora to conquer the Yaquis.

Basque genes, (Basques being an ancient pure race), are dominant to Indian genes. In Sonora, today, are found many fair people who descend from Ituralde's soldiers. It is easily in the realm of probability that Murrieta was of fair complexion, for many descendents of his family are fair-skinned people, to this day.

The stories of Murrieta's exploits and of his audacity, do not accord with the accounts of Love's, who claimed to have awed a hundred men by himself.

A man who beat his wife and ran from a ranch hand, (Iverson), could not have captured any of the men who had followed Murrieta. Men who had shot their way out of many desperate situations.

The men he shot down in cold blood in San Gabriel, were unarmed laborers. Because a man who has guts, has guts when he is a boy, when he is in the prime of life and when he is a feeble old man.

Love's ignominious behavior at San Jose, when he didn't even have the nerve to shoot a man in the back, proves very conclusively that all those heroic tales of his exploits are not true.

England had many outlaws and cut off arms and legs of all men caught stealing. When the authorities tired of seeing so many maimed criminals walking the streets, begging for food, they decided to transport them to America, where they could trade them for tobacco and thus get rid of them and make a profit.

The result was that the sweepings of Newgate and Bridewell prisons were brought to America. Each convict was worth a certain quantity of tobacco, which brought a good price in England.

England got rid of its criminals, but flooded America with thieves and murderers. They were the criminal element that drifted across the Cumberland Gap and into the free lands of the border states. In Texas, when they arrived, they stole every horse they could get.

Ironically, horse stealing, which was the first act the hungry gringos engaged in when they came to California, began to be frowned upon. There are histories replete with tales of vigilantes lynching horse thieves during a season of righteousness.

OLD MEN

In telling their tales of long ago, the old men mangled their dates, as is natural for the very old, when recalling fifty or seventy strenuous years. In the main, however, the recountals were scrupulously correct in delineating the methods, equipment, and lore of the vaquero. One cannot question the minute accuracies of the tales. They worked no injustices on what can easily be called a fine art.

To sum up, if these narrations of events as the old men told them never happened; if they did not, then others exactly like them did. The story of the vaquero is not history, nor is it fiction. It is better than either; it is the lore of the people.

Hunger, privation and sudden death were commonplace to those men who possessed the greatest skill on horseback ever developed on this continent.

Buried in the canyons of the Sierras are many old men who found a spring or a creek to water their animals. They came to settle on the wild lands and for many years developed their skills in the constant struggle to preserve their limbs intact in the handling of bronco horses and wild cattle. Men unknown and unsung, who did their best and in the end sank into an unmarked grave. The few who existed in the "teens" of this century had retired to muse on their experiences with a melancholy wistfulness.

Few of them ever recounted their personal adventures. They kept no diary, for they couldn't write. As a result, there are few dates given, as the old men relied on their memories when referring to events which had happened many years before.

My hope is to reconstruct the mood and spirit of those unsung men, the vaquero and the buckeroo. The belief in their culture was more important than the culture itself and my effort is to shed a light on their lives as completely as possible. "The truest histories are not always those that have really come to pass."

THE ORIGINAL COWBOY

As we have said, the Black who was brought to America and became the first cowboy was a cattleman in his native habitat. The Black of Africa held his cattle so important that the handling and tending of cattle was not allowed to the woman, only men handled cattle. When a boy had served his apprenticeship herding, he could step up into the rank of warrior. Cattle were thought so valuable, that their yield of milk or beef was inconsequential.

A man's wealth was counted in cattle. These people knew something of selective breeding. So important was this culture, that a man could describe an individual cow out of thousands and know if one were missing. Earmarks and dewlaps were used as marks of ownership. They had an extensive vocabulary of cattle terms and colors.

Some of the steers were broken to ride, others trained to race, still others were taught to charge the enemy in battle. So precious was the milk curds on which they subsisted, that it was never offered to strangers. Women were never allowed into cattle corrals. The herds were sometimes so large that they were divided into small groups and let out to different people. Some of the African Chiefs' greatest pleasures was to have his herds driven past for hours at a time. In fact, the African measured his wealth by the number of his cows, as the Red man in America measured his by the size of his herd of horses.

Jesse Stahl

Jesse Stahl

MULES

The Lord in his wisdom has provided the mule with a mouth of iron, so that when in danger he can ignore the trembling creature on his back and go his way to keep his feet no matter how the frantic rider pulls and tugs on the bit.

Riding a mule in the mountains is never joyful, but only a mule is capable of crossing over steep trails on which a horse would fall and break his neck. If managing a mule could cause the saintliest man to swear, the terrain of the Sierra in which we rode was so bad that it gave the mule the disposition for which he is famous or infamous.

Most of those we rode had first served as pack animals and had acquired the fearful habit of walking on the edge of the trail to avoid bumping their packs against the walls. This however, caused their rider to ride suspended over a precipice. The mules had learned that if they bumped their packs against the walls of the trail it would throw them off balance. Once thrown off balance, they would fall and if they did not go over the cliff, they would ever after lean away from the side of the trail and for that reason, when they were ridden by a man, they walked as if they were leaning outward.

Waiting Patiently

Yoked mules in Spain

HORSES

Horses were rarely or never hitched to a plow in Medieval Spain or Portugal. The horse enjoyed a privileged position, compared to that of the gentleman who rode him and whose grave he afterwards shared.

The idea of placing the horse in such a menial position as pulling a plow, was abhorrent to the nobleman. Plows were pulled by oxen or cows. There is a breed of big red cattle that are bred primarily for work on the farm. The vaquero rides a horse it has taken years to train. His reins held high, his eyes on the horizon. Men have ridden camels, elephants, buffalo, oxen, but on horseback only can a man be a caballero. He is an expert with hands of silk, that no teaching and all the practice in the world could not supply. "For what nature does not give, Salamanca cannot supply."

Horses ridden by such vaqueros as Juan Olivera, Emiliano Cordova, Don Victor Ortega, Teodoro Valenzuela, were distinct in themselves, faultlessly reined, yet each had their peculiarity of movement.

The development of any horse's schooling and learning follows a definite pattern which is based on the animal's conformation, temperament and sensitivity. To find this pattern is the rider's first step in training a horse, the sum total of the horse's character. His traits of character must be recognized and utilized to best advantage.

One vaquero can recognize in the horse the man who trained him.

I have often heard Adolfo Encinas say of the horse he was riding, "Este Caballo lo amanso Luis Zamora," (This horse was trained by Luis Zamora), without knowing who had trained the horse. He could recognize by the horses actions the hand of a master. The response of the animal to the rider's signals told the entire story.

Oxen and wooden plow in Spain

A VOICE IN THE WILDERNESS

It is thirty years now that I have been a "Voice Crying in the Wilderness." I have been protesting people riding "rimmy" saddles that cause horses to ring their tails; the teaching of innocent little children brutality by hitting horses over the head and to jerk on the reins so that the horse, in his own defense, travels with his jaws set, his head turned to one side, waiting for the jerk. The teaching of children that the only end of riding is winning a ribbon.

Children should not be put on saddles with sloping cantles, because they are made only for men who rope calves and must dismount quickly. I have advised the teaching of basic dressage, so that a child can stay on the horse's back, without throwing him off his center of gravity. I advise the mastery of horsemanship important and the winning of a ribbon incidental.

The child should be taught the functions of the bit, so that he can use it without hurting the horse, but attaining the result he seeks. The child should know the parts of the horse, its mouth especially; the importance of knowing when the teeth need attention, when the bit needs adjusting and the right bit to use.

BUCKING ROLLS

Years ago the saddles used on the ranches were mostly slick fork Visalia. About 1910, when the swelled forks began to appear on the ranches, the "old timers" would have nothing to do with them. They clove to the old slick fork.

The riders who changed over to the swell fork were usually young men who believed the wide fork helped them to stay on a horse; even if the older men said that the wide fork "beat a man to death" when a horse bucked.

Some of the young men, who could not afford a new saddle, solved their problem by attaching bucking rolls to their saddles. These were stuffed pads shaped like a pyramid, attached to the fork. By pressing his knees under and against them, the rider had much firmer seat on a bucking horse. but if a man were bucked out from behind them, he was almost sure to be thrown.

Nacho Montes owned a little bay horse that weighed less than seven-hundred pounds. Although not much more than a pony, he already had a reputation as a bucking horse. Augustine Hinio was riding him at Rose Station one day, when the little horse, which always traveled with his little ears laid back, lit into bucking. Augustine was a good rider, but the pony must have caught him unawares, bucked and sat him on top of the rolls. Augustine reached down and grasped the fork under the horn and weathered the storm.

Finally, the little horse stopped, out of breath and Augustine got back behind the bucking rolls, just as the crew arrived in time to enjoy the show, which made them laugh uproariously.

Jesse Stahl

Jesse Stahl

Snaffle Bits

BRIDLE BITS

My education in the history and use of the bridle bit began over sixty years ago, when I went to live with Don Leonardo Ruiz in Soledad Canyon. Whenever I rode the old buckskin or grullo he owned, I used an old bridle which hung in the blacksmith shop and which had not cost more than a dollar and a half. It served the purpose, for the old mustangs would have performed very well without a bridle, since one was thirty and the other was twenty-five years old.

I was perfectly satisfied with the equipment because I had yet to meet the fastidious vaquero and buckeroo, with his discriminating tastes in bits and spurs. Such men as those rode on the Tejon and Land Company ranches. I met them in later years after I had left the old man's ranch to shift for myself in the San Joaquin Valley. The old man gave me a saddle and a hip-shot, humped-backed mare. When she was saddled and ready to go, he led the way into the attic and after rummaging in an old trunk, he dug out two old silver-mounted bits and gave them to me.

They had been made by Madueno in Ventura and were keepsakes from the time when the Ruiz family had owned herds of cattle and horses and many acres of land. I did not know then how valuable bits made by Madueno were to become in the future. Fifty years later I was to see a Madueno bit sell for hundreds of dollars.

I got my first inkling of how much men valued the Madueno on the day I arrived at the Tejon Ranch, and unsaddled my horse. After I had put my saddle and bits in the tack room, Nacho Montes picked up the bits and looked them over, one was a spade and the other half breed. He held up the spade and said, "Te doy cinco pesos por este freno" (I will give you five dollars for this bit). Five dollars! Men worked for a week for five dollars in those days. I put out my hand and Nacho put a five-dollar goldpiece in it.

Excepting for the old men who would and could take a little time to give a touch of artistry to their work, the general run of bits were commonplace. That is to say, because all horses were broken in the same way, with a hackamore and a double reins, herding cattle, the same bit would work on one horse as well as on another of the vaquero's string. After being ridden by different men over a period of time, the horses naturally would be more or less hard-mouthed. Since they had all been broken to work on cattle, without the guidance of their rider, the bit did not have the importance the present day horse-show riders give it.

The old vaqueros as a rule owned but one bit and used it on all the horses in their string. (Excepting colts of course).

I remember the first bit I ordered from G.S. Garcia. It was a Las Cruces with three-inch conchas, engraved with a replica of the California State flag. I was the proudest kid in Kern County.

Old Toribio Cordova used a silver overlaid S shank. Don Antonio Levia used a Madueno spade. Years afterward, I encountered Don Antonio's bit in the collection of Rod Kelly, a horse trainer in the Sacramento area. Cheno (Nepomuseno Cordero) used a converted U.S. Calvary bit and so did Sutah Coway. Nacho Rodriquez used a ring bit and Louie Zamora, a spade bit, when he rode one of the older horses. Most of the time, however, he rode colts with a hackamore.

Adolfo Encinas used both half breed and spade. Eduardo Valdez was the most particular of all about his bits. They were made to order by A. B. Hunt. Oddly enough, though Eduardo trained and rode the best horses on the Tejon Ranch, he was the poorest roper there. He could ride into a corral and throw a loop all day and not rope a calf!

Bit makers of Magdalena, Sonora, Mexico.
Juan, Eduardo and Eduardo Jr.

During the "fifties" of this century, most towns had rodeos, with rodeo fans. They knew nothing of horse shows, which belonged in the East. It was after some effort that horse shows were established. Then the demand for bits began.

At first the show riders started to use the type of bits that were used by cattlemen and vaqueros. Unfortunately, they would not work, for the horsemanship of a horse show and that of a vaquero, were worlds apart. Even though they chewed tobacco, and wore "western" clothes, the show riders lacked the most important quality of the range rider of whatever race, "respect for his horse."

It was not until I had left the ranch and established a training stable on the outskirts of Bakersfield and had gone into the business of breaking horses for other people, that I began to learn about bits. The horses I rode, were not taught to work cattle and as a result they were pulled much more than they would be on a ranch. The result was sore, lacerated mouths which became a problem, a problem never found among horses on a ranch.

So thus began my search for bits to use on horses which I broke, for the person who rode them was by no means a vaquero. He or she was a novice, who rode on ''trail rides'' and in horse shows.

I was not long in the stable business before I learned that riding after cattle on a ranch was not even remotely similar to riding done by amateur pleasure riders. It was another ''breed of cats.'' Even though the ''trail rider'' and horse show rider wore ''Western'' clothes and used ''Western'' saddles and equipment, the problem was to fit the rider's hand and skill in handling the reins, to the bit.

At first it was hopeless. The riders, for whom I broke horses, had not ridden enough to develop the muscle which gives balance and could not be expected to ride like a vaquero, most of whom had ridden since childhood.

It took some time for this knowledge to sink in, but after a season of stress, I gave up the idea of the Vaquero way of riding — that is to keep the horse light. I found it better to teach the horse to bear a little on the bit, so the rider could ride enough on his reins to stay on the horse's back. The same thing occurs on a polo horse, when a poor rider plays. This idea brought a small degree of success. The problem was where to find a bit, because the bits used by vaqueros would not do.

I traveled to Mexico where I found a number of good craftsmen who still made bits. As a matter of fact, in each town of any consequence in those days, I found a bit maker who made bits for the local trade. For ten winters I went to Mexico and had bits made by one or another of those artisans. I would design a bit, then have a number made. I would bring them to California, and distribute them among the trainees.

At first they would be very successful, but by the end of the year, the bits were discarded. The next trip I would design another, only to have the same thing happen again.

The first bit maker I found was Eduardo Grijalva in Magdalena, Sonora. He had just come into town from an outlying ranch and set up a repair shop. His prospects were poor, when he ran out of guns and odd things to repair. He had made and repaired a bit or two on the ranch and was very handy with tools. I set him to making bits for me. His first bits were a little crude, but in time, by trial and error, he became quite an expert. One day I came upon an antique bit with a swivel mouthpiece. I brought it to Eduardo, who copied it. For a number of years that bit was quite popular until it was condemned by the judges.

In dealing with the people who used it, I came to the conclusion that the reason the bit was no longer effective and discarded, was that the perpetual pulling on the horse's mouth, hardened and killed the feeling in the mouth and as a result, made the bit useless.

In Hermosillo, I found an old bit maker, Ortiz by name, who made beautiful bits, but the tragedy was, he made only two bits for me and would make no more. He said he was too old. The two spade bits he made for me were the best spades I have ever owned.

One of them I gave to Nancy Williams, of Calexico, who was my pupil. She used it on a Palomino she showed very successfully. When she grew up and married, she kept the bit in the tack room of the feed lot her husband managed in Arizona. One morning the bit was missing! The thief had cut off the headstall and reins, and left every other bit in the room untouched. It seems that the only thing of value to him was the spade bit.

My next bit maker was Ibarra in Navojoa, Sonora. Navojoa is in mule country. The vaqueros there prefer a mule for a saddle animal. Ibarra made a spade with shanks that curved back, but since the mules are small, the bits he made were four inches wide. I had to take the bits to Eduardo to have them copied. The only man who could use the little bits was Jeff Wonnell, now living in Arroyo Grande. He still had the little bits and uses them on small-mouthed Arabs.

In speaking of mouths, while studying the Andalusian horses in Spain, I was surprised to find that the big Andalusian, the war horse, used a narrow bit, never more than four and one-half inches wide. I have brought the bits from Spain made for Andalusians and found that they were most often too narrow for Arabs or Welsh ponies.

In Guadalajara, the city in which the Charro had developed the most, I found several bit makers. They all had to be taught about the bit used in California, because their horse culture differs from that farther north. As a matter of fact, there are four cultures in Mexico, each differing one from the other. However, Panchito Munos was a skilled workman and he adapted himself to making fine bits. Those he made for me are still in service. Alice, the wife of Richard Smith, has one which she uses at the present time.

One day Grant Iverson told me about a box of antique bits that were being sold by Victor Leather Company. When I saw what the box contained, I was surprised to find Chilean bits, Argentine bits, Peruvian bits. All that morning I sorted out bits that I thought could be copied and used on a "Western" horse. Each of the bits had "Made in England" stamped on the mouthpiece, even the one that had a Spanish name stamped on the cheek. Some of the copies were used very successfully, especially on Arabs. Loren Vogt still has copies made of one. He tells me he has sold many of them.

In time all of the antique bits were sold by the Victor Leather Co. The last of them went to Clarence Chown at Rawhide College.

On my visits to Spain in talking to the dressage trainers there, I learned that whenever a rider needs a bit, he measures the horse's neck to decide the leverage he needs. He puts a bit on the horse and the leverage is so perfect that the horse cannot lift or lower his head, it will stay in one position. I watched the bullfighters on horseback (rejoneadores) put a horse through the entire Haute Ecole pattern levade, Capriole, etc. and then fight a bull on the horse without the horse ever opening his mouth, or ever "blowing up."

I bought several bits with the mouthpiece tapered from the shanks to the center. They had an inch-high sapo port, a bit which would be called "mild." But while the mouthpiece on all the bits was alike, there were about five different lengths of shank, from the very severe, to the comparatively mild.

I took an old cavalry S shank bit to Rafael Lopez and had him use the tapered Spanish mouthpiece in it. This bit has been the most popular of any I have designed.

ETIQUETTE

We were talking about the old days and Howard Rogers said, "I learned my ranch etiquette from old California men when I was a kid on the Irvine Ranch. From such men as Cleve Helm, who taught Jimmy Williams, Bill Goodwin, Len Thrall, George Studley, Ray Moreno and Juan Fuentes who trained polo ponies for Captain McKittrick."

I have found that the men who can do the most with horses are those who treat them with kindness. Never touch another man's horse nor his equipment, his saddle, nor his bridle.

Treat your horse with respect for his feelings and feed your horse before you feed yourself.

When going through a gate, never ride off and leave the man who opened it, afoot. Always wait until the man has mounted. Always leave a gate as you found it. If it is closed, close it again. If it is open, leave it open.

It is always good policy and thoughtful of a horse's comfort to loosen the cinch, lift the back of the saddle, so the air can circulate between the saddle blankets and the horse's back.

I worked for years on Santa Rosa Island. After I left there, I rode races with Jimmie Williams, who became a leading jumping horse trainer.

Horse Week in Jerez de La Frontera, Spain

THE SPANISH HORSE

After the Spaniards had developed their riding style, princes, knights, courtiers wanted to learn more of the haute ecole. As a result, the Spaniards, then ruling Naples, founded a school of equitation, called "La Maddelena" and it was in that province that the Haute Ecole, found to this day in Vienna, had its birth.

The fame of the Andalusian horse and the expertise of the Spaniards and Portuguese had reached all of Europe. Many foreigners eager to learn horsemanship, traveled to Naples and enrolled in the school set up to teach dressage, also to learn the art of fighting on horseback. Men went there to buy a horse of that noble breed to make a present of him to some reigning prince. In those days a stallion was the most appropriate gift one could offer in the courts of Europe.

There were men who were accepted as teachers of Haute Ecole with the idea of using them as instructors in the royal courts.

In 1580, the Archduke Charles, son of Emperor Ferdinand, undertook to create a new breed of horse of elegance. With this plan in mind, he selected a high plain in the Alps. Here he established a breeding farm. He sent his buyer Hannus Von Khevenviller with 5,726 guldens to Spain to buy the best horses. He bought thirty-three mares and stallions.

Hannus Von Khevenviller made two trips to Spain, in 1582 and 1584. These men were the founders of the Lippizaner breed of horse,

Dressage training in Cordova, Spain.

which exists to this day.

The French horsemen also journeyed to Naples to learn dressage of the Spanish School and enthusiastically translated the books on equitation into French. Francis the First would mount no horse for war or peace, other than his one-eyed black Andalusian. Oddly enough, the terminology of Haute Ecole used the world over, the piaffe, levade, passage, capriole, etc. is French.

The most famous horseman in France was Pluvinel, who was also an excellent writer on equitation. He stayed seven years in Naples to learn horsemanship.

In time the rage for racing put the Spanish horse in the background in France, his popularity declined. The last royal person to ride an Andalusian was Eugerlia De Monito, the wife of Napoleon III, but she was a Spanish princess.

After the French Revolution, there were no horses used in sports or pleasure, although Napoleon the First plundered Spain of its horses during the occupation of that country.

Testing fighting cows - Spain

Lippizaner

Andalusians in Spain

Antique saddles and bridles - Santa Paula

Bit Display at "The Mill" - Santa Paula

Spur display by Jim Layne - Santa Paula

OLD SPURS,
OLD BITS, OLD SADDLES

It all started with Lou Hengehold at "The Mill" in Santa Paula. I had known him years ago in Bakersfield and had stopped at his store to say "Hello" when I saw the saddle. It was a full stamped, slick fork, "Visalia" and it had been so well preserved that it still had the original stirrup leathers with the peculiar twist found on all old saddles of that make. Someone had taken loving care of it and no part had been changed. I breathed a "Thank you" to the man who had owned it, for I have seen so many of these fine old saddles ruined by fools who tried to "modernize" them by cutting down the cantles and changing the rigging and the stirrup leathers.

I already owned Eduardo Valdez's old Visalia, but I couldn't resist wanting this one. Lou had gotten it as a "trade-in" from a girl who wanted a modern one. Her grandfather had owned it. Lou let me have it for an old Visalia catalog. These catalogs have become scarce, and are "collectors' items." Illustrators use them for reference in their art work, which makes them valuable and much sought after, so Lou did not make such a bad trade after all.

As we stood there and lamented the passing of the old days in which these old saddles played so important a part, it suddenly occurred to me that an exhibit of old equipment might be of interest to a good many people. There were many collecting bits, spurs and pictures of the Old West. Why not saddles? Not only Visalias, but

Tony Araujo and Lou Hengehold, owner of "The Mill" in Santa Paula. Tony was cattle boss on the Tejon and is the last old time vaquero, he is 92 years old.

Author and Ernie Morris viewing bit display - Santa Paula

Porters, Hamleys, Wilsons, Morenos, Brydons, Garcias, Cuens.

I suggested to Lou that since he had the storage space and a number of old saddles, which combined with mine, they could serve as a nucleus for an exhibition in his store. "Yes," he said, "we could have it in conjunction with the yearly celebration here in Santa Paula." I said, "And we can invite the bit and spur collectors to bring their treasures."

Lou had a friend, Sheridan Wright, who was an expert on leather. In his spare time, he went to work on the saddles and got them into fine shape. We invited to our exhibit only those who could recognize quality and workmanship in silver mounted bits and spurs, and who added only the finest made articles to the collection. Such men as Jim Layne of Santa Barbara who collects Madueno bits and owns the finest collection of silver mounted spurs extant.

Bill Clark, who has many pictures of the West, Mrs. Catherine Haley of Ojai, who had a fortune in Ed Boeins, Stan Ruano of

Stan, Judy and author at Santa Paula

Fontana, who makes silver mounted bits, Ernie Morris of Templeton, the artist who brought his matchless paintings of vaqueros, together with reins, riatas and hair ropes, which he makes. Jim Gerber of Bakersfield, who brought many bits, spurs and artifacts, Dave Klesper of Rialto, bit maker, brought his work to display. Harold Daulton, manager of Rancheros Visitadores, brought a fortune in pricelss silver mounted parade saddles. Tom Ryder came from Silva's Saddlery in Sacramento with a fine display and Harry Connelly, who

Stan Ruano, Tom Ryder and Ernie Morris

runs cattle on Henry Miller's home ranch, "The Bloomfield," near Gilroy, came all the way to see the displays.

Every old-timer in Ventura, Santa Barbara area, who owned an old silver mounted bit or a pair of spurs, a riata, a pair of reins, brought them for the spectators to admire. Tony Araujo, cattle boss on Tejon Ranch and the one surviving old-time vaquero, was there from Bakersfield. He has never missed an exhibition.

Tommy Condley, who rode with me the last year (1927) that Miller and Lux was in existence as a cattle outfit, was there to reminisce of the old days. The Yanez brothers, good vaqueros of the area, Joe, Fred and Ray, came to see and admire.

There were two-hundred saddles, and at least five-hundred bits. The attendance has doubled every year and bids fair to become one of the major attractions in its category. Indeed our exhibition of old saddles and spurs was a huge success.

Stan Ruano in one of his pensive moods.

Skin of last Grizzly killed in Piru area

Stan, Arnold, Sue and Dan at "The Mill"

Sue, Florence and Judy

Antique saddles - Santa Paula

Jim Gerber on right with his display of silver-mounted bits.

Bit and spur display - Santa Paula

MISSION SAN CARLOS

The mission buildings which survived were roofless. The campo santo was weed grown, the Indian huts were mounds of adobe, sun warped and rain sodden in disrepair for years past. The shops where carpenters, blacksmiths, masons, weavers, shoemakers and tailors had worked when the Franciscans had taught, were no more. Their sites could barely be made out where the sage brush and brick wheat had grown among the ruins. The church itself was roofless and its wall half washed away. Bushes grew out of the cracks in the walls. The gardens and field were brush choked and the orchards were dead. The Indians in dogged hopelessness in a pitiless world had wandered away to starve in the hills or to be shot down by the whites, there to die in a prayerless, priestless vastness of an empty wilderness.

San Fernando Mission

Kino's Mission Tuluitama in Sonora, Mexico. Padre Garces' remains were found here after the disaster at Yuma.

OLD CALIFORNIA

The old man sat on a park bench, watching the girls go by. When an especially well shaped one passed, he would follow her with his eyes until she was out of sight.

A young man sitting on another bench across from him seeing the gleam in the old man's eyes, turned to his companion and said, "Las tardes son mas frescas que las mananas," (The evenings are cooler than the mornings), which means there is no fool like an old fool.

It is easy enough to criticize when one is young but it is nevertheless tragic for an old man who has survived not only his own times but the ideals of it, for there can be no loneliness like that of a man who has outlived his time.

Before the Gringos came, the governors of California often lamented that they could not accede to the pleas of their ijados and ijadas, (godsons and goddaughters) and their comadres and compadres, (sponsors for their children) as a good padrino (godfather) should.

They all wanted something. The women were as avaricious as the men. The godfathers and godsons wanted grants of land and the goddaughters wanted grants of land for their husbands to be. Yet, the owners of grants were all compadres or primos (cousins), to the governor. It was a matter of great pride for a man to be known as a god padrino, for in the event of a man's death, the compadre was ready to take the children to raise as his own. Actually, however, the padrino vowed to see that the babies (his ijado) followed in the path of Christianity, but most padrinos took the orphans into their homes. This practice was so established in California that before the coming of the Gringos, there were no orphanages here. There was no need for them.

Baja California Vaquero
He is covered with heavy leather against cactus and thorns.

Ruins of Pete Bergian's service station

FRENCH PETE'S

Pete Bergien was on San Emideo in 1919. We called him French Pete for he was a Canuck. He was very strong and one day attempted to hold a steer from on horseback with his hands without taking the turns around the horn. Of course, the steer pulled him out of the saddle and got away with his rope.

Pete took up a homestead near San Emideo's Salt Creek and when approached by the company to sell, he refused. He kept his homestead and set up a service station calling it "Mirage Service Station." Besides gasoline, he sold a little moonshine.

Finally, Pete disappeared from Kern County, but he left a monument. The walls of the service station having been made of cement are still standing along Highway 99, near the town of Mettler. Someone has painted the words "God is Love" on the walls.

Don Leonardo Ruiz

DON LEONARDO RUIZ

Along an abandoned road leading to the high desert, there is an old cemetery in the San Francisquito Canyon. On a hillside and across the arroyo, there is a grave far from all the others. The monument stands alone under a gnarled old oak.

On the monument is a picture of a bearded fine featured man smiling down on the old road. It is a kindly smile for he was of the old gentle race that once lived in California. May he rest in peace here in his last retreat, for his lifetime had been a succession of giving up his lands to cheating lawyers and going into the hinterlands.

His last ranch had been ruined by the water of a dam which broke and left the ranch covered with sand and killed his brothers.

THE YAQUIS

Back in the time of the Jesuits in New Spain, when Martinez De Ituralde began his conquest of the Yaqui Indians, a storm arose after the Jesuits destroyed an Indian Idol.

Martinez De Ituralde was the son of a Spanish nobleman and an Aztec "Princess." There still exists a family of Ituralde in Sonora. Oddly enough, while in California, the law of the Indies was in force. When Ituralde made peace with the Mayos and Yaquis, he made them presents of horses and saw to it that the Padres were careful to baptize their Indian prisoners before he hanged them, a very correct man, Ituralde.

It was by giving dresses to the women that the Spaniards made peace with the Indians. The women so wanted to adorn themselves, that they traded all their food for cotton cloth.

Before hanging the Indian Cacique, the Spaniards prepared his soul for entering into Heaven; by hanging him, they removed a barrier to the teaching of salvation. Shades of Torquemada!

It was in these mountains, the Spaniards met stone arrowheads, instead of points of burnt wood, often poisoned, which they had encountered so far.

In 1616 came the great uprising of the tribesmen throughout the Sierra, which caused much bloodshed and took many months of fighting to subdue.

It was the Pima Indians who accompanied Cabeza De Vaca and 80 years later, helped Ituralde with his conquests and two centuries later, fought on the side of Porfirio Diaz.

Diaz, Bojorques, Ibarra, are old names in that land. Descendants of these people are still found in California and in the area of Alamos, Sonora.

Several times in the history of the conquest, there have been women who aided the Spaniards. Marina, who helped Cortez and Louisa, who helped Ituralde.

One Cacique had renounced all but one of his wives. "But one day, while at another rancheria," says Padre Rivas, "he was disturbed by the Devil and took another man's wife." Later, he repented and scourged himself.

The Spaniards considered the Yaquis to be the most valiant, most belligerent and most independent of the Indians they met in the New World.

Nuno De Guzman, a killer of Indians, claimed them to be the fiercest of all the Indian Nations. Martinez De Ituralde said he had never found another Indian with the courage of the Yaqui.

The men who did the healing in the Plains Tribes were medicine men, but among the Hispanic Indians, they were Hechiceros, (Witch Doctors). They violently opposed the Jesuits, who believed them possessed of the Devil. Naturally, the native witch doctors were opposed to the priests, because they destroyed their influence over their people. "The forces of the Devil in the form of Hechiceros were always attempting to impede the progress of Christianity," so said the Padres.

The first Jesuits of New Spain were told by the Indians of a legend which report of their coming from the Far North, where the nights were two weeks long and where they had been dispossessed of their lands.

In Deboropa lived a bedeviled old Indian, who never attended church and held drunken brawls with a number of companions. It was he who killed Padre Tapia.

The Spaniards made armor for their horses, using a thickness of two bullhides, which arrows could not penetrate. The danger lay in an Indian throwing himself under the horse and stabbing him in the belly. A soldier heavily armored was lost if he ever fell from his horse.

The Captain, Martinez De Ituralde, impressed the Indians with his piety. They marveled at so courageous a man, kneeling humbly in prayer. He always said, "I learned from experience it is unwise to show fear (especially among Indians)."

TULE FOG

It was back in 1920 when Charles Smith, the cattle inspector, took me out to the 3C Ranch, (Carmel Cattle Co.) on the west side of the valley. Charlie was concerned because some cattle bearing the 3C had been stolen and the 3C brand had been converted into a B O Bar. The ranch was selling its cattle and I had been hired to go with each bunch that was bought and to see that they were vented.

Whoever had stolen the cattle and altered the brands, had done a very poor job. Anyone could see the old brand 3C even after it had been altered.

One day a man from Taft bought a bunch of cows and brought his wife and an old vaquero, Nacho Herman, to drive them. The man's wife, a very pretty girl, had a brown, part Arab colt, which she was riding with an English saddle.

It was very cold and a pea soup tule fog made visibility almost nil, when we left that morning. The Arab colt bucked for a long time with the pretty woman, but she rode him with a rein in each hand. When the colt quit at last and stood panting, the woman said, "Oh, he is very hard to ride when he does that jumping." She didn't know the horse had been bucking!

Well, to get back to the tule fog, we drove all that day and that night, left the horses and cattle at Lokern and stayed over night in Taft. The next day we finished the drive in Fellows, where we vented the cattle.

Nacho Herman
circa 1920

It was afternoon when I started back to the 3C through a thick fog. After I had ridden an hour across a wide flat, I was completely lost. Since I had been told all my life that a horse can always find his way home, I left the horse to choose his way back. He was a big-footed, hairy-legged buckskin that must have had a strain of work horse in his ancestry.

He was very enduring and had a fast, running walk. All afternoon, he headed into the fog and at dark we crossed a slough and went on. The weather was very cold and I rode standing in my stirrups, peering into the fog ahead. After what seemed an endless agony, the buckskin came to a gate and stopped. I dismounted and opened the gate, passed through, closing it again.

Over to the right was a shack in which a coal oil lamp burned and farther on, was a shed with tie stalls. I rode up to the shack and yelled, "Hello to the house." The door opened and an old man came out. "Is this 3C?" I asked. "No," he answered, "This is Juan Pump, Miller and Lux, put your horse up and stay the rest of the night." (It was two o'clock in the morning.)

I put the horse up and fed him then went into the shack. There was another man who was the vaquero. The old man who came to the door was the pumper. He harnessed and drove the mule which pumped water for the cattle. The vaquero fried some meat and made coffee for me. After I had eaten, they each lent me a quilt and I went to sleep in a straw filled bunk.

The next morning when eating breakfast, I said, "I wonder why that horse didn't take me on to the 3C, since it is a well known fact that a horse will always back track his way home."

"That's easy," the old man answered, "Fat Al Robinson was the buckaroo on the 3C before you went there. He was supposed to ride the range and look for stray cattle; but instead of working, he would come here and play pinochle with me. The horse had been tied up here in the shed and fed since November, so it was only natural that he should come here where he was fed." It was only a short distance to the 3C and I got there before noon, none the worse for having been lost in the fog.

A YOUNG BRONC RIDER

In 1918 Fred Rush, the superintendent of San Emideo Ranch had a son, Teddy, who rode a Shetland pony when he went out riding with the buckeroos. One day, when the boys had been teasing him, he went to the corral and got his pony.

He saddled him and put a strap around his flanks. Teddy then mounted and of course the pony bucked. When he was through, Teddy was still in the saddle. He dismounted, turned to the buckeroos who had been yelling encouragement and said, "All right, you S.O.B.'s, how do you like that?" He was only seven years old.

A year or two ago, I was staying with Jim Vaughn at Vacaville in Northern California. In talking with one of his customers, he told me that he knew a cattleman named Teddy Rush who ran cattle around Suisun Valley. We compared notes and it was the Teddy Rush we had teased when he was a little boy on the San Emidio Ranch. He promised to speak to Teddy, but when I met the man again, he said that Teddy has passed away.

DIA DE SAN JUAN

The Arabs called it Jerid and took it to Spain, where it was called Correr a la Sortija. It was brought to America by the first Conquistadores who played it here and left it as a legacy to all Spanish America.

It is still played in the older, more remote colonial towns in Spanish America. Though it has been forgotten in California, if it was ever played here, it means literally, "Run at the ring." The game is played by a man on horseback riding at a gallop, putting a reed, which he carries in his hand, through a ring hanging from a cross beam. It was El Dia de San Juan in the old town of Alamos, in the state of Sonora, in old Mexico. All the young men of the area had arrived on horseback to participate in the game, for a "rich" American had put up the prize money — twenty-five pesos (two dollars).

A pair of upright poles had been set up on a level spot. A cross piece had been nailed across the top. From the cross piece there hung a number of ribbons, each of a different color and attached to the end of each ribbon was a two inch ring. On a rise of ground were seated a group of the prettiest girls in Alamos. Each girl wore a ribbon in her hair and a sash of the same color around her neck. The ribbons she wore corresponded in color with one hanging from the cross beam.

The riders rode a high horned; steep, cantled saddle on a little horse, for the old Mexican breed had not yet been crossed out.

The first boy to stab a ring was an American, whose parents were vacationing there. He dismounted, and bashfully knelt before the girl with the same colored ribbon as the one on the ring he had speared. She placed the sash over his shoulder and he kissed her hand. He was her escort for the day.

After the last ring had been speared and each boy had walked off with a pretty girl, the game of Correr al Gallo, (run at the rooster), began. I was eager to see this one because it had once been very popular in California. Old men had told me stories about it; of how they had won the prize at some fiesta. Don Jose Acosta, my friend, brought a rooster and buried it up to its neck in the ground. Then a rider would start home a distance away and just before reaching the rooster, lean down and try to grasp its neck. The show was productive of much laughter because two boys fell off and a saddle turned. One horse kicked at the rider and went off bucking. None of the boys were hurt physically, although the crowd jeered them. None even got near the rooster.

At last a boy appeared on an old buckskin gelding which ran a straight line at a slow gallop. The boy had evidently been in training for the event. Be that as it may, he managed to grasp the rooster and ride off with the prize, twenty-five pesos, (two dollars).

CAST THY BREAD . . .

This story was told to me by Manuel, an old Miller and Lux buckaroo, who had spent years riding as a trooper with Pancho Villa during the Mexican revolution. In one of the battles, in which the insurgents were dispersed, he had made his escape to the border and entered the United States.

He worked on the ranches here and one day after I had been absent from Bakersfield for about twenty years, I came back to town and parked on "L" St., the old skid row. I had just stepped out of the car when I saw a man on crutches approaching. As he neared, I recognized him. He was my old companero, Manuel. His face was drawn and haggard and I saw he was a sick man. When I asked what caused his sickness, he answered, "I am sick because I am going to die." "Pues uno tiene que enfermarse para mirir," (and one has to get sick before he can die). It was characteristic of him to speak that way because he was the most unemotional of men I have ever known.

I surmised from his appearance, that he had not been eating regularly, so I invited him to eat with me. After we had found a restaurant that served Carne Asada, (broiled meat), with rice and refried beans, we sat down to dine. The carne (meat), was tender and the beans and rice, which we ate by making a scoop of a flour tortilla, were very satisfying.

Manuel told me this story; "In speaking of death," he began,

"No man can escape his destiny and no man can choose the place where he is to die. Only God can decide that. I will tell you a story of the Revolution. There was a pochi, (A Mexican born in California), who had been mistreated here by a Gringo and had taken revenge, exactly how, I do not know. But whatever the case may have been, he made his escape to Mexico and since his only way of surviving was to join Villa's guerillas, he found himself a soldier of the Revolution.

He was a taciturn man who spoke little and seemed to brood on his past injuries. One day he wrote a letter for me and since his people had originally been from Sonora, the state in which I was born, we became companieros.

He was accepted among the guerrillas because he had defended himself against abuse. Ordinarily, they care little for Pochis. They

Mexican Rancheros
Picture from
"The Scalp Hunters"

knew he would hang as Estevan Cano had been hanged for defending himself against assault. In fact, in time he became a captain. But I am getting ahead of my story.

In those days, there was no sanitation, as there is now, and the conditions under which we campaigned were very primitive. Many of us who were raised under those conditions, succumbed.

In one of the engagements, we captured two Gringos who had been in the opposing army. How they had survived, we never knew.

They were both suffering from dysentery. Soldiers of the opposing army were often shot but when the Gringos were brought before the Colonel, he took one look at them and said, "Don't hurt them, but do not let them escape." He knew he wouldn't have to shoot them, that these men would not last long and since there were no doctors or

The Devil's Highroad
(Camino del Diablo)

medicines they would die soon enough and he could then avoid an international incident. He could wait until disease killed them.

The pochi's name was Horatio and one night he asked me to help him. He wanted to steal his horse out of camp on which one of the Gringos could escape. When I asked why he would help one of the people he hated, for if he gave his horse away, he may never get another, he said, "Well, I was born in California. My parents were of the old Colonial stock and I went to school among the Gringos. In those days there were only a few Mexican families in each town. There were only five in ours. The Gringo teachers were very kind to me and I made friends with two boys who became my chums. They were Harry and Norman, for no matter what kind of people one is thrown into, he will make friends with one or two. We played "hooky" together, sneaked into circuses, swiped loquats and oranges, as kids will until I left school and they went on."

"When I saw this poor devil doomed, if he couldn't get a doctor and the only doctor to be found was across the border in the United

States, I just couldn't let him die! That night we managed to get the horse, mount the gringo on him and head him for the border. I think he made it, for his horse never came back.''

"How about the other Gringo?'' I asked.

"Oh, he was from the wrong state, we let him stay there.''

In those days, remember, to lose your horse was almost sure death, for you were at the mercy of any group of mounted enemies.

Life was cheap and death was often sudden, babies died like flies and the average life expectancy was seventeen years. In that time, before antibiotics, gangrene, exposure, hunger, thirst and bullets took their toll. Even when one had a horse, mule or burro, the chances of surviving were thin indeed, and without a mount on which to escape, so much less as to be almost nil; yet here was a man who would give his horse away!

In all probability, Manuel would have suffered and regretted his act of generosity in giving up his horse, but such was not the case. The next day, one of our patrols, scouring the neighboring ranches, came upon a hacendado driving a band of horses and mules out of the area to save them from the insurgents. The patrol commandeered them and that night drove them into our camp. There were enough horses to mount each man and pack mules to carry our equipment. The bread cast upon the waters had returned.

Tamalera
(Tamale maker)

Serenata
(Serenade)

THAT KID

I always referred to him as "that kid", but when he did something deserving of approbation, I would praise him by saying, "That's my kid. That's my kid." (accent on the my). Nothing I could say gave him greater pleasure. He lived with me for years, and I look back to the pleasure his companionship gave me.

He came to me when it was the time of hunger in America, during those bleak depression years in California; when starving men roamed the 48 states, begging for food at back doors, or pawing through garbage cans. Bread lines stretched for blocks in the great cities.

There were no jobs, so I went to live on an old ranch that had been tenantless for years. At least I would have a place to stay. I repaired the fences and built a shack. I could shoe and break horses. I hoped to find a few to break or shoe.

One morning, a little man, who had the map of Ireland on his face, walked up to me. "I live in that house" he said, pointing to a hill about a mile away, "and I can't pay the rent because I have fourteen kids, and they take all I make. They are going to put me out tomorrow. Can I camp in your pasture?" His statements were not altogether true, because I learned afterwards that he was an alcoholic and spent his money on drink. Besides, he didn't like to work.

"There is a corner of this ranch that is cut off by the Callaway

—417—

Canal, about two acres, which I do not use. You may camp there," I answered. The next day he moved his family on to the land I had indicated. Somewhere, he found two abandoned bus bodies, which he moved to the place. He used one as a kitchen and the other for a bedroom for himself, his wife and the smallest of the children. The rest of the fourteen each had a box half-filled with excelsior in which to sleep.

Anyone who had passed a winter in the San Joaquin Valley will know how cold it gets, but those kids were tough. The family had been camped there for a week, when one morning, a little boy came running up to me, as I was building a corral.

"Someone is shooting in your field," he said. "I told them to get out, but they wouldn't pay any attention to me."

I said, "You stay here, I'll run them off." I jumped on a horse and rode down into the pasture and told them to get out, which they did. I rode back to the shack where the little boy was waiting for me.

His little face was drawn and looked older than mine and his belly stuck out like those in the pictures of the children of India, who have starved to death.

I was riding a colt for the daughter of a dairyman. Her boyfriend drove the delivery truck. Every few days he would come by and leave milk, cream, butter, eggs, whatever he had left over. These items were very welcome, since they cost me nothing. Besides, I had no money. I turned to the little boy and asked his name. "Clyde," he said. I weighed him on a fish scale and he weighed only 26 lbs.

"Will you mind me if I let you stay here with me?" "Sure, I'll mind you" he answered eagerly. "Well," I said, "drink that milk in the bottle." He took it up and emptied it.

I said, "I will pay you fifty cents a month." He stayed with me until he entered high school. Every morning he would go by on his way to school, collect his fifteen cents lunch money and a nickel extra. At that time, one could buy a big candy bar for a nickel. He would come every day after school until the day I bought him a pair of shoes. He went home and the next morning appeared without them. His mother had taken the shoes and given them to his sister!

Winter was setting in and rather than let him sleep in a cardboard box, I told him to ask his mother's permission to stay with me and sleep in the house. I could buy him another pair of shoes and he could visit his mother barefooted and put on his shoes after he was back at the stable.

I had started a stable, and named it "The Bar O," because I had borrowed everything to start it. I asked Dr. Gundry, who boarded a horse with me, what I could do to help the poor, little, undernourished child. Doctor Gundry's heart was as big as himself, for all of his gruffness. He said, "Feed him as well as you can, come down to my office." He gave me a big supply of vitamins to give the boy.

In time, his little belly began to recede as his little chest began to grow. I rigged up a weight on pulleys and put handles on it, where he could exercise every day. I also encouraged him to take tumbling and calisthenics in school.

One day the teachers wanted him to take part in a play, but in order to make him presentable, the teacher gave him a bath. This made him very angry. But every Sunday night afterwards, he would get a tub, fill it with water and scrub himself. He felt he was too big for a woman to bathe him.

It is a great privilege for a man to watch a child grow and develop. I never had to scold him. From the beginning I could never tolerate a "sassy" kid or one who lied. The few times I had to discipline him, I did it by "firing" him. I would say, "All right, you are not going to mind, well, go home and stay and don't darken my door again." He would go home crestfallen. The next morning, on his way to school, he would pass the stable, singing at the top of his voice, "I ain't got no use for women. A true one may never be found." All this to attract my attention. I would call to him, give him his fifteen cents lunch money and his extra nickel. Then I would say, very seriously, "You can come back, but you aren't on the payroll. You can just hang around." That afternoon, he would rake the yard and stay tentatively.

In a day or two, we would forget he had been "fired." One day I "fired" him and when he came back, I said, "You are getting to be a big boy now. I shouldn't have to "fire" you. If I don't have to from now 'til Christmas, I will give you a horse." At that time, one could buy a horse for five dollars. My stable business had improved and I traded horses. One day I sold a horse and got another and a pretty five-year old burro, to boot.

This was about July. About September, he said, "If you will give me that burro, you won't have to give me a horse for Christmas."

"Yes, but you've got a long time to go yet before Christmas, you may be fired. Besides, I don't want you riding a burro. I'll show you what to do with him. Get your saddle, (he had a little saddle I had given him) a light hackamore and a lasso." I saddled the burro.

"Now," I said, "mount him, get a rein in each hand, and squeeze your legs."

The burro stood quietly, while I put a loop around his flanks. But when I pulled the loop up tightly, he let out a bawl, bogged his head, and went off bucking and bawling like a horse. Something I had never seen a burro do before.

The boy was sitting on the bucking burro easily, riding on his balance. From that day on, we used the burro for nothing else, but for the boy to practice riding. The more he bucked, the better he bucked, until no one who tried him other than the boy, could ride him.

One day I brought out an old Tejon vaquero from town to watch the boy ride the burro. After the show was over, he said, "That boy could ride a bucking horse." From then on, whenever anyone brought in a spoiled pony or little horse, "The Kid" rode him.

VARMINTS

The vaqueros with whom I rode in my youth came from many origins and often had interesting backgrounds. The stories about their early life always fascinated me and kept me around the embers of the campfire, when I should have been in my blankets, sleeping. This is a story told me by a vaquero who rode on the great Terrazazas Haciendas in the state of Chihuahua, in old Mexico.

"Rattlers were not the only varmints which menaced us. In dry weather, scorpions and centipedes crawled out of the adobe walls of the houses we lived in. At night, as soon as we blew out the candle, we could hear them on the floor. They sounded like paper rustling. They would scurry into the dark whenever we lit a candle and we never put our feet on the floor in the dark, for fear of being stung.

Here, one never comes in contact with scorpions or centipedes, unless one works in ditches, tunnels, or mines. But in my native town, we lived in adobe houses. Scorpions and centipedes live in the walls of all adobe houses. They were the poisonous variety, much smaller than the kind we find in California, which are not very poisonous. Those in the town where I was born had killed many people, especially children.

There is a story told in a region where the scorpions are very poisonous; there was a cell in the city prison from which no man ever came out alive. After a series of deaths, the reason was discovered – a scorpion was the killer! Once this fact was established, the firing squad was discarded. From then on, men who were condemned to death were locked up in the "Celda Del Alacran," (scorpion cell). The scorpion killer would sting the man while he slept. The poison was so deadly, death was instantaneous and thus was eliminated the wastage of cartridges.

The dusty little adobe town, where I was born, slept in the sun for most of the year, except when a cloudburst in the mountains would bring a crescenta (flood), roaring down the arroyo. The torrent would wash dens of snakes out of the hills and when the water spread over the flat land on which the town was built, it would deposit hundreds of diamond-back joruba, (humpbacked) rattlers. They would infest the houses, sheds and chicken houses.

There would be an epidemic of snake bites among dogs. The snakes would give the inhabitants many frights before the hogs, which roamed the town and acted as scavengers, ate all the snakes.

The only industry of the area was cattle raising, but the herds were small because it took leagues of desert range to support a cow. The people of the town were so poor, that when a couple were married, they were classified into those who would eat every day and those who would eat every other day.

The cattle roaming the desert became very wild, and a vaquero from that desert country was very skillful in outwitting his charges. I wanted to escape this poverty, so I crossed the border into New Mexico. I found work there and was happy, chiefly because New Mexico fascinated me.

Of all Hispanic peoples, those of New Mexico are the most friendly. They are also the most indifferent. They often never bother to learn English. In this respect, they are like the French, who do not try to learn a foreign language. In New Mexico, if one must speak, it must be Spanish or not at all.

When the War came, the recruiting officers soon learned about this quirk of theirs and did not ask too many questions, but signed them up as soldiers. I went to the recruiting office and tried to enlist. I was not asked many questions and soon found myself in the army and before I knew it, I was in Germany. The officers assumed I was native born. After the war, I got citizenship papers and came to California where I went to work for Miller and Lux.''

MECHANIZATION

Mechanization came swiftly to the Tejon Ranch after the Roaring Twenties. When I first worked here, the Ridge Route, (now Route 5), had just been finished. Cars were few and we drove cattle up and down Highway 99. Whenever we met an occasional one, toiling up the grade in low gear, with the radiator boiling, we would ride ahead of it and push the cattle to one side, to let it go by. This did not seem to bother the drivers, because to cross the mountains from Grapevine to Castaic was a day's journey.

As time passed and cars became more numerous, the Model T Ford of Don Jesus Lopez, the manager of The Tejon, gave way to another more modern one and by the early thirties, one or two of the vaqueros owned a car.

Don Toribio Cordova told a story of how Sutah Coway, the Indian roper, got into a car after it started, couldn't get it stopped. The car careened in a circle in a field. Don Toribio took down his riata and was preparing to lasso it when it ran into a ravine and stopped. Later Sutah drove cars and tractors and became an expert mechanic.

Howard Rogers on "Two Grand"

Forsman and Rue, cattlemen.

Terry & Monica Stockton marking ears

Arnold, Jack, Tony & Chucker

Arnold Rojas and Jack Hitchcock
in Reno, Nevada

Chuck Hitchcock
at Grisedale's Branding

MODERN CATTLEMEN

Some twenty-five years ago, I published a list of old time vaqueros and buckeroos who had long since gone out of existence with the big cattle outfits.

However, there are still many cattlemen in the west, though not on the operating scale they were fifty years ago. In one way or another, they have managed to put the cattle business on wheels with trucks and trailers. Nevertheless, they are still a skilled breed of men and women and what is remarkable of late years, many girls and women are riding horses and working ''manfully'' on ranches.

In view of this circumstance, it would be remiss to neglect mentioning some of the modern cattle people of our mountains.

Terry Stockton, Mrs. Jim Gerber,
Tony Araujo, Jim Gerber

Jack Sarret at Grisedale's

They never got too big for Daleen Sarret

Monica Stockton, a good hand, kept busy marking

AFTERWARD

If, as I tell my story, I say little as to my compelling motive, it is only that my reader can easily discern it.

If I make light of the events which occurred, they were still far removed from normal experiences. Yet, that which I saw, and learned, is of profound interest to my readers and gives an insight into the character of the Westerner.

I am convinced that these stories will add to human knowledge in a way which makes it of value not only to people who ride and train horses, but to the student of history as well.

The stories which lie unfolded within these pages are an untold epic of courage, endurance and loyalty. Occasionally there was risk and danger, but mostly, there was hardship which the vaquero suffered, although the vaquero, being young, did not consider it a hard life. Cold, frosty mornings in the San Joaquin, long, hot, stifling days in the desert, driving cattle through cactus forests into the mountains over trails which wound for many miles over the ridges of the Sierras. Long, weary rides when the pain between the shoulder blades became a day long agony. Heat, cold, hunger, thirst, were all in a day's work.

Years after, when the big cattle outfits had gone out of existence, occasionally one would encounter an old saddle which had done service fifty years before and recognize an old friend, for the old saddle brought back memories.

Some of them had been "modernized" by cutting down the cantle and changing the rigging. Common decency compelled one to acquire them, when discovered, in order to save them from what one would look upon as little short of desecration.

The result was that I took it upon myself to save as many of the old "kaks" as I could, so I traded for or bought outright, every one I found that had the original rigging and the Visalia twist in the stirrup leathers.

Perhaps it was the pitiful condition of the old missions which had influenced me to collect old saddles. The old adobes stand, in most cases, forlorn and in ruins, the bountiful orchards are gone. Behind one mission in a weed-grown field, survive five scrawny trees, an apricot, two olives and two figs, of the vast orchards the Padres planted.

The priests long gone, in sorrow and defeat from the scenes of their labors. The gentle Indians who met rape, abuse and genocide are no more. Indians who swarmed around the missions where there were enough neophytes to stand shoulder to shoulder to form a corral around a herd of ten thousand cattle, have faded away. Even the enormous heaps of bones which were left when the great herds of long-horns were slaughtered for their hides, are gone to make fertilizer.

For years the incoming immigrants would cross fields covered with heaps of bones of the cattle which had multiplied in the seventy-seven years since Don Juan Bautista De Anza and Don Gaspar De Portola brought the first cattle to California.

Part IV

OBSERVATIONS

Mesilla Valley — 1905

NOSTALGIA

We were sitting on an old-fashioned porch in Bakersfield. Dusk was falling on the town as we watched the mass of traffic rush by. But without seeing it, we heard only its howl as it rushed up the freeway between rows of trees.

We spoke of many things; for we were no longer drifters, no longer youths to whom the future meant only the next payday, when we were young and able to ride into camp sitting erect in our saddles to hide our exhaustion after a stretch of sixteen hours on horseback. We thought in those long ago days of our youth that we were masters of our fates, that we could build our futures and foresee what would happen. But now we had come to realize that we were infinitely unimportant in the great scheme of things. We had learned that only the present is certain. The rest depends on the Big Boss Upstairs.

We were looking at the present day Bakersfield. But were seeing with a nostalgic eye, the "Old Cowtown" of seventy years ago; when scores of vaqueros and buckeroos swaggered along the streets of the town, for thousands of head of cattle ranged the surrounding plains and mountains. The oilfields on the West side were booming and Bakersfield did not need to take a back seat to any other town for wildness.

Between Bakersfield and Sumner (East Bakersfield) there was an open country. The circus, when it came to town, pitched its

Man on left unknown, man on right is Jim Campas

tents on the corner of 19th and Union Avenue. The Tegeler and the Southern were the best hotels in town and the gourmet restaurant was the French Cafe. One could get a meal there for forty cents.

A man went to a hotel, got a room, took a shower, then pulled the mattress off the bed, set it on the floor, took the fan (each room was supplied with one) set it in the window so that the air would blow over him and lay down on the mattress and tried to sleep through the terrible hot nights with clouds of mosquitoes buzzing over him.

In the late afternoon, the people would come out of their houses and sit on their porches and wait until their houses cooled down enough so that they could go to bed; for the summers then were worse than they are now. The Ridge (99) Route was still in the future. It was a long day's journey to travel from Bakersfield to San Fernando by way of Elizabeth Lake and Bouquet Canyon.

The big cattle ranches were still intact because the farmer could not always get water. It was not until the deep-well turbine pump was invented or developed that the agriculturist came into his own in the southern San Joaquin Valley. There wasn't enough water in the canals for everybody who needed it. The big ranches began to gradually disappear and the land which was used to run cattle was put into cultivation. Even The Sinks of Tejon, where a band of wild horses roamed was planted to cotton.

The vaqueros would ride into town, their horses keeping step to the clink, tap, clink, tap of their spur chains and tapaderas. There were many runaways. The teamsters were in the habit of leaving their teams standing and going into the saloon for a drink. The horses would tire and start home without their driver and before they had gone far, they would be running wildly down the street. Then the vaqueros would give an exhibition of their skill with a riata by roping the runaways.

An oldtimer told me of an experience he once had on a runaway colt on the streets of Bakersfield. He was twelve years old, when one day his father told him to ride into town and get something or other. He had forgotten what. His family owned several horses, among them a gentle colt which the boy and his sister often rode. Eager to go into town, the boy hurried to the barn and picked the first hackamore he found and went out to the pasture and caught the colt. He put on the hackamore and saddled the animal, mounted and headed for town. In town he left the colt at a hitching rack and went into the store and bought the article he had come for.

He left the store, walked out to the horse and mounted. He headed for home down 19th Street. After he had ridden about a block, a dog chasing a cat frightened the colt, which jumped sideways and broke into a run. The boy pulled on the reins. They parted and left him with a piece of hair rope in his hands and no control over the horse which was stampeding madly down 19th. Luckily, two vaqueros were riding into town. They turned into 19th when they saw the colt coming toward them. They separated so that the colt would run between them and took down their reatas, made a loop and waited.

As the colt came abreast they yelled, *"Agarrate, agarrate!"* (grab hold, grab hold). In those days any boy raised on one of the ranches understood some Spanish. He clutched the horn in a death grip and hung on. The vaqueros threw a loop around the colt's neck and racing their horses beside him, gradually brought him to stop without hurting the boy. After they had dismounted and helped him fix his hackamore, the boy rode home, none the worse for his adventure; but ever afterward, whenever he saddled and bridled a horse, he examined carefully the hackamore or bridle before he put it on the horse. For as the saying goes, *"Los golpes quitan lo bruto,"* which means that, "Hard knocks teach wisdom".

We talked far into the night, bringing back to mind the fellows we had known; because we had liked them, we remembered them.

Alfred Fraga, the descendent of Portuguese celts, who spoke Castillian so well that he liked to go among Hispanics and surprise them with his fluency in the language; because his bright red hair, snub nose and freckles made them think he was a sure enough gringo.

There was "Injun Pete" (Mariano Sanchez), the pure-blooded Yaqui Indian. He came from the most warlike tribe ever encountered by Spanish Conquistadores, but was one of the best-natured men I knew. He always wore a wide grin on his face. He was the father of Joaquin Sanchez, the rodeo clown who was known for his cold nerve in taking mad Brahma bulls away from the cowboys who were thrown and helpless. In speaking of his dad, Joaquin once told me, "My dad rode all the horses in Cuff Burrell's bucking string, just to see if he could ride them and none of them bucked him off."

A boy came to work on San Emideo and earned the name of Salome Bill, perhaps he came from Salome, Arizona. Hank, the foreman, gave him a big bay horse called Bill. He was a good cow-horse, but he had his eccentricities. If his rider let him walk off on a loose rein in the morning when he was first mounted, old Bill would remain horizontal and docile. But if his rider turned him to the right or left, Bill would buck. If he bucked, as this

George Randall, Ojai, Calif.
"El Gringo Bonito"

Nicolas Firfires, Montecito, Calif.
One of the few artists to accurately depict
the California Vaquero.

writer has good reason to remember, the person on his back would think that his backbone was coming out the top of his head. Once this writer got on Bill with his Levi jacket buttoned all the way up. In the storm, the jacket was hooked onto the horn and all the buttons were torn off but the top one. He also pounded his ribs against the horn. They were so sore that he couldn't ride straight for a month.

The foreman warned Bill about the horse's peculiarity. Salome only grunted. He saddled Bill, led him out into the yard. He mounted, laid the rein on Bill's neck and turned him around, then he laid the rein on his neck again, but this time Bill started bucking. He bucked around the yard for a long time. At last, out of breath, he stopped. Salome was still in the saddle. Hank asked why he had tried to turn Bill around instead of letting him walk off. "Oh," he answered, "I wanted to see if he could buck as hard as you guys said he could."

There were many of the vaqueros and buckeroos who couldn't ride a bucker no matter how mild the buck. But such men usually had an infinite patience and could turn out the best working cowhorses. Sutah Coway roped beautifully and never missed, unless he was in a bad humor. Then he would miss either because he didn't like the boy who was tailing for him, or wanted to be ordered out of the corral. He was never a bronc rider.

Nepomuseno Cordero could never ride a bad one but he turned out some of the best-mouthed horses on Tejon. Don Jesus, the boss, said (facetiously, of course) that Nepomuseno's legs were too short for his body and his behind was too big and too broad, that when a horse got it out of the saddle, it was too heavy to get back in. But Cheno, as we called him, was so good with colts that the boss always gave him the most promising ones on the ranch to ride.

Eduardo Valdez could never rope, but he rode the best horses on the ranch and in a pinch he could ride a pretty good bucking horse. He stayed on the White Wolf for many years. When he retired, this writer bought his old Visalia saddle.

Adolfo Encinas was never a bronc rider, nor ever wanted to be one, but when he threw a loop he never stopped to see if he had caught. He turned his horse toward the fire and took his turns around the horn. His riata had eyes. He rode colts for Roland Russell Hill who ran the Tehachapi Cattle Company and turned out many good Morgans. Russell told me that Adolfo was one of the best men with a colt he had ever known. As a matter of fact, Russell said, the horses Adolfo turned out, had too light a mouth, because when riding the colt through brush, if a branch happened to swing back and hit the colt's rein, the colt would spin around. Nevertheless, he put out some of the best Morgans the Hill brothers owned.

Salvador, for instance, was expert in all the skills of the vaquero's work. He was a good bucking horse rider, he was a good roper, he could put a good mouth on a horse, he knew cattle, he could shoe a horse and he was even good at cooking. One day when he was gathering cattle on the east side of Breckenridge Mountain, Salvador, Jim Polkinhorn and two other men were camped at Mill Creek. I dropped in on them and had supper. Sal had cooked it. He had made biscuits. They were so good that

I can still remember how good they were. I still have a pair of rawhide reins and a riata he made. I keep them hidden because I have been offered so many inflated dollars for them that I'm afraid I will some day weaken and sell them.

Another good man and a complete vaquero was Bill Nichols. He was an Indian from the Kernville area. He rode colts on San Emideo and turned out good horses. A colt fell over backwards with him. He was taken to the hospital and died on the operating table. He was a very quiet man. One could ride by his side all day long and the only word he would say is "Yes" or "No".

Bert Hobbs would brag all day long of the broncos he had ridden, until he bored Hank, the foreman, so much that Hank undertook to cure him by getting him bucked off. Hank gave him Tango Annie who would buck at intervals all day long. Bert saddled Annie with an old slick fork saddle, put a snaffle bit with split leather reins on her and mounted. Once firmly seated, he crossed the reins in his left fist and took a firm hold on the horn with his right hand. Tango leaped into a buck and swapped ends, then bucked off around the yard. When she quit, we rode off toward Pleito Ranch. Before the morning was over she bucked three times, but she could never catch Bert asleep. She never bucked him off during the months Bert rode her. But neither did Bert stop bragging. Someone, I think it was big Ed Norton who told me, that Archie Reed, sometime later, finally succeeded in riding the buck out of Tango Annie.

Tony and Jim Campas were fifteen and sixteen years old, respectively, when I first went to Tejon Ranch. Under the coaching of Salvador Carmelo both became first class bronc riders. I remember Tony making a beautiful ride on "Hell-to-Set" at a rodeo in Lebec. We became friends the first time I met them and have been friends ever since. Tony lives in Cuyama Valley and Jim lives here in Bakersfield.

Freddie and Willie Lamas were little guys but they were mighty on a horse. It took a good horse to buck either one of them off. Freddie has passed away, but Willie lives in Pumpkin Center surrounded by his sons and grandsons. Johnny Puget,

Ernest Seeley   Robert Grisedale

the little Frenchmen, still lives on Real Road in Bakersfield. Angel Montanio, whom we called *"Chango"* (Monkey) worked for Rafael Cuen on the chuckwagon. He was the son of Santos Montanio, the good chuckwagon cook.

Uel Matthews, a boy from Orange County wandered up this way and got a job on San Emideo. He used to ride Liver-eating-Johnson, the mule. That is, he sometimes rode Johnson, because the mule sometimes threw him. He worked on only one ranch, San Emideo. When he left he went back to Orange and married. Years afterward I met his brother who told me that "Booger", as we called him, was the father of a big family and very prosperous.

Old Jim Gorman was one of the good gringo vaqueros in the country. He as also the crankiest. He descended from an Irishman who came to America during the famine in Ireland. On arrival here he enlisted in the army and served at Fort Tejon. Gorman Station is named after him. Old Bob Bowen, Turner and Billie Rose were good gringo vaqueros.

We must not forget Charlie Hitchcock, whom we called Curley, when he worked at Rosedale Ranch. During his stay there he bought a Model-T Ford and left it to Providence to help him find a way to make payments of thirty dollars a month. Providence in the form of a Kansas cowboy named George Knowles came to his aid. George taught Charlie how to rope Tule elk and to pull their teeth.

Fifty-five years later the two were on a hunting trip in the High Sierra. They were sitting by the campfire having a nightcap when George turned to Charlie and said, "Johnson", he always called Charlie, "Johnson", "Do you remember when you had to make payments on the Model-T Ford and I showed you how to rope elk and how to pull their teeth? And how I sold the teeth for you so you could make payments?"

"Yes", Charlie answered.

"Well, Johnson", George said, "I've got something to confess. You know I sold these teeth for you but I didn't get thirty dollars for them. I got fifty dollars." Chuck, Charlie's son, told me this story, but he didn't tell me what Charlie answered.

Rawley Duntley was an oldtime cattleman who lived on Oak Creek. He had more activities in Lancaster than in Bakersfield. But he was well known all over the county. Another little fellow who didn't make much noise was Rafael Sanchez. He was a good little bronc rider when he was sober. Archie Reid from Honolulu was another good little bronc rider. He was a ranch bronc rider. I say that because many of the boys who never missed a rodeo in town wouldn't ride a colt on the ranch. Some of the boys from the mountains would come down and ride on the ranches. Claude Caldwell, Pinky Reed, young Bob Bowen worked for the Land Company at times.

Remick Albitre and his brother "Dutch" would come down for the rodeos. Remick was at his best as pick-up man at the old fairgrounds. He and his horse Truck were always at the right time. I liked to sit in the grandstand and watch Remick work. Whenever something happened that amused him, I could see his grin from up in the grandstand. Jimmie and Bautista ("Boy") are the only brothers left in the Albitre family.

I often meet Doug Silica in the Pleasant Grove area when I go north to visit Bobby Ingersoll in the Sacramento Valley.

Years ago, on weekends, Salvy Rodriguez would put on a little rodeo. There was always the same group of contestants who showed up to the ride. Most of them worked on ranches, but didn't seem to get enough work during the week. Jim and Tony Campus, Dutch Albitre, Joe Garcia, Johnny Puget, Buster Clark, Tommy Condley, Alfonso Valenzuela, Vic and Bob Huntington, Pete Rivera, Wille Lamas. There was not always a paid attendance. As a result, the bronc riders didn't always get paid. If they didn't make any money, they had a lot of fun. However, those little rodeos were more risky than the big ones, because the arena was made of parked cars or was an open field which some farmer had good-naturedly lent for the occasion. One time Sal put on a rodeo on the McManus Ranch in a cornfield. The corn stalks had been cut at a slant and stood up about three feet with a sharp spearlike edge. Willie Lamas remarked that if some cowboy would be thrown on one of those stalks he would be impaled. Luckily no one was hurt, because all the riders hung on for dear life.

The watching of the vaqueros and buckeroos, that is, young ones, strengthened my belief in Guardian Angels. However, many of the boys who started their career riding in those little rodeos later made good in big time rodeos.

Often around the campfire we would talk about our ambitions and how we would run a ranch if we had owned one; but we never became cattle kings, because their day had long-since passed. Cattle kings had flourished as long as the land they used was free and they paid no taxes on it. When the cattleman had to own the land on which he ran his cattle and pay taxes, he did not last long. Already, in the times of which we speak, ranching was diversified. The cattle outfits also ran sheep, raised hogs, alfalfa and other crops. About the only chance of advancement the vaquero or buckeroo had was to get the job

Jim Campa and Frank Martinez
The gray horse is "El Horcado".

Sal Carmelo

of the foreman. But that chance was remote, indeed. Foremen were a special breed of men who were hired for their experience, their ability to handle men, their knowledge of cattle and their reliability.

Many foremen became legends in their own time and they lasted on the jobs for many years. Don Jesus Lopez, sixty years, Rafael Cuen, fifty-four years, Joaquin Feliz, forty years, Catarino Reese, forty years, Russell Hill, fifty years, Johnny Green, thirty years. A foreman was known far and wide. Men from Nevada, Utah, Oregon, Idaho had heard of Marks Parks and Henry Battor on the Miller and Lux Ranches in California. Most vaqueros and buckeroos rode the range because they liked horses. Most of the talk around the fire was about them. A rider would often talk of owning a dream horse. Now and then one would leave to ride in rodeos, like Johnny Drayer, who followed the ciruits. That was long before rodeos as they are today, existed. Nowadays good performers make big money. Some fly from one show to another in their own plane.

It was romance which made the vaquero and buckeroo leave the ranch. When he left, it was to get married; for as the saying goes, *"Para cada oveja hay una pareja"* (For every Jack there

Bill Cantleberry and his wife, Lena.

Teodoro Valenzuela   Dan Castro

Frank Urrea   Rawley Duntley

is a Jill). Women were scarce, but somewhere, somehow, the buckeroo found a woman who would have him. Then arose the problem of making a living for her. The thirty dollars a month he earned on the ranch was too little. The newlywed had to get a job in the oilfields or in town. One or two married men worked on the ranch, but that was because there were camps where a family could live. Those jobs were scarce.

Although one sees women riding in horse shows, teaching riding, running stables, competing most exclusively against other women in both English and Western classes and sees them working around corrals and on ranches today, it was not so in the old days. I do not believe that a woman saw romance on the ranches in those days, where she lost her femininity pumping water, feeding pigs, carrying stove wood, sometimes having to chop it, busting suds over a washboard and a tubful of steaming, soapy water and using outdoor toilets. Today there are women horseshoers and women veterinarians.

Arnold Rojas being presented with buckle on his eightieth birthday by Reined Cow Horse Association. Reno, Nevada, 1976

Photo by - Bill McNabb, Jr.

EARLY NOTES

After the placer mines had gradually become less productive, the "miners," who did not have the enterprise to have made a success at the mines, began moving down the coast to "squat"on the old Spanish and Mexican land grants and dispossess the rightful owners who had been guaranteed the title to their lands by the United States Government.

After those outrages had been committed and the lands along the coast had been usurped, the mobs of hungry land seekers swarmed into the San Joaquin Valley. The Great Valley, in wet years, was an immense pasture on which thousands of wild horses, wild cattle, deer, elk and antelope roamed. The entire valley during wet seasons became a carpet of flowers in which lupines, poppies, blue bells and buttercups bloomed.

A man could ride for five hundred miles, from the Grapevine to the foot of Mount Shasta and never be out of sight of wild horses, wild cattle, elk, antelope and jack rabbits.

The rabbits were not exterminated until the farmers planted orchards. The rabbits destroyed the young trees. To protect the trees, the farmers organized rabbit drives. The farmers would construct a corral of wire mesh with long wings on each side. Hundreds of people in buggies, carts, wagons and on horseback would congregate at a given point and drive the rabbits into the

Soda Lake - Carriso Plains

Elk Hills in the background.

Cholame, San Luis Obispo County, Calif.

corral. Then three or four men would enter the corral and beat the squealing animals to death.

After one drive near Bakersfield, some men cleaned the rabbits, loaded them into a rack and shipped them to a tamale factory in Los Angeles to be made, so they said, into chicken tamales. Sometime later the word got about that the government had prohibited the factory from calling tamales made with jackrabbits, "chicken" tamales.

The early "land grabbers", as Stevenson called them, took much of the flat lands. With the exception of a few Mexican grants which skirted the Tehachapis and the Coast Ranges, it had all been free land. They left only the foothill and the Sierras for the small homesteaders. The big land owners let the land lie fallow and ran cattle on it. It was better, in a way, for the land because if the homesteaders had settled the better portions, they would have tried to farm it. They would have starved out during the dry spells and left the ground they had plowed to grow weeds and for the wind to blow away, just as they did on much of the prairie lands in the East.

Before the railroads came, the valley transportation was by wagon. Freight cost sixty dollars a ton which made the enormous grain crops, in good years, worthless.

The coming of the railroad ended the open range and the great bands of wild animals. The era of the gang plow and the twenty mule team came into being.

It was during that period the "jerkline skinner" (teamster) was the aristocrat of the ranch bunk house. Twenty mule teams, horses or mules, pulled the gang plows, the multiple grain wagons, the logs out of the mountains, in long trains to the coast. A team of twenty mules pulled two wagons loaded with grain, a tank wagon and two feed racks mounted on wheels. Five vehicles, one behind the other, across the valley, over Cottonwood Pass to Paso Robles.

The "Fresno scraper" pulled by four mules hitched abreast, built the numerous ditches, canals and levees and leveled thousands of acres which were planted to alfalfa.

However, the "sand lapper" did not always make a crop. Winters came in which there was no rain. It was not until the deep-well turbine pump was developed that the farmers came into their own. One farmer leased one hundred and sixty acres from a ranch which embraced four "Spanish" grants in its four hundred thousand acres and made more money from his cotton crop than the ranch made from its cattle on the four "Spanish" grants in one season.

Frank Lane's Relics of long ago.

A COWBOY'S HORSE

During the late 1920's and early 1930's, feral and Indian horses, which had been gathered on the ranges of New Mexico and Arizona, were shipped into Kern County and sold here. Of the hundreds which were bought, many were young enough to be developed into useable horses, though many were "sand-locoed", after they were well-fed on grain and alfalfa, they gained from two to three hundred pounds, even when their teeth showed them to have attained full growth, that is to say, over seven years of age.

All horses running on desert ranges go through periods in which grass becomes scarce. During these periods, the horse licks up every blade of grass he can find and in the process, swallows a quantity of sand. During these periods of scarcity, the horse never finds enough forage to fill his belly and as a result, the sand he swallows becomes a ball and stays in his belly. When some one undertakes to break the horse, he finds that when he becomes heated, he develops peculiarities of behavior. This writer believes that the sand must press on some nerve in the horse's anatomy which causes severe pain, because it becomes frantic and goes crazy. Sometimes the horse will buck; sometimes he will stampede; sometimes he will fall over backwards. All have attacks of madness. All sand-locoed horses this writer was ever familiar with, died suddenly and when they died, he had them cut open, never failing to find the lumps of sand in their bellies.

However, crazy behavior was not confined to New Mexico and Arizona broomtails. The Kern County Land Co. and the Tejon Ranch had horses which were often erratic in their behavior, to say the least.

Reminiscing of that time long ago, brings to mind an experience I had with a horse which had a habit of kicking at the stirrup.

Back in the early 1930's, I ran the Bar-O-Stables on Pierce Road in Bakersfield. After I had been teaching kids how to ride for a year or two, I learned that a child will learn much faster if mounted on a good horse, especially on one that has learned to assume responsibility, like an old cowhorse that had worked cattle. My problem then, was getting a number of old vaquero horses as mounts for the children. Therefore I had a talk with Remick Albitre, who knew all the ranches and most of the horses in the mountains. I told him that I needed a number of old ranch horses that were too old for the strenuous work of the mountains and old enough to be ridden by children.

As a result of our talk, Remick would periodically haul in a truck load of horses, which I bought. I culled them and kept the best for schooling the kids. The rest I advertised and sold. There was a demand for them because they were reliable.

One day, in one of the truck loads Remick brought, was a sturdy sorrel which at once attracted my attention. He was not a big horse, but he was well ribbed, with high withers and stout hairy legs. Evidently he was a horse out of a wild or range band. Remick told me about each horse, in turn. Each one he said, was gentle, but when he came to the sorrel, he said, "Now a 'cowboy' can ride that horse" and he grinned.

In a way he emphasized the word 'cowboy' and the way he grinned, I gathered that the sorrel was not by any means a kid's horse and that I would have to find a cowboy before I could sell the sorrel.

After I had sold the surplus horses, I saddled the sorrel, mounted and rode him around. I pulled logs with the horn of the saddle and found that somebody had been 'cowboy' enough to make a working horse out of him,.

One day I worked him into a sweat and as I was riding along, he suddenly "cowkicked" and hit my spur and broke the spur leather. The next day I saddled him and tied him to the hitching rack. After he had been standing there for a few minutes, he suddenly kicked at the stirrup and caught his foot on it. He struggled until he fell and while he was down, I took the saddle off.

There as a fat man in Bakersfield with whom I had had an argument about four dollars which I never got. He had forgotten the argument, but I had not. He came out to look at the sorrel that I had for sale. He needed a horse for the man who tended his cattle. I saddled the sorrel and rode him around. I dragged a few logs to show him how well he worked with a rope. Then I explained very clearly that the horse was definitely not a "kids horse," that he was one a cowboy could ride.

He bought the sorrel and that afternoon brought a trailer and hauled him away. Two days later, he was back, in high dudgeon. It seems that the man for whom he bought the horse, knew the animal. The minute he saw him he went into hysterics. He said the horse was an outlaw and that he wouldn't ride that S-O-B for a hundred dollar bill. He said the only man who could ride him was Jack Sarret.

I stood pat and would not take the horse back. I said that I had not mis-represented him and if the man who rode for him wasn't cowboy enough to ride the horse, it wasn't my fault. In that way, I settled the debt of the four dollars which was owed to me.

This all happened over forty years ago. The other day, I was at Chuck Hitchcock's Training Stables in Shafter. Jack Sarret was there and we talked about the sorrel horse. Jack said, "That horse was scared to death of a saddle strapped to his back and

Old Freckles

would become frantic with fear." He came out of a shipment of horses from New Mexico. A boy bought him and although the horse was full grown, when he came here, after the boy fed him on grain or alfalfa, he gained two or three hundred pounds. The boy never put a saddle on him. He rode him bareback all the time he owned him. My Uncle, Gene Sarret, bought the horse and took him to Poso Flat. One day Gene Sarret saddled him in the corral; the horse bucked Gene off and tore half the corral down. Gene traded him to me for a cow and I rode him for long time, until Remick bought him and sold him to you."

THE CATTLE

The enormous profits to be gained in the trade for the pelts of animals lured the first dauntless Frenchmen into the wilderness of North America. Men who quailed at neither hardship nor danger, who ventured into the camps of Sioux, Blackfeet, Chippewa, even the Apache and Commanche and came out alive. Those far-ranging Frenchmen, while trading and trapping for furs, explored much of the present United States and Canada, from Quebec to Vancouver and from the Arctic Circle to the Gulf of Mexico. They have left the names on the map of North America. As far west as California we have the names of Lebec and Rubidoux to remind us of the voyaguers and the coureurs du bois.

Yankee skippers, no less intrepid, sailed out of Boston, Salem and other New England ports into the turbulent Atlantic to the tip of South America, to fight storms and adverse winds around Cape Horn, into the Pacific and north to the remote, god-forsaken ports of California, to trade for hides or tallow. It was a voyage which often lasted two years and involved eight thousand miles of travel, contingent on the will of the wind.

Since 1519, Spaniards from one generation to another, had pushed slowly northward to established missions and ranches as far as Sonoma, north of San Francisco Bay. Cattle had been multiplying into many thousands since Don Gasper De Portola and the Franciscans had brought the first ones into California. Over the years the rancheros had developed an industry based on the cattle which they raised for their hides, since there was no market for the meat. Every year the rancheros slaughtered many herds of steers in the matanzas (slaughterings) and only the hides were saved. The meat was left to rot. True, Indians in the wilds of the surrounding areas salvaged much of it, still most of it was left for the bears, coyotes and buzzards.

The early California culture was based on the longhorn Spanish cattle just as the Plains Indian's was based on that of the buffalo. The hide of the longhorn steer had a "thousand" uses. Besides being used as "banknotes" in trade with the Boston skippers, the hides were made into leather, which already was famous as "California oak-tanned leather," riatas, latigos, bridle-reins, hobbles, alforjas, which the gringos called "kyacks," water buckets, coverings for saddle trees, lacings for chairs, beds, couches and a thousand other uses.

Because of the absence of nails, the beams in the old mission buildings were lashed together with strips of rawhide which have held to this day. And now after two hundred years they still hold. Now and then, in the more remote parts of the Sierra, one will come upon an old corral, its poles still held firmly to the posts with rawhide, some long-forgotten vaquero lashed there a century or more ago.

The country teemed with wild animals, which nobody hunted. Grizzly bears, antelope, elk and deer roamed unmolested; for the Californiano was no hunter. A man could ride days through herds of game that had never heard the sound of a gun. Indeed, it would be years before "sportsmen" would succeed in wantonly destroying the wild life of California.

Except for an occasional grizzly bear which vaqueros roped and sledded into one of the towns for a bear and bull fight, wild animals roamed at peace. As late as 1919, twelve antelope ranged the highest desert on the Liebre Ranch near Neenach. Don Toribio

Cordova watched a man shoot down all twelve, one after another. He then got into his car and drove away before Don Toribio, who was on horseback, could reach him. He left the dead animals for the coyotes. He was most probably a "sportsman".

Sheep had come into the country from New Mexico, but they were raised mainly for their wool. The Californiano was a beef-eater and if he ate any other meat than beef it was because he had no choice.

As we have said, the Yankee windjammers brought in goods which were traded for hides at five hundred percent profit. Little money changed hands, for there was little to buy. True, the rancheros used many Indians as servants and laborers. They were never paid, but they were clothed and fed. Quite often their lot was much better on the ranch than it would have been in the wilds.

It was not until the Gold Rush, when people swarmed into the state, the cattle became valuable for their meat. By that time the era of the sailing ships and the Boston skippers and the hide trade had passed out of existence.

After 1849, thousands of ships lay rotting in San Francisco Bay, abandoned by the crews who had fled to the Gold Fields. Of the hordes of people that had burst upon the fair land of California, a few, comparatively, were fortunate, but many more, instead of finding gold, found only disappointment and if the tales of the wild mining camps had a little truth, many met a violent death. All were blind to the real wealth of California, which was its soil. It was not until the disappointed had turned to cultivating it that they found its prosperity. The first comers met an open-handed hospitality from the natives until the gringos started committing outrages. Then the natives began to retaliate.

Contrary to the lies told of them, the people the gringos found here were a hard-working lot, the men as herdsmen and the women running a household under primitive conditions. The girls married at fourteen or fifteen and started raising a family. Sometimes they had as many as twelve or more. Half the babies died at infancy; but the population grew despite infant mortality, which was about ninety percent. The average life expectancy was thirty-five years, though there were cases where a man reached an extreme old age.

Bruno Contreras lived to be well over a hundred years and Avelino Martinez died at the age of one hundred and ten. If a child lived past the age of seven years, he was sure to reach manhood. The epidemics which wiped out the Indians did not have the same effect on the Hispanics. A measure of European blood gave them some immunity.

Baja California Tack

SADDLES AND BRONCOS

After they had established the missions in Alta California and the herds of cattle began to increase, the padres taught the Indian they found here to be vaqueros. While teaching them the three "R's" (roping, riding and rounding-up) they also taught them to make the equipment they used in their work; saddles, ropes, both rawhide and hair, reins, hobbles, jaquimas and bosals. But most important of all, they taught the Indians the use of the tapa-ojos (blindfolds). For the tapa-ojos was the most indispensible piece of equipment in the vaquero kit bag. Without the blindfold, he could not mount the fighting broncos, which were as fierce as a wild cat and would strike, bite and kick. Indeed, many wild mustangs killed themselves in the breaking. The way the broncos were broken in, was by no means gentle. A vaquero rode into the corral, threw a loop around a bronco's neck and dragged him out of the herd. After the bronco had choked down, a vaquero put a tapa-ojos over his eyes, adjusted a hackamore on his head and hobbled his forelegs. Then the vaquero let the bronco get to his feet so he could saddle him. Once mounted and seated firmly in the saddle, the vaquero lifted the blindfold, whereupon the startled bronco lit into bucking. If the mustang failed to throw his rider and bucked until he was exhausted, it was most likely that he would never buck again. Most wild horses

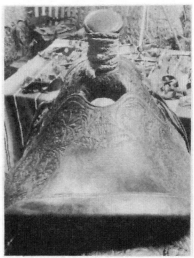

Fine old saddles at "The Mill".

gave up after the first struggle--I use the masculine pronoun because the vaquero of that era never rode a mare. Mustangs, however, never gave up striking, kicking, or biting; so in order to avoid being struck, kicked or bitten, the vaquero used tapaojos until the mustang got tame, that is, if he ever got tame. Blindfolds were used on some of the meanest broncos for a year or more.

The packing industry, which was so important during the Gold Rush period, when bands of mules were used to carry goods into the mining camps, would never have succeeded without tapaojos, because no mule of that era would have allowed himself to be packed without a cover over his eyes.

The more cautious vaqueros would lace a limb of a tree across the saddle behind the fork, to extend about a foot on each side of the horse. This was done because the mustangs often threw themselves and the limb would prevent the bronco from crushing its rider's leg or rolling with the saddle.

The two hundred odd head of cattle which Portola and De Anza had brought into California to start the mission herds increased to over a million and a half by 1840. Before 1846, when

Saddle Displays
at "The Mill"

the gringos came into the country, the Governors had made over a thousand land grants. The vaquero was the most important figure in the economy of the country.

As we have said, the padres taught the horse culture they had brought from the missions in Baja, but once in Alta California, the culture, perhaps because of the difference in climatic conditions, began to change and develop into one peculiarly Californian. The skeleton tree used in the tropical country began to acquire a cover which was not detachable, like the mochilla or armas used in Sonora and Baja.

The saddle first encountered by foreign travelers here was a stout skeleton tree. The padres had taught the Indians how to carve a tree, to cover it with bull hide and to sew the hide around the tree with deer skin. The Indians learned to pad the seat with sheep or bear skins for comfort. But it was a long time before the saddle used by the vaqueros in California was covered permanently with leather. There are still some old saddles in this writer's collections which were made during the transition period and are still semi-skeleton saddles.

It was the Sonorans who finally settled the type of tree that was to become the famous Visalia, Lewis, Davis, Garcia, Marteral and Ledesma saddle of the West.

Once the rancheros were established on the grants, bit, spur and saddle markers began to flourish in the towns. By the time the first gringos began to write of California, the rich rancheros were riding very elaborate silver mounted saddles, with silver mounted bits and spurs, if one is to judge from the illustrations of Walker and other artists who were in California in the 1830's. Twain, Bret Hart and Marryat all depict the early saddles and tell the viciousness of the early Californian mustang.

California has had through its history many skilled saddle craftsmen. Unfortunately, they did not survive the depression of the early thirties. But, of late years, they have had a rebirth. After the horse shows became popular, the saddlemaker came into his own again. Today saddlers are flourishing over the entire country.

Hot Iron

RODEO

The "Rodeo" or roundup is one of the oldest operations known to pastoral peoples. Since time immemorial, nomads of Asia have been making roundups (gigantic circles of mounted men), either to entrap game or to gather cattle.

A rodeo starts from the center or hub. The riders fan out and ride in different directions like the spokes of a wheel to form a circle. When each rider has reached a designated spot, he stops and waits until all the riders are placed in the form of a circle. This is the rodeo. To "rodear" means to encircle. When each rider turns his horse toward the center, or hub, which is called the "rodeo ground" and drives all the cattle he encounters toward it. As the rider progresses, the circle becomes smaller and smaller and the bands of cattle join until by the time they reach the rodeo grounds they are one huge mass.

Then the work of parting out the beef steers begins. Of course, not all roundups are made by using a full circle; quite often only segments of a circle are used to make a rodeo. At all rodeos a number of interlopers will turn up running with the cattle. Odd animals which always provided amusement to the men. Burros which had learned to steal milk from the cows and by stubborn persistence had in the end forced a cow to adopt them. Each burro walked beside the cow's calf like a brother.

Cattle on the San Martin Ranch

Whenever another animal got near, the burro would lay back its ears and drive it away. Frantic deer leaped from one side of the herd to the other until they found a way out. Now and then an elk would be in the bunch. But he would rush straight ahead and out of the herd and soon be out of sight. Furtive coyotes, not sure what to fear most, angry cows or the grinning vaqueros who sat their horses and threw their lazos at them, but always missed, for a coyote is the hardest thing in the world to rope. The coyotes paid no attention to the numerous rabbits, which was their main source of food.

Don Toribio Cordova told me that once a mountain lion had been caught up in a rodeo. But he charged out of the herd before they tried to lasso him - a feat which would have been most interesting to see, if it had been successful. Oddly enough, although the vaqueros uncoiled their ropes and threw their loops at everything that walked, they never bothered the burros. Vaqueros had had one for a childhood playmate and found them faithful servants. Besides, they were inoffensive creatures that had done service to man and were considered animals of great wisdom.

Besides, the burro, like the ox, was blessed. The burro had carried the Savior and oxen had breathed upon the Babe to keep Him warm when he lay in the manger.

Jim Rocha cutting at El Tejon Ranch, Fellows, Calif.

Branding

Doug Silicz - February, 1981

Branding in Nevada - This is a Miller and Lux looking horse.
Photo by - Adrian Atwater, Nevada State Highways Dept.

Bill Schwindt and Ray Yanez. Ventura Fairgrounds - 1953

VAQUERO HORSES

Once the padres had established the missions and the cattle and horse herds, it did not take the Indian tribes of the Great Basin, the Shoshones, Piutes and others long to learn that the California mustang was a superior animal. This knowledge brought raiding parties of Indians sweeping over the passes of the Sierras to drive off horses from the ranches and missions. This raiding went on for years, without seeming to reduce the numbers, though it has been estimated that over a period of twenty years a hundred thousand horses were stolen from the ranches and missions. Still the myriads of mustangs were countless, even after thousands were driven over cliffs to drown in the ocean and Sonoran vaqueros trapped other thousands and drove them over the Devil's Highroad to Mexico.

These fine horses made fine riders. The first Yankees who came around Cape Horn found superb horsemen who were confident in their ability, vain in their silver saddles and sure in their expertise in handling horses. A legend of their horsemanship and some adobe missions and ranch houses are all that remain of the Hispanic era in California.

However, the tradition of the old Spanish horsemanship did not die altogether. The gringos adopted it through the period of the great ranches. There were many men who made good spade-

Martin Aquierre, Manuel Machado and Francisco Figueroa - at the old plaza in Los Angeles. These three horsemen are men of substance, their equipment is well made, their horses are well bred, even the mule is an aristocrat, the period is between 1880 and 1900.

bit horses. And now-a-days, when the cattlemen have put the cattle industry on wheels and each vaquero or buckeroo is given a pick-up and trailer to haul his horse, a lunch and a canteen, there are still good men who try to put out a good horse, even though there is hardly enough work for the horse to earn his keep. The old Spanish mustang is no more. Many types and breeds of horses have come and gone since Padre Serra and De Anza brought horses into California, but there are still men in the West who take pride in turning out a reined horse.

In California, Oregon, Nevada and in parts of Idaho, Wyoming and Arizona a boy fell heir into a system of horsemanship which was distinctively Californian, a tradition of Spanish equitation. The tradition of the faultlessly reined horse, of the spade bit and of the sensitive hand on the bridle rein. He learned to ride almost as soon as he could walk and instinctively developed that skill, which is the heritage of the Californian rider. Here in the West, a rider is judged by his skill in handling a horse, for of all the boons which the bow-legged god of horsemen can grant, that of the delicate bridle hand is most precious. A vaquero with hands that signal, but never hurt is the most admirable among horsemen.

Time, patience and forebearance went into the training of the vaquero horse. On the Tejon Ranch, during the period in which Don Jesus Lopez was the *MAYORDOMA*, the colts were given to ride to only men who were able to train a colt. The men who rode colts were always proven vaqueros. Of course, each man had his particular way of handling the colt and of teaching it how to work cattle. Basically, however, the methods of handling a colt were generally all the same.

In spite of all which has been written about the "West" the vaquero or buckeroo was, after all, a laborer and his horse was a work horse. Of course, the foreman kept his eye on the colt and his rider. Foremen were efficient and conscientious men and would never let a man spoil a horse. However, the vaquero or buckeroo, if he was any kind of man at all, had pride in his ability and would take great pains in handling the colt. Most vaqueros or buckeroos would ride their colts about once or twice a week and then only on days when there was no hard riding to be done.

West side of valley at Salt Slough.

Bridle Horse

Joe Yanez
1902 - 1978

Don James
Washoe Indian

In spite of all this care, however, at the end of the first year though the colt was most probably still in the hackamore, he was already a very useful animal and his rider could do all the work required on him. The second year he was in double reins and could do any work the old vaquero horses could do. From that time on he learned more every day and became a finished horse when he was straight up in the bridle.

"Wet saddle blankets make a vaquero horse", the old men always said. It seemed the more the colt worked, the more he learned. After each day's ride, the colt became more eager to turn after a cow. It was better for the colt to be tired after each day's work, but by no means exhausted, because if a colt were to become exhausted, he would be a dead-head for the rest of his life. Some ranches were known far and wide for having horses which had been ridden too hard when they were colts. Good vaqueros would never work on such ranches.

However, a colt which has steady work will not "sour". The different tasks in the day's work on the ranch varied. The colt

Bill Schwindt, Ray Yanez, Joe Yanez and Cook.
1948

carried his rider out on a circle, then drove the cattle between him and the rodeo ground to join those being held there. He helped hold the rodeo, turned back the beeves that would break out and drove the fat steers which were parted out to the *PARADA*, then helped drive the steers to the field where they were held overnight, if there was a field or pasture in which to hold them.

Working a colt, that is, spinning and turning the animal when there were no cattle to be turned, was frowned upon on the Tejon Ranch in those days. It was also a good way to get fired and a sure way to spoil a horse. To spin an old vaquero horse that already knew how to work, was the height of stupidity.

It is said that a horse cannot learn to work cattle or to rein without cattle and that is true in a sense, because working cattle gives a horse a reason for turning and so long as the horse does his work without interference from his rider, so long will he do it willingly.

Road to San Emideo

BRIDLE HORSES

True, we lament the passing of the "Old West" and the old-time vaquero and buckeroo. But the fact remains that there are still good men in the West and many of the ranches still retain their original acreages.

The modern rider is still expert, expert in so far as the extent of his system of working goes; and he is much better mounted. The modern cowhorse is much better bred than most cowhorses of seventy years ago; that is, in most cases. Today, horse-breeding is much too expensive for a rancher to breed scrub horses and the modern day cowhorse is almost pure throughbred, if not entirely so. The present-day cowhorse can move much faster, although they are worked too young in this writer's opinion.

The vaquero's occupation differed from other crafts, in that the range rider acquired a body of knowledge which he enlarged, as he gained experience. The more competent he became, the more averse he was to depart from traditional methods. The lore of horsemanship, bits and the bitting of horses is a rare wisdom, which all men who ride horses seek--sometimes in vain.

What little knowledge I have of horses and horsemanship is a legacy of an old California gentleman who, out of the kindness of his heart, seventy years ago, took a skinny, orphan kid, put him on an old buckskin mustang and taught him the rudiments of riding. In giving his instructions, he taught the boy to be gentle, patient, and humane and to love and respect his culture. It was there that the boy came under the spell which he will carry to his grave and never be happy again away from the company of horses.

The old gentleman's generosity with his knowledge has helped this writer through a lifetime of handling horses in different capacities: as a vaquero on the ranches, as a teamster in grading camps, as a packer in the mountains, as a horseshoer and a horse dentist, during which time he has tried to be true to the legacy.

I remember many of the old gentleman's sayings. One of them was "To be perfect, any movement of the horse must be elegant. Movement must flow, be a complete action in itself; for the key to riding is simplicity, that is to say, balance."

To see skilled vaqueros work was the great event of my boyhood. I was twelve years old with eyes that were new to a spectacle which was still an art which had developed to perfection in the centuries since Cortez had landed on New World shores with the first sixteen horses.

As I grew older, after I had spent years riding with vaqueros, I formed my notions of the grandeur and hardships of the range riders' life. And when the era of the open range ended, I mourned that a beautiful phase of California history had died.

They were so sure of themselves and so wholly expert, those men who admitted me into the brotherhood of horsemen. I never admired men more and ever since I have striven to be serious and stalwart like them.

Looking back over a period of seventy years to the times when we were boys starting to ride on the ranches, I remember the many occasions when I got through a tough spot with a horse by the advice of one of the older men. We could never have learned to handle colts without their help. Sometimes just a word or two would solve the problem.

One morning (it was three o'clock and still dark) I was trying to put the bridle on a gray horse. Every time I tried to put the

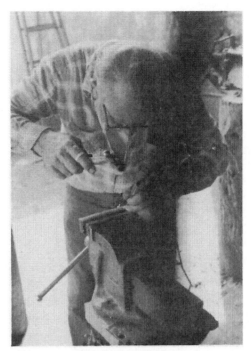

Fine Hand Work

The old master, Eduardo Grijalva of Magdalena, Sonora
Mexico making one of his handtooled bits.

bit in his mouth he would pull back. When suddenly out of the dark a voice called, *"Ensenya le el freno, vale"* (Show him the bit, pal.) It was Luis Zamora's voice.

I held the bit in front of the horse and after a few moments he put his head in the bridle and took the bit, as a result of Luis' suggestion. I was able to leave camp with the rest of the vaqueros. Blundering kids were often laughed at, so it behooved them to think for themselves and try to act as mature as they could.

One of the best of the older men was Luis Martinez. He never laughed at the boys' mistakes, but often tried to suggest ways to solve a problem. Old Luis, unlike most of the men of that era who came into the Valley to ride for Miller and Lux, had seen better days. He could read and write both Spanish and English and as a boy had known both comfort and wealth. His father had owned herds of horses and cattle and Luis had been sent overseas to study horsemanship in Spain and Portugal. His father's hope had been that Luis would become an officer in the elite Guards of the dictator, Porfirio Diaz. All officers in this regiment were the sons of rich *haciendados* (big land owners) and served without pay. But the revolution had come. Luis' father had been left penniless and Luis had come to California in one of the trains loaded with cattle stolen from Mexican ranches.

He had stayed on the ranches because he had horses to ride and had refused all offers of advancement. He rode the best mouthed horses on the ranch.

Often when he and I were riding alone, he would tell me of what he had learned in Spain, and of the tradition and the horse culture which has come down to us through the ages.

Moreover, he was articulate enough to explain the mechanical principles of bits and what effect different leverages had on the mouths of horses. It was he who explained the types of necks and why one bit would work on one horse and not on another.

I have remembered much of what he said because I have always carried books and I made notes in the blank pages of those

Eduardo Grijalva   Juan Grijalva making a bit.

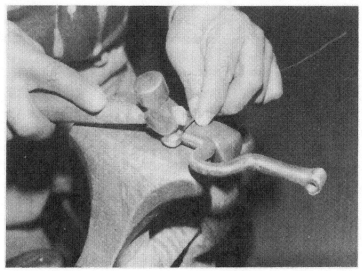

Skilled hand-inlaying of copper.

I carried in the bedroll. The following is preserved from that long ago lesson. It was back in the second decade of this century, over sixty years ago that the events which I am going to relate happened.

We were riding for Miller and Lux on the chuck wagon. That day, Old Luis and I had accompanied Rafael Cuen, the cattle boss, into Bakersfield to get a buckeroo who had come from one of the company ranches in Nevada. We got back to Corn Camp, which was were the vaqueros stayed, late that night.

The next morning, the new buckeroo, husky young fellow, carried his outfit which was in a bag, to the corral. He pulled the saddle, bridle, blankets and chaps out of the bag, spread them out on the ground and waited for "Old Jake" to give him a string of horses. Meanwhile, Luis and I caught a horse and saddled it. The rest of our string was awaiting us at La Panza Ranch where the chuck wagon was stationed.

In a few minutes, Cuen strolled by. As he passed, he gave the new buckeroo's outfit a fleeting glance; but in that glance, the cattle boss had learned what kind of a buckeroo the new man was, from what part of the West he had come and what kind of horses he could ride. The new man's outfit was an open book for all to read.

The well-worn, but well cared for, slick fork saddle with its bucking rolls, told that its owner was prepared to ride to a finish any horse that essayed to buck him. The bars of the mane-hair cinch gave further evidence of spur rowells having been hooked into them when some Nevada horse had bucked with the man who wore them.

The latigo which had been wrapped around the horn to hold the turns when a rope was wound around it, had deep grooves worn into it. The stirrups were linked inside with thick sole leather and tied to the stirrup leather so that they could not turn. It was the outfit of a proud, experienced man who could hold his own in any company of vaqueros.

However, one object struck an odd note in that buckeroo's outfit and that was his bit. A short-shanked, low port affair, commonly called a "grazer". It was not in keeping with the rest of the outfit.

Cuen gave the new man a string of six horses. When he had saddled one and turned the others out to drive to La Panza, we mounted. Driving the loose horses ahead of us, we headed for the chuckwagon some fifty long, hot dry miles ahead.

As we rode abreast, the loose horses ahead of us, Luis told the new man the names of the horses and their virtues, if they had any. "They are all good vaquero horses, but they are beginning to get old. Three of them were broken seven or eight years ago."

"Why would the boss give me old horses? I don't mind if a horse bucks me off once in a while, as long as I don't have to prod him along. I never thought they were so particular out here, even if this is spade bit country."

"It was the grazer bit," Luis answered. "If you put a five-pound bit on a ten-pound mouth, the horse will learn to bear on it and the result will be a hard-mouthed horse. These horses have been worked with cattle so much that they work without the need of guidance from their rider. They would work just as well without any bit."

"My bit was stolen at a rodeo in Elko," the new man said. "I ordered one from Garcia, but it hasn't got here yet."

I was a kid then and prone to ask foolish questions. "Why would Old Jake be so hard to please?" I asked. "A bit is just a bit." As we rode abreast across the flats, over the Temblor Range, across the Carrizo Plains to La Panza, Old Luis gave me the following explanation of bits and bitting.

"There has always been much disagreement among people who ride horses in respect to the merits of the high port bit and the low port bit; and it will go on until people are taught the principles of bitting. While I do not wish to sound arrogant about which mouthpiece is best, I shall give my reasons why I will not use a low port with little leverage. Popularly called a 'grazer'."

"A bit with a low port and little leverage is to some people a "mild" bit, but actually it is a VERY SEVERE BIT and the reason that it is a VERY SEVERE BIT is that a horse will disregard it to the extent that a hard pull is required on the reins. From the very beginning, the horse will resist the pull until his mouth gets harder and harder, then it is not long before the horse has learned that by bearing on the bit his jaw will become numbed. And since there is no more feeling, he can do whatever he pleases regardless of his rider's pulling and tugging on the reins. And that is the end of the rider's control over the horse."

"Then the rider will shop for a bit with more leverage, that is, a bit with longer shanks; and he is wrong again. Because with more leverage, the sooner the horse's jaw will become numb because of the stronger pressure on the jaws."

"The spade or high port bit was used on the ranches because the horses were often overridden and became exhausted. As a consequence, they lay on the bit in order to brace themselves. It seems that they could go a little farther if they had some support. If the rider on a tired horse was using a low port bit

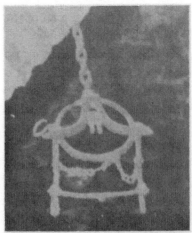

An old ring bit used on mules in Mexico.

This bit hangs at the entrance to the Cathedral in Seville, Spain. It is said to have been given to Alfonso the Wise by a Moorish King.

with little leverage, the horse would bear on it and once he got the habit, he would never get over it."

"Years ago when the big ranches still ran cattle, the foremen were loath to hire a man who used a grazer bit because the days were long and the horses were ridden hard and were sure to bear on a bit which they disregarded from the beginning. The end would be that the horse would become hard-mouthed. A horse begins by disregarding the bit, then by bearing on it and then ends up by stampeding with his rider and a stampeding horse will go over a cliff or bluff. Besides, in a sixteen-hour day of bearing on a bit, a horse will cut his tongue in two without knowing it and the rider won't know it until his attention is called to the stream of blood pouring from the horse's mouth."

"Split reins are another cause of spoiled mouths; for no matter how careful a rider is, sooner or later he will accidently drop one of his reins and the horse will step on it. The hard jerk on the horse's mouth will cut the tongue in two."

"A tour through the equestrian museums of Europe with their display of bits will tell the story of ancient horsemen and their problems . Their biggest problem with the horses was the bits, because they were the medium with which they controlled their horses in the heat of battle. Horses were only used for fighting in wars in those days."

"Down through the ages men have sought a bit which would control a horse, but never found it - because the more a horse's mouth was pulled on, the harder his mouth became. From bitter experience, men, through trial and error, have developed high port bits, spades, rings, half-breeds, serrated nose bands, spiked chin straps, long-shanked bits, curved-shanked bits and solid-cheeked and loose-cheeked bits; but never solved the problem."

"There is no need today for the trigger-reined horse. As a matter of fact, there was no need for him during the cattle ranching days in California during the last two centuries, unless the rancheros went out to fight Indians - which was a remote possibility."

Andy Jarequi always rode a good horse.

"A good cow horse will work a cow or drive one out of a herd without guidance of his driver just as a dog will work sheep. The reined horse was needed in the days when men fought each other on horseback and the outcome of battles was decided on the merits of the contending riders and a rider's life depended on the dexterity of his horse. To be sure, the old Californians delighted in a trigger-reined horse; but that was because their ancestors had been Spanish Cavalrymen and rode reined horses; and since those men took great pride in their heritage they continued the custom of making their horses as silk in their riders hands. They used a high port and considered it best because it taught the horse to never bear on the bit and as a result he never got hardmouthed."

"Although it entailed much time and patience, those old-time riders had plenty of time and plenty of horses. If a horse was not finished this year, he could be finished the next. By the time the horse was in the bridle, he and his rider knew each other so well that there was perfect communication between them. The horse could read his rider's mind. It took time to train the horse to perfection in the hackamore and then another period in the double reins before he was considered to be perfectly reined. It did not take more than a few rides to find out if a colt was a knothead. And since there were thousands of horses that could be had for the taking, he was quickly discarded and another was tried."

"However, there are certain horses in sports which must depend on their rider's guidance. Polo is one game where a horse must be guided, because if the horse anticipates his rider's wishes, he can turn on a back stroke and collide with a rider in the opposing team."

"The old-time ranch horse and the modern show "stock horse" are worlds apart. A trainer in the course of a day's "warm-up" in the exercise arena will pull a horse more in one hour than an old-time vaquero on a ranch would have pulled his horse in a year. Bits which were used on ranch horses did not work on show horses. Slowly, by trial and error the trainer of show horses has learned which bits will work best on those horses and such bits are being produced by such men as Eduardo Grijalva and Stan Ruano, Gordon Hayes, Dave Klesper and Mike McDowell. Likewise, the horse which the vaquero broke was between four and five years old and does no longer exist, The colts today are two or three years old."

"So much for the modern horse; the well-reined horse has been in use since time immemorial."

"The victories by men mounted on light horse over men mounted on heavy horse is a well-known fact of history and has been done many times through the centuries. The Crusaders brought horses they had captured to Europe, which were a marvel to the heavily armored knight of the period. If they had looked closer, they would have found Spanish Moors riding A La Jineta in Spain next door, so to speak. They had been riding light horses in Spain since the eighth century."

"It was a marvel to the old vaqueros why they would find a perfect horse in size and conformation among bands of scrubby mustangs. *Un Doblon Entre Reales Sencious* (a doubloon among simple reales), or a pearl among swine.''

The secret belongs to the Maker of good and faithful horses. Perhaps the current of fine blood ran hidden until it pleased the god of horsemen to bring forth a good horse.

Sonora Vaquero

THE FEAST DAY
OF SAINT FRANCIS

It was the fourth of October in Magdalena, Sonora, Mexico. The old mission town was crowded with Yaquis and Papagos who had come to celebrate the feast day of Saint Francis whose image lies in the church. The Yaqui chief and I were sitting on a bench in the plaza contemplating the remains of Padre Eusebio Francisco Kino which had been unearthed in this plaza and left exposed after a kiosk had been built over them.

He was the missionary who had pushed the frontier into Sonora and Arizona by establishing mission churches and "little cattle ranches" in the uplands of Pimeria Alta. It is this Jesuit to whom we are indebted for establishing the cattle industry in what became in time the Western United States. He spent many years exploring the bleak, inhospitable, waterless waste which came to be known as the Colorado Desert. He was the first explorer to envision a route overland across the Devil's Highroad to California and the Pacific. It was Padre Kino who charted the trail for Padre Francisco Garces and Don Juan Bautista De Anza who opened the route across the Colorado River and the terrible sand dunes to the missions of California.

I observed to the chief that the Papagos were all big and fat, while the Yaquis were small and thin. "Yes", the chief said, "but many of the men you see here among the Papagos are

Caborca, Sonora - Kino Mission

actually Yaquis who escaped across the border into Arizona after one or another of the numerous battles they fought with the federal troops or the blood-thirsty Rurales of Don Porfirio Diaz, who was an Indian, but wanted to be a *criollo*. He tried to prove it by persecuting the Yaquis. He took their land and gave it to the *haciendados* (large land owners), many of whom were gringos. The gringos brought mercenaries with machine guns to slaughter the Yaquis. Nevertheless, before he was through, Don Porfirio was to learn that the Yaqui was hard to whip and could give as much as he took. He would never give up his land. A Yaqui is tough."

"A Yaqui will run all day beside a horse and when the horse lies down and dies, the Yaqui will run on and on. The Yaqui, unlike his kinsmen the Apache and the Commanche, does not use a lance on horseback. He is a mountaineer and fights on foot. He likes to charge his enemy waving a machete, running to close with him as he learned to do through the centuries of fighting the iron men of Spain. When captured, if he ever is, he will brace his body against the "dobe" wall so that the bullets of the firing squad cannot topple him and he dies singing the Yaqui death song, "*El Yaqui que sabe morrir*" (The Yaqui who knows how to die).

"For the Yaqui, in his fights through the centuries, has never learned to give or receive quarter."

The chief pointed to a young man who was dancing a *Pascola*, the famed deer dance in which the dancer wears a beautifully made deer head strapped atop his head and imitates the motions of a frightened deer.

"That boy is a Yaqui, he was born in Arizona and went through high school there and is a veteran of the Second World War. He does not resemble most Yaquis because he is fat. And he is fat because in the States the people eat much and work little, while here in the Bacatete of Sonora we eat little and work much; and for that reason they are big and fat and we are small and thin."

But whatever little the Yaquis ate, that little was extremely nourishing, because they were all fine physical specimens. Their slender bodies suggested thin steel cables; and whenever one strode by I would think, "I'm glad I don't have to try whipping him," and wish I were thin and wiry like him.

Pasqual Michel on a fiery horse three days before his death.

Pasqual Michel: a good man, a good horse, a good outfit.

PASQUAL MICHEL

Pasqual Michel and John Fernando Michel, in company with three other men, were pioneer cattlemen in the Hanford area of the San Joaquin Valley. In a period of less than two years the group paid $56,000 in freight bills to the Santa Fe Railroad. For many years, John Fernando was a cattle buyer for Miller and Lux with authority to ship carloads of cattle on Henry Miller's banking account. In later years he reclaimed land in the Goldberg district and raised grain and other crops.

John Fernando had a wide knowledge of the area in which he lived and was able to supply information to historians doing research on early day happenings. He died in Hanford on July 1, 1950 at the age of eighty-seven.

Pasqual B. Michel moved to Southern California and became famous as one of the finest horsemen in the West. In Pasadena he established a livery stable on Dayton Street. He made a name for himself by driving in the chariot races at Tournament Park, in Pasadena on New Year's Day. He won second place with a cash purse of $2,500.

The horses driven in those chariot races were thoroughbred running horses. The only way the driver could control the horses was for him to place his feet against the fore part of the chariot and lie back horizontally. This action was to provide enough

Pasqual Michel in New Years Day chariot race, 1904. Michel came in second, but won it the next year - 1905.

Pasqual Michel won this race at Tournament Park, Pasadena on New Years Day 1905.

leverage to hold the racing horses on their course. This writer's uncle, Jim McFall, drove horses in the chariot races and used the method just described.

This writer knew the worthy Michel family as a child in Pasadena, my birthplace. My brother, Rafael Rojas, was a boyhood chum of Fernando, Pasqual Michel's son.

Pasqual Michel's greatest wish was to train horses. He was so expert in his work that the banker, Marco Hellman, engaged him to manage his horse program. Mr. Hellman bought the best reined horses he could find on the ranches of the West and gathered a group of expert riders. While Michel was in charge, Mr. Hellman's riders won many trophies and ribbons in horse shows and fairs. In establishing this group of horsemen, with Pasqual Michel as manager and often teacher, Mr. Hellman saved the old California tradition of horsemanship from being forgotten.

Fernando, Pasqual Michel's son, "the horseman of the family," as his brothers called him, was superintendent of Rosedale Ranch for the Kern County Land Company during the "forties" and "fifties". I have a picture of him driving four Kern County Land Company mules, hitched to the Miller and Lux chuckwagon.

Fernando Michel driving four Kern Co. Land Company mules hitched to the Miller and Lux chuck wagon carrying a number of old Teion Ranch Vaqueros. About 1948 or '49 this was the last horse

Riding in the wagon are a number of old Tejon Ranch vaqueros, who had grown too old to ride a horse.

Pasqual B. Michel died in Los Angeles on May 30, 1934 at the age of seventy-three. *DIOS LO TENGA EN VERDADERO DESCANSO.* He sleeps in the Old Mission Cemetery in San Gabriel.

I am indebted to his son, Walter G. Michel, for much of this material. He came to my house one day, like a memory out of the past and gave me heretofore information about his father's history. And I thank him, for his father was a man whom I have admired since I was a boy.

Fernando Michel, son of Pasqual on a good horse.
1930

JOAQUIN MURRIETA

In all the countries of America once ruled by Spain, now and then one will come upon groups of people living apart from the rest of the population; and only they knew how they got there and settled on that spot. They lived their own lives, speak their own language or dialact and have little to do with their neighbors.

These people descend, sometimes from fugitive Jews, sometimes from fugitive Arabs or Moors. Their women are always beautiful, with olive complexions and long-lashed "gazelle" eyes. In escaping from the Inquisition, behind them is a tale of bribing high officials in Spain to keep their lives and a meager portion of their once-vast wealth, of bribing ship's captains to take them aboard and away from sure death in the flames of the *Quemadero*.

How they managed to keep the captains from throwing them into the sea, no one knows. Spanish ship's captains believed in their "Christian" duty to destroy all "heretics" fleeing from the flames of the Inquisition; but not, however, before slitting their bellies open to see if they had swallowed any gold. Perhaps the passage   money was held by some great lord until the fugitives landed in America.

However that may have been, descendants of those people are found in isolated spots of Spanish America.

There is another group of people distinct from those mentioned above who are also clannish and aloof. They differ from the others, however, in that they have never been fugitives. They have always been stout Christians. As a matter of fact, they guarded the padres and the Cross from Vera Cruz to California. These people descend from the Basque *conquistadores* who came to New Spain with Hernan Cortez or Panfilo De Narvaez. One can trace their paths from the Gulf to the Pacific. Such people were the Murrietas, the Duartes, the Feliz, the Ybarras, the Aquirres and the Valenzuelas. They settled around the old town of Real De Alamos and the town of Fuerte, which means fort and along the Fuerte River. Most of these people were fairskinned. They are called *blancos* (whites) in Mexico.

For generations they had raised horses, mules and cattle and fought off Yaqui and Mayo Indians. Horsemen before the Lord, they were expert in the use of the rawhide riata and in the trapping of wild mustangs. They came in a close-knit group to California, but after a short time in the fields, the gringos drove them from their claims. this group then turned to trapping wild horses in the San Joaquin Valley. Thousands of wild horses roamed the Great Valley when the gringos took possession of California. The tame or domesticated horses in the herds which belonged to the rancheros, that could be handled easily, were stolen by the gringos and driven into the prairie states. Many a Civil War mount had come from the ranches of California.

The wild horses were left to run on the plains until the Sonorans began catching them and driving them south of the border where they brought a fair price. This practice with the business of packing supplies with mules into the mining camps in the Sierras, brought them a living. These men were honest ranching people and not horse thieves, as one writer claims. The wild horses had no owners; as a matter of fact, the *rancheros*, who owned the ranches along the western rim of the Great Valley, often gathered in large groups and drove great bands of wild mustangs over cliffs to drown in the ocean. This was done to get rid of them and save grass for the cattle.

These rancheros welcomed the wild horse hunters and even aided them in gathering the mustangs. It must also be remembered that the Sonorans who came in the Gold Rush were cousins or near relatives of those who had come with Portola, De Anza, Fages, or Rivera. In view of this circumstance, there was no friction between the established rancheros and the newcomers. Only a person who has handled horses can visualize the heartbreaking toil of capturing and taming broncos enough so they could be driven for a thousand miles across the most desolate and arid desert in North America.

The drive took sixty to ninety days, depending on conditions. The horses the vaqueros rode had to be broken on the trail and had to be hog-tied before the men could put shoes on them. Water had to be carried across the Devil's Highroad, which was part of the route, in rawhide bags on horses which were broken to carry a pack on the trail. The drives were made in the fall and winter, because the thermometer rises to one hundred and twenty-five degrees in the summer. The thirsty wild bands had to be night-herded to keep them from turning back to their home ranges.

Of these groups of men, Valenzuelas, Feliz, Duartes, Murrietas, who were driven from their claims in the Mother Lode country, none but Joaquin Murrieta stayed there. He stayed until he had killed all the gringos who had lynched his brother and raped his wife.

The rawhide riata was the best weapon of offense in avenging himself, for unlike a gun, it made no noise. In the hands of an expert such as Joaquin, it was a simple matter to cast a loop around a man's body and drag him against a tree and thus breaking his neck. He managed to kill all his wife's ravishers but one. He escaped to Texas and stayed there until he died.

Murrieta's method of avenging himself struck such terror into the hearts of the gringos that the instant one saw a vaquero approaching, the gringo would take his rifle out of its scabbard and cover the vaquero until he was out of range, for it is a well-known fact that most men who commit atrocities in gangs at night are brave only when they are in gangs. When alone in broad daylight they are meek. This retaliation for wrongs done him on the part of Murrieta, nevertheless, put a stop to the wholesale lynching of Mexicans in Northern California.

After his work of vengeance had been completed, Joaquin Murrieta went back to Sonora and died in Cucurpe. His name had inspired such dread that other men took advantage of it whenever they took something away from the gringos, on riding away from the scene, would call out, "*Yo soy Joaquin*" (I am Joaquin). At times there were five Joaquins taking back from the gringos property which they had been robbed of in the invasion of California. All robberies were attributed to a "Joaquin" even if they were committed on the same day and five hundred miles apart.

It was the "Joaquins" who caused the governor to commission Harry Love to cut off some Mexican's head and swear it was Joaquin Murrieta's. Love and his posse rode aimlessly over the state, supposedly looking for Murrieta. When the time given him to find his man was near an end, Love returned to Los Angeles where a large number of Sonorans had settled. It was not hard for him to find a man among them who, not knowing Love's motives, could give the information that some of the Murrietas were trapping mustangs in the vicinity of Tulare Lake.

Love rode by forced marches to Cantua Creek northeast of the present town of Coalinga and found a large group of vaqueros trapping wild horses. Among them were a number of *rancheros* of well-known families; men who could witness any atrocities Love or his posse would commit. He withdrew his posse until he learned that most of the horse hunters had left for Sonora with their captive bands. He returned to Cantua and found five unarmed men camped at the creek; he and his men shot all five in the back, cut off the head of one and the hand of another and departed for San Francisco.

On the way Love captured a member of an old ranchero

family. The man was unarmed and rode upon the posse unexpectedly while hunting strays. Love tied the man's feet under his horse's belly. While crossing a river the captive's horse fell and the man drowned; another needless murder on Love's part.

There are many versions of the history of Joaquin Murrieta; they all differ on many details. After crediting those written by Joseph Gollomb, Walter Noble Burns, Rollin Ridge, Frank Latta. two versions written in Spanish and one wherein Murrieta is called the *Bandido Chileno*, after hearing numerous campfire tales in which Murrieta was the main subject, this writer has come to the conclusion that they all agreed on one point and that is: No man in California met with more injustice than Joaquin Murrieta and out of the whole dreary tale of rapings and lynchings, there is one fact and that is: An honest man was not given justice.

Since this writer was a small boy he has heard numerous tales of Murrieta from old men who lived in the latter part of the last century. And if those tales disagree with those he has read, he has this to say, "When it comes to campfire tales, one man's word is as good as another's. For legends are often accepted as truths and facts often accepted as legends. The result is that history is often not true, but is accepted as fact."

GRIZZLY ROPERS

Of all the creatures that roamed the plains and mountains of the Far West, the truculent, irascible California grizzly was the most dangerous. In fact, he was the fiercest animal in the Western Hemisphere. The grizzly often weighed half a ton and had the speed of a race horse. A female with cubs was even more to be avoided than the male as she was extremely bad-tempered and would charge anything that would threaten her offspring.

The vaqueros who rode out to rope a grizzly knew the risk involved in bearding the one animal, the great *Oso Pardo*, to which all other creatures of the wild gave way.

It was only when the need for one arose, a bear-and-bull fight, that the young men ventured out into the wilds to confront the terrible grizzly.

First, they selected a horse which would be reliable under all circumstances. Next the saddle and the bridle were inspected and repaired if neccesary. Most important of all was the rawhide riata which everyone used in that era. A *riata para lazar osos* (a riata for roping bears) was braided from choice rawhide. The strands were cut from only the back of the steers hide. After being carefully braided, each individual strand was pulled so that there would be no looseness, the riata was then pulled through four holes bored about eight inches apart in a hardwood post. After the riata was pulled through the four holes for many aching hours, it was smoothed into shape and became a live thing in the roper's hands. All the stretch was thus taken out of it. The *riata para lazar osos* was not much thicker around than a modern fountain pen. The reason the vaqueros used a thin riata was that the bear could grasp a thick riata much more easily than he could a thin one. The riata was greased for the first thirty feet of its length to make it even more difficult for the bear to grasp. Since a grizzly weighed more than the little mustangs of that era, he could easily pull a horse into reach of his claws. The vaquero would also grease his horse's tail to prevent the bear from holding the horse and mauling both horse and rider.

My uncle, Jim McFall, was born in 1850 and lived through the period when bears were still plentiful in California and a plague to the sheep and the cattle ranchers.

He once spoke of the practice of bear roping. "If there are four or more ropers and each man can put a loop on one of the bear's legs, the bear can be spread-eagled successfully. It is better to have more than four men because if one man misses or his rope breaks, another man can catch the leg before the bear can turn and charge. If the bear charges, the ropers must get out of the way. Roping bears was dangerous work and horses were often mauled."

Most of the time the vaquero left the grizzly discreetly alone and often rode out of his way to avoid meeting one.

I have an antique spur in my collections with rowells seven and one-fourth inches from point to point. It has two steel coils resembling clock springs on the shanks. When the rider's horse was in motion these coils would ring. The sound would alert any bear which happened to be on the trail. The bear would move away from the strange sound and thus avoid a meeting with the man on the horse. The sound also would be heard by the bear when the rider was at a distance, enough so that the bear would not be startled by the sudden appearance of the rider.

BAD WORDS

There is no incident in this work which has not occurred; no character which was not known on the ranches. All the names in this work can be identified today. Contrary to most "Western" themes, the vaquero was pretty much of a gentleman.

I still remember the occasion when Dick Kelly suffered an embarrassing half hour one day when he called an old friend an "Old F-----," in the hearing of his friend's wife.

Dick and his friend Boggs had ridden the range together for years, when finally Boggs had married and moved to another part of the country. That year, February 1926, we were on the Carrizo Plains. The chuck wagon which operated the year around in Kern, San Luis Obispo and Kings County was stationed at the Pimentel Ranch. We were finishing breakfast, when a car drove up and a man and a women got out and walked toward the group of vaqueros who were drinking their last cup of coffee around the cook's fire. The woman followed close behind the man, but stopped behind the wagon while he approached the group around the fire, shaking hands with each one. Dick Kelly who was stooped behind the coffee pot, with his back to the wagon, looked up, saw his friend and yelled, "Boggs! you old F---, what are you doing here?", just as Mrs. Boggs walked up to the fire and heard her husband called an "Old F-----". Dick saw that she had heard him. His face turned red with embarrassment. He turned around and leaving his coffee, walked to where his horse was tied, mounted and rode off. I joined him. As we rode off in the direction of The Painted Rock to gather cattle, he said, "I didn't know Bogg's wife was around, when she came up to the campfire I said, 'Boggs, you old F-----, what are you doing here?' and his wife heard. That was an awful boner."

I don't think any man today would have such a bad half hour as poor Dick had, even though he was one of the best gringo vaqueros in the country and a man among men; for one never heard foul language spoken in the presence of a woman whether she was a lady or not.

DEVIOUS ARE THE WAYS

Sometimes a small boy will try so hard to become expert in the skills of the vaquero, that his effort will delight the eye of the beholder and bring forth no end of chuckles. A boy will decide that he will become a vaquero and it is a distinct pleasure to watch his efforts in realizing his ambition.

One day while I was in the stable business in Bakersfield, I put on a dinky, little rodeo for the entertainment of the youths who visited me. The entire bucking string consisted of three horses and a mule. I gathered a number of goats for the boys to rope.

One Sunday morning the boys appeared to ride, high schoolers most of them. At that time if a boy living in the mountains wanted to go to high school, he would have to come to Bakersfield and live there while he attended school. There were only three of four high schools in the county then. Among the boys, there was a husky, broad-shouldered youngster about fifteen or sixteen years of age. He drew my attention because on getting out of the car the boys had come in, he ran up to where the horses were in the chute and mounted one. When the horse had quit bucking, he jumped off and ran back to the chute, pushed the boy, who was getting on the horse aside and climbed on it and rode it out. He repeated the performance on all the horses. The kids brought the horses back and rode them and the mule over and over again as long as they would buck, then they merrily got into the car and went home. That was my first meeting with the husky kid, Doug Silicz. His father ran cattle up on the South Fork. Bob Snow who went to school with Doug, told me the following stories of how Doug got his practice in learning to be a buckeroo.

Doug, Ray Stanfield, and another boy found a district where there were many dogs which would chase cars. The trio would drive up into the Northeast district of Bakersfield at night. While one boy drove, the other two would straddle a front lamp of the car. Whenever a dog would chase the car they'd rope it. How many times they were bitten taking their ropes off, I was never told. But they got a lot of practice . Most ranch boys aspired to be bronc riders so the first thing they would do was make for themselves a pair of bronc riding spurs. Then arose the problem of trying to find a horse to try the spurs on. In their hunt the trio went to the fairgrounds where they found an old albino horse. Doug immediately led him out of his stall and mounted him. Of course he tickled the horse with his new spurs and in the process cut him a little. For, inadvertently, Doug had left a few sharp points on the rowells. The result was that the next morning when the horse's owner came to saddle the albino to ride in a parade, he found him marked by Doug's spurs. It was out of the question to ride the horse in the parade. The owner stormed and fretted. He asked questions but no one ever told on Doug, who smiles slyly when someone asks him if he remembers the albino horse.

One time at a show, for some reason or another, Doug grabbed his saddle horn. A spectator at the other end of the arena yelled, "Hey, let go of that horn!" Doug rode around the arena and when he came to where the man was, said, "When I bought this saddle I bought the horn, and I grab it whenever I feel like it."

The boy's efforts to learn their trade brought good results. Doug was a foreman on a ranch in the wheatland area of north Sacramento for many years. Ray Stanfield was superintendent of the Land Ranch Company and now is manager of Fat City in the Salinas Valley. Bob Snow owns his own ranch and runs cattle in the Granite Station area.

Tejon Indians in town for Frontier Days - 1933.

POKER FACE

In my stories of long ago I have often spoken of the Indians of the Tejon and their chief, Juan Losado. But the Indians are gone forever from the little adobe village on the Tejon Ranch. The little group of houses in Tejon Canyon which made up the Indian village are forlorn and empty. The adobes where fugitive Indians found refuge and a home for many years, are deserted. Some of the roofs have fallen in and the sturdy grapevine which had been coaxed into an arbor to provide shade has withered and died. For the *acequia* which brought water from the creek has long been dry. Most of the Indians have died and are buried in an old Indian graveyard. The few who survived, moved away. The men who lived there and made so important a contribution to the labor force on Tejon, are no more. It is a sad thing to contemplate, but they were good people and the best vaqueros in the world.

I always admired them for their dignity and their ability to control their features so that no sign of emotion ever showed on their faces. If they were ever afraid, they never showed it. Their faces remained dead-pan, excepting of course, when something amusing happened, for contrary to the stereotype of the glum-faced Indian, they laughed often and long. In fact they were always joking.

True, on their visits to town, they sometimes got in the slammer; but that was because they had imbibed of the joy-juice and while under the "influence" drove a car. Captain Leroy Galyen, of the Highway Patrol, had his hands full with the frequent accidents on the "Suicide Stretch" of the old Ridge Route, Dead Man's Curve and the Grapevine Grade. Narrow, crooked, steep, it was a tough route to drive, even for a sober man; and the captain would tolerate no drunk driving. Anyone caught was sure to make the hoozegow. Otherwise, the Indians were harmless and law-abiding.

Even the chief once had a little difficulty. Old Juan was invited to dinner at the home of a Bakersfield business man. After dinner and a few glasses, the old chief decided to walk to his hotel to clear his head. Since he was about ninety years old, he naturally tottered a little. An alert patrolman picked him up and took him to the jail. When the sheriff, Johnny Loustalot, saw him, he roared, "Take that old man back to his hotel and put him to bed." The next day the chief appeared in Judge Frank Noriega's court. When the judge saw him waiting patiently, he invited the chief to come sit on the bench with him so that they could talk over old times. That afternoon the chief drove back to Tejon in his buckboard, with his dignity still unruffled.

One day, back in the early thirties, Vance Brite, the chief criminal deputy in the sheriff's office, came to me and asked me to take charge of the Indians from Tejon who were coming to Bakersfield to take part in the Lion's Club Rodeo and Celebration. I was in the stable business on the outskirts of town and in a position in which I could handle the assignment. I had corral space and they could camp on the ranch. Accordingly, I sent word to chief Juan Losada that if the boys would come in, I had been promised an eagle feather war bonnet and a buckskin costume for each man. They were very sensitive about their appearance when depicting the early days of our country.

Most Indians who came in had ridden the range on Tejon for years and were seasoned vaqueros. Only two of the group were teenage boys. One of the boys, I noticed, had very little to say, though the others made delighted comments on the elegance of the costumes which I unpacked and issued to each man.

I had borrowed horses to mount the Indians from Cecil and Earl Pascoe. I let each man pick his own mount, but I gave a gentle-looking horse to each of the boys. The older vaqueros, I figured, could take care of themselves. We all mounted and rode to Chester Avenue, where I went to look for the man who was marshalling the parade. He told me where I was to take my position. I rode back to the Indian group, but when I got there I found an atmosphere of hilarity among them. Something had happened. I turned to Augustine Hinio who was grinning the widest and asked, *"Que Paso?"* (What happened?) "The wind blew Canuto's war bonnet over his face and the horse bucked. Canuto stayed with him, only his feet went through the stirrups. Jim and Bob stopped the horse and helped him get his feet out. The horse bucked so high, I could see the roofs of those sheds under his belly", Augustine explained.

"How is it that these kids can ride so well?" I asked.

He grinned again and said, "The kids on Tejon Rancheria have been corraling the Tejon horses on moonlit nights and bucking them out."

Then I understood why the Tejon boys were such good riders and the Tejon horses so prone to buck.

A year or two later, while Canuto was paying me a visit, I got an impromptu invitation to ride in a parade. Participation in all community events was always good publicity for my business. I agreed to ride and since I had two costumes with war bonnets, the next morning Canuto and I got ready. I had two beautiful pinto colts I was riding for an oilman, so Canuto and I saddled them.

The two colts were red and white and very gentle. I knew they would be cowed in the crowds of people and would follow the horses ahead of them. There had been other times when we had borrowed an unbroken colt out of pasture and ridden him through crowds of people. The colt would crowd close to another horse and go right along. Jimmy Albitre had ridden green colts in several of our parades. A horse in a strange place will very seldom cut up. We did not have time to shoe the pintos, because to shoe a horse to ride over pavements and streetcar rails entailed a number of things. First, we had to fit the shoe to the horse's foot, then take the shoe to a welder and have him weld borium on the heels and toes. A horse shod with borium will not fall, even if he steps on a slippery rail, because borium is one degree less hard than diamond and will cut the steel of a streetcar rail.

The line of march was down Nineteenth Street. When we got to L Street, the horses ahead of us made the street wet and slippery. Canuto's colt stepped on a rail and slipped and slid, trying to get his balance. Canuto left his reins loose to give the horse a chance and staring straight ahead, sat the horse until he was straightened up again. We did not notice, but a number of people from Chinatown were among the spectators.

The next day I went down L Street, which was the old skid row and a Chinese came up to me and said, "Indians, he come from China." Another friend, a Japanese said, "That poker-faced Canuto did not bat an eye when that horse almost fell with him." Canuto with his dead-pan face had stolen the show again.

Of course, we would never undertake to ride across the river bridge nowadays; but Bakersfield was a much smaller town then and we could ride down 99 without getting killed.

TOMMY

My recollections of little Tommy Condley have always been pleasant, for he is a genial little Irishman. He has always been "Little Tommy" because he is not much over five feet, but husky and almost as broad as he is tall.

The first time I met him was at a little, dinky rodeo Sal Rodorigus had put on. Tommy turned to me and asked, "Do you think I ought to get on that horse?" (A bronc standing in the chute).

"Sure," I said, by way of encouragement, "get on him, he won't do much."

I don't remember whether Tommy rode the horse or got bucked off. It was his first time on a bronc. He was never afraid and would get on anything.

In those days, the early twenties, George Foote had a rendering plant on Brundage Lane. He bought every horse that anyone wanted to get rid of. Horses too old to work, crippled, or spoiled in the breaking were sold to Foote to be rendered into chicken feed and fertilizer.

One day Tommy came to me and said, "George Foote has bought a bunch of horses that have been spoiled. If they can be ridden, he could get a lot bigger price for them than he could for chicken feed. He wants me to see if they can be ridden. I want you to snub them for me."

Truly - "The lack of imagination is the guardian angel of the bronc rider."

We went to see the horses. They were big stout animals, seven or eight years old and weighed from twelve to fourteen hundred pounds each. They look like horses out of a bucking string. They were horses that someone had tried to break and had not suceeded. Max Enderley raised horses like these out on the desert near the Liebre Ranch. Stout animals with a lot of coach-horse blood in them. I shook my head in doubt. But as I have said, Tommy would get on anything that wore hair and had four legs, confident his gardian angel, who protects the fool-hardy, would keep him from getting his neck broken.

I snubbed the first one. When Tommy was seated firmly in the saddle, I turned the horse loose. He squatted for an instant then threw himself over backwards. But the angels had their arms around Tommy, for he wasn't hurt.

We tried another horse but he fell over backwards. I didn't want to see Tommy killed so I refused to snub any more horses. I advised Tommy to let those horses go while his neck was still in one piece. I also advised that the angels could get tired of holding their arms around him and to quit while he was ahead. Foote hadn't bought those horses for chicken feed prices (one cent a pound) if the owner could have sold it to anyone else. Foote gave us two dollars and we went on our way. He had proof enough for he rendered the horses that afternoon.

In those days, partnerships were made on the spur of the moment. One could meet a man in the pool room, in a bar or on the street, start a conversation and after a few moments, join forces and leave town together to seek work on the ranch or in the oilfields, Some of those partnerships, made so abruptly and without forethought, often lasted many years or even a lifetime.

I remember I once joined forces with Tommy to go into the mountains to buy horses.

George lent us a little white horse about fourteen hands high which turned out to be one of the toughest horses I ever knew.

He must have had some Shetland in him because he was sturdily built and shaggy.

Tommy rode and I drove my car which was an old 1919 model Dodge. I had bought it for a hundred and fifty dollars and it was one of the good cars I have owned.

The first day we made Poso Flat where we stayed with Rafael Marvis. Rafael had another Dodge, just like mine, parked under a tree. After I had told him I was mechanic enough to keep my car in running order, he asked me to get his to run. It had been sitting under the tree for over a year. I worked all day, but never got the car started.

The next day we left and went up into the mountains around Glennville. After a week, we had bought about twenty horses. Some were old vaqueros' horses which had become too old to ride in the mountains. Some had turned out to be buckers while some were cripples or misfits the ranchers wanted to get rid of. We paid from two to five dollars for each of the horses. Sometimes a rancher would give us a horse on the condition that we take it away.

On the return journey we camped at Granite Station. The Bigots ran the station at the time. We bought a dozen eggs and scrambled them with potatoes and proceeded to eat. But, the eggs were bad and as a result, we were ill the whole night.

When we got back to Bakersfield, we sold the horses to Foote and made a little money in the sale. The little white pony which Tommy had ridden for ten days was still going strong when we arrived. He was one tough little horse.

One day we took in a tall, thin, gangly old man who was broke and out of a job. He said he had ridden in Nevada and Arizona, but he was so old that no one would hire him. A drifter, like many others of that era, he was senile, helpless and trying to survive. He was of the gaunt, lean southern mountaineer type who never got fat. We could see that he had been on short rations for many days. His spare, old body was a book in which we read of a hungry childhood and manhood of hard work and cheap

A corral in the Sierras.

wages. He had tried for a job on the ranches but no one would give him a job riding. After we had seen him on horse, we knew why.

We advised him to try for a job as a pumper with the Land Company or Miller and Lux. On the big ranches the pumper harnessed and hitched the mule which supplied the motive power for the pump which lifted the water from the well and filled the troughs with water for the cattle. The mule, hitched to a beam, traveled in a circle and was blindfolded in order that it would not get dizzy. Over a period of time, the mule would stop when he got to the spot in the circle farthest from his driver. But, when he heard the footsteps approaching, he would start again. One pumper made himself a slingshot; henceforth, everytime the mule stopped, he would pepper its' rump with pebbles, thus out maneuvering the mule.

There was usually a rider in the camp with the pumper. Since the pumpers were always very old men, they often got attached to the mules and would quarrel with the animals. One would hear them grumbling and muttering. but they treated the animals well and fed them morning and night.

At some pumps, as at Painted Rock, there were two pumpers who were brothers, one thin and one fat. They kept four mules going all day. They were very conscientious and would hitch the mule before daylight. But, old Frank wanted a job riding.

I remember one night I wanted to go to the circus. The old man tried to talk me out of going because he was afraid I would spend all of my money and we would not have any left for grub. In the end, I bought a pound of coffee so, as Frank said, that at least we wouldn't be out of coffee.

Tommy and old Frank went to Nevada to look for work. Tommy got a job riding and Frank worked as a cook. When Tommy got back to Bakersfield, he told us that Frank was getting breakfast one morning when he stepped out of the wagon onto a wheel which was covered with ice. He slipped and fell on his head and was knocked unconscious. He was taken to a hospital in Elko where he laid twenty days in a coma and then died.

All Tommy could tell the authorities was that he knew the old man as Frank Young and that he didn't know where he came from or if he had any relatives. The old "loner" had died as he had lived, alone.

Tommy disappeared from Bakersfield. One day, years later, he appeared at my stable with Buster Clark. He had been in the army and had served in Germany and in the Arab countries throughout the Second World War. He and Buster worked together on ranches until Tommy left and went to live in Ventura where he married.

THE MIMIC

The ancestors of Don Jesus Lopez had come to California in the expedition of Don Juan Bautista De Anza; a circumstance which made Don Jesus very proud of his heritage. There were few schools in the Los Angeles of his boyhood and the few that existed were poor indeed. Don Jesus learned the little they had to give and by his own efforts through reading old books written in the Castillian spoken in the time of Cervantes, he educated himself.

He had a tradition to uphold; therefore, he took great pains to pronounce his Spanish clearly and distinctly, with all its inflections. It was the way of speech of the old Californians, so aptly described by Richard Henry Dana in his "Two Years Before the Mast". To the Indian vaqueros who spoke bluntly and in monotones, the old Don's way of speech was a mannerism which amused them. In fact, they became quite expert in mimicking him and the best mimic on Tejon was Juan Gomez, the one-legged vaquero.

Early one morning Don Jesus had arrived at the vaquero camp and led the men out to gather the beef herd which was running in the home pasture. As he sent each man out to bring in the beef he cautioned him to be sure to drive the steers very slowly so that they did not lose flesh. Tom Eveleth, the cattle buyer, had come to Tejon to select the prime beef.

That afternoon at two o'clock the work of parting out the fat steers was finished and the vaqueros had come in to eat. When the vaqueros worked cattle Don Jesus ate at the vaquero camp. He took Tom to the foreman's house to wash. The vaqueros washed up at the bunkhouse and then crowded around the cookhouse to wait for the bell. As the men were waiting, Juan gave a, "Harumph" to get their attention and began to send out each man to make the rodeo just as Don Jesus had done.

He signaled out Adolfo and said, "*Tu Adolfo me los arreas despacio, muy despasito hijo.*" (You Adolfo, my son, drive them slowly, very slowly.)

Juan had imitated Don Jesus so well that the men were roaring with laughter, when Don Jesus and Tom came around the corner of the cookhouse. They had been listening. Tom was having a hard time keeping a straight face. Don Jesus, with an amused gleam in his eye said, "Juanito, my son, you have forgotten Mr. Eveleth and me, let me hear you send us out". Juan, nothing loath, sent Mr. Lopez and Tom out just as he had sent the other men, while Don Jesus lent a critical ear. Then he said, "Juanito, I believe you are as good a mimic as my cousin, Leo Carrillo."

FORTY YEARS
A HORSE DENTIST

AUTHOR'S NOTE

This article was written for "The Western Horseman" and published in the August 1982 issue.

I wish to thank Mr. Chan Bergen for permission to reprint it in this edition of "Vaqueros and Buckeroos".

Through the years we rode the range and worked on cattle ranches, we knew nothing about care and floating of horses' teeth. It was something the ranchers did not know or did not care about. If any horses were born with mouth defects, they did not survive on the range. If they were underdeveloped by the time they were old enough to be broken in, the rancher disposed of them, either sold them for chicken feed or destroyed them.

Horses with defects such as "parrot mouth" could not graze because their incisors did not meet. The result was they starved to death when feed was short or never developed into a useful horse. It depended how badly their jaws were deformed. There were so many good, fully developed horses that most ranchers never bothered with crippled or defective animals. This writer, in the early 1920's bought good horses for two dollars each.

A horse bred on the range will have to roam for many miles when grass is scarce. This makes the horse tough and develops his muscles. The rancher needs a tough horse that will stay under him throughout the longest day. He has no use for one that will play out and leave him afoot on the range miles from home and shelter.

It was not until I went into the stable business in the 1930's that I learned about floating teeth and how important it was for the horse. Although the care of the teeth had been an old custom in the eastern states. Kentucky, Tennessee, Maryland and Virginia have developed many good "mouthmen" or Veterinary dentists.

One day an old gentleman drove into my place of business and asked if I had any horses that needed floating. I didn't know what "floating" meant and Mr. Heath, who was the old gentleman, explained that floating consisted of rasping the sharp edges of the horse's teeth and thus smoothing, so that they would not interfere with the horse's chewing. I told the old gentleman I would ask and if the owners of the horses wanted it done, for him to return in a few days. A week later Mr. Heath returned and we set about working on the horses, since the owners had given their permission. Thus began my education as a horse dentist.

The old gentleman was a southerner, a native of Mississippi. At first I held the horses, but after he had done those at my stable, he would come to get me to help him. Then he would let me float one or two. I also would practice on every horse I got on the place.

As time passed, I developed a professional skill and the old gentleman told me what to look for in a horse's mouth that needed correcting. He taught me to read a mouth, that is, how to tell a horse's age by the cups in his teeth and the Galvain's Groove and also by the slant of the front teeth and   their shape. He showed me what to take off the teeth and how much, because if one takes off too much, he will offset the teeth and the horse won't be able to chew his food properly. The result would be a loss of weight. As we came to different problems, he taught me what to do to correct them. Of course, different horses have different problems, which are the result of domestication or ill-advised breeding. In Europe, a stallion cannot be bred without the approval of government veterinarians and it should be that way here.

Even a horse that has a bad neck, that is, an elk or pig neck, is gelded. Horses with swan necks are preferred.

The basic problems with a horse's teeth are the edges, which cut into the sides of his mouth, or interfere with his chewing. They must be ground off with a "float", which is a rasp on a handle long enough to reach the back teeth. The horse's teeth develop these sharp edges because the upper jaw is wider than the lower jaw. A condition which causes the teeth to wear at an angle.

Other problems are "wolf" teeth, which grow up against the upper molar or "grinder". They do not interfere with a horse that has ridden with a hackamore or curb bit. But nowadays, the snaffle bit is used extensively and when a horse is pulled with a snaffle, the mouthpiece is pulled against the upper molars. If there is a "wolf" tooth, the mouthpiece will drive the tooth into the flesh and cause pain.

Horses that rear and fall over backwards, or refuse to run on a tight rein, are, on examination, sure to have "wolf" teeth. A race horse must be taught to "lie" on the rein, so that one will support him. A horse cannot run if the rein is loose and "wolf" teeth will prevent him from bearing on the bit.

Throughout the years that I practiced horse dentistry, I found many interesting cases where the extraction or cutting of a tooth cured the horse of a bad habit.

Once, in Calexico, I met a man at "Augies", where bets are placed for all the race tracks in the country. In the course of our conversation, he said,"I have a colt that is bred to run, but he will not run, I wish I knew why." "I can tell you why," I said. "Your horse has 'wolf teeth', which prevent him from bearing on the bit."

"Will you look at him?" asked the man. "I will pay you, if you will."

"Where is the colt?" I asked.

"On the ranch that has the last date grove, west of El Centro, on Eighty."

I was leaving for the horse show circuit. In a few days, I got to the ranch and found the colt in a little paddock. He was a fine type of thoroughbred. I had a little trouble catching him. Two colored men were unloading hay and they helped me. Once I got my hands on the horse, he proved to be gentle and let me open his mouth. Sure enough, he had two big "wolf teeth". I pulled them and wrapped them in paper, putting them into the glove compartment of my pickup. I was headed for Seattle, Washington and forgot all about them.

That fall, when I got back to Imperial Valley for the winter, I walked over to the border to "Augies". I met the owner of the colt. When he saw me, he rushed up and shook my hand, asking, "What did you do to that Chestnut colt? He won his first three starts."

"I pulled his 'wolf' teeth. Remember I told you he had them. In fact, they are still in my pickup."

We walked across the border into Calexico, where I had left the pickup. I looked into the glove compartment and there they were. I gave them to the man, who was delighted and handed me a twenty dollar bill!

Another time I arrived at a large jumping horse stable. I had been floating the horses for a long time. The owner, a good jumping horse man said, "that horse fell over backwards with me."

I said, "You went to pace him before you came to the jump and pulled him."

"Yes", he said, "How did you know?"

"He has 'wolf teeth' and when the mouthpiece hit the 'wolf' teeth, he fell over. That happens all the time." In a joking way I said, "You should do like all the other good jumping horsemen. Wait until I come around and inspect the horses' mouths before you ride them."

"From now on, I'll wait until you get here before I ride any of the colts," he said.

Another time, a young trainer whom I had known all his life, was riding a horse with a spade bit. The horse would throw his head sideways and upward, when the rider pulled the reins. It was not because of poor horsemanship, as the rider had been trained by old Cleve Helm, one of the best trainers. I watched awhile and said, "Bring that horse over here." The boy rode over, dismounted and removed the bridle. The horse had abnormally long "tusks" or "canines". The upper canines were hooking into the braces of the spade bit. When the bit was pulled, it would hang on a tooth and cause the horse to throw its head. I had a pair of nippers, which I kept very sharp.

I caught the tooth close to the gum with the nippers, then I rotated the nipper as a person rotates a tool to cut pipes, until the tooth was gradually cut into two. I cut the tooth in this way, so that it would not shatter. If one makes only one cut, it's likely to shatter and pieces remain in the gum and work their way into the flesh, causing much pain.

Colts are often born with a tooth sticking out and cutting through the cheek. Parrot mouths are about the worst the dentist encounters, because there is no possible cure. People who are buying a horse neglect to look into its mouth and as a result have a parrot-mouthed horse foisted upon them. Some don't know enough to look into its mouth.

Once I came to the barn of a very successful trainer. Upon my arrival, he immediately hurried to me and said, "I want you to look at a mare. She hasn't eaten much since she came here, about a week ago." The mare had won a number of Championships in the East and was considered a valuable animal. I opened her mouth and looked into it. I have never seen one as bad as it was. The upper jaw overlapped the lower about an inch. But the worst part was that the first molar in the upper jaw had had no wear and it had grown so long that it was cutting through the lower jaw as a result.

I cut the protruding tooth and rasped the edges of the upper jaw. When I had finished, he said, "Done?" I said, "I am but you are not. The best thing for you to do, is to load that mare into a trailer and take her to a veterinarian, who can cut the back tooth on the lower jaw, which has grown as much as her front molar. It is probably boring into her skull." He put her into the trailer and hauled her to a "vet", who had the facilities for the operation. He told me later that the back molar was as long as the front one I had cut off.

The mare lived a few years longer, but there was no way to cure a parrot mouth. One may relieve a little pain. There are many cases in my experience, wherein a horse's performance in the show ring or his health and well-being has been greatly improved by having his teeth cared for. Every horse has a different mouth and a different problem. The good Lord did not make two sands on the seashore alike so it follows that no two mouths will be alike. The condition of the teeth has an effect on the horse's chewing and consequently, on his well-being and his behavior under the saddle.

One can walk into a corral and a glance at the dung will tell the condition of the teeth. A skinny, rough-coated horse always has bad teeth. If one will watch a horse working, the way he moves his head in response to a pull on the reins, will tell the condition of his teeth. When a dentist looks into a horse's mouth, he can tell from what part of the country it came. Horses from the Blue Grass country, with its limestone formation, will always have very good, hard teeth and seldom need floating more than once in a lifetime - if at all.

Horses from the Northwest, Oregon, Idaho, Montana, Washington, have good teeth. The New Mexico, Arizona horses have teeth worn down by the sand in those desert states.

Colts should be examined as yearlings, two-year old and three-year olds, for irregularities in their teeth. A colt starts shedding its milk or baby teeth, about two and one-half years of age. Sometimes racing colts are floated as yearlings, but it is hardly worth while, as they shed their teeth between the ages of three and four. That is the colt's worst time, because the loose teeth give them pain when they eat and the permanent teeth are too short to grind the food, The wolf teeth should be removed, however.

A horse should be examined very carefully when he is five years old, because by that age, he has his permanent teeth and if there are any irregularities, they should be corrected. "Floating" is simply rasping the sharp edges of the teeth and making them smooth. It is easy to take too much off. I found horses that had been "floated" by an inexperienced dentist, who had done this and the horse was not grinding his food. The result was that the food passed through the horse largely unchewed. We could see that, by examining his stools in the corral. One small rasp to remove that which is bothering the horse, no more. Now and then one finds a horse with lower teeth, which are cutting the tongue because the edge of the lower teeth is sharp on the inside.

Nowadays girls make up the crew around the barns and in one respect they are better than boys, because they are seldom combative. They have a gentler hand than boys and horses react to good treatment, although girls are seldom strong enough to compare with men in the heavy work. Nevertheless, I would much rather have a girl help me than most boys.

Speaking of help, I remember an incident which was amusing. Through the years, I have learned that the big stables that have many horses, have those which are the best broken. A horse in a chicken-coop corral, will more often give trouble.

As I grew older and of course not so strong, I would pass over those "barnyard savages" as they are called, because they would exhaust me in doing just one horse and since everyone for whom I had worked recommended me, I got many calls I did not want. I always refused, until one day, I met a lady who would not take "No" for an answer. She called several times and Bill C., who was learning to float, answered and told her I wasn't in. One morning she appeared at the place and since there was no escaping, I agreed to go to her place and do her horses, even though I didn't want to do so.

I asked her if there was anyone who could catch the horse for me and she said, "If I am not there, my daughter, who is seventeen, will catch them for you."

That afternoon, I said to Bill C., "We might as well go out there and float those horses. That lady won't let us alone until we do." "Yeah, I guess so", he answered. We drove about twenty miles to the place. As we drove in, we saw a little girl about nine or ten years old, in shorts and bandana waiting by the corral. The animals consisted of three mules, four burros, a Shetland pony and three or four old horses. They were all very poor and I saw the reason. The woman had been feeding them sour oat hay, which the stock would not eat, so had lost weight.

I did not see the woman or her daughter, so I turned to the little girl and asked, "Where is the lady or her daughter and who is going to catch the horses for me?" The little girl said, "I am." So I turned to Bill who is six feet six and winked, then I said to the little girl, "O.K. Get your pretty, little, lily white hands on a halter and catch one of those mules." The little girl was small for her age. She took a halter and walked into the corral. The mule she was going to catch, snorted and whirled around. The little girl took the end of the halter shank and hit the mule on the rump, holding up the halter. The mule turned around, walked up to the little girl and put its nose into the halter. The little girl had to jump up to buckle the halter behind the mule's ears. I looked at C and he looked at me.

We floated three of the horses. The mules, burros and Shetland didn't need it. When finished, I went to the little girl and handed her a ten-dollar bill. I said, "Here, Honey, the show was worth the price." She immediately left on a bicycle and before we had finished washing our tools, she was back with an armful of candy.

Incidently, I have never floated a Shetland, or ever found one that needed it. The reason is, that the Shetland, through the

Arnold Rojas - Carrizo Plains, June 1983

ages, had to survive on the cold, barren Shetland Islands and the ponies that had bad mouths could not live. As a result, only those with good mouths grew to maturity. It is the horses with defects, which are undermining the breed. These should not be bred, but unfortunately, they are.

The old time Californian with his thousands of mustangs, did not bother to float his horse, if he had known how to do so.

As I have said, tame horses are petted too much and are the worst to float. They have been allowed to do as they pleased and do not like one to "float" them.

One day, at a horse show in Santa Barbara, an old man walked up to me. He obviously had a "hangover", for his hands were shaking. He said, "Have you got a dollar for cigarettes?" "Dad", I answered, "here are two dollars. Go over and get a 'shot' of whisky to settle your nerves. Then come back." In about an hour, the old man returned. He had had a "shot" and felt much better. I gave him three more dollars and said, "Now Dad, go over and get some ham and eggs, under your belt." He left and just as he walked into the cafe, Frances E. came up to me and said, "Have you found me a groom?" "Francis," I said, "I have found you a man who can put your horses into form. He is one of the best grooms in the business. Take him home with you, feed him well, find plenty of work for him. Don't give him any whisky and I guarantee he'll have your horses into shape for showing. He has just gone to get breakfast."

After a while, the old man came out of the cafe. I called him over and introduced him to Frances. She took him to her ranch where he got her mares in shape, repaired and painted her barns and fences.

One day I stopped at Anderson's in Buellton and saw Frances there. She said, "I have a mare I want you to float." I went to her ranch and there was the old man. He led out the mare and I proceeded to float her teeth. While I was busy "floating", she suddenly struck me with her right foreleg. Luckily, she hit me as her leg was going up, but even then, she knocked me six or seven feet. I was not hurt and I picked myself up and proceeded to continue "floating" her. The old man said, "Wait a minute," got a blanket and threw it on the mare and buckled it at the throat, pulled it around and dropped it in front of the mare, like an apron. "She won't strike now," he said. I finished "floating" her and she never struck through the blanket. One never gets too old to learn.

Once at a horse show, in Northern California, I was walking by a group of stalls, when the trainer called to me and said, "Come over and sit down and tell us a story." I went over and sat down. The trainer said, "We had to take that little mare out of the class. She was bleeding."

I asked, "Did you look at her mouth?"

"No, would you do that for me?"

I got my tools and opened the animal's mouth. The sharp points on her teeth had made ulcers on her cheeks on each side. That was where the blood was coming from. I floated and smoothed her teeth, so that they would not cause bleeding. Also, I put salt into a Bull Durham sack and tied it to the mouthpiece of her bit. I told the trainer, "Let her stand all day with the salt in her mouth. It will dry up the wounds so that they will not bleed and tonight you can ride her in her class."

That night the little mare went through the class like an angel and won the Championship! Even afterwards, the owner would say to me, "You saved the championship."

There have been many such incidents wherein floating has so changed a horse's behavior, that over the years I have gotten the reputation of being a "wizard". But it was just "common sense" which I used in handling the animals.

Once, Sheila Varian, who is a top horse woman, asked how I managed to float a horse without the animal "cutting up" and I told her that one must approach any animal in a completely pacific attitude. That is to say, to have complete peace in his system. In order to float a horse, one must approach the animal in a complete spirit of peace, harmony and serenity. The horse will sense this and let himself be "floated". The first thing to remember, is not to fight the horses, because the man will not win. Force cannot be used in floating horses. If the dentist will grasp the animal by the soft part of the cartilage on the nose and hold it until the horse relaxes, he will be successful.

The old gentleman who taught me to "float" always said, "Get under the horse. If he strikes and hits you coming up, he will knock you away, but if he hits you on the downstroke, you will never float horses again. So by all means get close to the horse."

The first indication of bad teeth are "cuds" (particles of unchewed food) which the horse drops from its mouth and can be found in the manger. When this occurs the owner of the horse should lose no time in getting the horse's teeth floated, because "cuds" indicate that the horse is not chewing its food and if neglected is sure to have an "impaction", another name for colic which is often fatal.

ROPERS

Some years ago I was traveling south of the border. I was driving on the Pan-American Highway, which parallels the cobbled old Spanish Road in the state of Jalisco, when I saw five vaqueros moving up on a big Brahma bull. To all appearances they were going to rope him, because all had their ropes with a loop made in their hands, ready to throw. The bull weighed more than the combined weight of the little horses and mules they were riding. Two were little mules and three were little horses.

"This," I said to myself, "I've got to see."

I drove off the highway down to where the men were riding. I shut off the motor and got out to speak to them. Two were *Huichol* Indians and the others were native Mexicans of the area. All five carried ninety-foot *maguey* ropes. All rode the big-horned saddle of Central Mexico. Their bits were also typical of the area and carried a chain instead of a curb strap. Two of the horses were ridden with a bosal. All wore the big-rowelled spur of that region, strapped over rawhide *huraches* (sandals) and all wore straw hats. These men were poor working men from all appearances.

One who seemed to be the leader asked, "Do you have music in your car?"

"Yes, I have the radio."

Sonora Mule

"Bueno," he answered, "We will have a fiesta in your honor, after we doctor this bull."

I parked the car under a tree along the old Camino Real and walked out to watch them rope the big Brahma. One man made an enormous loop and rode out to where the bull was standing. The vaquero threw his rope. The big loop, instead of settling around the horns, passed them and settled around the neck. When the vaquero jerked up the slack, the bull started off, pulling the little horse, who sat back on his haunches in an effort to hold, but slid along the grass. However, small as the horse was, the bull could not pull his weight long and soon choked down and fell. The other men quickly put their ropes on the bull's legs, two loops on the front legs and two on the back legs. Thus, with the four little animals holding, the bull was held down while the man who caught him by the head doctored him.

"There are tricks in all trades," I said to myself.

That evening the people who lived along the old Spanish Road, danced to the music of the car's radio. After I had eaten breakfast with them, I drove on with their wishes, that I go with God.

Sonora Mustang

It seems to me that all the men and boys in the rural districts were expert ropers. The reason for it was that their only boyhood toy was a miniature rope made of the fibers of the *maguey* plant which grows abundantly in that area. Every chicken, pig, dog, cat and goat is used by the children to practice roping. The animals have been roped so much that when they see someone whirling a loop, they do not run. They just stand and let themselves be caught. Even little boys are expert ropers.

I saw many examples of roping skill.

I was driving to the town of La Barca, Jalisco. Coming upon a little meadow, I saw a number of animals being herded by a small boy. There was some burros, oxen, goats, a horse or two and a few milk cows. I was passing through them when I saw an especially fine ox among them.

The people down there were taking pains to match their oxen and one sees some fine, well-matched yokes.

I stopped the car and, taking my camera, stepped out to take a picture of the ox. People from foreign countries are strange to the animals of Mexico. One feels it in the dogs and other domestic animals. The ox would not stand, he shied away from me, even when I called, "Oh, Oh" as the people do to stop them. Suddenly a little boy stood before me and asked, *"Quiere que se lo laze?"* (Do you want me to rope him?) I put my hand in my pocket and pulled out a fifty-centavo piece and said, *"Sí"* (Yes).

He whirled and threw a little, thin maguey rope and as it settled around the the ox's horn, he said, *"Aquí está."* (Here he is).

I gave him the money and he said, "Do you want me to rope the other, his mate? He is behind the bushes."

As I pulled out another fifty-centavo piece, he led me behind some bushes and there was another ox, fully as majestic as the first. It was a matter of one whirl and one throw and the ox was roped. I gave him the fifty-centavo piece and went on my way.

That Saturday I met him in the town's plaza. He brought his father over to show him the *turista* (tourist) who had given him a whole peso.

Young Vaqueros

BOBBY AND JIMMY

They came during the 1930's when millions of people were broke and hungry.

About a year after Clyde had come to live with me, there appeared one morning, two, little, undernourished, undersized boys. They timidly stood at the gate, not sure they would be welcome. They were barefoot and naked except for a pair of shorts. The sun had burned their bodies a dark brown.

What a terrible misfortune, or unconscionable neglect, in this, the richest country in the world, had permitted these tots to sink into this condition? Hunger shrieked from their eyes, from their peaked little faces, from their shrunken little bodies.

Neither boy was seven years old and neither weighed twenty-five pounds. Already want had stamped a grim, dogged resolve on their wizened old men's faces, a determination to stay alive, to find food enough to kill the gnawing pangs of hunger and keep body and soul together. This instinct to survive, which is in all God's creatures, had brought them to my door. They were on the hunt and I was a prospective food provider. I could read their minds because I had been hungry like them. Only I had been cooped up.

I had spent my childhood in an orphanage where I had been starved and from want of food, had become an idiot in my boyhood. It was not until I was grown and had sufficient food when in some way, somehow, a miracle of nutrition had occurred in my body and cleared away the mental block which had kept me roving the country and in the lowest paid ranks of labor throughout my youth and early manhood. Truly, a man is what he eats.

I knew the little boys were Clyde's brothers, but I went through the routine with which I always met the kids he brought home to play with him.

"Who are these guys?" I asked. "My brothers, Jimmy and Bobby," he answered.

"Are they good guys?" I asked. "Oh, yes!" he assured me.

"Okay," I said, "they can stay around and play with you."

The little boys grinned. Things were looking up.

After Clyde had lived with me for several months I learned that of all the food I cooked he liked macaroni with onions, cheese and scrambled eggs the best. So, when I asked him what we should have for dinner, he said, "Macaroni, Rojas! Macaroni with cheese and eggs."

Beans, macaroni and rice were all we could afford to eat in those days and we were lucky to get those items. We feasted on meat when Mr. and Mrs. Felix Galtes gave a barbeque. The two boys would hide in the thistles nearby and Clyde would supply them with steaks.

Macaroni seemed to be the most filling and this is the way I prepared it. I put lard in a skillet and browned the macaroni first, then I added onions and then tomatoe sauce. When it was done I added cheese. Then I would scramble a dozen eggs and add them to the macaroni.

Sometime before the advent of the Story kids, Doctor Edwards, the veterinarian, had given me a little Buff Bantum rooster and three little hens. As time passed, people who had chickens they wanted to get rid of would give them to me. Since bantams are the busiest little chickens and the best of mothers. I soon began to meet with a little hen with a brood of toy chicks,

Clyde Story breaking his
first colt.

for they stole their nests and since I never gathered more eggs than I needed for a mess, I soon had fifty or more chickens. Incidently, when I moved away from Pierce Road, Clyde, Jimmy and Bobby gathered over a hundred and fifty little Bantams.

To get back to the kids, when the food was ready, I would set it on the table and say, "All right, you guys eat this up, but be sure to clean up when you get through." When I got back, the dishes would be washed and the yard would be raked by way of thanks. They would come to play with Clyde and have an occasional meal with us but, small as they were, they understood that Clyde had priority and they did not impose. From that day on they were part-time boarders.

They would go across the street and rake up around Ham's Service Station and Ham's mother would feed them. Whatever they got in the way of food they shared with each other. Adversity had taught them to feel for others.

They had been dealt cards by hands other than their own and were making the best of it. They bore their hard lot without whimpering and without complaining. Suffering had made them men when they were yet babies, for they acted like men. I always had a respect for them even when they were children. All three survived hunger to serve their country. When they grew up, they went into the service. Clyde to the Marines and Bobby to the infantry.

Jimmy says, "I went into the 'Maweens," (He has a slight speech impediment.) "and the D.I. says to me, "Story, is this boot camp tough for you?" and I said, "Sir, this boot camp ain't one-tenth as tough as my old man was."

Bobby said his worst trouble was keeping from being promoted to second lieutenant in the field while he was still in action in Korea. "That's a sure way to get killed," he said.

Many riders wore long underwear winter and summer because "shorts" will curl up and chafe the riders legs. Besides, "long johns" were warmer in winter.

The sight of "long johns" always struck a humorous chord in Bobby Story. One Fall, Bobby Story and Ernie Sanchez were staying with me while they were going to high school. They were earning their keep by helping me and making themselves useful after school.

One sunny day, just before the cold weather set in, I dug out my winter underwear and hung them out on the line to air in the sun. I went back into the house and was sorting out more clothes when I heard the boys laughing at something which must have been very funny from the noise they were making. I went out to see if they were in some mischief.

They were standing at the clothes line and laughing uproariously at my underwear hanging there. I put on a serious look and walked out to them and said, "All right, you two jokers, get your lily white hands on a pitchfork and "muck out" those stalls you have been neglecting for the past week. That will cure you of making fun of people's clothing." Still laughing, they walked off to find the pitchfork.

Bobby never forgot the incident. When he had grown up and was fighting for his country in the sub-zero cold of Korea, he was issued long woolen underwear. He must have thought of me and his boyhood in Bakersfield for, when he came back from the war, wounded, he brought two sets of long woolen underwear. He brought the package and handed it to me with a sly grin. I opened it and held out the underwear and Bobby broke into a laugh. After all those years, Bobby was still amused at the sight of "long johns".

DESERT RIVER

The Santa Clara begins as a desert stream and flows for many miles through a sterile landscape. On the map of California, it is called the Santa Clara River, but the Hispanics who named it called it an *"arroyo"*, which means creek. At first it is a tiny rill born of a spring which seeps down a canyon in the mountains which border the southern rim of the Mojave Desert in Los Angeles County. For many miles it is a little creek lined with watercress and shaded by cottonwoods and willows. Here and there along its course, where it spreads out to make a swamp there grows *Yerba Mansa* (anemopis californica), a medicinal herb.

Like all the desert streams, it has its moods. Sometimes it flows on the surface for many miles. Then suddenly it plunges underground and leaves its bed dry and dusty. Then suddenly again, it rises to the surface. Periodically, a storm will blow up out of the Gulf of Cortez and a cloudburst will occur on the desert. The Santa Clara will become a raging torrent and carry everything in its path - houses, barns, chicken coops, horses, cows, goats, sheep and dump them into the ocean miles away near Point Magu. The torrent cuts deep gashes in the earth, tears out lemon and orange orchards and generally spoils the ranches in its path.

Along the course of the Santa Clara there are many monuments to broken dreams. Dreams of optimists who filed homestead, built shacks, starved out and left the shacks for time and desert winds to blow down. The abandoned homesteads tell the story of a couple who filed on a homestead and stayed until the wife could stand the poverty, hardship and lonliness no longer and left. The husband stayed until hunger drove him away to seek a livelihood elsewhere.

Roofless, weatherbeaten walls of shacks stand forlorn. The windows and doors long since carried off; succeeding numbers of scavengers have combed the premises, taken everything of use or value. Nothing remains but rusty pieces of tin. Even the discarded bottles have been carried away; the burning desert sun paints glass with rainbow colors. Along the course of the stream a cloudburst has left a house hanging over a bank. The gash cut into the earth has made the ranch worthless.

There is a model ranch sitting next to a hillside. It has an elaborate dairy barn and a silo which never harbored anything but rattlesnakes. There is also a mill along the creek, the wheel of which never turned; the water in the creek never rose high enough to turn it. Farther down the canyon the creek flows past heaps of adobe, once walls where Rogers, the immigrant, found food and help after his escape from Death Valley. Once there were beaver meadows the length of the canyon, but succeeding cloudbursts washed them out, only sand remains. The Santa Clara flows between the beetling walls of Soledad Canyon until it reaches Saugus, where the waters of Bouquet and San Francisquito Canyons join it. Farther on, it is joined by the waters of Piru Creek which drains the Lockwood and Mootaw Valleys high into the Tehachapis.

As it nears Santa Paula, the valley through which the river runs, broadens and lemon and orange orchards appear. Here the stream passes the Camulos Ranch, the oldest of the western ranchos. Paradoxically, it has survived cloudbursts, dry years, wet years, booms and depressions and still sits serenely in the midst of its orange and lemon groves. When at last the Santa Clara reaches the lovely little town of Santa Paula, it ceases to

Santa Paula

be a desert stream; for the eastern half of the town is hot and dry; the western half is cooled by the ocean breezes. The coast is only ten or twelve miles away.

Santa Paula is an old town whch has not yet been spoiled by urban renewal. It has fine old buildings and shady streets. True, there is a sprawling shopping center. There are many oldtimers who are not in any great hurry and prefer to shop in the older part of town, where men still call each other by their first names and take a little time to chat and reminisce - a custom consecrated by time and usage. Santa Paula is an oasis after the burning desert.

The advent of collectors of silver-mouthed bridle bits in the last thirty years is a phenomenon which has amazed people who have an interest in horses and horse shows. Thirty years ago, after horse shows had become established in California, men suddenly started collecting bits, spurs, saddles. The bits collectors sought, were those that has been used on ranches by vaqueros and buckeroos and made by master craftsmen in the years the cattle industry was paramount in California. Men paid ten times more for a bit than it had cost the original buyer. This writer remembers ordering a bit and a pair of spurs from Garcia Saddlery in Elko,

The work of Mike McDowell

Ring Bit owned by Jim Gerber

Old saddles in a corner.

This collection of bits belongs to Jim Layne of Santa Barbara. It is the best collection this author has ever seen.

Nevada in 1919. I paid sixty dollars for the two articles, which meant two month's wages. I got thirty dollars a month on the San Emideo at the time for riding the range. My grandson rides on the same ranch today and gets five or six hundred dollars a month. Recently he paid two hundred dollars for a bit which means he gets a much better bargain than his old granddaddy did sixty years ago.

Some of the old bits have been sold for a thousand dollars, which makes me hope that those old men who made them don't turn over in their graves. Today, paradoxically, new bits are sold for much less than old bits. After men began combing the ranches for bits, they began to disappear into collections and never seen again.

One day it occurred to me to suggest to Lou Hengehold of Santa Paula, that he have an exhibit of old saddles, bits, spurs, chaps, ropes and pictures. And that is how Mr. Hengehold came to offer his place of business for the exhibition, the first of its kind. True, there are many antique shows, but those antiques are for sale, whereas the exhibit at the "Mill" was strictly non-commercial. It was a gathering of history buffs who would show their treasures, like mothers showing their babies to one another. The collectors, Lou and I invited responded eagerly. We had our first show five years ago. All the exhibitors brought others with them. The result is that the exhibition has grown every year.

In July, Santa Paula has its early festival when all inland California is burning up in the heat of summer. Because Santa Paula is always cool in July, it can have its big parade. Lou Hengehold, owns an enormous building called "The Mill". Here he stages his annual exhibit of western artifacts and invites the collectors of saddles, bits, spurs, chaps, ropes and other articles used on the cattle ranches of the West. He also invites western artists and collectors of paintings and photographs.

The artifacts must pertain to the actual West. That is, California, Nevada, Oregon and parts of Idaho, Wyoming, Utah and Arizona. All the exhibits must show that they have been used by vaqueros and buckeroos and must be in useable condition.

Some very fine examples of hand-carved leather craftsmenship and fine inlaid silver will be brought to be displayed. This exhibition is the high point of the festival.

There are to be seen Visalia saddles, Moreno saddles, Wilson Saddles, A. A. Cuen saddles, Hamley saddles, Lewis saddles, Porter saddles, Garcia saddles, Brydon Brothers saddles. Some of these saddles are still in fine shape, though they were made a hundred years ago.

There are Madueno bits, Gutierrez bits, Pini bits, A. B. Hunt bits, Figueroa bits, Rodriguez bits, Morales bits, Biacan bits, Manuel bits, Steve Clark bits, Goldberg bits, Juan Estrada bits, Jesus Tapia bits, Eduardo Grijalva bits, George Ortiz bits, Harry Malone bits.

There are chaps made by Porter, Kelly , Lewis, Hamley. Riatas made by Tony Araujo, Salvador Carmelo, Ernie Morris, Sherman Wright, Guadalupe Valencia. There are collections of spurs made by the men who made bits. All bits and spurs are beautifully silver-mounted and engraved.

There are many photographs taken many years ago when the cattle industry was paramount in Southern California. There are many western paintings done by western artists. In fact, Ernie Morris brings his work every year and Stan Ruano, the bit maker, comes every year with his creations.

Lou Hengehold's exhibit at "The Mill" in the month of July is truly a western history buff's paradise and is the outstanding entry of the festival. Every year more people hear of the exhibit and the number of exhibitors has doubled each year. This year there was hardly standing room for the spectators, although the display area has been enlarged often.

Santa Paula is the ideal place for this exhibit because it has a Spanish heritage. Since the coming of the Franciscan Padres, cattle have run in the Sierras surrounding the town; for the historic San Bonaventura Mission is a short distance away. The vaqueros and buckeroos who rode in this area were the best in the West. A few very old men who have herded cattle here still survive and always put in an appearance at the exhibition.

SHEIK

For many years during the time I owned the Bar-O Stables on Alfred Harrell Highway below China Grade, the Haberfeldes kept their horses with me. Every spring I hauled the horses to the Haberfelde ranch near the Jack Ranch and every fall I hauled them back to my stable in Bakersfield for the winter.

The first time I brought them down from the mountains I unknowingly left one behind. He was hidden in a gulley in some bushes. Mr. Ed Haberfelde sent me back with the trailer to get him. "He's my father's old Gelding," he said, "He likes to stay off by himself, often hidden in a clump of bushes."

When I got back to the ranch in the mountains, I searched the pasture and, sure enough, I found him standing quietly behind some buckeyes. He was more of a roan than a gray, as I caught him and loaded him into the trailer, it struck me that I had seen this horse before. He was vaguely familiar. His flat croup and high withers told me that somewhere in his ancestry there was a blooded sire, although his ears and Roman nose said "Mustang". I cudgeled my brain. Where had I seen this horse before? Mr. George Haberfelde had told me that he had raised the horse, so he could not have been on any of the ranches on which I had worked. Some horses have personality, other's don't. This horse would not easily been forgotten.

The next morning, after I had brought the horse to the stable, I turned the gray out with the other horses. I turned all the horses out every morning, so that their stalls would dry out and they could exercise.

A few days later, a man who wished to buy a horse, called up and said he was coming out to see the one I had for sale. All the horses were in the pasture, I picked up a rope amd walked out to catch the horse. When I got close the horses threw up their tails and ran off, except the gray horse. His name was Sheik. He was by himself, as usual and stood while I walked up to him and put the rope around his neck. He would never run from a person trying to catch him, even when the other horses with him ran off. I put a loop around his nose and jumped on his back. As I mounted, the loop fell off his nose. I didn't need it, the old horse knew what I wanted and set out at a gallop after the horses. From the way he went about it I knew he had wrangled horses many times. Even when one broke out, he took after it and brought it back. "This is an old vaquero horse, some man who knew his business about making a good horse, broke this one." I said to myself.

One day Jim Waldon, who was the secretary of our goat roping and polo club, came out to the stable. He had no more than parked his pick-up and walked to the gate, when he looked up and exclaimed, "Why there's old George," pointing to the gray horse Sheik. "Do you know that horse?" I asked, "I've been trying to place him. It seems to me that I've seen him somewhere before." "His sire was the Tejon Ranch Arabian stallion and his dam was a Nevada mustang mare," Jim answered, then went on to tell me the history of the old gray horse.

"Years ago, about 1925, George Haberfelde had a very good roan mare which pulled the cart in which his merchandise was delivered to his customers. She was a very willing animal and worked in the cart for many years. "During the Kern County Fair, the Tejon Ranch management sent the Arabian to be exhibited at the Fairgrounds. He was probably the only Arabian in the county at that time. The roan mare was stabled at the fairgrounds and since she was in season, some joker stole the stallion out of the stall and bred the mare.

"Some eleven months later," Jim went on, chuckling, "after the mare had foaled, the surprised Haberfelde sent the mare and colt to the Smith and Record ranch at Granite Station. In time, either Cliff Record or Hugh Smith broke the gray colt. He turned out to be such a good mountain horse that the ranchers would hide him so that Haberfelde would not take him away. He would slide down a steep mountain side on his haunches and work his way down with his forelegs. In the end, Haberfelde took the horse away to his ranch, but by that time he was a first class vaquero horse. "And that is the end of the story of the old gray horse." Jim finished, still chuckling. No wonder the horse seemed familiar. The Tejon Arabian had marked him just as he did all his foals on the ranch and I recognized the mark.

The horse stayed in my stable for years. I was the only one who rode him because each one of the Haberfelde boys, George and Steve, had his own horse. When they grew up and no longer rode their horses Mr. George Haberfelde sold them to me. All except the old gray, Sheik. "I will not sell you that horse," he said, "I am going to give him to you. And so that you will not have to sell him, I'm going to send you a check for twenty-five dollars each month, so you can feed him." The check came every month until the old horse died.

When I sold my stable in 1949, I said to Jim Waldon, "What am I going to do with the old horse, Jim? I'm selling my place and I don't want to leave the fellow in strange hands." "Bring him to my place, I will keep him until he dies." Jim answered. For years afterward, I would see old Sheik in a parade with some little girl riding him. Jim would let a little girl exercise him since he was very gentle.

He got so fat he waddled; what with the kids feeding him and his way of working Jim's sister. Jim would feed him in the morning, Sheik would finish his hay, then he would walk up to the gate and put his head over it and whinny. Jim's sister would give him another flake of hay. This would happen at night too, after Jim had fed him. Jim would protest to his sister, but to no avail. Jim went out to feed him one morning and found that the old horse had died in the night.

CATTLEMEN TODAY

Many years ago, with the help of Remick Albitre, now deceased, and Jesse Stockton, also deceased, I made a list of the cattlemen and riders of the surrounding Sierras. Many of them have been mentioned here in stories or photographs. There have been changes—many have passed away or moved away.

I prevailed on Bob Snow and his gracious wife, Ramona, to compile another list of present day cattlemen and riders of the Sierra. Of course some of these names have appeared in the first list, but they are names of people who are still in the cattle business or have ridden the range. I hope it meets with the readers' approval.

Glenn Record	David Olds	Jane Davidson
Ginger Record	Frankie Olds	Ellis Snow
Jack Sarret	Orin Olds	Alice Snow
Mitch Holmes	Alan Jacobs	Herb Queen
Robert Grisedale	Judy Jacobs	Warren Stockton
Eva Grisedale	J. F. Williams	Jess Stockton
Grant Grisedale	Jim Ben Williams	Marion Stockton
Dan Albitre	Nona Williams	Frank Stockton
Dorothy Albitre	Kyle Williams	Ralph Stockton
Robin Malofy	Corinne Williams	Irving Stockton
Henry Gardette	Will Williams	Trent Stockton
Harry West	Thea Nash	Mark Stockton
Walter Burke	Jack Davidson	Terry Stockton

Peter Stockton
Monica Stockton
Ted Brown
Harry Brown
Roy Brown
Julien Bigot
August Bigot
Alex Bigot
Marvin Maddux
John Rofer
Robert Woody
Ward Woody
Henry Bohna
Roy Bohna
Pike Bohna
Joe Weringer
Ed Rutledge
Roy Rutledge
Jim Rutledge
Jules Villard
Bill Rose
Bill Jaughin
Cathy Bernard
Larry Moore
Jeff Stone
Mary Stone
Julia Martin
Benton Martin
Roscoe Martin
Alice Martin
Jim Beard
Fred Beard
Guy Hughes
Dottie Hughes
Carver Bowen
Jeff Bowen
Cindy Bowen
Russ Carver
Mabel Carver
Frank Smoot
Jim Smoot
Clint Smoot
June Smoot Sanchez
John Wafford
Hugh Smith
Charlotte Nash Smith
Clifford Record
Hazel Record

Ted Bernard
Arron Caldwell
Nancy Caldwell
Dr. Charles Booth
Judy Booth
Al Richardson
Clara Armstrong
Frances Stockton
Albert Darling
Karl Johnson
Glenda Johnson
Roderick Jameson
Margie Albitre
Milton Rudnick
Roger Bias
Sandra Bias
Bill Douglas
Pleasant Martin
John Beard
Mark Rudnick
Bill Rankin
Lawrence Snow
Gary Snow
Ronnie Knudsen
Bud Silicz
Daisy Silicz
Evalyn Farnsworth
Elmer Keuchel
Delphine Keuchel
Jim Buley
Dr. S. Woody
Stonewall Woody
Elmer Woody
Stevie Cherbonno
Robert Snow
Ramona Snow
Nathan Carver
Skinner Hardy
Gene Sarret
Deidre Lavers
David Lavers
Jack Lavers
Betty Lavers
Max App
John App
John App, Jr.
Kenneth Mebane
Bill Carver

Mona Carver
Louie Mebane
Bruce Mebane
Dwight Mebane
Buck Vincent
Jim Vincent
Marion Vincent
Jim Dean
Rita Dean
Karl Klein
Walter Klein
Oscar Klein
Duane Fitter
Delores Fitter
Ron Dilday
Darlene Dilday
Wilbur Studer
Winnie Studer
Ken Sayder
Julie Ann Sayder
John Fachen
John Hershey
Jay Hershey
Jo Gardener
Dick Gardener
Pearl Hitchcock Shirley
Marcellus James, Sr.
Remick Albitre

LETTERS & ARTICLES

Reprinted here are a few of the letters I have received over the years, all of which have given me much pleasure. I have included them and two reprinted articles that might be of interest. One of the articles is about a man that influenced my life. The other article is a review that was written several years ago on one of my books.

Aug 10, 1982

Dear Rojas:

In retrospect, over a long career, with many experiences, there is one I note with especial pride and it is my association with you & I have a sincere admiration for what you have achieved in your life by dint of application and the employment of a genuine talent &

Certainly this latest book of yours attests the pride I feel toward you and your most noteworthy accomplishments & Bravo!

Thanks, indeed for your kindness in sending it to me. I shall go through it with real pleasure and the honor I take in knowing you &

A man I most honor is, one who has hoisted himself to a pinnacle by his own boot straps &

The only merit I take in knowing you is that I had the perception to note yours.

Thanks again,

Jim Day,
Cambria, Pa.

P.S. Fingers too stiff now for a typewriter, though I did pound one for many years. JD

August 7, 1964

Dear Chief,

No favors to ask this time. I just want to congratulate you on your last book,
THE VAQUERO. I'm a great reader. I'm sure I've read over a thousand books on all
subjects & I honestly never read one I enjoyed more than this. This, along with your
other 3 books, give loads of most interesting information on the vaqueros that can
be found no where else. Your books have a ring of authority & authenticity found in
very few others & you have a litterary style equal to any I've ever seen. This sounds
too much like flattery but I mean every word of it. Each of your books is better
than the last & this one is the best. I only wish you had said more about Sonora &
Baja California but what you did say about them cleared up some questions I've wondered
about for a long time. The drawings are good, too, in this one. I'm glad you found a
good artist.

Even more than for the book itself I must congratulate you for your courage.
Parts of the book are very contrivercial on subjects that some people get very
emotional about. Such a book is almost certain to stir up a hornet's nest & it
already has. I read a review of it in the El Paso Herald Post which started out,
"This book diserves a review if only to warn the reader." From there he launched
into a bitter condemnation of you saying you were an opinionated fool writing from
nothing but blind prejudice & imagination. All he talked about was the first section
entitled "Loyalty" in which you compared the yaquero & the cowboy. Appearantly that
made him so mad he didn't read any more. But as you know, I've been studying the same
subject for several years. I've been to Baja California & other parts of Mexico &
I'm a great lover of history. In school I took a course in the history of Spain &
another in the history of Mexico. The Spanish history started about 1000 B. C. & came
down to Francisco Franco & the Mexican hostory started with the Spanish conquest &
came down to the present day. I read both books thru twice. I've also read Pablo
Martinez's history of Baja California & several histories of the Jesuits in Baja &
Sonora, a history of the Franciscans in California & several other more complete
histories of California, a history of New Mexico & a history of the United States.
All this history & my own experience bares you out in all you say. You mentioned
some things I didn't know before but I know all you say is true. It's high time
someone told the whole truth on this matter, always more interesting than fiction.
I admire anyone who will stick his neck out when there's a good reason.

The American cowboy has been more written about than any other character in the
history of the world. I've read at least 100 books on the subject myself & would like
to read just as many on the vaquero but they aren't available. For some reason it's
been over looked. It makes a very warped picture of American cattle ranching.
Thousands of books on cowboys & only 6 or 7 on vaqueros ! We need many more & you
must be the only one in the world now living qualified to write them. Maybe some old
vaqueros still around know the subject well enough but they don't have the ability
to put it down on paper. The book jacket says you're working on another book. I
hope it's true. I'm looking for all I can find about vaqueros & will buy anything
you put out whether one more book or 10 more. Congratulations again. I hope this
one is a financial success, Thanks for autographing it for me.

Sincerely,

Henry Schipman, Jr.

Arnold Rojas
P.O. Box 773
Wasco, CA 93280

Dear Mr. Rojas;

Recently my brother in Santa Paula loaned me his copy of your fascinating book, <u>These</u> <u>Were</u> <u>The</u> <u>Vaqueros</u>, to read. Now, upon its completion, I hasten to write you a letter of congratulations for a hard job well done. The material of that book could only have been written by a man like you who lived it and I appreciate that. Thank you for all that you said.

My interest in the Tejon country was first kindled in 1931 when, as a boy of thirteen, I saw it for the first time across Antelope Valley from the town of Sandburg on the Old Ridge Route when our family made—made its first trip from Los Angeles north to Yosemite National Park by automobile.

That interest was intensified in 1939, '40 and '41 when my dad and his brother and we male cousins camped for all or part of each of those summers at the Tom Barnes place at Bronco Flat. On some of the Auto Club maps it is called the Quinn Ranch, after Virginia Quinn.

We had many adventures those summers such as camping overnight at Marble Springs after a long hike across the mountain, seeing and shooting at coyotes and rattlesnakes, trying to hike along the face of the Tehachapi Mountains from Bronco Flat to Gorman to mail a letter to my girlfriend. On that trip my brother and I were caught by the one legged cowboy you mentioned in your book, Juan Gomez, and escorted in a pickup truck to where we could see old Highway #99 and told to leave.

Years later, in 1954, my wife and I bought a vacation place in Frazier Park and my interest and knowledge about the Tejon Ranch grew with each book I read about the area. In 1971, with a permit from Tejon management, my two sons and I relocated the forgotten site of the Chumash village of Castac (Kaš-tɨc) on the northeastern shore of Castac Lake. Since that time I have archaeologically dug and screened the site for the Tejon people and recorded all of the beads, arrow heads, fish bones, pottery bits, etc. that we recovered. This mass of material is now being analyzed in the Archaeology Department at the University of California at Santa Barbara. Eventually our findings will be published for public consumption.

Now, can you see why your book was so fascinating to me? It fills in where Frank Latta, A.l. Kroeber, Earle Crowe and Griffen and Woodward, etc. leave off. Some day soon I would like to meet you face to face. In the meantime, may I ask you favor or two in the

the form of a few questions?

1. Did you meet or know of an Indian named José Juan Olivas who lived for a time on the Tejon (about 1918+)? He was Castac Chumash, that is, born at Castac Lake, and probably the only Castaqeño who might still be alive.

2. You list Frank Alviso as one of the old time cowboys that you knew. Apparently he lived for a while at the old Duck Hunter's Lodge located on Dryfield Road at the eastern end of Castac Lake as a gate keeper. Do you know if he is still alive and/or where he or his wife might be living? I would like to interview him about the lake.

3. Could you identify the exact location of Cerro de los Borregos on San Emidio Ranch and Loma del Avenal on Tejon? They are mentioned in some of the ethnographic notes collected on Tejon and San Emidio by John P. Harrington for the Smithsonian Institute in Washington D.C. between 1913 and 1923. Did you meet J.P. Harrington or hear about him when you were a ranch employee? He owned a Model T Ford but his young wife drove it for him in those days.

I understand through my brother in Santa Paula that you will be in Santa Paula on July 15th, 16th and 17th at the store owned by Louis Hengehold, a mutual friend. Therefore, I am sending him over to buy at least two more copies of your book, one for me and the other for an archaeologist at the University of California at Santa Barbara who is also steeped in the Chumash people and their history.

My wife and I are planning to return to Southern California early in the fall. We will be staying at our Frazier Park place some of the time. If it is possible then, I would like to request an interview with you somewhere in Wasco or at any other convenient meeting place because I have a number of other questions to ask you, if you don't mind.

Oh yes, I am a retired teacher of Geography and Anthropology who spent most of his career at Los Angeles City College in Los Angeles but who has now moved to Coos Bay, Oregon to enjoy these golden years away from the frantic life and the crowds of Southern California.

Very sincerely yours,

David L. Jennings

Enclosure

WESTERN MEDIA
CONSULTANTS

May 13

Dear Chan Bergen,

        I've been meaning to write ever since I saw
your reference to Arnold Rojas' book 'Vaqueros and Buckeroos'.
I'd seen a review of the book in an old Western Horseman and
I'd written to the address given there asking to buy a copy
but I've had no reply. If you'd be so good as to send this
letter to ~~xkxxxx~~ whoever is selling the book and ask them to
send me details of how much money they want, or better still
asking them to Air Mail me a copy and I'll pay for the book
and the freight with a U.S. money order by return post (you
can guarentee them that I am polite to women, kind to children
and pay my bills promptly).

Best Regards,

Chris Hector
Iona Rd.,
Bunyip, 3815
Victoria,
AUSTRALIA

Iona Road Bunyip 3815   Telephone (056)295551

Henry Schipman, Jr.

WESTERN ILLUSTRATOR AND WRITER
644 WEST COURT AV.
LAS CRUCES, NEW MEXICO 88001
524-4412

Oct. 29, 1980

Dear Chief,

What a nice surprise to find when the 2 books of yours that I ordered came that you had autographed both of them for me ! That adds a great deal to their value to me. Thanks a million. These 2 books really look great. You found much better artists to illustrate them than your first books.

To repay you for the autographing I sent you these 3 books of mine. I autographed them. They're nothing compared to your books but I hope you find them interesting.

You asked me to tell more about what the Texans said about your books. It has been several years since I read the reviews of your books in the paper and I don't remember all the details but ofcourse any book about Calif. vaqueros is bound to be unpopular with most Texans. I don't remember now whether I read it in the Las Cruces paper or the El Paso paper but Las Cruces is only about 40 miles from El Paso. The forward of your book on the origins of the vaquero, written by someone else, said you corrected "a mountain of apochrapha" on the subject, which you did, but the Texans didn't want to be corrected. They wanted to go on believing the apochrapha. The reviewer resented your speaking of Texas as part of the South instead of the West, saying Texans had never really learned dale roping, saying the vaquero represented an older culture than the cowboy, that the vaquero had influenced the cowboy but hadn't been influenced by him, etc. That's about all I remember. It was an unfavorable review but I don't think that will bother you.

If you have any old spurs, bits, reatas, saddles, etc. that you would like to give or sell to my vaquero museum let me know. I get things for the museum in 3 ways: I buy them, accept them as gifts or take them on loan. In any case I lable each thing and tell who it's from. If it's loaned I say on the lable that the owner loaned it to the museum and ofcourse the loaner can take it back any time.

One thing I'm anxious to get is an old-time, California half breed bit. I have some spade bits and some ring bits but no half breeds. By the way what's the Spanish name for a half breed bit ? It wouldn't be "freno mestizo" would it ?

Also I'm anxious to get a real, old-time, extra wide, extra fancy California horsehair cinch with a big, fancy horsehair tassel in the middle and a big, fancy leather pad on each ring. Ofcourse I'd like to have a whole California center fire saddle with the cinch on it or several of them if they weren't all alike but even then I'd like to have an extra California cinch to hang up by its self. If you have any of these things or know of anyone who has them and is willing to sell them, give them to my museum or loan them please let me know. Vaya con Dios.

cincerely,

Henry Schipman

23 Oct. '81

CHIEF ROJAS
C/O Ruano Custom Bits
17852 Miller Ave.
Fontana, CA. 92335

Dear Chief Rojas:

Would like to order your two books: THESE WERE THE
VAQUEROS and VAQUEROS AND BUCKEROOS.

Enclosed is a check for $43.90, per my phone conver-
sation to Judy Ruano covering the two volumes at
$20 each; plus $2.40 and $1.50 for postage and tax.

Found the article VAQUEROS AND BUCKEROOS in HORSE ACTION
NEWS, July 1981,super interesting and important.

Keep up the good work in keeping the record straight
for us much later "Vaqueros and Buckeroos."

Best regards,

Alec Blasco-Ibanez
618 S. Lucerne Blvd.
Los Angeles, CA. 90005
Tel.: 213-939-1326

CLAUDIO M. MASI DE VARGAS MACHUCA

Señor
Arnold Rojas
c/o Chuck Hitchcock
620 Munzer Street
SHAFTER
93262 California
U.S.A._____

Milan, 24th November 1980

Mi querido amigo,

First of all let me apologize for having written to
you so late to thank you for the gift of the two bits
you made to me in Reno during the Snaffle Bit Futurity Show, but back home the business has taken me
back.

I hope as I told you next time I am in California
to see you and your collection, by the way could I
have your private address and phone number or should
I keep writing to this one?
I am sorry not to write to you in Spanish but at my
office nobody types it.

I have read in your book that you have gone through
one of the books written by one of my ancestors, you
are very lucky because in our library I have not found
the book you mentioned; I have called a Spanish cousin
to see if he had it in his library, but also he does
not have it. I must say that your books are wonderful
and by reading them made me dreaming the past like I
were there.

I hope to see you next year. To you and to your wife
my best wishes for a merry Christmas and a happy New
Year.

your Claudio

CARROLL
SADDLE COMPANY

McNEAL, ARIZONA 85617   PHONE 602-364-8138

July 6, 1981

Arnold Rojas
PO Box 773
Wasco, Calif. 93280

Dear Arnold Rojas:

Glad you liked the article on vaquero gear.

We lost Ed a couple of years back. He went to give a seminar
in B.C., stepped down from his horse, and died immediately.

Was to see our mutual friend, Ray Rich, about two months ago.
Had a very pleasant visit, although a short one, with him.

Ed's book was butchered by the publisher. You know that the
gentling process is important to the horse, but all this and
more was cut out of the original MS. A shame!

But the book is authentic. I am certain that ed, if he were
still alive, would appreciate your endorsement.

Looking forward to more of your stories in H&R, I remain,

Cordially yours.

J. Carroll

J. C. DYSLI DIPL. ING. ETH.   TIERZUCHTBETRIEBE AG

SEKRETARIAT + ADMINISTRATION:
Lic. iur. Max Schummer, 8008 Zürich
Florastrasse 38, Telefon 01 - 32 76 06

BANK:
Schweiz. Hypotheken- und
Handelsbank Zürich

ZUCHTBETRIEBE + LANDWIRTSCHAFT:
8321 Gündisau. Telefon 01 - 97 40 86

Mr. Arnold R. Rojas

c/o Chuck Hitchcock

620 Munzer Street

Shafter, Calif. 93263

U. S. A.

Gündisau, January 12, 1976

Dear Mr. Rojas,

I have seen your new book "These were the Vaqueros" and I would
like to acquire a copy very badly, since I collect and read everything concerning the art of the old Vaqueros, either in Spain or
in California. Also, I think I am the only European, who trains
horses this way on a professional basis, and I can tell you, that
this venture was not accompanied by the help of our European established, so-called classical Horsemanship. I'm doing it since ten
years now, and only lately has success and apreciation started to
compensate me for my long and never-resting patience in introducing
this fine old art of horsemanship. Unfortunately, not many will be
able to acquire it, since it seems that nobody has the time and
patience for it anymore. Some US professional horsepoeple have seen
my horses work and they pretended that I would be able to compete
in any stock horse class over there at the West Coast. This helps
to know, that I am on the right track.

Anyhow, I heard, that you have published some other books too.
Would it be possible, that you give me the titles of these other
books too. I'm sure to order some of this list. Also, I shall
send you the money right away, as soon as I have your answer and
the prices of each book.

In respect of your work towards the benefit of an old art I remain
with my most sincere regards

yours very cordially

MR. JEAN-CL. DYSLI
"Gundisau" Ranch
CH 8321 Gündisau
Switzerland

It was through the courtesy of the editors of *"Western Horseman"* magazine, that I was able to include this fine tribute to Lee M. Rice, Master saddler, Western artist, author, and above all, a kind old gentleman. He was one of the first to encourage me to write.

I thank Chan Bergen, the editor and Kurt Markus, the author of the article for their permission to include the story in this volume.

They Saddled the West

LEE M. RICE
and
GLENN R. VERNAM

by KURT MARKUS
Western Horseman Magazine

RIDING THE TRAILS

I AM NOT the right person to write Lee M. Rice's obituary. I had never met him, nor talked with him on the phone. I have no personal memory of his face, not even from a family snapshot. And while I will say a few words about a man who has been more a part of this magazine than I have been, I wish for him that Will James — an acquaintance of his—or Maynard Dixon—also a friend—were alive to send him off properly. Theirs would be eulogies you'd remember, for they could have colored a life-size remembrance of Lee, a man Idaho saddlemaker Bob Kelly describes cleanly yet powerfully as a "fine gentleman of the old school."

When Lee Marvin Rice died in Clovis, Calif., on January 14, 1984, he was 91. With him went a legacy that cannot be shoveled over. Although his wife is still living (they had no children), Lee is survived by his work, a collection of words and drawings that go a great distance to tell us how it was in his cow country West and in an oblique way, something about Lee Rice. His subjects were saddles, saddle making, and saddlemakers and it can be safely written that few men, if any, commanded greater knowledge.

But to label Lee Rice a historian and let him go at that would be to discredit the true shape of his soul. Lee Rice knew saddles because he built them. And he was buddies with numerous makers of the highest reputation. Yet what placed Lee into his own league was that he knew what a good saddle felt like from butt-to-leather experience, years of cowpunching that gave him an empathy for the men who used saddles as part of daily life.

Levi Strauss & Co. employed Lee's talents frequently before and after WWII. The booklet of "Western Horse Lore" was both written and illustrated by Rice.

Lee grew up in the Kings River country near Fresno, Calif., on a family-owned ranch. Like many other horsemen from the Californio tradition, Lee benefited from both urban and cattle-raising cultures; there was enough country in the early 1900s to get lost in, yet cities with universities and museums were never far away. Perhaps it is this combination of lifestyles that produced what we think of today as a more refined horseman, the Californio, and what gave men like Lee Rice the opportunity to not only experience ranch life but equip them to translate that experience into words and pictures.

Following a two-year hitch in the Army, catching the tail end of World War I, Lee returned from France and Belgium in 1920 to work for the Capital H outfit on the San Joaquin River. By this time, Lee had uncovered a talent for drawing, which he cultivated for a short time in France with professional studies at the University of Toulouse and continued stateside when he took up with the painter Maynard Dixon in 1923 in San Leandro, California. There was commercial work for Levi Strauss & Co., in San Francisco, and illustrating assignments from saddleries, some of which Lee Rice worked for at the time or later was employed by.

A boyhood friend, Leon Akers, recalls a trip he and Lee took to the Visalia Stock Saddle Co., in San Francisco after the war: "My dad told me to go and order a complete outfit for myself—and I took Lee along for company. Well, when we got back home, Lee turned around and went back to Visalia and got a job." It was the beginning of a career that would span many decades and give young Lee Rice a focus and determination few men seldom acquire. And it was his assortment of talents that made him the ideal man for a task he was seemingly destined to trace.

I have only bits and fragments of Lee's life scribbled in scattered notes taken from a few people still living who knew him well, and from a stack of correspondence several inches thick that Lee answered for Western Horseman readers. I can't make a laundry list, step-by-detailed-step of Lee's doings and say with certainty when he attended the University of California at Berkeley or when he met Will James or when he built saddles for Visalia, Olsen-Nolte, or Goldsmith. He was primarily a saddle maker, and the drawing and research and writing were hobbies, you might say, that occupied his time away from the shop. He was never the type, say friends like Ray Holes Sr., of Grangeville, Ida., to talk about art theory or mix with artists who weren't of the West. Instead, his mind was on saddles and cowboys and how they

Ray Holes
SADDLE COMPANY
GRANGEVILLE, IDAHO 83530
Area Code 208/983-1460

Catalog No 80   Price $2 00

Catering To The Working Stockman

Lee Rice was personal friends with Ray Holes and with other Holes family members—as well as with the craftsmen employed by Ray Holes—for many years. The Ray Holes Saddle Company catalog is peppered with Lee's pen-and-ink drawings, acquired by Ray over the course of their long friendship.

influenced each other, and how, if a man knew what to look for, a saddle could tell a history of a region and the man who rode it.

It is this story-telling blend of fact and speculation that makes the Lee Rice/Glenn Vernam book, "They Saddled the West," a classic. Published in 1975 by Cornell Maritime Press, it is the standard reference book on early saddles and saddle makers, illustrated with photos and drawings by both Rice and Vernam. Our Western Horseman office copy reflects repeated use, and whenever we get an inquiry from someone who has a saddle they can't identify, it's the first stop, and oftentimes it contains an answer. Rice and Vernam collaborated on what is as much a history of the cowboy West as it is a history of saddle making.

Unfortunately for anyone not already owning this masterpiece, the book is now out-of-print.

The first article Lee submitted to Western Horseman appeared in the January/February 1942 issue (the magazine was published six times a year at that time), and 32 years later his last piece was printed. Between were 30 stories which he routinely illustrated with his own drawings. Additionally, he answered saddle-related questions for the magazine for 20 years; copies of his replies were filed in the editorial secretary's cabinet, and the correspondence reflects Lee's generosity to a fault. No matter how brief the reader's description of a saddle, nor how extensive an answer they requested, Lee gave all he knew without compensation. His attitude was that he learned from the letters and he was happy to have them.

Lee Rice's final years were not good. He had major surgery more than once for a brain tumor and his ability to draw and write was seriously impaired. Still, he carried on. A nephew, Harold Qualls, says there's a manuscript in Lee's belongings which is two-thirds completed, recounting the early range wars. Lee had apparently been researching the topic for 35 years, compiling fact wherever he could locate it. At this point, no one has taken a full inventory of the Lee Rice collection. Because Lee seldom worked in any other medium except pen-and-ink or pencil, there have been no collectors outside of his immediate circle of friends, and it's difficult to guess if his art will fetch handsome prices now that he's gone. But then, to his friends, his work has always been treasured beyond dollars.

This is not the last you'll hear of the late Lee M. Rice, either in this magazine or elsewhere. His contribution is too large to dismiss with a few graveside remarks and a recitation of the "Cowboy's Prayer." Those who knew him were lucky. I feel the loss of deprivation, of knowing I shall never meet him, and he now becomes part of the legend of the West which haunts us all.

"Nevada Roundup Wagon, 1895." They Saddled the West, Cornell Maritime Press, 1975

This review appeared in the *"Horse and Rider"* and was written by my friend Don Pitts, a Texax Cowboy, years ago.

By DON PITTS
Horse and Rider Magazine

THESE WERE THE VAQUEROS By Arnold R. Rojas; 528 pages; $15.90. It has been a point of humor and disgust among writers of the West that in order to be published one must have a New York City address. Granted, those city folks may be fine writers, but they are prone to inaccuracies, embellishments and downright lies. They have never seen the West, but they know that romance sells, so they have made long hours, cow manure and rotten horses appear romantic.

In essence this problem still exists, but Mr. Rojas, an old-time vaquero himself, has produced a book off the private press. Now he must sell it. This may be difficult, because most reviewers will not consider such books. This is also unfortunate, because These Were The Vaqueros is undoubtedly one of the finest portrayals of cowboy life in the far west ever to appear in print.

Not a literary masterpiece, there are inconsistencies, redundancies and occasional lapses of organization. But if a book is to be discarded solely on that basis, literature has lost touch with humanity. This book has found humanity and reveled in it.

Mr. Rojas did not intend to produce a book on how to train horses, how much better the old days were, or even to document an area's history. he just wanted to tell it the way it was, and he did so beautifully.

"Don Pedro was a famous roper and his special skill was roping hogs." Maybe you're laughing, maybe you're not but that is a direct quote from the book. Okay, what modern cowboy would lower himself to roping hogs? What modern cowboy could rope a hog? It is an interesting concept, but not so interesting as the story of Don Pedro himself.

What was it like to be a vaquero? "He didn't remember how long the horse bucked because he lost consciousness. When he came to, one of the sailors was pouring water on him and told him he had found him with his body hanging on a horse's side and the spurs hung in the cinch." Or perhaps the reader might be interested in the stories about rattlesnakes, which the vaqueros usually killed with their riatas.

One such *quento* (tale) involved a group of cowboys who, upon awakening one morning, were horrified to see a rattlesnake sleeping on the feet of one of their companions. Carefully getting their riatas, they sneaked up on the reptile and started giving it a furious thrashing. The victimized vaquero naturally was aroused by the painful beating, and seeing the snake, kicked his feet. The deadly serpent flew up in the air and landed right on top of . . . Well, I won't bore you with all the details, but there are quite a few good snake stories.

Can you learn some helpful tips from reading this book? Sure! Gold that has been buried a long time exudes dangerous fumes. When digging up treasure, one should always pour vinegar on the gold. Remember that the next time you're playing around with exhumed bullion.

Looking for horsemanship? "Louis Lopez, the best reinsman that ever rode on the Tejon, never started to bit up a colt until the moon was full. Horses bitted when it (the moon) was tender were invariably hard-mouthed runaways." You like the moon business? Okay. The riata was taken from a steer that was slaughtered when the moon was right. However, adding to the quest, "The strongest ropes were made from hides taken from steers that had died from hunger." It must have been a real trick to get a steer to succumb to starvation under the right moon.

There are other bits of advice of great importance. For example, a lion (cougar) attacks on the third night. There is a story of a man who had been kept awake by a lion for two nights. A friend advised him to leave the camp, which he did, but he left his coat on a rock. When he returned the next day his coat was shredded.

More tips? Never change clothers when breaking a mule. The sound of the cricket decides the worth of the bit. Why, this book even tells you how to avoid the evil acts of *brujas* (witches). Each fact is substantiated by stories.

Speaking of *brujas*, there is a full complement of headless horsemen, ghosts and spirits, and a fantastic *cuenta* about the consumption of ostrich meat.

There are stories about vaqueros, caporals, rancheros, and banditos, from Joaquin Murrieta to M. R. Valdez. There is even an account of the introduction and evolution of the horse and its training in America, all as seen through the eyes of the old vaquero.

When considering modern books, it is amazing that this one contains not a single curse word. For example, when discussing the spoken word, he states: "Picking up Spanish as spoken by the vaqueros, who use an unchaste expression for anything for which they do not have the term, is like picking up English from an Australian cattle station hand." Readers who have even a rudimentary knowledge of behind-the-barn Spanish are probably laughing on the floor at this reference, but the author is to be commended for not succumbing to the temptation of actually printing that "unchaste expression."

The feelings of the vaquero toward his horses and their training are viewed in great detail. Little facts like smoke arising from the wooden saddle horn as the roper slipped his dally bringing applause are also included.

Finally, Mr. Rojas reminds us that the vaqueros weren't only of Spanish and Mexican decent. There were also blacks, Indians, Europeans, and the native mixture of them all.

They were our ancestors, or men like them, and us, even if you have never waited for a steer to die under the right moon. They were skilled, tough and sensitive members of what we call the human race.

Now many have vanished, taking most of their culture with them. Arnold Rojas, now 78 years old, could not allow himself to die without knowing that the vaquero would be remembered. Mr. Rojas, thanks to you, they will be.